The Romans

New Perspectives

ABC-CLIO's
Understanding Ancient Civilizations

The Ancient Maya
The Ancient Greeks
Ancient Canaan and Israel
The Aztecs
The Romans

Forthcoming

The Ancient Celts
The Ancient Egyptians
Ancient Mesopotamia
The Incas

The
ROMANS

New Perspectives

KEVIN M. McGEOUGH

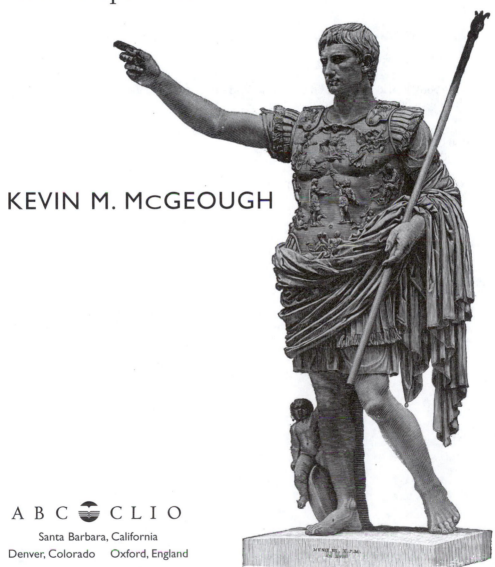

A B C ● C L I O

Santa Barbara, California
Denver, Colorado   Oxford, England

Library of Congress Cataloging-in-Publication Data
McGeough, Kevin M.
  The Romans : new perspectives / Kevin McGeough.
      p. cm. — (Understanding ancient civilizations)
  Includes bibliographical references and index.
  ISBN 1-85109-583-7 (hardback : alk. paper) — ISBN 1-85109-588-8 (e-book)
1. Rome—Civilization. I. Title. II. Series.
DG77.M4 2004
937—dc22
2004020737

08 07 06 05 04 10 9 8 7 6 5 4 3 2 1

This book is also available on the World Wide Web as an e-book.
Visit abc-clio.com for details.

ABC-CLIO, Inc.
130 Cremona Drive, P.O. Box 1911
Santa Barbara, California 93116-1911

This book is printed on acid-free paper.
Manufactured in the United States of America.

Dedicated to my parents

Contents

PART 3:   CURRENT ASSESSMENTS

Series Editor's Preface

In recent years, there has been a significant and steady increase of academic and popular interest in the study of past civilizations. This is due in part to the dramatic coverage—real or imagined—of the archaeological profession in popular film and television, and to the extensive journalistic reporting of spectacular new finds from all parts of the world. Yet, because archaeologists and other scholars have tended to approach their study of ancient peoples and civilizations exclusively from their own disciplinary perspectives and for their professional colleagues, there has long been a lack of general factual and other research resources available for the nonspecialist. The Handbooks to Ancient Civilizations series is intended to fill that need.

Volumes in the series are principally designed to introduce the general reader, student, and nonspecialist to the study of specific ancient civilizations. Each volume is devoted to a particular archaeological culture (for example, the ancient Maya of southern Mexico and adjacent Guatemala) or cultural region (for example, Israel and Canaan) and seeks to achieve, with careful selectivity and astute critical assessment of the literature, an expression of a particular civilization and an appreciation of its achievements.

The keynote of the Understanding Ancient Civilizations series is to provide, in a uniform format, an interpretation of each civilization that will express its culture and place in the world as well as the qualities and background that make it unique. Series titles include volumes on the archaeology and prehistory of the ancient civilizations of Egypt, Greece, Rome, and Mesopotamia, as well as the achievements of the Celts, Aztecs, and Inca, among others. Still more books are in the planning stage.

I was particularly fortunate in having Kevin Downing from ABC-CLIO contact me in search of an editor for a series about archaeology. It is a simple statement of the truth that there would be no series without him. I am also lucky to have Simon Mason, Kevin's successor from ABC-CLIO, continue to push the production of the series. Given the scale of the project and the schedule for production, he deserves more than a sincere thank you.

JOHN WEEKS

Acknowledgments

I would like to thank everyone at ABC-CLIO for their help in preparing this manuscript; it could certainly not have been accomplished without the help of the entire team. Scott Horst and Giulia Rossi have done an excellent job in preparing the illustrations. Cisca Schreefel did a wonderful job catching mistakes big and small. Gina Zondorak has also been helpful in the editing process. Martha Whitt has gone out of her way to facilitate the transformation of an error-ridden manuscript into a book. During the writing stage Simon Mason provided critical feedback and support; many thanks are due him. Many others at ABC-CLIO whom I did not have direct contact with have also helped and they are just as deserving of thanks. Finally, John Weeks must be thanked for suggesting this project in the first place and recommending me to ABC-CLIO.

On a personal level, this book could not have been written without the help and support of my family and friends. My parents have been generous in their support as has been my sister. Matthew Rutz, Spencer Allen, Benjamin Porter, and Jennifer Jacobs acted as valuable sounding boards throughout the writing of the manuscript. Jeremiah Peterson provided both assistance and access to his substantial personal library. Theresa Musacchio gave generously of her time, especially assisting with technical matters, and Prescott was always there to keep me company. Thanks go to all of them.

Kevin M. McGeough

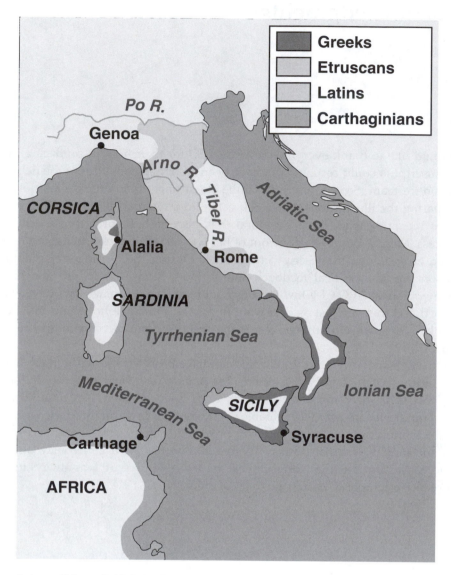

Italy, ca. 600 B.C. © ABC-CLIO, Inc.

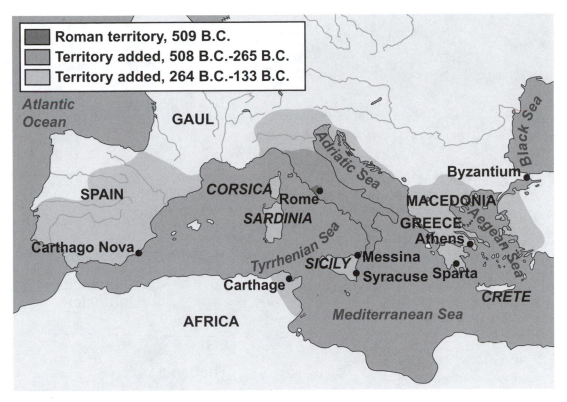

Legend:
- Roman territory, 509 B.C.
- Territory added, 508 B.C.–265 B.C.
- Territory added, 264 B.C.–133 B.C.

Atlantic Ocean

GAUL

SPAIN

CORSICA

Rome

SARDINIA

Carthago Nova

Tyrrhenian Sea

SICILY

Carthage

Messina

Syracuse

Adriatic Sea

MACEDONIA

GREECE

Athens

Sparta

Byzantium

Black Sea

Aegean Sea

CRETE

Mediterranean Sea

AFRICA

Growth of the Roman Republic, 509–133 B.C. © ABC-CLIO, Inc.

The Roman Empire at its height, A.D. 117. © ABC-CLIO, Inc.

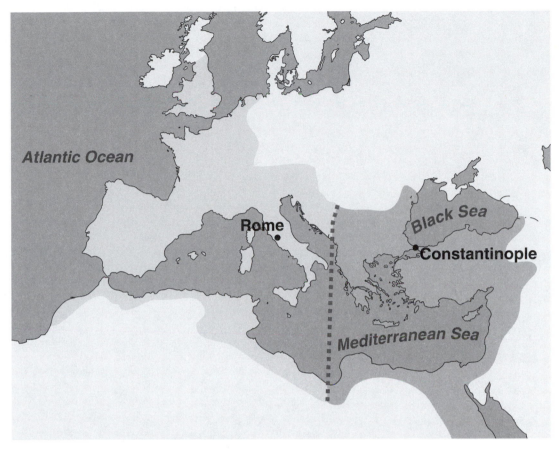

Division of the Roman Empire, East and West, third century A.D. © ABC-CLIO, Inc.

PART I

Introduction

I CHAPTER I
Introduction

WHY ARE WE FASCINATED BY THE ROMANS?

Something about Roman civilization still captivates people today. North Americans and Europeans frequently encounter images of ancient Rome or images derived from Roman times. Everybody knows what a gladiator is and most people can recognize Roman images without having had formal education on the topic. Most people know that Julius Caesar was a famous Roman leader, even if they do not know much about Roman history per se. As any History Channel viewer could attest, documentaries abound on the subject of Rome. Likewise, movies about Rome have been popular since the days of the silent film. The success of the recent film *Gladiator* is further proof that films about the Roman era still appeal to a broad audience. There is probably no single reason that Roman civilization has remained a popular topic, but it is worth identifying the aspects of Roman civilization that have seemed relevant in modern times.

The Ben Hur chariot race re-created in a nineteenth-century print. (Library of Congress)

The crowd gives "thumbs down" to a defeated gladiator in the Colosseum, Rome. Engraving after a nineteenth-century French painting. (Library of Congress)

One of the more intangible aspects of Rome that intrigues modern people is the idea of Roman excess. Roman civilization was generally a very conservative and moderate society. But popular imagination has created a Rome of brutal violence, lewd sexual activity, and an unquenchable appetite for luxury. There is, of course, some truth in these characterizations, even though the Romans were not really as shocking as some sources suggest. But certainly some aspects of Roman life are very prominent in popular culture. Gladiatorial combat and violent entertainment are of huge interest. Many modern cultural critics have drawn parallels between Roman blood sports and modern sports like boxing and wrestling. But such parallels are overstatements, because killing people as an entertainment spectacle is not acceptable in modern culture. Yet there is something fascinating about the idea of killing for entertainment that viscerally affects people today. Likewise, stories of the emperors (often based on uncritical reading of only mildly "historical" accounts) have misled mod-

Thomas Couture, *Romans of the Decadence*, 1847. (Réunion des Musées Nationaux/Art Resource, NY)

ern audiences about the reality of Roman civic virtues. Perhaps the most extreme example of this is the motion picture *Caligula*, which portrays Roman society as less chaste than Roman moralists would have us believe, based on uncritical readings of the author Suetonius.

On a less popular level, the study of Rome is interesting for what it can reveal about the roots of modern institutions. Many aspects of modern everyday life originated in Roman times. For example, the names of the months and days are based on Roman designations. In fact, the modern calendar is based on the Roman calendar, although it has undergone significant changes. The names of the planets are derived from the names of Roman gods. Arches and concrete—technologies perfected by the Romans—are still found in buildings today. Also, many Catholic readers may well be shocked to see the pre-Christian origins of some of the officers of the papacy.

That leads to another area of relevance of Roman times in the present: Christianity originated in Roman times. Although it developed from older Jewish traditions, early Christianity should be understood within its Roman context. The traditions of Jesus and all of the writings of the New Testament can be firmly dated to the Roman period. A good understanding of Roman civilization can help Christians understand more about their traditions and better understand the writings and concerns of the people who played formative roles in early Christianity. Likewise, Judaism was fundamentally transformed by its encounter with Roman civilization. Indeed, many aspects of modern Judaism

The Connecticut Avenue bridge in Washington, D.C., utilizes concrete and round arches, both of which were pioneered in Roman architecture. (Library of Congress)

The Los Angeles Coliseum evokes comparisons with the design of the Roman amphitheater and the circus (hippodrome). (Douglas Slone/Corbis)

A re-creation of entertainment taking place in the Circus Maximus, Rome. (Pixel That)

Tourists look at the fragmented colossal statue of the Emperor Constantine, in the Capitoline Museum, Rome. (Benjamin Rondel/Corbis)

can be said to have originated in Roman times. The study of Roman-period Judaism and Christianity is itself a discipline, so this book will not provide extensive detail on that topic. However, to understand early Christianity and Second Temple–period Judaism, a strong understanding of Roman civilization is essential.

Another aspect of modern life that has been fundamentally influenced by Roman times is language. Latin is the basis of the Romance languages and is a distant relative of English and German. Until the 1970s, the study of Latin was an important part of any education. More than just helpful for comprehending Latin literature, the study of Latin can provide a better understanding of modern language. Because language is the fundamental orienting principle for the way people think about and understand the world, a better understanding of language can help us to better understand ourselves.

A NOTE ABOUT THE DATES USED IN THIS BOOK

The dates used in this book might appear strange at first. B.C.E. and C.E., rather than B.C. or A.D., are used throughout. For practical purposes, B.C.E. is exactly equivalent to B.C., and C.E. is exactly the same as A.D. But from a theological perspective, the distinction is very important, although it is not something that most readers would consider. Because the term *A.D.* is an abbreviation for the expression *anno Domini,* which is essentially a profession of Christian faith, the use of B.C. and A.D. can, although usually unintentionally, exclude non-Christians. So, although Roman studies more commonly use B.C. and A.D., there is a general movement away from that terminology in archaeology. On a less politically correct note, most readers are aware that the abbreviation "c." or "ca." stands for the Latin *circa* "about." *Circa* means that the exact date is not known, but a fairly accurate approximation can be made.

HOW DO WE KNOW ABOUT THE ROMANS?

On a very basic level, it is important to recognize the sources for what is known about the Romans. Modern scholars are extremely lucky because a huge amount of data is available for the study of ancient Rome, arguably more than for any other ancient civilization. We never forgot the Romans; this civilization has always been part of the cultural memory. Unlike Mesopotamia, which disappeared from popular consciousness for centuries, Roman civilization has continued to play a primary role in Western intellectual traditions. Partly because of this, and partly because of the nature of Roman remains, modern scholars have three major kinds of sources for the study of Roman civilization: textual, archaeological, and art-historical. This book uses all three types of data to present a broad overview of Roman civilization.

Roman-period literature has provided one of the most important sources of information for the study of Roman civilization. Although countless volumes of Roman literature have not been preserved, a substantial amount of preserved documents still survives. The importance of these documents in medieval Islam and Renaissance Europe guaranteed their preservation in one form or another. A variety of types of Roman literature exist, mostly in Latin or Greek. Among these are historical writings, literary writings, religious writings, treatises on science and philosophy, and many other types of writing. All of these sources can and have been used by scholars to reconstruct Roman civilization and preserve its traditions. Most of the existing copies of this literature come from hand-copied documents that date to periods after Roman civilization had waned. But occasionally ancient editions of these texts can be found. One of the most notable caches of ancient texts was discovered in 1752 in Herculaneum. But this is unusual because the materials the Romans used for writing did not preserve well in the Italian climate due to the combination of heat and humidity.

A more recent development in the study of Roman civilization is the use of archaeological materials. Information gained from archaeological excavations is substantially different from the kind of information that can be gleaned from ancient writings. Roman archaeology is a well-established discipline, and much has been learned from the excavation of Roman sites throughout the Mediterranean region.

Related to the archaeological evidence (although it should be distinguished from it) is the art-historical evidence. Techniques for the study of art have been successfully employed in the study of Roman civilization. The focus of art history is different from that of archaeology, even though both kinds of evidence are artifactual. Although different methods and tools of interpretation have been employed in researching ancient Rome and Roman art, the knowledge that has been gained through the various methods is an important component of the study of ancient Rome.

SOURCES OF INFORMATION ON THE ROMANS

The centuries of research on Roman civilization have created a vast amount of scholarly tools and secondary literature. This huge body of work can be quite intimidating at first, so this book provides a map of sorts to Roman scholarly materials. What follows here is a guide to the major tools used by Roman studies scholars in their research. At the end of this volume is an annotated list of some of the major English-language treatments of Roman topics. The bibliography at the end of each chapter should also be considered. These works are not usually directly referenced in the body of the chapters, but it is important to be aware of the sources used for the information presented. Scholarship is a continuous process of building on what has been done before. This book should be used as a reference tool for Roman scholarship. No claims are made concerning the originality of this work, so I want to acknowledge the sources used and the much greater contribution they have made to the field by having provided new ideas and analyses. The ideas in this book are mostly not original; rather, they reflect an understanding of the centuries of previous scholarship on this topic. One last warning before you begin: None of these lists should be considered complete, but they will provide enough information for getting started.

Journals

Many scholarly journals are dedicated to the study of Roman civilization. Most of these journals presuppose that the reader already has a fairly strong knowledge of Rome, and the articles are geared toward a scholarly audience. That should not cause the reader to become intimidated. After getting used to scholarly styles of writing, readers will find that the articles are not that difficult after all. Journals intended for popular audiences are also very important, even to professional archaeologists. What makes popular journals so important is that frequently these forums are the first places where new research and excavations are published. It is important to read them to keep up-to-date. The following is a presentation of some of the more prominent (and mostly English-language) journals, but this list is by no means exhaustive. The best way to discover new journals and to get a taste for what they have to offer is to check the bibliographies of books and articles.

There is a long tradition of journal publication among the various national schools in Rome (see chapter 3 for the history of research in the field). These schools publish various journals, collections, and monographs and are important sources of information on current research projects. The American Academy in Rome publishes *Memoirs of the American Academy in Rome*. The British School publishes *Papers of the British School at Rome*. Both of these publications are written primarily in English. French-language resources include the French School's *Bibliothèque des écoles français d'Athènes et de Rome* and *Mélanges de l'École français de Rome, Antiquité*. The German School's *Mitteilungen des Deutschen Archäologischen Instituts, Römische Abteilung* is an important German-language resource.

Many universities publish their own journals devoted to Roman or classical studies. In the United States, *Yale Classical Studies* and *Harvard Studies in Classical Philology* are published by Yale and Harvard respectively. The Johns Hopkins University Press publishes the *American Journal of Philology*. *California Studies in Classical Antiquity*, published by University of California Press, is useful as well. In the United Kingdom, prominent university-based journals include *Proceedings of the Cambridge Philological Society* and the *Oxford Journal of Archaeology*, although neither is devoted entirely to Roman matters.

A number of journals are devoted solely to scholarship on Rome. For general articles as well as useful book reviews, look to the *Journal of Roman Studies*. More specifically related to archaeological matters is the *Journal of Roman Archaeology*, published annually. For those specifically interested in ceramics, the *Journal of Roman Pottery Studies* will be important. The *Numismatic Chronicle* and the *American Journal of Numismatics* are geared toward the study of coins, but not exclusively Roman coins.

More common are journals devoted to classical studies in general. These publications typically concentrate on Greek and Roman subject matter, but many also include studies on other aspects of the ancient world or on the communities that used the Latin language. A host of publications that contain the word "classical" in their title are available, including *Bulletin of the Institute of Classical Studies, Classical Bulletin, Classical Folia, Classical Journal, Classical*

Philology, Classical Quarterly, Classical Review, Classical World, New England Classical Journal, and *Acta Classica,* to name a few. Other important resources include *Ancient History Bulletin, Antiquities Journal,* and *Transactions of the American Philological Association.* Important journals that deal with the study of the past in general and frequently feature important works on Roman civilization include *American Journal of Archaeology* and *Past and Present.*

Popular periodicals devoted to the study of the ancient world are numerous. Perhaps the most prominent popular publication, occasionally presenting Roman materials, is *National Geographic.* The magazine *Archaeology* is widely available and frequently publishes articles relating to Roman archaeology. *Archaeology Odyssey* is a similar publication but is less readily available. Both *Near Eastern Archaeology* and *Biblical Archaeology Review* concentrate on the Near East but frequently publish articles on Roman-period materials. The Italian *ROMArcheologica* is a prominent publication, and even if one does not read Italian, the photographs are well worth perusing.

Electronic journals are becoming more common in Roman studies and will doubtless only increase in popularity. The *Bryn Mawr Classical Review* is a free journal located at *http://ccat.sas.upenn.edu/bmcr.* Other E-journals include *ARACHNION: A Journal of Ancient Literature and History on the Web, Classics Ireland, Cultures and Classics, Electronic Antiquity: Communicating the Classics, Scholia,* and *The Stoa.* Most of these journals can be found by typing the title into a search engine like Google or Yahoo!. One warning, however: a slow Internet connection can make downloading E-journals quite frustrating.

Reference Books

Two of the most common formats for reference works on Rome and the classical world are a dictionary and an encyclopedia. These types of books provide alphabetic listings on various topics. Arguably the most prominent English-language book of this type is *The Oxford Classical Dictionary* (1996), edited by Simon Hornblower and Antony Spawforth, now in its third edition. By the same editors is *The Oxford Companion to Classical Civilization* (1998), which provides encyclopedia-length entries on most facets of Greek and Roman life. Also by Oxford is *The Oxford Companion to Classical Literature* (1989) and the smaller (but much more affordable) *Oxford Concise Companion to Classical Literature* (1996). Available for a very low price is *The Wordsworth Classical Dictionary* (1996), reprinted from the 1852 dictionary compiled by William Smith. Although outdated, this book is an unbelievable bargain, and for the most part, it is still useful for quick reference. An extremely useful German-language reference tool is *Paulys Realencyclopaedie der classischen Altertumswissenschaft.* An English-language edition is currently in preparation (only the first volume is available), titled *Brill's New Pauly Encyclopedia of the Ancient World.* For the study of Roman religion, Adkins and Adkins' *Dictionary of Roman Religion* (1996) is useful and available at most bookstores.

Reference books are available in other formats as well, but only two of them are cited here; other good titles are cited in the guide to further reading located at the end of this book. For history, there is no better source than *The Cambridge Ancient History.* Another fundamental tool for students is the three-volume series *Civilization of the Ancient Mediterranean: Greece and Rome,* edited by Michael Grant and Rachel Kitzinger.

More specialized reference works on a number of topics are available. Perhaps the most important work for the study of Rome is the *Corpus Inscriptionum Latinarum,* begun by Theodor Mommsen, which collects Latin inscriptions. Selections taken from this volume are normally cited with the abbreviation *CIL* and the number of the inscription from within the volume. Guides to Roman topography are also available. Richardson's *Topographical Dictionary of Ancient Rome* (1992) is good. More in depth is the six-volume *Lexicon Topographicum Urbis Romae* by Eva Steinby, as well as the *Lexicon Topographicum Suburbium Romae.* Those interested in the study of the history of the republic should also be aware of T. Robert S. Broughton's important work, *Magistrates of the Roman Republic.* The importance of this work cannot be overstressed.

Reference works that provide tools to use with the secondary literature on Rome are also available. An important tool is the *Dictionary of Bibliographic Abbreviations Found in the Scholarship of Classical Studies and Related Disciplines* (1983) by Jean Wellington, which provides lists of the abbreviations used by scholars. Although this may not seem important, it is very difficult to keep track of all of the different abbreviations used in Roman studies. Another important type of guide to the secondary literature is the bibliography. There are many monograph-length bibliographies devoted to classical studies, with different goals and organizational schemes. Three useful volumes are *Classical Scholarship: An Annotated Bibliography* (1986) by Thomas Halton and Stella O'Leary, *Classical Studies: A Guide to the Reference Literature* (1996) by Fred Jenkins, and *Ancient Greece and Rome: A Bibliographic Guide* (1995) by Keith Hopwood.

Anthologies of Classical Sources

A prominent genre of book used in Roman studies is the anthology. Anthologies of Roman texts tend to be organized in one of two ways. One way is to organize the anthology as selections of writings from specific authors, to give the novice reader a taste of Roman literature. The other way is to take selections from classical sources and present them in a manner that illuminates certain aspects of the history and civilization of Rome. This type is known as the thematic anthology. The purposes of these two types of anthology are different. The first type exposes the reader to literature. The second type, while still offering the reader an exposure to literature, also brings out certain themes of Roman civilization. Some of the better anthologies include David Cherry's *The Roman World: A Sourcebook* (2001), Basil Davenport's *The Portable Roman Reader* (1951), and Naphtali Lewis and Meyer Reinhold's *Roman Civilization Sourcebook 1: The Republic* (1966). But by far, the anthology used most frequently in classrooms is Jo-Ann Shelton's *As the Romans Did* (1988).

Series

A number of series of books can be helpful for the study of Roman civilization. The quintessential series dedicated to the study of Classical literature is the *Loeb Classical Library,* published by Harvard University Press. This is an extremely useful series, dedicated to publishing the original Latin and Greek writing alongside the corresponding English translations. The red-colored volumes contain Latin language, and the green volumes contain Greek. Each book provides the text in the original language on the left page, and the accompanying translation is found on the right. Also included in each volume are a critical apparatus and good introductory materials. These books are the standard of the field in the English-speaking world.

For those who do not read Latin and Greek, there are several other series that publish ancient literature. *Penguin Classics* are always good translations, and usually the volumes include excellent introductory essays. These books are probably the best introductory translations of ancient literature. Very inexpensive translations of ancient literature are available as *Dover Thrift Editions.* Although this series typically uses out-of-date translations (translations so old that they are legally considered public domain), the low price makes them a viable option for interested readers.

A number of monograph series are devoted to Roman studies. Two important series are *Papers and Monographs of the American Academy in Rome,* published by the American Academy in Rome, and *Journal of Roman Archaeology Supplemental Series,* published by the *Journal of Roman Archaeology,* both of which publish monographs on Roman issues. Another series that is quite good is the Classical Association at the Clarendon Press's *Greece and Rome: New Surveys in the Classics,* which publishes short books on a variety of subjects. So much has been written about Rome that it is impossible to list all of the academic series here.

Many series of books devoted to nonspecialist audiences can be helpful in learning about Rome. *Shire* books, by Shire Publications, provide easy introductions to a variety of topics in archaeology. Also good is the *Interpreting the Past* series, published by the University of California Press/British Museum. These books are dedicated to popular audiences but are written by experts in the subject covered. They are easy to read and accurate. The *Discoveries* series, published by Harry N. Abrams, Inc., Publishers, also includes a variety of easy-to-read books on a variety of archaeological topics and is often available at museum giftshops and large bookstores.

UNIVERSITIES AND RESEARCH PROGRAMS

Many research programs are available in North America and Europe for the study of Roman civilization. (For a list of graduate programs in the United States, see *http://www.williams.edu/Classics/Grad_Programs.html,* and for programs throughout the rest of the world, see *http://www.classics.cam.ac.uk/ Faculty/departments.html.*) The first requirement of a research program is an undergraduate degree, which can be specifically in Roman studies, or in a related discipline, such as history, anthropology, ancient languages, or art history, just to give a few examples. It is not necessary for students to specialize until they reach the graduate stage. At this level, students generally specialize not only in Roman studies, but also in a specific aspect of Roman studies, such as Latin or archaeology. A master's degree is usually only a one- or two-year program, sometimes involving the writing of a thesis. Most PhD programs in Roman studies no longer require a master's degree, but a master's nonetheless provides a valuable experience and requires a far smaller time commitment than does a PhD. If you have a master's degree in Roman studies, you would be qualified to teach at some schools (although usually not at research institutions) and to work in museums or other specialized institutions. However, most active scholars in Roman studies have a PhD or are in the process of working on one. This is quite a serious commitment, involving the writing of a dissertation. In North America, students are expected to continue with class work while working on their dissertations, but in Britain it is more common just to jump right into the dissertation.

It is also worth pointing out that no matter what level of formal education in Roman studies is desired (if any at all), learning languages is one of the most important things to do in preparation. Roman scholars should know Latin and Greek, and some specialize in other languages as well. But the ancient languages are not the only ones that are important to learn: A working knowledge of other modern languages is equally important. For Roman studies, scholars should be able to operate in Italian, French, and German. These languages (along with English) are the major scholarly idioms of Roman studies, and those who are unable to read them are excluded from a vast amount of scholarly work. So, one piece of sound advice is to start learning languages as soon as possible. Language study can only help the researcher or the scholar.

Organizations

Outside of (but related to) the university setting are scholarly organizations dedicated to the study of Roman civilization and the classics in general. These groups typically publish newsletters and/or journals, organize conferences, and provide other services for members. Usually there is a membership fee, but this varies considerably from organization to organization. The members of such organizations typically are academics, but it is not unheard of for members of the lay public to be involved. Some of the more important organizations in North America and the United Kingdom are *American Philological Association, American Classical League, Archaeological Institute of America, Association of Ancient Historians, Centre for Roman Studies, Classical Association of Canada, The Classical Association, Classical Association of Scotland,* and *Women's Classical Caucus.* There are a number of regional organizations in the United States devoted to the study of classics, including *Classical Association of the Atlantic States, Classical Association of the Middle West and South, Classical Association of New England,* and the *Classical Association of the Pacific Northwest.* Many states have their own classical studies organizations as well.

Online Resources

Typing "ancient rome" into an Internet search engine will generate literally hundreds of links. A few of the more useful free sites for studying Roman civilization are listed here. Be patient when trying to find these sites—Web pages change and servers can go down. By the time this book is published, many of these links may have already expired. But typing some of the key words of the links into a search engine should help to find the sites if they still exist. Most of the Web pages listed here have been stable for some time now, so try the supplied link first. However, do not feel limited to these sites—have fun and follow the links.

Sites that provide links to other Roman Web pages are among the first types of Web pages with which the beginner scholar should become familiar. These sites will open up the Internet for you and start you on a useful trail to finding what you are interested in. An excellent resource is *Electronic Resources for Classicists: The Second Generation (ERC2)*, located at *http://www.tlg.uci.edu/~tlg/index/resources.html*. This Web page offers links to a variety of electronic resources available for classical studies, from university department Web pages to discussion groups. Educators may be interested in the links to educational materials for kindergarten to college-level studies. A similar resource is *Internet Resources for Classicists*, located at *http://www.sms-va.com/mdl-indx/internet.htm*. *Corax: A Classics Hypersite*, at *http://omni.cc.purdue.edu/~corax/*, is also a good place to start. A Web page that also has links to sites dealing with other aspects of the ancient world is *Links to Classical Material*, at *http://www.vuw.ac.nz/classics/links.html*.

General information about Rome is available at a number of sites. Start with *ROMARCH*, located at *http://acad.depauw.edu/romarch/*. At the time of this writing, *ROMARCH* offered access to good discussion groups and a clickable map feature that provided links and ratings of sites. Another good site is *Lacus Curtius: Into the Roman World*, located at *http://www.ukans.edu/history/index/europe/ancient_rome/E/Roman/home.html*. This site provides a gazetteer to Roman sites (and photographs), along with some important public-domain works available in their entirety. Many aspects of Roman society are discussed at *Richard's site about the Roman civilization*, located at *http://main-vision.com/richard/Romans.html*.

Another important type of Web page is the virtual library. This is especially useful if one does not have access to a library with substantial Roman materials. Without a doubt, the most important virtual library (for classicists) on the Internet is *Perseus*, currently located at *http://www.perseus.tufts.edu*. This site is remarkable for the sheer number of classical writings offered, most translated into English. It is an excellent site for quickly looking up a source, because it is so easy to navigate. *Perseus* also has virtual exhibitions, although these do not change very frequently. *The Latin Library* at *http://www.thelatinlibrary.com/* also offers a good virtual library of Latin texts, although they are all written in Latin. Latin readers may also find *Bibliotheca Latina*, at *http://polyglot.lss.wisc.edu/classics/biblio.htm*, to be useful. The *Internet Ancient History Sourcebook* at *http://www.fordham.edu/halsall/ancient/asbook.html* provides translations of Roman texts organized for classroom use.

The Internet has many resources that can help one to acquire Latin-language skills. A dictionary, study aids, and some Latin texts can be found at *Latin Language and Literature* at *http://www.csbsju.edu/library/internet/latin.html*. A variety of materials that can assist the Latin scholar can be found at *Tools of the Trade* at *http://classics.rutgers.edu/resources.html.* Latin teachers may find *The Latin List* listserv useful for contacting other Latin teachers; it can be found at *http://www. geocities.com/Athens/Styx/1790/index.html.* Similarly useful is *Latinteach* at *http:// www.latinteach.com/.*

Many sites are dedicated to specific topics in Roman civilization. A timeline of important events in Roman history, from 2000 B.C.E. to 300 C.E., is available at *www.exovedate.com/ancient_timeline_one.html.* An online encyclopedia of Roman emperors, *De Imperatoribus Romanis,* is available at *http://www. roman-emperors.org/startup.html.* The best resource for the study of Roman law is *Roman Law Resources* at *http://www.iuscivile.com.* Roman (and other historical) weights and measures can be converted into their metric equivalents at *http:// www.convert-me.com/en/.* Roman dates and numbers are converted into the numerical system at *http://www.guernsey.net/~sgibbs/roman.html.*

Museums and Tourism

One of the truly great aspects of studying ancient Rome is the accessibility of the ancient artifacts and architecture. Many Roman archaeological sites are open to tourists, and the remains are awe-inspiring. Archaeological sites of other cultures are often nothing more than holes in the ground or modern reconstructions of ancient buildings. Roman construction, however, was so strong that many buildings have survived to the present. When visiting a site, it is possible to actually walk through buildings that the ancient Romans inhabited. Rome is an excellent tourist destination, and there is a strong emphasis on ancient remains within the local tourist industry. But also worth considering is a visit to Roman-era sites in other parts of the world. Often, these Roman-era cities are far less crowded with tourists than Rome, and there is more freedom to wander and explore. Sites in Israel (like Caesarea) and Jordan (like Jerash) are wonderfully preserved, giving the visitor a good sense of what Roman life was like. Similarly, visitors to Egypt have the chance to discover the substantial Ptolemaic and Roman-period remains, which make up the vast majority of tourist destinations.

Museums provide another opportunity for people to experience Roman material culture. There are so many museums with Roman exhibits, it is impossible to list them all here. A good approach is to browse through travel guides for the city you are visiting. Good travel guides will have lists of museums with a description of their collections. A list of museums with links to home pages can be found on the Web at *http://www.vuw.ac.nz/classics/depts.html,* but this list is far from complete. The sheer volume of surviving Roman artifacts has meant that such artifacts can be found in museums throughout the world.

PART 2

Roman Civilization

II CHAPTER 2
Location of Roman Civilization and Environmental Setting

An important first step in any archaeological investigation is to understand the physical environment in which the ancient people lived. There are several reasons why this is imperative. The natural environment is the stage on which human action plays. The constraints imposed by and the possibilities made available by certain environments have a fundamental effect on the humans who live in them. For example, Bedouin living in the Sinai and Americans living in New York City obviously would have different access to resources and different environmental constraints. In comparison with New Yorkers, the Bedouins' resources are scarce, but the Bedouins' freedom of movement and living space are much greater than that of New Yorkers. The same is true in regard to ancient civilizations. To comprehend an ancient culture, it is important to understand what its environmental constraints were.

The environment also affects what is preserved in the archaeological record. Some materials survive better in different conditions than others. For example, the bog marshes in northern Europe are damp enough to preserve human bodies—so well that many "bog men" have survived from the late Bronze Age to the present. The Egyptian climate is well suited to the preservation of papyrus, so it has been possible to retrieve much Egyptian writing. Depositional processes also affect sites as a whole. A volcanic eruption preserved the Roman cities of Pompeii and Herculaneum in their entirety. In contrast, the constant occupation of the city of Rome has obscured much of its archaeological material. An archaeologist must understand how the physical environment has affected an archaeological site before making any conclusions about that site.

The study of the ecosystems in which ancient humans lived is so important that a whole subdiscipline of archaeology is devoted to it. Environmental archaeology seeks to understand human interaction as part of an ecosystem. Rather than focusing only on artifacts (objects created and used by humans), archaeologists now study plant, animal, and geological remains. Using a variety of scientific techniques, archaeologists can reconstruct the environments in which humans lived to understand how humans affected and were affected by their environment.

This chapter provides a broad overview of the environmental setting of Roman civilization. The enormity of the Roman Empire meant that ancient Roman civilization encountered many different ecosystems and environments. These issues are explored in the following sections.

The ruins of Herculaneum, Ercolano, Italy. (Roger Ressmeyer/Corbis)

LOCATION OF ROME

Rome, as a geographic term, can refer to two very different entities. Rome was and is a city, located in modern Italy, on the Tiber River. But Rome also designates an ancient empire, a large geographic region with constantly shifting borders that encompassed many distinct climatic zones. The two uses of the name *Rome* indicate an intrinsic connection between the city and the empire. Rome was seen as the center of Roman civilization—the region from which power and authority radiated out toward the rest of the empire.

The earliest occupation of the city seems to have been in the middle Bronze Age; however, the remains from this time are meager. From that period on, the city of Rome has been occupied almost continuous, making archaeological excavation difficult. Certain areas (such as the Forum) preserve ancient remains. And certainly new construction can uncover new archaeological evidence.

Rome was founded on highly productive fertile soils, 20 km inland. This region is typified by irregularly shaped spurs (hills), which were formed by tributary rivers of the Tiber that had cut through the plains. Roman traditions held that Rome was founded on seven of these spurs, but the traditions are not consistent about which seven hills. The four largest spurs (on the left bank of the Tiber) are known as the Quirinal, the Esquiline, the Caelian, and the Aventine. Each of these spurs ended in a knoll that was also referred to as a hill. The most

A map shows the extent of the Roman Empire during the time of Constantine the Great. (Library of Congress)

A view of the Roman Forum. (Library of Congress)

important three knolls were the two at the end of the Esquiline called the Palatine Hill and the Velia Hill and one at the end of the Quirinal called the Capitoline Hill. The low-lying floodplain on the east of the Tiber and north of the Capitoline Hill is called the Campus Martius (Field of Mars). During the Republican period, this space was left open for military and legislative assem-

A model of ancient Rome, with the Colosseum in the center. (Araldo de Luca/Corbis)

blies. During the empire period, it was gradually filled with public buildings. At its height in the Roman period, Rome was one of the largest cities in the world, measuring from 3 to 5 km across at any given point. More information on the development of the city of Rome is located in chapter 9.

GENERAL NATURAL AND CULTURAL SUBDIVISIONS

The Roman Empire encompassed a vast number of different geographic regions. (For the history of the growth of the Roman Empire, see chapter 4.) As the Roman Empire grew, it encountered a number of different environments to which it was forced to adapt through a variety of means. But Roman culture actually developed out of its relationship to its immediate environment. That environment was what is now known as Italy and the Mediterranean. It was this environment that had the greatest influence on the development of Roman life. Following is a discussion of three discrete regions (southern Italy, the Mediterranean, and northern Italy), including some mention about the environments of the Roman provinces.

Southern Italy

The city of Rome is located in southern Italy, an area also referred to as peninsular Italy. The dominant geographic feature of peninsular Italy is the Apennines mountain range. This mountain range divides southern Italy in two halves. The eastern side is often referred to as the Adriatic side (because it borders the Adriatic Sea) and the western half is referred to as the Tyrrhenian side (because it borders the Tyrrhenian Sea). On the Adriatic side, the coast is low and sandy and the waters are very shallow. The area around Venice is the only area that allows access to oceangoing vessels. The western coast, on the other hand, is broken up by bays and gullies and provides natural positions for anchorage. One of these western coastal features, the Golfo di Napoli (Bay of Naples), is dominated by Mount Vesuvius. The Golfo di Taranto (Gulf of Taranto) separates the "heel" and "toe" of Italy.

The Tyrrhenian side has a much more stable system of rivers than the Adriatic side. This allowed easy communication throughout the region (Hughes 1998: 104). Both the Tiber and the Arno Rivers are navigable and both have predictable courses. The rivers on the Adriatic side are less predictable and dry up in the summer months. This posed serious problems with communication and transportation, especially in pre-Roman times, when river and water transport was the easiest means of travel.

Rome's favorable position on the waterways facilitated its rapid development. The city is situated on the left bank of the Tiber River (whose source is in the Apennines), about 22 km inland from the sea, in a region known as Latium. Rome's distance from the sea prevented the development of a significant harbor, but this distance also made the city less vulnerable to attack by sea. Rome's vantage point on the Tiber was a nodal position. From this spot, access could be easily gained to many of the other rivers, especially because this was a particularly calm stretch of the Tiber. The Arno River, which also has a source in the Apennines, flows west consistently. From a transportation and communication perspective, Rome was in the very center of southern Italy.

Climate.   The climate of southern Italy is distinct from that of northern Italy. It is a Mediterranean climate, a climate common to most of the land directly situated around the Mediterranean Sea (see page 25). This climate is very conducive to human habitation. The winters are mild and the summers are hot. Rain can be quite heavy during the winter months, but from June to August there is next to no precipitation. On the Adriatic side, rivers dry up completely during these months.

Volcanoes

Italy is a region that has experienced much volcanic activity. It is home to Europe's highest volcano, Mount Etna, which towers at 3,323 m in height. Located on the east coast of Sicilia, this volcano has erupted at least ninety times in recorded history and probably many other times as well. More infamous is Mount Vesuvius, which erupted on August 24, 79 C.E., covering Pompeii and Herculaneum. Vesuvius is the only active volcano in continental Europe. It rises from the Plain of Campania to a height of 1,277 m. Its base is 48 km wide, making it quite large. Vesuvius has two summits, the highest of which is Vesuvius proper.

Soil. Much of peninsular Italy (especially Campania, Latium, and Tuscany) has very productive soil. Extinct volcanoes and crater lakes are typical of this region, which makes the earth well suited to agriculture. Volcanic soils create natural fertilizers and thus provide a rich environment for plant life. (See sidebar above.)

Flora. The flora of southern Italy is Mediterranean. It is well adapted to the climatic extremes of the region and is a fruitful natural resource. Vineyards and olive groves grow well in this climate and are found throughout southern Italy. Grapevines and olive trees were introduced to the region in antiquity and are quite destructive to the soil and to other kinds of plant life. It takes a long time for vines and olive trees to grow into productive resources after their initial planting. Once they have grown, however, it is difficult for other flora to grow in the same area. Other kinds of plant life in southern Italy include fig trees, pomegranate trees, date trees, and almond trees.

Fauna. Animal life in Italy is much less rich than in the rest of Europe. Until human encroachment, the rest of continental Europe was teeming with wildlife, including deer, elk, bison, bears, boars, and wolves. Italy has (and had) only a small amount of these animals. Wolves and wild boars are present in Italy's mountain ranges. Bears roamed the countryside at one time but were hunted to extinction long ago. Foxes are common, and in the Alps, marmots, chamois, and ibex can still be found. Italy is home to many bird species, including eagles, hawks, vultures, buzzards, falcons, quails, woodcocks, and partridges. In addition, migratory birds use Italy as a seasonal home.

Typical of Apennine Italy is the variability between lowland plain and hill, a feature that was well suited for transhumance. Transhumance involved the seasonal movement of pigs and sheep (rarely cattle) between the farmlands and the hills. The hill regions provided ample food for the flocks, and their close proximity to farmland made the journey short and easy. This allowed small agricultural communities to feed their flocks from wild growing plants,

Vineyards below a Tuscan hill town. (Jay Syverson/Corbis)

which meant the communities were not forced to use their crops as fodder. Pigs and sheep provided several benefits, such as wool, meat, and milk.

The Mediterranean

The Mediterranean Basin is the geographic region bordering the Mediterranean Sea. The ecosystem throughout this landmass is broadly consistent. Despite this fact, the Mediterranean Basin is not often studied as a holistic unit, because it encompasses sections of southern Europe, North Africa, and Asia Minor. Since Braudel's important work, *The Mediterranean and the Mediterranean World in the Age of Philip II,* was published, historians and archaeologists have recognized the importance of understanding how the distinct nature of this ecosystem affects human habitation. The United Nations Educational, Scientific, and Cultural Organization (UNESCO) recently recognized the importance of viewing the Mediterranean as a whole and has developed a project called the Blue Plan, on which it bases economic and social planning for the region (King 1997: 3–4).

Although most scholars recognize the utility of thinking of this environment in terms of the Mediterranean, few agree on the exact boundaries of this area. King (1997: 5) has suggested that it may be better to view the Mediterranean as an experiential entity, rather than one whose borders can be drawn on a map. As a general rule of thumb, however, the Mediterranean region should be understood as the landmasses surrounding the Mediterranean Sea that share a consistent climate.

The Mediterranean Sea.   The Mediterranean Sea is the common denominator of the surrounding lands characterized as Mediterranean. The ancient Romans called it *mare nostrum,* which means "our sea." The sea is about 2,509,000 sq. km in area, and about 3,600 km in length (from the Straits of Gibraltar to the coast of Israel). Its width varies, reaching a maximum of approximately 1,100 km. The depth varies considerably—the maximum depth is about 5,150 m, and the average depth is about 1,501 m. Its major source is the Atlantic Ocean.

The Mediterranean is surrounded almost entirely by land, except for the opening at the Straits of Gibraltar. Islands of various sizes are peppered throughout. Because the sea is landlocked (oceans do not affect it), tides are very calm. Currents are much more apparent and familiarity with them was essential for ancient seafarers. On a local scale, the currents tend to run counterclockwise up against the shores of various locations. The landlocked nature of the sea contributes to its salinity (Hughes 1998: 103). This, along with its high rate of evaporation, makes it a very salty body of water, much more so than the Atlantic Ocean. An undersea ridge divides the Mediterranean into two basins (Hughes 1998: 102). The ridge runs from Tunisia to Silicia, dividing the sea into an east side and a west side.

Climate.   The climate of the region is similar to climates such as those of California and western Australia, so "Mediterranean" can refer to a specific climate as well as to a region. The Mediterranean climate is subtropical, and its most noticeable characteristic is that it has only two seasons rather than four. The region has cool, wet winters and very hot summers with droughtlike conditions. The wettest period is from October to May, and the hottest months are June to August, although this is not entirely consistent throughout all of the Mediterranean.

Precipitation is variable throughout the region; some areas receive much more rain than others. Averages of the annual rainfall are basically meaningless; the amount varies widely from year to year (Perry 1997: 36). However, even in the wettest months, rainfall never occurs in great quantities. From a meteorological perspective, the Mediterranean climate has three times the amount of winter rainfall than summer rainfall, but this is a gross oversimplification. Often, the rain comes in massive torrents, and sometimes a large proportion of the annual rainfall arrives in a single day. This creates difficulties for farming. The region's rainfall cannot be considered a dependable source of water for crops, even though the precipitation statistics make the rainfall seem consistent throughout the course of a year (Perry 1997: 36).

One climatic feature that makes the Mediterranean region so pleasant, despite the high temperatures, is the winds. Cool breezes moderate the hot summer temperatures, making the atmosphere feel much cooler than it actually is. However, the winds can be quite destructive. Winds known as the mistral bring a fire hazard to southern France each year. The fire hazard can be expected yearly because of the predictable nature of Mediterranean weather patterns. The winds follow consistent patterns of movement, and their direction and speed can be generally predicted for each season. In antiquity, the predictability of wind patterns made sailing on the Mediterranean dependent on the season (Perry 1997: 36). For example, in the late Bronze Age, the ancient city of Ugarit in Syria had laws regulating how long foreign merchants could stay in the port, because if they stayed beyond a certain month, the winds would prevent them from sailing home!

Soils.   In general, the soils of the Mediterranean region can be considered quite productive and well suited to agriculture (Hughes 1998: 98). But in the higher elevations, the mountainous topography of the Mediterranean Basin creates mountainous soils, which are very thin and subject to erosion. Because the climate is somewhere between temperate and tropical, Mediterranean soil tends to have the best qualities of soils found in either of these climatic zones.

   Two major soil types are found in the Mediterranean Basin: *terra fusca* and *terra rosa* (Hughes 1998: 98). Terra fusca is dark brown in color and tends to be present beneath forest environments; it is nonacidic. Terra rosa soil derives its name from the reddish color of the soil (caused by the presence of iron oxides). Terra rosa also tends to be very heavy and has large amounts of clay.

Terracing.   A method that farmers in hilly environments have used since ancient times is terracing, a technique that reduces the problems caused by erosion. Terracing is a process in which the shape of hillsides is altered to create flat surfaces for cultivation. The slope upon which soil can run off is reduced, helping to control erosion, and water is kept on the "terrace," thereby maximizing water use. Terraces have been used throughout the Mediterranean from the end of the Bronze Age to the present. They pose a particular problem for archaeologists, because their ongoing construction prevents any possibility of dating them. Modern farmers in the Mediterranean have begun abandoning terracing as a method of erosion prevention. The farmers often do not replace terracing with another form of erosion containment, and this has led to severe soil degradation (Rendell 1997: 53).

Flora.   The Mediterranean region is closely associated with an ecosystem known as Mediterranean Woodland. Evergreen shrubs and very small trees typify the Mediterranean Woodland. The trees can survive the intense heat of the Mediterranean summer because of their hard leaves, called sclerophyll. In droughtlike conditions, these leaves resist drying out by closing the pores that allow evaporation. When rainfall occurs again, the pores reopen.

   The flora of the Mediterranean is also well adapted to the effects of fire. Because of the sometimes intensely hot breezes, brush fires are fairly frequent. The indigenous plant life has adapted so that it can regrow after a fire. Indeed, the wild plant life of the Mediterranean is well suited to the region's extreme temperatures.

   The vegetation found in the Mediterranean today is very different from that which was present when humans first moved into the region. Much of the original vegetation of the Mediterranean has been replaced by other types of vegetation because of human interference, such as deforestation (Faulkner and Hill 1997: 255). For example, olive groves and vineyards have mostly replaced evergreen, oaks, and pine trees, once the most common forms of plant life in the area. Areas not currently cultivated by modern humans are covered with dense shrubs, called *maquis* or *macchi*.

Northern Italy

The entire Italian Peninsula should be considered a geographical unity, distinct from the rest of Europe. The Alps bound Italy on the north. Although there are numerous crossing points through the Alps (on which travel has occurred since antiquity), the Alps nevertheless created a natural barrier between Italy and continental Europe. Despite northern and southern Italy's general geographic unity in relation to Europe, important ecological differences exist between the two regions, specifically with respect to topography and climate.

Topography. Unlike peninsular Italy, lowland plains dominate northern Italy. Mountains surround the plains, and the land is more even than in the south. The major river in the region is the Po, which cuts through a large floodplain. The Po flows eastward and runs 652 km into the Adriatic Sea. With its tributaries, the Po River creates about 965 km of waterways. In pre-Roman times the floodplain flooded frequently. This problem was solved in Roman times through the digging of canals. The other major river in continental Italy is the Adige. It enters Italy from Austria and flows east into the Adriatic. Today, alluvial deposits are slowly elevating the beds of both the Adige and the Po from the mountains.

Climate. Northern Italy has a climate much more similar to central Europe than to southern Italy. Mediterranean climates (see previous section) do not extend far beyond the areas bordering the Mediterranean Sea. Northern Italy's climate is much colder, with very severe winters. Summers are severe in the other direction, with quite hot temperatures. Rain falls evenly throughout the year—northern Italy does not experience the annual drought that southern Italy does.

Flora. Further differentiating northern Italy from the south is that the olive tree does not grow in this region. Viticulture is not as successful in this environment. The whole region is very heavily wooded. Coniferous and deciduous forests are the most common woodland flora in this region. Chestnut, cypress, oak, fir, and pine trees can all be found in Italy.

The Provinces

The nature of Roman expansion meant that the Romans encountered numerous kinds of ecosystems beyond those present in Italy today. Although for the most part, the Romans can be said to have exported Roman culture and ways of living throughout the empire, this must be understood within the context of different environments. Furthermore, the cultures Rome encountered as it expanded were cultures that had developed under different environmental conditions. A detailed geographic study of each area of the Roman Empire would require volumes; only a brief mention will be made here.

The Romans eventually controlled almost all of Europe, including England. Europe is a large geographic expanse consisting of very different climatic zones. It is a highly fragmented continent, with many peninsulas and geologically complex islands. The continent has, for the most part, a radial drainage pattern, which means that most streams flow out from the center. Although Europe has a predominantly northern climate, the warm seas that surround the continent create much more moderate temperatures. Before human activity cleared it away, Europe was covered in woodland vegetation. Most of Europe was dominated by coniferous and deciduous flora, with tundra vegetation present in the highest elevations and in most northern locations.

The areas of North Africa that fell under the Roman sphere of influence were mostly regions with a Mediterranean climate. Beyond this fruitful zone, North Africa consists of desert zones with sparse populations. Egypt, which fell under Roman influence with Augustus, is an exception. The Nile delta (Lower Egypt) is a rich environment created through the interplay of the Mediterranean Sea and the Nile, forming sandy ridges. The Nile valley (Upper Egypt) is an extremely rich and agriculturally productive region, formed by the regular inundation of the Nile (until the construction of the Aswan High Dam).

The Levant (modern-day Israel, Jordan, Syria, and Lebanon) is another Mediterranean climatic zone. This region was part of the Fertile Crescent, which runs from the Levant down to between the Tigris and Euphrates Rivers in Iraq. This was (and is) a very productive region, rich in natural resources. Its strategic position as a landmass connecting Asia and Europe with Africa has made it an extremely volatile location politically.

ENVIRONMENTAL TRANSFORMATIONS

The environment of Italy has been significantly transformed since Roman times. Italy has one of the worst pollution records in the European Union. Sulfur dioxide emissions have decreased at a rate far lower than that of the rest of Europe. These emissions do great damage to buildings, and much of Italy's ancient architecture has been damaged and is still threatened. Marine environments are also changing in Italy. A process called eutrophication became so rampant in 1988 and 1989 that the government declared a state of emergency. Eutrophication is a process by which dissolved nutrients build up in a marine environment, leading to algae growth. Unchecked algae growth depletes the water of oxygen, killing animal life in the water.

On a more positive note, deforestation is decreasing in Italy. There has been a significant decline in human encroachment into forested areas. The government has also attempted to preserve forests through a park system. About 22 percent of Italy is forested, and this is likely to increase somewhat. All of these environmental changes mean that archaeologists cannot assume that the ancient Romans lived in the same ecological environment as modern Italians.

In 1981, the second-century bronze equestrian statue of Emperor Marcus Aurelius was re-moved from its location on the Capitoline Hill because of the damage caused by air pollution. (Bettmann/Corbis)

However, scientists still hotly debate whether environmental change is caused primarily by humans or by independent, uncontrollable phenomena.

Archaeological evidence suggests that from about 200 B.C.E. to about 400 C.E., the climate warmed up on a global scale. How can archaeologists know this if the Romans lacked the technology and desire to record temperature? Ancient temperature can be estimated from various kinds of evidence. The amount of carbon isotopes in the atmosphere fluctuates through time, presumably be-cause of variations in solar activity. During the Roman period, the amounts of carbon isotopes were consistent with those found in the atmosphere during better-documented warming periods. The science of palynology, or pollen analysis, yields similar results. Taking pollen cores allows one to learn the rela-tive amount of different kinds of pollen in the atmosphere at a specific period of time. The ratio of amounts of kinds of pollen is directly related to tempera-ture (Greene 1986: 81–85). Palynology informs us that there was a period of warming during Roman times. Tree rings also provide important information about climates. The width of tree rings is affected by temperature and is con-sistent globally. This makes the redwoods in California a particularly useful tool for the study of ancient Rome. The California redwoods are trees with long life spans, dating from well before the Roman period until the present. Comparison of the tree rings from archaeological sites with those from California (with known dates) constitutes an important dating system called dendrochronology (see chapter 3). It also allows us to deduce climatic variability in the past. All of this archaeological evidence suggests that the Romans had a relatively warm environment.

Another climatic change observable from the archaeological record is soil erosion. Palynological evidence from the Roman period indicates that extensive deforestation occurred (Greene 1986: 86). In addition, geomorphological studies have shown that from about the second century C.E. onward, sediment deposition in rivers increased, a fact that is consistent with deforestation and increased agriculture. It is important, therefore, to remember that although many similarities exist between the environments of ancient and modern Italy, one should not assume that the environment has remained static since the Roman era.

BIBLIOGRAPHY

Adkins, Lesley, and Roy Adkins. 1994. *Handbook to Life in Ancient Rome.* Oxford: Oxford University Press.

Braudel, Fernand. 1972. *The Mediterranean and the Mediterranean World in the Age of Philip II.* Siân Reynolds (trans.). New York: Harper & Row.

Cornell, Tim. 1995. *The Beginnings of Rome.* New York: Routledge.

Cornell, Tim, and John Matthews. 1982. *Atlas of the Roman World.* New York: Facts on File.

Faulkner, Hazel, and Alan Hill. 1997. "Forests, Soils, and the Threat of Desertification," pp. 252–272 in *The Mediterranean: Environment and Society.* Russel King, Lindsay Proudfoot, and Bernard Smith (eds.). New York: Halsted Press.

Greene, Kevin. 1986. *The Archaeology of the Roman Economy.* Berkeley: University of California Press.

Hughes, J. Donald. 1998. "Land and Sea," pp. 89–133 in *Civilization of the Ancient Mediterranean: Greece and Rome.* Michael Grant and Rachel Kitzinger (eds.). NewYork: Charles Scribner's Sons.

Keller, Donald, and David Rupp (eds.). 1983. *Archaeological Survey in the Mediterranean Area.* Oxford: BAR International Series.

King, Russel. 1997. "Introduction: An Essay on Mediterraneanism," pp. 1–11 in *The Mediterranean: Environment and Society.* Russel King, Lindsay Proudfoot, and Bernard Smith (eds.). New York: Halsted Press.

Perry, Allen. 1997. "Mediterranean Climate," pp. 30–44 in *The Mediterranean: Environment and Society.* Russel King, Lindsay Proudfoot, and Bernard Smith (eds.). New York: Halsted Press.

Proudfoot, Lindsay. 1997. "The Graeco-Roman Mediterranean," pp. 57–74 in *The Mediterranean: Environment and Society.* Russel King, Lindsay Proudfoot, and Bernard Smith (eds.). New York: Halsted Press.

Rees, Sian. 1987. "Agriculture and Horticulture," pp. 481–503 in *The Roman World.* 2 vols. John Wacher (ed.). New York: Routledge & Kegan Paul.

Rendell, Helen. 1997. "Earth Surface Processes in the Mediterranean," pp. 45–56 in *The Mediterranean: Environment and Society.* Russel King, Lindsay Proudfoot, and Bernard Smith (eds.). New York: Halsted Press.

White, Keith. 1970. *Roman Farming.* Ithaca: Cornell University Press.

III

CHAPTER 3

Historical and Chronological Setting

HISTORY OF RESEARCH

The history of research on Rome cannot be understood as the development of one discipline. From its earliest days, Roman scholarship has been multidisciplinary, involving philology, literary studies, archaeology, and many other methods of analysis. The vast amount of evidence available for the study of Rome, as well as the fact that Roman civilization was never lost or forgotten, has meant that many methods have developed for using the vast amount of available information. What follows is an overview of the main themes in the history of Roman research, from the dissolution of Rome to the present.

The Medieval World

The city of Rome shrank from prominence when Constantinople and Ravenna became the new capitals of what had once been the Roman Empire (Moatti 1993: 16). Many of the treasures of the city were taken to other locations. The population shrank, as did the physical size of Rome. The population moved off of the hills (the traditional center of Roman occupation) and into the valleys of the Tiber. Christianity had made Rome's temples obsolete. These religious sanctuaries fell into ruins, and people were kept away by the notion that these locations were haunted. Other cult places (like the Curia and the Pantheon) were converted into Christian churches. Rome was no longer part of the present—it was part of the past.

During the medieval period, Islamic civilization became an important intellectual center for learning and study. Many of the classical writings were preserved in Islamic sources and studied in this environment. Scholars have assumed that Roman learning was lost at the hands of barbarian invaders who squandered it during the medieval period. In fact, much of this learning was preserved and incorporated into Islamic culture. The study of the relationship between classical writings and medieval writings in Islam is in its infancy now, but this work should provide an interesting perspective on both cultures.

In Europe, tourists and pilgrims kept the memory of Roman civilization alive. Tour guidebooks were the main locus of medieval intellectual work on Roman civilization. Rome's prominent place in the history of Christianity made it a natural destination for pilgrims. And essential for these pilgrims' visits were guides. One of the most famous of these guides that survives today is the *Einsiedeln Itinerary*. Named after the Swiss monastery in which a copy was found, this work records eleven walks that pilgrims could take through Rome to view monuments and inscriptions (Moatti 1993: 21–22; Osborne 1996: 386). Originally dating to the eighth or ninth century (Osborne 1996: 386), itineraries like the *Einsiedeln* became very popular in the twelfth century. Arguably, however, the most important medieval guidebook to Rome was the *Mirabilia Urbis Romae*. Probably dating to the twelfth century, this book lists various monuments and recounts stories of early Christianity and ancient Rome (Sperling 1996: 551). What makes this work so important is that it formed the basis for many later guidebooks (Kinney 1996: 760). These later books were basically general guides to the city. They tended to demonstrate very poor understanding of history and concentrated on the location of visible inscriptions (Moatti 1993: 22). Latin was still a prominent language of learning, and often, these pilgrims could read Roman inscriptions (although often the vocabulary and ideas were obscure to them). The descriptions of Latin inscriptions in these guidebooks are useful to modern scholars, especially because many of the inscriptions have not survived to the present.

Ancient Rome became an important political symbol during the period of the Avignon papacy (Moatti 1993: 24). From 1309 to 1378, papal authority moved to Avignon and was under French influence. For Italy, the home of the Church for centuries, this created a crisis of identity. In the vacuum left by the departure of the Church, Italians looked to new identities rooted in a time before Christianity; in this case, they looked to ancient Rome. Interest in ancient monuments grew, sites were looted, and the antiquities trade grew alongside the changing sensibilities of what it meant to be Italian. Scholars and politicians brought ancient Rome into popular discourse. Perhaps the clearest manifestation of ancient Rome's new presence in the political discourse of the time was the political career of Cola di Rienzo (1313–1354). He was a politician who called for the restoration of the Roman Empire in Italy (Moatti 1993: 26). In 1347, Cola di Rienzo was elected "tribune of the people"—a political office that had not existed since Roman times (Moatti 1993: 26). After his election, however, Cola di Rienzo behaved bizarrely and tyrannically. Eventually he was deposed and executed by the Roman population. Although usually in less extreme forms, ideas of ancient Rome would play a prominent role in Italian politics and nationalism, especially in times when the power of the Vatican waned.

The Renaissance

Medieval Rome's deterioration began to reverse after the papacy returned to Rome. The Church became an important force in the restoration of the city and the retrieval of ancient monuments and documents. At the same time, new sensibilities toward learning and education spawned greater interest in classical history. The achievements of Greek and Roman civilization became highly valued in this period. A sense developed that the learning of these civilizations had been lost, and scholarly endeavors were initiated to recapture the lost information or to protect elements of the Greco-Roman world that had been pre-

The interior of the Vatican Library, Rome. (Library of Congress)

served. The dominant theme in these scholarly attempts was collection. Collection of ancient documents, artifacts, and data about the past was the fundamental goal of Renaissance-period Roman studies.

For modern Roman studies, the collection of ancient documents was arguably the most lasting achievement of this period. Latin and Greek inscriptions throughout Europe were recorded, and some of these editions are still important today. However, the collection of ancient writing (in Europe) can actually be said to have begun by a commission of Pope Nicholas V, who was pope from 1447 to 1455. In 1453, when the Turks captured Constantinople, Greek scholars fled to Italy, bringing with them their interest in ancient texts. In response, Nicholas V ordered that Greek manuscripts be purchased (Moatti 1993: 32). Under Nicholas V, the Vatican Library grew into a great library. Translations and commentaries of ancient texts were commissioned and great classical writers (such as Ovid and Livy) were rediscovered. Particularly noteworthy were the editions of Vitruvius's architectural treatise produced at this time, which played an important role in the development of Renaissance architecture (Moatti 1993: 33).

The study of ancient Rome did not always meet with papal approval. Indeed, the personality of the reigning pope and upper-level members of the

The sixteenth-century "Villa Rotunda" by Andrea Palladio shows the influence of the Romans on Renaissance architects. (Library of Congress)

Vatican certainly played a role in the manner in which Roman studies persisted. Perhaps the most notorious example of conflict between the Church and Roman scholars involved Julius Pompanius Leto and the organization he founded, known as the Roman Academy. The organization held elaborate Roman-style banquets and held meetings in the catacombs (Moatti 1993: 34). Although Leto took the title of *pontifex maximus* (an honor reserved for the pope at that time), it was the republican and political sentiments of the Roman Academy that likely led to the Church's disapproval (Rowland 1996: 967). In 1468, Pope Paul II tried this group for heresy. However, after a prominent trial, Leto wrote a long defense of the academy and they were found innocent (Moatti 1993: 35). After the trial, lectures given by Pompanius on ancient Rome became extremely popular (Moatti 1993: 35). In 1471, Pope Sixtus IV allowed the restoration of the Roman Academy, and it lasted as an organization until the sack of Rome in 1527 (Moatti 1993: 35; Rowland 1996: 968).

It was not just the collection of texts that was important at this time. Collection of artifacts was made possible by the exploration of ancient ruins and the new popularity of museums. The discovery of the Golden House (Domus Aurea) of Nero led to a new craze for studying Roman architecture. The wonderful murals and statues preserved within became important influences in Renaissance art (Moatti 1993: 38–39). Figures as important as Raphael were inspired by the ancient artwork. In fact, in 1515, Raphael was appointed commissioner of antiquities, and through this office he formed a team to map ancient Rome and undertake restoration projects (Moatti 1993: 51).

The discovery of artifacts led to the need to develop institutions in which to house them. Museums became important centers for antiquarian studies, although normally, they took the form of temporary displays of artifacts held by institutions that did not specialize in the preservation of the past. In 1471, Pope Sixtus IV opened an exhibit of some of the Roman collection from the Vatican. This collection on the Capitoline Hill was of great interest to the public and popularized the collection of all things Roman and ancient.

The related discipline of early Christian archaeology began with a ground collapse in 1578 (Moatti 1993: 54–55). The collapse revealed some of the many catacombs lying beneath Rome that were used by the early Church community. In 1593, Antonio Bosio began somewhat systematic excavations of the catacombs. The fruits of his explorations were published in 1632 in his work *Underground Rome* (Moatti 1993: 55). These early excavations played a role in the religious controversies of the time (Moatti 1993: 55). Various groups claimed that the evidence discovered was proof that their church was most similar to Paul's church, thereby legitimizing their church over others.

These religious controversies, normally described as the Reformation, led to the division between Protestantism and Catholicism. The rise of Protestantism directly affected the study of Classical literature. Latin, as the language of the Catholic Church, had been a priority of study among scholars. The rise of Protestantism, however, emphasized the Greek culture of the New Testament, and subsequently, ancient Greek texts became the focus of Protestant scholarship (Christiansen 1995: 41).

Collecting knowledge of ancient Romans was also an important new development in Roman studies at this time. Scholars desired to record large amounts of information on all aspects of ancient life, and their main goal was to preserve this information. Aspects of everyday Roman life, economic matters, and matters of governance all were very important. Machiavelli (best known for *The Prince*) gained notoriety for commenting on contemporary political activities and personalities through his uncomplimentary comparisons with the Roman institutions described by Livy (Christiansen 1995: 41).

Enlightenment and Romanticism

History classes often make the transition from the Renaissance and Reformation periods to the Enlightenment and romantic periods seem very clear-cut. The traits associated with these periods, however, changed slowly and gradually. With respect to attitudes toward the past, a few underlying traits typified this transition. Christian archaeology was the dominant area of interest associated with ancient Roman studies, mostly through the search for relics. Museums were established and excavations organized. Along with the rise in museums at this time, the foundations of the modern discipline of art history were built.

The popularity of museums developed throughout the Enlightenment. Private scholars and artists frequently made their collections available to the public for viewing. But the Pio-Clementino Museum (which was open to the public once a year) was perhaps the most influential museum in terms of Roman studies. This museum was situated in the Vatican and was begun by Pope Clementine XIV. It was completed by Clementine's successor, Pius VI (Oresko 1997: 174). Pius was an avid collector who had granted himself first rights to any ancient materials discovered (Moatti 1993: 67). He organized excavations in the Latium region and had the Vatican's collection catalogued. The finished catalogue consisted of seven volumes. The Vatican and other institutions were privy to the wealth of artifacts appearing from the many excavations of Roman buildings that had begun at this time. Sites like Domitian's Palace and the Tomb of the Scipios were discovered and excavated, revealing splendid architecture and wonderful pieces of art.

These artistic excavations paved the way for the development of the discipline of art history (at least in relation to ancient studies). A scholar of particular note was Johann Winckelmann (1717–1768), who is often viewed as the father of ancient art history (Potts 1996: 1200). The restoration of artwork, in Winckelmann's point of view, should be based on the study of other ancient pieces, not upon the artist's whims (Moatti 1993: 83). Winckelmann believed that to compare and understand ancient art, it was important to categorize artistic works by their dates of creation (Ceram 1959: 14–15). His *History of Ancient Art* divided antique art into four distinct periods. The Ancient period was the period of Archaic Greece, the Sublime period was the fifth century B.C.E., the Beautiful period was the fourth century B.C.E., and the Decadent period was the Roman period (Moatti 1993: 82). Most of Winckelmann's identifications were wrong (Johnson 1989: 15). The identifications were important, however, for their methodology of classification, which Winckelmann established (Johnson 1989: 15).

Napoleon's conquest of Italy accelerated the development of classical studies, but at the same time it undermined local Italian efforts. The Treaty of Tolentino (1797) allowed the French to remove Roman artifacts from Italy, a practice that had begun with the French occupation of Rome (Moatti 1993: 86). Many of these artifacts were moved to the French Museum of the Republic, opened in 1801. In 1815, however, many of these items were returned to Rome. The artifacts that were not returned became part of the Louvre's collection. Under Napoleon, the study of antiquity developed methodologically. During his campaign to Egypt, Napoleon established a team of scholars to record and draw artifacts and sites (as well as local flora, fauna, and inhabitants). These records were so carefully composed that they are still valuable tools in modern scholarship (especially in the study of sites and artifacts that have not been preserved). Napoleon's team of scholars brought scientific illustration and recording techniques into vogue as tools for the study of the past.

After the defeat of Napoleon, international interest in Roman archaeology did not abate. Various national institutions were established in Italy with the express purpose of studying Roman monuments. In 1829, the Institute of Archaeological Correspondence was established by King Ludwig I of Bavaria and Frederick III of Prussia (Moati 1993: 118). After the Franco-Prussian War of

Excavations at Pompeii and Herculaneum

When Mount Vesuvius erupted on August 24, 79 c.e., it preserved the cities of Pompeii and Herculaneum in all of their glory, as they were on the very day of the eruption. The excavations of these two cities have been extremely productive and important in the history of Roman scholarship and in the development of archaeology as a discipline.

The writings of Pliny the Younger preserved an eyewitness account of the eruption, so the existence of these cities was never completely forgotten. Actual excavation of the cities, however, did not begin until centuries later. In 1549, a nobleman ordered water channels dug in the region to provide water for his nearby villa (Stiebing 1993: 147). The workers dug through Pompeii, discovering antiquities and inscriptions. But these were of no interest to the nobleman, and the area was ignored until 1709.

At that time, a peasant digging in hopes of finding a well was disappointed to hit marble. An Austrian general constructing a villa nearby bought the land to acquire the marble for construction. The general ordered workers to expand the trench that the peasant had dug, exposing the theater of Herculaneum (Stiebing 1993: 147). The general's team emptied out the theater completely, working until 1716. Excavations stopped between 1717 and 1737, when Vesuvius started erupting again and Spanish forces drove the Austrians out of the region.

In 1738, excavations resumed, now under the direction of Rocco Giocchino de Alcubierre (Stiebing 1993: 148). At this time the site was identified as the city of Herculaneum. Tunnels were dug beyond the theatre, which had previously been excavated, and many of the antiquities found were melted down for precious metal. In 1748, excavations at Herculaneum were halted and the team moved to Pompeii to continue work. But the finds there were not as spectacular, so the team returned to Herculaneum shortly afterward.

When Karl Weber (a Swiss architect) joined the team, he was determined to map the tunnels. His attempts at recording the excavations were sabotaged by the dig director, Alcubiere, who did not think this was a productive effort (Stiebing 1993: 150). In 1750, the team found what is now known as the Villa of Papyri—one of archaeology's greatest discoveries. An amazing group of bronzes was unearthed, as were Roman copies of busts of Greek philosophers. It was also found to have a library filled with rolls of carbonized and preserved papyrus. Most of these documents were philosophical writings, but about 800 of the 1,800 that were discovered have yet to be opened.

In 1763, Pompeii was identified and all efforts were concentrated there. The excavations from this point on focused on creating an area where tourists could visit. Numerous publications began to appear that furthered the public excitement over the finds. And, when Napoleon seized Naples in 1806, excavation efforts were doubled.

The Pompeii excavations entered a new, more scientific phase when Giuseppe Fiorelli was appointed director in 1860 by the new king, Emmanuel II (Stiebing 1993: 159). Fiorelli began a journal to document the work at Pompeii and took a greater interest in recording procedures. He ordered all of the previously excavated areas to be completely cleared and he mapped the entire city based on the town walls. The map was divided into nine sectors, and Fiorelli's team began systematic excavations by sector. They stopped the practice of excavating by tunneling along streets, into the doors of buildings. Rather, the team began excavating from the top down, attempting to preserve some remains in situ and to record the provenance of artifacts.

A plaster cast of a human body found at Pompeii. (Library of Congress)

In 1864, the first plaster cast of an ancient Roman person was made (Stiebing 1993: 168). When Vesuvius erupted, it trapped many people within the city. The ash hardened around the bodies, and when the flesh deteriorated, a mold of the body was preserved in ash. When plaster was poured into the tops of these human molds, it was possible to make casts of the person in the position in which they died. The ash preserved so well that often facial expressions and clothes are visible in the casts, creating one of the most haunting types of archaeological remains.

Since 1927, excavations have continued at Herculaneum. Preservation is much better there because the ash is much harder, better protecting the remains from other disruptive processes. Herculaneum is buried much deeper than Pompeii, a fact that made the preservation far more extensive. The wealth of data from these two sites is phenomenal, providing moderns with an amazing view of what life (and death) was like in the ancient world.

1870, this became the German Archaeo-logical Institute. The French had also remained active in Italy, even af-ter Napoleon, and the French School of Rome was founded in 1873. Roman studies had become an international en-terprise during this time. Scholars from a variety of countries in Europe com-posed histories of Rome in German, French, English, and other languages (Chris-tiansen 1995: 43), which made the field more available to scholars without a com-mand of Italian or Latin. Per-haps the culmination of this scholarly trend was Edward Gibbon's *History of the Decline and Fall of the Roman Empire,* which is a masterpiece of the English language.

Edward Gibbon, author of *The Decline and Fall of the Roman Empire.* Engraving after a portrait by Sir Joshua Reynolds. (Library of Congress)

The Rise of the Italian State

The effect on Roman studies of Italian unification at the end of the nineteenth century cannot be overemphasized. From 1852 to 1860, Italy went through a period of violent unification. Under the force of Count Camillo Cavour, Italy was transformed from a group of absolutist city-states to a unified nation. Cavour curried favor with France (especially with Napoleon III) by entering the Crimean War on the side of France and Britain. After the Crimean War, Cavour and Napoleon deliberately provoked a war with Austria (which held much of northern Italy) so that France could be justified in fighting against Austria. After France defeated Austria and entered into a separate peace with it, Giuseppe Garibaldi, an Italian nationalist, began securing territory in Italy through military domination. Eventually, though, Garibaldi capitulated to Cavour's forces and joined a union with north Italy. In March of 1861, after Italy had been formally unified, Victor Emmanuel II was named king. In 1870, Rome was declared the capital of the new nation of Italy.

With this new proclamation, Rome was rebuilt, a process that would destroy many Roman monuments. But at the same time that ancient monuments were being destroyed by new construction projects, Emmanuel II acted to preserve Italian heritage through a number of institutions (Moatti 1993: 124). Emmanuel II established the Italian School of Archaeology in 1875 based on the other na-tional schools for Roman study. And in 1889, the National Museum of Rome was founded in the Baths of Diocletian.

The Victor Emmanuel monument in Rome. (Paul Thompson; Eye Ubiquitous/Corbis)

Within this context of Italian nationalism, Italian scholars were generally trusting of classical accounts. German scholars, however, approached the classical authors from the opposite direction. The work of German literary historians at this time was greatly influenced by an attitude of skepticism. Germans tended to be critical of all ancient texts and very interested in the methodology of the study of history (Christiansen 1995: 44). It was at this time that biblical criticism developed, and German scholars seriously questioned the accuracy of the scriptures. The same movements were afoot in German classical studies, which strongly contrasted with Italian readings of the sources. Arguably the most influential of these minimalist scholars was Theodor Mommsen, who, in 1862, published the first volume of the *Corpus Inscriptionum Latinarum*. Mommsen's work frequently involved the application of methodology derived from other historical fields to the classical texts. Although German and Italian scholars may have differed in their approach to historical inquiry, both groups saw Rome as a model of successful nation-state unification. Like Italy, Germany at this time was not a nation-state, but rather a series of smaller, yet affiliated local polities. German scholars like Mommsen saw the study of Rome as a useful tool in modern political discourse (Christiansen 1995: 45).

Outside of Germany and Italy, scholars in the larger European nation-states also saw ancient Rome as a model for informing contemporary political thought. With both France and England gaining imperial power throughout the world, the study of Rome was informative for the proper and successful

Pitt-Rivers

Born in 1827, Augustus Henry Lane-Fox, who later changed his name to Pitt-Rivers as a condition of a bequest, would become an important figure in the development of Roman archaeology. The same bequest that led to his name change made him the owner of substantial amounts of land in southern England. This land was rich in Roman remains, and Pitt-Rivers would devote much energy to the study of these materials. He concentrated on what he called "native" constructions from the Roman period. This was important archaeological evidence relating to the other side of Roman imperialism, from the perspective of the conquered peoples. While working on these remains, Pitt-Rivers pioneered the practice of section drawings, in which stratigraphy is recorded as it remains along the walls of the trenches. Pitt-Rivers was convinced that it was important to study the context in which the artifacts had been found. When he died in 1900, he had pioneered many new recording methods, some of which formed the basis of methods still used in the field today.

maintenance of imperial conquests. After German and Italian unification, scholars in France and England would similarly view the Roman Empire as a political force worth emulating.

The Professionalization of Archaeology

The beginning of the twentieth century saw archaeology develop into a legitimate academic discipline, alongside the social sciences. Archaeology became the work of scholars rather than wealthy antiquarians (although many were both). Theoretical issues became much more prominent in archaeological research. Archaeology had become a legitimate academic profession and required specialized skills and education.

Archaeology, as it developed until World War II, was dominated by the use of evolutionary models, especially for comparative purposes. The idea of unilinear cultural evolution, in which every culture advanced along the same steps, underlay many academics' understandings of the past.

Along with the development of new theoretical perspectives came the development of improved excavation methods. One of the most important proponents of a more scientific excavation method was Sir Mortimer Wheeler. Wheeler was a British archaeologist, and although he was not a Roman specialist, the methods he innovated are still fundamental to Roman archaeological excavations today. Although his innovations cannot be described in detail here, it should be noted that he introduced excavation techniques that gave archaeologists much better control while digging. (Wheeler's volume on this topic, *Archaeology from the Earth*, is widely available.)

Sir Mortimer Wheeler with a colleague. (Hulton/Deutsch Collection/Corbis)

Fascist Uses of Rome

World War II temporarily halted archaeological excavations throughout the world. But the political situation in Italy leading up to World War II had actually increased the prominence of archaeology, although this archaeology was based on morally troubling motivations. Just as the romantic nationalists of the nineteenth century used traditions of ancient Rome to excite Italian sensibilities, Mussolini's Fascist party adapted symbols of ancient Rome to inspire the populace. For example, Mussolini adopted the Roman symbol of the eagle and spoke of the need to revive the Latin language as a means of restoring the glory of ancient Rome. In his orations, Mussolini emphasized that the Italian state he led was strongly connected to ancient Rome.

Under Mussolini, state archaeological institutions were given the explicit goal of demonstrating the connections between ancient and modern Italy

Mussolini addresses the Fascists in the Colosseum, Rome. (Library of Congress)

(Moatti 1993: 130). Several archaeological projects were planned under the dictator's supervision. The Augustan city was to be fully restored, as well as the Via del Mare—the road from Rome to the Mediterranean. From 1937 to 1938, Augustus's 2,000th birthday was celebrated. This celebration involved the restoration of his mausoleum and a related exhibit (Moatti 1993: 132). As they had during the Avignon papacy and the unification of the Italian state, conceptions of ancient Rome had been employed in the service of articulating Italian identity.

World War II to the Present

After World War II, when archaeological work was revived out of the shadow of fascism, new goals and new methods were introduced into the discipline. Roman archaeology ceased to be a tool of the fascist state and lost its prominence in public policy. But the destruction caused by World War II had revealed many ancient remains, and ancient Rome was very much on the minds of the public.

Evolutionary models of culture still dominated archaeology. However, the horrors of genocide in World War II substantially checked the development of biological determinism as a means of understanding human history. Culture-area studies came to dominate archaeology immediately following the war. Area studies involved the categorization and study of discrete cultures, bound by specific geographic regions. At this time it became common to specialize in the study of a particular culture, rather than in archaeology in general.

In the 1960s and 1970s, scientific and social scientific methods were introduced into archaeology. Processual archaeology sought to separate archaeology from the study of history. The goals of a processualist were more similar to the goals of hard scientists than to those of historians. Processualists sought to understand the behavior of ancient humans (normally through anthropological or scientific models) rather than to just describe it. Essentially, processualist archaeology (often also called "New Archaeology") is very rooted in evolutionary models and functionalist explanations for human behavior. The reaction to this movement, called post-processualism, created heated debates in the 1970s and 1980s. Post-processualism cannot be easily explained or defined because it involves many different methods and approaches. In general, post-processualists viewed humans and their behavior as too complex for scientific models to be successfully applied. Although post-processualism rejected the explanatory laws of processualism, it also returned archaeology to the study of history.

The most striking feature of Roman archaeology since World War II is its pace. Incredible amounts of work have been accomplished. In fact, although it was possible to summarize the achievements of all the medieval archaeologists in a few paragraphs, it is impossible even to begin to summarize the achievements of the twentieth-century scholars in so little space. The rest of this volume is devoted to the description of the results of this endeavor.

ROMAN CHRONOLOGY

One of the first steps in gaining an understanding of the past is to understand the chronological framework used in reference to the particular civilization of interest. Scholars of Rome usually divide the Roman period proper into three distinct phases: the regal (or monarchical) period, the Republican period, and the imperial period. These periods are discussed in more detail in chapter 4. Each period is based on the prevailing form of government in Rome during that period. According to ancient historians, the regal period began in 753 B.C.E. and ended in 509 B.C.E. The Republican period lasted from 508 B.C.E. until about 29 B.C.E. The imperial period began shortly after the end of the Republican period, and 476 C.E. is usually considered to be the end.

Archaeologists and historians employ two distinct types of chronology—absolute chronology and relative chronology. Absolute chronology is based on actual dates. Dating the period of the Republic from 508 B.C.E. to 29 B.C.E. is an example of absolute dating. In contrast, stating that the Republican period comes after the regal period is an example of relative dating. Relative chronology bases chronology on the relationship of artifacts and events with other artifacts and events. For example, in Jordan, archaeologists can determine that a site is a Roman-period site if certain kinds of glass artifacts are found. In a case like this, an archaeologist can date the site to the Roman period (as opposed to the Hellenistic period or Byzantine period) but would not be able to determine a specific date for the site.

Roman archaeologists have much data for both absolute and relative dates, especially when compared with other areas of study. Think of how many documentaries you have seen that try to redate the construction of the pyramids or an event from biblical times. Roman chronology is fairly secure in contrast. The wealth of classical sources and Roman calendrical interests provide scholars with many absolute dates. Taken with the vast amounts of archaeological excavations that have produced relative dates, Roman studies benefits from a wealth of chronological information. Following are some examples of the ancient and modern sources for Roman chronology.

Roman Systems of Dating

The chronological framework upon which modern scholars base their understanding of Roman history is that of the Romans themselves. More is said about Roman calendrical techniques in chapter 10, but issues of Roman-year reckoning are important for understanding chronology and its associated problems.

The most consistent method of identifying a year in ancient Rome was through the name given to the year. The name of the year was not numerical but was based on the names of the consuls who reigned in that particular year. This system is very cumbersome and can be quite complicated when first attempting to study Roman history. Although the list of consuls goes back as far as 509 B.C.E. (the beginning of the Republic), historians do not trust the information for the time before 300 B.C.E. (Adkins and Adkins 1994: 337). And because the Roman year was actually much shorter than a solar year (until the Julian reforms of 45 B.C.E.), there are problems with converting consul dates into absolute dates.

There were two types of year calculations that were better known among the general population of Rome. Occasionally, emperors would designate the name of a year after themselves. But even more important to the general population was the *indictio*, which was the annual tax assessment. From about 287 C.E. on, the indictio was numbered in five-year cycles; after 312 C.E., it was numbered in fifteen-year cycles (Adkins and Adkins 1994: 337). This kind of timekeeping was important for all Romans to be aware of, and records of the indictio can be useful in historical reconstruction.

Numismatics

Numismatics, the study of ancient coins, is a subfield of Roman archaeology. Much has been written on this subject, and more is discussed about coins and their place in Roman economy in chapter 5. Coins last very well in the archaeological record, and because there is writing and/or imagery on every coin, they are very easily identifiable.

Roman coins can be useful for dating, but there are certain problems with their use in this manner. Coins can provide a *terminus post quem* ("the date after which"), which means that they can be used to identify the earliest possible date for the stratum in which they were found. If a coin can be dated to a certain year, its context must be later than that year. But because Roman coins had such a long circulation life, the context in which the coin was found could be many years after it was minted. Furthermore, because coins are so small, it is very easy for their initial context to be disturbed by depositional or archaeological processes. Therefore, archaeologists have to be very careful about the provenance of coins.

Typology and Seriation

Typology is one of the most important concepts in archaeology. Derived from the natural sciences, typology refers to the classification of artifacts according to their features. It is assumed that artifacts with similar appearances and properties have some intrinsic relationship, so it is considered worthwhile to organize them accordingly. Creating typologies is a necessary component of archaeological information management. Archaeologists are confronted with a huge amount of data. The best way to control these quantities is to simplify and organize the data.

Related to typology is the concept of seriation, which incorporates evolutionary concepts into the classification schema, based on the principle that the styles and forms of objects evolve over time. Seriation also presupposes the principle of stratigraphic superpositioning, which suggests that an object found above another object comes from a more recent time than the lower object. The first objects found in an archaeological excavation are, theoretically, the most recent (although this is not always the case). Likewise, the lowest objects at a site are the earliest. By comparing the relative depositions of artifacts, then comparing this information with that of other sites, archaeologists can build seriated typologies of artifacts. It then becomes possible to date a site or architectural feature relative to other sites with the same artifacts. This principle is most frequently used in ceramic analysis (see chapter 9) and architectural analysis.

The principles of typology and seriation are fundamental to any archaeological study. They allow archaeologists to understand the particular site being excavated in the context of the rest of the culture area. For Roman studies, typologies are well established, making relative chronologies fairly easy to produce, given enough research time.

Radiocarbon Dating and Other Scientific Techniques

Scientific methods have revolutionized archaeologists' ability to date material remains. Radiocarbon dating (also known as carbon-14 dating) is probably the best-known method of scientific dating commonly employed by archaeologists. In 1949, Arnold and Libby published a paper in *Science* that detailed their ability to date objects of a known date, independently, by the amount of radiocarbon in the artifacts. This paper revolutionized archaeological research.

Radiocarbon dating is based on the observation that neutrons produced by cosmic radiation react with nitrogen in the earth's atmosphere to produce carbon 14. This carbon isotope is absorbed in organic materials, but ceases to be absorbed when the organism dies. Carbon 14 is unstable and gradually decays after it is no longer absorbed by the previously living matter. According to Libby, this rate of decay is stable, and it takes 5,730 years for half of the C-14 in organic materials to decay (this is known as half-life). The object can then be dated by the scientific examination of the amount of radiocarbon isotopes present. The dates sent back by the lab are only statistical approximations (each date also has a standard deviation). But with enough carbon dates, an archaeologist can greatly reduce the margin of error, so that any organic artifact (made of material that was once living) can be radiocarbon dated if it was carefully excavated. This is a useful method of analysis for objects dating between 50,000 B.C.E. and 1,500 C.E.

However, radiocarbon dates must be calibrated. Libby had thought that the amount of carbon-14 isotopes in the earth's atmosphere had always been constant. This assumption has been proven wrong; changes in solar activity and in the earth's magnetic field have made the amount of carbon isotopes variable throughout history. So, to produce accurate dates, radiocarbon dates must be compared with evidence derived from other scientific methods.

Dendrochronology is one such method; it is basically the study of tree rings. Tree rings are the concentric circles that can be seen in a tree trunk and that represent the tree's annual growth. Because these circles develop based on various climatic phenomena, specialists have developed methods of comparing the rings of different trees. By comparing the rings of different trees with those of trees that were felled on a known date, it is possible to establish absolute dates. This method has been particularly useful for Roman studies in the European periphery.

LITERARY OR FOLKLORIC EVIDENCE OF USE FOR INTERPRETATION OF ROMAN CIVILIZATION

Scholars of ancient Rome are particularly fortunate in the wealth of textual evidence available for the study of Roman civilization. The writings of classical authors have been preserved in numerous formats and provide an unparalleled source of information about Roman life and history. Taken in tandem with archaeology, these literary sources for the study of Rome are invaluable. More is said about Roman literature in chapter 10, but for now, it is important to point out some of the historical and mythological sources that have played particularly important roles in the development of Roman studies.

Roman Historians

The Romans had a strong tradition of historical writing. From about the third century B.C.E., authors writing in Latin composed works describing historical events. Parallel to this was an equally rich Greek-language tradition of historical writing, which often provided an outsider's perspective on Roman history and personalities. It is not possible to provide an overview of the vast amount of ancient historical sources here, but some important characteristics of Roman history writing should be mentioned.

The ancient histories that have survived most frequently do not survive as complete compositions. Because of the accidents of preservation and transmission history, full sections of otherwise well-preserved works are often missing. Often, historical accounts are known about only because they were quoted at great length in the works of other writers. So it must always be remembered that the historical sources, while quite rich, are also very incomplete.

One of the striking features of ancient-history writing in Rome is the explicit moralizing. Since about the nineteenth century, historians have attempted, with varying success, to remove moral judgment from their accounts of the past. But for the Roman historian, it was an important aspect of the writing. The lives of figures of the past provided lessons on moral behavior, and this was an important motive for historical study.

Roman historians were not only interested in moralizing. Frequently they worked directly with archival materials. Most of the records of public archives have long been lost, so the only source for these records is in the writings of the historians. Ancient historians sometimes quoted these documents at length, in effect preserving the records and allowing us to read them. The same can be said for major documents such as treaties and law codes, which are, almost exclusively, preserved embedded in larger historical narratives.

Roman Mythology

Mythologies that have been particularly useful (and controversial) in the study of Roman civilization are the myths about the foundation of Rome. These stories revolve around the eponymous founder of Rome. Eponymous founders are individuals who were traditionally held to be the sole founder of a city and usually blended together mythical and historical aspects. The eponymous founder was the means by which a culture situated itself in relationship to other cultures. It was a simplified understanding of a complex situation. Eponymous founders are also often found in family lineages. In a family lineage, the eponymous founder is the earliest ancestor (although such a thing can never be known), and it is from this person that family identity is constructed. A famous example of eponymous ancestry that is still familiar to modern audiences is Jacob in the Old Testament. He is credited in the Bible as the founder of the nation of Israel, and all Israelites are said to have descended from him. Similarly, his brother Esau is the eponymous ancestor of the nation of Edom.

Romulus and Remus. The story of Romulus and Remus is perhaps the best-known myth of the foundation of Rome. The name *Romulus* suggests that the story is a myth. Romulus is a back-formation (a word derived from another word but claimed to be an earlier form) of the name *Rome*. A vestal virgin (a priestess of the goddess Vesta who was prohibited from sexual intercourse) was impregnated by the god Mars. She gave birth to Romulus and Remus, twins, but King Amulius (the vestal virgin's uncle, who had deposed her father as king) did not want any claimants to his throne, so he ordered the children to be left to die by the Tiber River. The children did not die, however. A she-wolf suckled them (an image depicted in numerous artistic forms from Ro-

Romulus and Remus being suckled by a she-wolf. Bronze sculpture in the Capitoline Museum, Rome. (Corel Corporation)

man times to the present) until a herdsman named Faustulus took them in and raised them as his children.

When the children grew up, they were recognized as the sons of the vestal virgin. They deposed their great-uncle (the man who had had them left to die) and reinstalled their grandfather as king of Alba Longa, a city near Rome. Romulus founded a city on the Palatine Hill. Remus founded a city on the Aventine Hill. The twins began to quarrel during the construction of the cities, and eventually Romulus killed Remus.

The myth goes on to describe how Rome developed as a city. Romulus encouraged Rome's growth in several ways. He welcomed criminals and runaway slaves to settle on the Palatine. His most famous attempt at demographic expansion is told in a story commonly referred to as "The Rape of the Sabines." In this tale, Romulus invited the Sabines (a neighboring people) to watch games held at Rome. While the Sabine men watched the games, Roman men carried the Sabine women off and raped them to produce heirs. War between Rome and the Sabines ensued, but eventually the two cities came to a mutual peace.

The Aeneas Legend. Another story told of the foundation of Rome is derived from the Greek epic poem *The Iliad*. Aeneas is the only Trojan hero to have survived the Trojan War, and there is some reference in the poem that his descendents will eventually rule Troy. After the Trojan War, Aeneas wandered the Mediterranean. He had a son named Romus, and when Aeneas founded the city of Rome, he named the city after this son. The character of Aeneas seems to have been very popular among the Etruscans and at Lavinium. The components of this story that made it popular in Rome were twofold. First, it established that the Romans had an ancient pedigree (in the ancient world, older is better) dating to the Trojan War. Second, it demonstrated that the Romans were not Greeks and had had a history independent of Greek heritage (Cornell 1995: 65).

Evander. Yet another story involves Evander (sometimes said to be the son of Hermes) and his movement of people from Arcadia to the Palatine. Since Evander's name means "good man," it is likely that Evander is not a historical figure. At the Palatine, he supposedly founded a new city and established rituals related to the worship of the Greek god Pan. Other tales tell of how Hercules visited Evander at the Palatine and killed a monster for him, leading Evander to found a cult for Hercules at the site. There are numerous stories about Evander and his various heroic deeds relating to Roman history, but most of them stress some fundamental connection between early Rome and Greece.

BIBLIOGRAPHY

Adkins, Lesley, and Roy Adkins. 1994. *Handbook to Life in Ancient Rome.* Oxford: Oxford University Press.

Bloch, Raymond. 1960. *The Origins of Rome.* London: Thames & Hudson.

Burnett, Andrew. 1991. *Roman Coins.* Berkeley: University of California Press.

Ceram, C. W. 1959. *Gods, Graves, and Scholars.* New York: Alfred A. Knopf.

Christiansen, Erik. 1995. *A History of Rome: From Town to Empire and from Empire to Town.* Aarchus, Denmark: Aarchus University Press.

Cornell, Tim. 1995. *The Beginnings of Rome.* New York: Routledge.

Cornell, Tim, and John Matthews. 1982. *Atlas of the Roman World.* New York: Facts on File.

Cowell, F. R. 1980. *Life in Ancient Rome.* New York: Perigee Books.

Crawford, Michael. 1982. *The Roman Republic.* Cambridge: Harvard University Press.

Deiss, J. J. 1966. *Herculaneum: Italy's Buried Treasure.* New York: Crowell.

Dorey, Thomas (ed.). 1966. *Latin Historians.* London: Routledge & K. Paul.

———. 1967. *Latin Biography.* London: Routledge & K. Paul.

Dupont, Florence. 1989. *Daily Life in Ancient Rome.* Christopher Woodall (trans.). Cambridge: Basil Blackwell Ltd.

Friedländer, Ludwig. 1910. *Roman Life and Manners under the Early Empire.* London: Routledge & Sons, Ltd.

Gardiner, Jane. 1993. *Roman Myths.* Austin: University of Texas Press.

Gjerstad, Einar. 1962. *Legends and Facts of Early Rome.* Lund: C.W.K. Gleerup.

Grant, Michael. 1958. *Roman History from Coins.* Cambridge: Cambridge University Press.

———. 1971. *Roman Myth.* New York: Charles Scribner and Sons.

Greene, Kevin. 1992. *Roman Pottery*. Berkeley: University of California Press.

Hayes, John W. 1997. *Handbook of Mediterranean Roman Pottery*. London: British Museum Press.

Johnson, Stephen. 1989. *Rome and Its Empire*. New York: Routledge.

Kinney, Dale. 1996. "*Mirabilia Urbis Romae*," pp. 759–760 in *An Encyclopedia of the History of Classical Archaeology*. Nancy Thomson de Grummond (ed.). Westport: Greenwood Press.

Kraus, Theodore. 1975. *Pompeii and Herculaneum: The Living Cities of the Dead*. New York: Harry N. Abrams.

MacKendrick, Paul. 1960. *The Mute Stones Speak: The Story of Archaeology in Italy*. New York: St. Martin's Press.

Mellor, Ronald. 1988. "Roman Historiography and Biography," pp. 1541–1562 in *Civilization of the Ancient Mediterranean: Greece and Rome*. Michael Grant and Rachel Kitzinger (eds.). NewYork: Charles Scribner's Sons.

Moatti, Claude. 1993. *The Search for Ancient Rome*. New York: Harry N. Abrams.

Ogilvie, R. M. 1976. *Early Rome and the Etruscans*. Atlantic Highlands: Humanities Press.

Oresko, Robert. 1997. "Culture in the Age of Baroque and Rococo," pp. 139–176 in *The Oxford Illustrated History of Italy*. George Holmes (ed.). Oxford: Oxford University Press.

Osborne, John. 1996. "Einsiedeln Itinerary," pp. 386–387 in *An Encyclopedia of the History of Classical Archaeology*. Nancy Thomson de Grummond (ed.). Westport: Greenwood Press.

Pallotino, Massimo. 1991. *A History of Earliest Italy*. Martin Ryle and Kate Soper (trans.). Ann Arbor: University of Michigan Press.

Potts, Alex. 1996. "Winckelmann, Johann Joachim (1717–1768)," pp. 1199–1200 in *An Encyclopedia of the History of Classical Archaeology*. Nancy Thomson de Grummond (ed.). Westport: Greenwood Press.

Rowland, Ingrid. 1996. "Roman Academy (Accademia Romana)," pp. 967–968 in *An Encyclopedia of the History of Classical Archaeology*. Nancy Thomson de Grummond (ed.). Westport: Greenwood Press.

Samuel, Alan. 1998. "Calendars and Time Telling," pp. 389–396 in *Civilization of the Ancient Mediterranean: Greece and Rome*. Michael Grant and Rachel Kitzinger (eds.). NewYork: Charles Scribner's Sons.

Scullard, H. H. 1961. *A History of the Roman World 753 to 146 B.C.* London: Methuen.

Shelton, Jo-Ann. 1988. *As the Romans Did*. Oxford: Oxford University Press.

Sperling, Christine. 1996. "Guidebooks to Rome (after 1500)," pp. 551–552 in *An Encyclopedia of the History of Classical Archaeology*. Nancy Thomson de Grummond (ed.). Westport: Greenwood Press.

Stiebing, William, Jr. 1993. *Uncovering the Past*. Oxford: Oxford University Press.

Vag, David. 1999. *Coinage and the History of the Roman Empire*. 2 vols. Chicago: Fitzroy Dearborn Publishers.

IV

CHAPTER 4

Origins, Growth, and Decline of Roman Civilization

This chapter provides a historical overview of Rome. What follows is a framework of the major historical events that occurred throughout Rome's long history. This account is short and is not meant to be exhaustive. Rather, it should be used as a beginning step in one's study of Roman history. A broad perspective of the flow of Roman history will help provide a structure for future investigations. The sheer volume of works written on Roman history can be overwhelming, and many of them assume a basic level of knowledge. This section provides that level of knowledge. After reading it, it will be possible to peruse a more detailed work on Roman history and understand the major arguments that are made and situate the discussion within one's own broader perspective. The major events and people in Roman history are described to give a sense of how they all fit together in the larger narrative of Roman life. However, the descriptions that follow should not be considered complete. For example, numerous volumes have been written on the Punic Wars, yet here they are discussed only in brief.

Furthermore, the discussion that follows represents a history of important individuals and events. Scholars now recognize that histories involving only these subjects are inadequate. History is no longer considered just a recounting and analysis of events and activities of major political figures. History should be more nuanced, involving discussions of all aspects of ancient lives. Archaeology can help this endeavor by providing information on how everyday people lived—a perspective that is presented in later chapters. However, historians who work without a thorough knowledge of emperors, battles, and other political events are doing themselves and the scholarly world a disservice. Although a given history is not just the history of political events, it does not mean that that facet of history should be excluded.

After reading this chapter, it is hoped the reader will understand some basic themes of Roman history. This chapter offers the opportunity to learn about the difference between the republic and the empire, about the wars with Hannibal, and about the lives of famous Romans such as Julius Caesar and Caligula. It is also important to keep this chapter in mind as a reference tool for any further study of Rome. Roman history is long and complex, and it is often difficult to keep the names and events straight. This chapter is a reference tool that can help in quickly learning about (or remembering) many concepts that are central to understanding Rome.

ORIGINS AND EARLY DEVELOPMENT OF ROME

Locating the origins of a particular cultural group or phenomenon is a difficult task. It is not easy to determine when one culture begins and another ends. And if an account does look simple—be warned! It is probably an oversimplification. Histories of origins are intrinsically more complicated than a simple reading might lead one to believe. Frequently, such accounts are used to justify the beliefs and values of those writing them and to justify the reality of the time of the account's writing. In the case of ancient Rome, the situation is particularly difficult because of the relative paucity of sources, as opposed to the tremendous amount of source material available for the later periods. This section on the origins and early development of Rome provides a basic framework for understanding the nature of early Rome. Chapter 11 treats the scholarly controversies about early Rome.

Iron Age Rome

It is somewhat arbitrary to begin a history of Roman civilization with the Iron Age settlements, but there are strong breaks between the late Bronze Age cultures and later cultures in this region. Around 900 B.C.E., large settlements appeared on previously unsettled soil. The material culture of the early Iron Age suggests that numerous local groups had arisen. Unlike the late Bronze Age, which was relatively uniform in Italy, regional variation in the early Iron Age was considerable. The appearance of cremation burial related to a cultural horizon referred to as Urnfield culture was the dominant trend in the late Bronze Age. In contrast, Iron Age Italy had a variety of burial practices and customs and a variety of identifiable, regional cultural groups. Iron Age culture can be characterized as many distinct local cultures with a variety of different traits.

One of the most important of these local groups was the Villanovan culture, which was first identified in 1853. The culture is named after the site at which it was first identified (Villanova near Bologna). Naming a cultural group after the first site of identification was a common practice in the archaeology of prehistoric periods. The most notable feature of Villanovan material culture is the use of distinctive urns for the burial of their cremated dead. The urns were biconical and covered with a lid (either a bowl or a helmet). They were placed in deep shafts and covered by stone slabs. Sometimes the ashes were kept in terra-cotta models of huts, which likely represented the kind of dwellings in which the Villanova people lived (Bloch 1960: 69). Evidence for wattle-and-daub huts that may have resembled these terra-cotta models has been excavated from numerous sites. Usually the dwellings are clustered together in defensible positions. Often the Villanovan culture is viewed as a precursor to Etruscan culture.

Rome itself has archaeological evidence dating from the middle Bronze Age. But substantive remains are preserved only from the end of the Bronze Age and the beginning of the Iron Age (Cornell 1995: 51). These remains belong to what scholars call the Latial culture (see Table 4.1 for the chronological distinc-

Table 4.1   Latial Culture Chronology*

Phase	Dates	Terminology	Preserved Burial Types
I	c. 1000–900 B.C.E.	Protovillanovan	cremation
IIa	c. 900–830 B.C.E.	Villanovan	cremation and inhumation
IIb	c. 830–770 B.C.E.	Villanovan	inhumation
III	c. 770–730/20 B.C.E.	Villanovan	inhumation
IVa	c. 730/20–640/30 B.C.E.	Orientalizing	inhumation
IVb	c. 640/30–580 B.C.E.	Orientalizing	inhumation

*Adapted from Cornell 1995: 50 (*Table 1*).

tions). In the earliest phases at Rome, these remains are manifest in a number of urn burials. The urns are circular jars, buried in a pit, and distinct from Villanovan remains. Other, nearby sites provide information on the Latial culture, but this is still mostly funerary evidence. The site of Osteria dell'Osa has yielded hundreds of tombs to archaeologists since the 1970s. This cemetery, dated to the Latial IIA phase, consists of both cremation- and inhumation-style burials (Bloch 1960: 75–77; Cornell 1995: 51). Differences in grave goods are assumed to be related to the status of the buried individual, although gender may also have been a determining factor in the nature of burial used. The evidence for the living members of the Latial culture is less well preserved. Settlements were small, with very little differentiation in structures and material culture (Cornell 1995: 54). By the IIB phase, the settlements became larger, leading this period to be characterized as proto-urban. Moving back to Rome itself, some evidence for huts dating to phases III and IV has been excavated, indicating the continued occupation of Rome by the Latial culture (Bloch 1960: 69–71; Cornell 1995: 57). Later Roman historians seem to have written about the cultures of this period, but there are no documents contemporary with this period.

Rome and the Etruscans

The relationship between Rome and the Etruscan city-states is very unclear. Later Roman historians seem to have had a love-hate sensibility toward the Etruscans, and modern scholars have radically different opinions on the nature of Roman-Etruscan connections. Some see the origins of Roman civilization as deeply rooted in Etruscan civilization. Other scholars see no connection between the two. It seems most likely that the answer lies in the middle of these two extremes. The Etruscans lived in very close proximity to the city of Rome, and no doubt the interactions between these two peoples were influential in both directions.

Whatever the exact nature of contact between these two groups, it is worthwhile to present an introductory overview of the Etruscans. From about 800 B.C.E. to 300 B.C.E., the Etruscan culture flourished. Between the Arno River and the Tiber River, and against the Apennine Mountains, the Etruscans lived in the region now known as Tuscany. Although Herodotus states that the Etruscan people immigrated to Tuscany from Lydia, modern scholars tend to be-

Etruscan mural paintings from the Tomb of the Fortune Tellers. (Archivo Iconografico, S.A./ Corbis)

lieve that they were indigenous to the region. Since the 1980s, it has been in vogue among archaeologists to assume internal causes for change rather than mass migrations of people, so one should be careful about those who dismiss Herodotus's accounts out of hand. They may just be following current academic trends rather than fully accounting for the available data. Linguistic evidence is helpful in resolving this debate.

Most of the Etruscan cities (such as Veii and Tarquinii) were located inland, but within a day's reach of the coast. The sites were set upon hilltops in very defensible positions. Most of the wealth of the Etruscans came from agriculture (owing to the rich volcanic soil) and from mining the rich deposits of copper and iron. Trade, especially with the Greeks, further provided wealth to the ancient peoples of Tuscany. This region was intensely rich, and it was in no small part due to the natural resources that Etruscan civilization prospered. At the same time, the contacts with the Greek world provided the Etruscans with the best of the Greek and Near Eastern civilizations.

Governance of the Etruscan city-states bore a close resemblance to early Roman governance. In fact, it is often assumed that the early Roman city-state system was modeled after the Etruscans (Bloch 1960: 105; Crawford 1982: 29; Ferril 1988: 46–47; Starr 1953: 15). Others suggest that the city-state arrived via Greece (Pallotino 1991: 118). This is possible, but it must be noted that the city-state system had been a common form of political organization from as far back as third-millennium Mesopotamia. A king ruled each city, and each city was bound to the rest in what scholars traditionally call a "loose confederation." Although political authority certainly manifested itself in this kind of city-state system, religious authority may have been likewise oriented on this model. There is evidence that the city of Volsinii may have been a kind of religious center at this time (Grant 1978: 14–15). Within a city-state type of confederation, it is common for different cities to have different kinds of authority over other cities. So it is not implausible that Volsinii may have been a religious capital, yet other cities may have had more political or economic authority.

The Regal Period

The history of the regal period is fraught with problems. It is very difficult to tease out facts from the ancient historical accounts of that time. Certainly the origin accounts are mythical (and are discussed in chapter 11). Ancient sources speak of seven kings ruling Rome in the regal period (see Table 4.2). The first of these kings was the mythical Romulus, who, according to tradition, founded Rome on April 21, 753 B.C.E. Following Romulus were six more kings. Historians pick and choose between the kings they believe were historical figures and those they believe were mythical. In general, historians are more trusting of the later kings in the lists as opposed to the earliest. However, the dates of 753 B.C.E.–510 B.C.E. are usually considered relatively trustworthy by historians, but not precisely accurate (Scullard 1961: 30–33). The accounts of these seven early kings represent attempts by ancient historians (writing in later periods) to identify the origins of particular Roman institutions. For example, the third king, Tullus Hostilius, is said to have founded the Senate house.

The processes involved in the selection of a king have not survived to the present; however, it is known that kingship in the regal period was not hereditary (Crawford 1988: 30; Ferril 1988: 47). Scholars have suggested that the king was selected from the upper officials who served the previous king. Evidence for this is based on the observation that a king and his successor were often linked by marriage. The daughter of the reigning king, it is reported, was frequently married to the king's chosen successor. This evidence is very problematic. Genealogical data from ancient sources are often not trustworthy. The

Table 4.2   Traditional Dates and Ethnicity of the Seven Kings of Rome

Name	Regnal Years	Ethnicity
Romulus	753–715 B.C.E.	Various traditions
Numa Pompilius	715–673 B.C.E.	Sabine
Tullus Hostilius	673–641 B.C.E.	Latin
Ancus Marcius	641–616 B.C.E.	Sabine
Tarquin I	616–579 B.C.E.	Etruscan
Servius Tullius	579–534 B.C.E.	Various traditions
Tarquin the Proud	534–509 B.C.E.	Etruscan

links between the seven kings of Rome may indicate the attempts on the part of later historians to make sense of the connectedness of these individuals. The information available about these kings is also very explicit about indicating that they were not ethnically Roman. Whether this was true is unclear. It is interesting that the accounts of the Roman kings suggest Latin, Sabine, and Etruscan origins—this is probably indicative of an ancient society composed of people of varying backgrounds and where ethnicity (if such a concept can be said to have existed) was fluid and complex.

The kings called "Etruscan" have been of particular interest to modern scholars of Rome. King Tarquinius Priscus (Tarquin I), accounts claim, brought Etruscan culture to the city of Rome (Bloch 1960: 101; le Glay et al. 2001: 24; Heurgon 1973: 141–143). This same king is the supposed initiator of the many early public works projects. It is unclear exactly how much these claims are based on early traditions and how much they are based on early historians' desires to explain where Etruscan influences in Roman society came from. Modern historians have traditionally taken the rise of Tarquin as indicative of an Etruscan conquest or domination of Rome (Ferril 1988: 47; Grant 1978: 23). They have regarded the evidence as suggestive that the Etruscans had a hegemonic influence over Rome and often refer to this time as the Etruscan period. Recently, Cornell has challenged the long-held belief that regal Rome ever experienced an Etruscan period. He suggests that Tarquin was not Etruscan and that his (and his successors') reigns do not represent an Etruscan domination of Rome (Cornell 1995: 156–159). Cornell's ideas are not conventional but they are important to consider. He illustrates that the long-held notion that the Tarquins ushered in a new era is based on minimal evidence. Whether or not the reigns of Tarquin and his successors represented an Etruscan incursion, there was likely a strong link between the Roman and Etruscan cultures.

The last king of Rome was supposedly Lucius Tarquinius Superbus (Tarquin the Proud), who is said to have come to the throne after assassinating the previous king. As the story goes, Tarquin the Proud was an unpopular and unjust king. Problems arose when his son Sextus raped Lucretia (the virtuous wife of Sextus's cousin, Collatinus). Lucretia killed herself (in virtuous Roman fashion), and popular anger toward Sextus led to rebellion. The Tarquins were expelled in this rebellion and Rome became a republic. It is probable that at some point around 510 B.C.E., the Roman governing system did switch from a monarchy to a republic in a rebellion. However, the impetus for the rebellion, the rape of Lucretia, seems more like a Roman or Greek literary invention than an actual event.

Rise of the Roman City-State

How do the events recorded by Roman historians compare with the archaeological record of the time? Most scholars think the two mesh together fairly well. The archaeological record of the period suggests that the site of Rome expanded in the mid-seventh century, becoming more heavily urbanized. This is consistent with other sites in the region. Larger, more urbanized sites are often associated with the rise of what has been called the city-state system. This was the major organizational system of the Etruscans as well (see the previous section on the regal period). The city-state usually consisted of a large settlement, with a defensive position and communal areas within the city itself. Cemeteries and farmsteads were outside of the settlement proper. Governance was local and centered in the city.

Theories of how the city-state came to be the dominant mode of settlement in Italy at this time are many. The fundamental difference among the various theories is the rate at which scholars assume change occurs. Some suggest that city-states are founded all at once (Gjerstad 1962). Others suggest that urbanization occurs gradually (Cornell 1995). Rate of change is a problem in historical and scientific fields in general (e.g., the debates surrounding Stephen Jay Gould's notion of punctuated equilibrium, which suggests that change occurs very quickly between periods of change and very long periods of stasis) and is not likely to be resolved anytime soon.

The archaeological evidence for city-state settlements and the historical evidence for the kings of Rome are consistent with each other. Although the details and personalities of the kings of the regal period may not represent real, historical personages, the institution of kingship within the context of a city-state form of government probably accurately describes the regal period.

THE ROMAN REPUBLIC

The beginning of the Roman republic coincides with the expulsion of the Tarquins from the city itself. With the forced exit of the Etruscan monarchy came the formation of the republican form of government. Whether or not the expulsion was an actual historical event at this stage, history can now be discussed more confidently. A description of the new form of governance can be found in chapter 7.

Concomitant with the rise of the new form of government was the rise of an order of people known as the *plebs* (or plebians). In contrast to the patricians (elite families who claimed descent from the original senators chosen by Romulus), the plebs were a heterogeneous group of underprivileged people who organized themselves into a collective political unit (see chapter 6). In 494 B.C.E., the plebs withdrew from the city of Rome (likely on account of mounting debts) and gathered on the Sacred Mount. There they voted to create their own governing body—the *concilium plebis*. This event, according to ancient historians, led to the codification of Roman law in the "Twelve Tables." These laws gave equality to all citizens but also formalized the differences between the two orders. Modern scholars often refer to the conflict between these two groups as "The Conflict of the Orders," of which more is said in chapter 6.

The Latin League and the Conquest of Italy

As Rome grew in size, it found itself in conflict with numerous neighboring Latin cities. These cities had banded together centuries earlier for shared cultic and religious purposes. With Rome's rise to prominence, this league of cities took on a militaristic aspect as well (Ferril 1988: 50). Modern scholars refer to this organization as the Latin League, although it must be mentioned that this was not a name used in antiquity. The exact nature of this organization is not well understood, nor is the sequence of events that led to war with Rome. It is clear that the Latin League went to war with Rome sometime after 504 B.C.E., and victory was gained by the Romans at the Battle of Lake Regillus in 499 B.C.E. The causes of the war were probably rooted in Rome's growing economic and military might.

Although Rome had been victorious in 499 B.C.E., relations between the two entities did not normalize until a formal treaty was agreed upon six years later. The *foedus Cassianus,* between Rome and the Latin League, was formed in 493 B.C.E., marking the end of the Latin War (Crawford 1982: 43; Ferril 1988: 50). Named after the Roman consul who was instrumental in its creation, the treaty viewed Rome and the rest of the league as equal partners, with Rome the only city able to call all of the cities to war. It established certain rights between the citizens and established a system of common defense. Spoils of war were divided, giving half to the league and half to Rome (Cornell 1995: 299). The conditions of the treaty were preserved by a summary in the writings of Dionysius of Halicarnassus.

Perhaps some of the motivation behind the foedus Cassianus was the desire for mutual security (Walbank et al. 1989: 282). Migrations of people known as the Volsci, the Sabines, and the Aequi led to attacks by these peoples against Roman and Latin territory. Throughout the fifth century, Rome was forced to fend off attacks from these three groups and various others. It is difficult to determine, from the accounts preserved by Livy regarding this period, what were historical events and what were literary tales. It is clear that war prevented the region from gaining stability for the first half of the fifth century. Through the second half of the fifth century, however, the raids of the Volsci and Aequi became more infrequent, and those of the Sabines seemed to have stopped completely.

The Veientine Wars. While the raids of the Volsci and Aequi tapered off, Rome and the city of Veii (15 km north of Rome) soon became entrenched in a serious conflict. These cities had had an uneasy relationship since the regal period, engaging in occasional warfare (Walbank et al. 1989: 294). In the latter half of the fifth century, conflict between the two states broke out over the control of transportation routes along the Tiber River. For both cities, prosperity was based on their central location on major trade routes, and securing access to these routes was a necessary step in ensuring that that prosperity would continue (Cornell 1995: 310; Grant 1978: 49; Huergon 1973: 181). Three wars were fought relating to this issue. The first Veientine War lasted from 483 B.C.E. to 474 B.C.E., the second from 437 B.C.E. to 435 B.C.E., and the third from 406 B.C.E. to 396 B.C.E. The length of this third war led to a reorganization of the Roman military (Grant 1978: 51 [also see Cornell 1995: 313]); to accommodate the length of time, Roman soldiers were kept away from home (see chapter 7). The series of conflicts ended when the Romans captured the city of Veii in 396 B.C.E., after a long siege.

The Attack of the Gauls.　After the conquest of Veii, Rome was poised to become the most powerful force in central Italy when an old threat reasserted itself. For centuries, bands of marauding Gauls had come across the Alps. An ambiguous term, *Gaul*, in general use, can refer to any Celtic or German tribe. Here, the Gauls were marauding tribes who attacked Rome from the north. These attacks were sporadic and of little consequence, given the preponderance of intercity conflict throughout the period. But in 390 B.C.E., one army of Gauls managed to penetrate the Roman heartland all the way to the River Allia, according to Polybius. Since the Romans were used to fighting in phalanx formation (see chapter 7), the Gauls were able to defeat the Roman forces by surrounding and overpowering them in hand-to-hand combat (Grant 1978: 52).

After this easy victory, the Gallic army entered Rome. Most of the population of Rome had already fled, but Livy tells of some who remained behind. Livy recounts two stories of the Gauls' entrance into Rome to illustrate the valor of Roman citizens even in the face of defeat. The first story describes the Gallic plunder of the area surrounding the Forum. Upon entering the patrician houses that had not been boarded up, the Gallic army was struck by the majesty of the Roman citizens and mistook them for statues. But when one Gaul tugged on the beard of a Roman, the Roman responded by striking the Gaul with a staff. The Gallic response was to kill all those remaining and burn down the houses.

The second story told by Livy is of the garrison that held Capitoline Hill. The Gauls attempted a night raid against this last group of Romans. They moved up the hill secretively, undetected by the Roman watch. But, according to Livy, the sacred geese of Juno noticed them and began honking. When the Romans heard this commotion, they used the chance to slay the Gallic invaders. Eventually, however, the forces on Capitoline Hill were forced to surrender because they had run out of supplies. Whatever the truth of Livy's accounts, the Gauls left Rome after being paid a heavy ransom and plundering much of the city (Walbank et al. 1989: 308).

Scholars do not agree on how the sack of Rome affected the republic in its immediate aftermath. It is uncertain how much the attack weakened Rome economically. Crawford suggests that the incident had almost no impact on Roman development, and that the renovation of the Servian Wall twelve years later indicated that Rome's wealth lay undiminished (1982: 39). Cornell also sees the quick economic recovery of Rome as evidence that this disaster was not as catastrophic as the ancient accounts suggest (1995: 318). The fact remains, however, that this wall was built for primarily defensive purposes, and that construction did not begin until twelve years later. The construction of the wall suggests a fear of attack, and the long time that elapsed before construction began suggests that Rome was impoverished. For years it was assumed that the Gauls destroyed many historical documents at the time of the invasion (including annals from the regal period). But scholars have become more inclined to believe that these records never existed at all. The sack of Rome must have caused a terrible economic crisis at first, but certainly it was not long before the republic was running smoothly again. Security became a central concern of the republic, as did territorial expansion.

The First Samnite War.   From 343 B.C.E. to 341 B.C.E., the Romans were at war with the Samnites. The term *Samnite* refers to a group of tribes organized in a federation of villages, occupying south-central Italy (Grant 1978: 62). In 354 B.C.E., a treaty had been established between Rome and the Samnites. But Rome's alliance with the city of Capua brought them into conflict with the Samnites in 343 B.C.E., according to Livy. By 341 B.C.E., the war had drawn to a close, and a new treaty was established, guaranteeing the previously held lands and alliances of both sides. This alliance with the Samnites would later prove beneficial in Rome's development as the supreme power in Italy. But peace with the Samnites would not last.

The End of the Latin League.   Allied with Rome since the foedus Cassianus of 493 B.C.E., the Latin League became concerned that Rome's powers were growing too strong after the war with the Samnites (Cornell 1995: 348; Crawford 1982: 41). It is likely that in the years following the Gallic sack, Rome had been inconsistent in honoring the terms of the treaty. There may have been occasional war with the Latins, but the evidence for these conflicts is not as clear as some scholars suggest (Pallotino 1991: 132). It is certain that in 340 B.C.E., the Latin League revolted against Rome. Probably an attempt to check Rome's growth and expansion, the revolt proved futile. Rome utterly defeated the Latin League in 338 B.C.E. (with the help of the Samnites), and the reorganization of the Latin states strengthened Rome's position immeasurably (Crawford 1988: 19; Pallotino 1991: 129).

Rome disbanded the Latin League and organized the Latin towns in a manner that prevented them from allying themselves against Rome. In essence, ac-

---

The Legacy of Alexander the Great

When Alexander the Great of Macedon died in 323 B.C.E., he left behind a huge empire, stretching from Greece to the Indus Valley. However, he did not leave behind a clear successor and until 281 B.C.E., the empire was contested by the *diadochoi* (the Greek word for "successors"). The diadochoi competed with one another for control of the divided empire and those related to Alexander by blood were killed off quickly. The most important successor was Ptolemy, who gained control of Egypt. Eventually, however, both empires were absorbed into the Roman Empire. All of these territories that had been conquered by Alexander were Hellenized, which is to say the regions had been greatly affected and transformed by the encounter with Greek culture. The absorption of these Hellenized regions into the Roman Empire brought Greek practices into even greater prominence throughout the empire.

cording to Livy, all the Latin towns were assimilated into Rome. The Latin cities were made into *municipia,* some of which were fully incorporated into the Roman state with full rights of citizenship (Heurgon 1973: 200). Others had all rights of citizenship with the exception of the right to vote (Heurgon 1973: 200). The designation of cities as municipia instantly made large portions of Italy Roman. Rome further entrenched its power by encouraging the elites of these municipia to participate in Roman social and economic life. Indeed, ties of marriage and finance integrated the Latin cities into the strict social hierarchy of Rome. By marrying the interests of municipia elites with those of Rome, the Roman state gained a powerful hegemony over large sections of Italy. Revolt from the municipia no longer was a concern, because the municipia saw themselves as Roman, with commercial and social interests dependent on the Roman state's prosperity. And because tribute usually took the form of manpower sent to the Roman army, the Latin cities lost their independent military forces.

Furthering Roman strength in Italy after 338 B.C.E., Rome greatly increased the policy of establishing *coloniae* (colonies). Coloniae were settlements created where none had existed before. Particularly, they were set up in strategic military or economic regions. Locations of Roman weakness quickly became locations of Roman strength (Crawford 1988: 21; Grant 1978: 45, 60). Furthermore, by displacing large segments of the population and establishing them in new areas, Rome weakened internal opposition. These new colonies became completely dependent on support from Rome.

The Second Samnite War.   Roman interests began to conflict with Samnite interests again in 328 B.C.E. with the foundation of the Roman colony at Fregellae (Cornell 1995: 352). In 327 B.C.E., Rome (upon request from its ally Naples) again went to war with the Samnites. The Caudine Forks was the site of tremendous Roman military loss in 321 B.C.E. Although scholars do not agree on the scale of devastation, the Roman army was forced to surrender (Heurgon 1973: 207). But when the republic refused the terms of surrender, the war began again. In 303 B.C.E., the war came to an end without a clear victor.

During the second Samnite War, the Romans constructed the Via Appia (the Appian Way), a major road between Rome and Capua. This was not the first major road leading to Rome; in fact, Rome's position at the crossroads of many trade routes provided it with strategic advantage from its inception. But the Via Appia can be considered the first massive public roadway built to facilitate military traffic (Grant 1978: 63). Although previous roads had been gravel and were constructed simply, the Appian Way's construction was a monumental undertaking, involving a significant amount of engineering activity. Here can be found the beginnings of Roman intercity infrastructure.

The Third Samnite War.   By the outbreak of the third Samnite War, Rome had most of Italy under its control. In 298 B.C.E. the Samnites, along with a coalition of Etruscans, Gauls, and Umbrians, went to war with Rome in an attempt to check its growing power (Heurgon 1973: 209). The major defeat of the Samnite

A section of the Via Appia near Rome. (Pixel That)

forces came in 295 B.C.E. at the Battle of Sentinum. In 290 B.C.E., the Samnites surrendered to Rome and became assimilated under greater Rome. Within a few years, a similar fate befell the Etruscans and Gauls.

The Pyrrhic Wars.   After the third Samnite War, Rome controlled most of Italy south of the Po Valley. But it would be Rome's victories in the Pyrrhic Wars that would secure Roman domination over a conquered and unified Italy (Cornell 1995: 364; Ferril 1988: 52). The background of these wars was Rome's relationship to the neighboring Greek regions. Alexander of Epirus (a Greek mercenary) had formed a treaty with Rome in 334 B.C.E. to prevent Rome from interfering in activities among the Greek cities, including Tarentum, and Rome had mostly honored that treaty.

However, when the construction of Roman colonies began in Greece, Tarentum declared war on Rome with the backing of Pyrrhus of Epirus (a relative of Alexander the Great). In 280 B.C.E., Pyrrhus landed in Italy with a huge expeditionary force. Pyrrhus won his early battles, but at huge costs to his army (which included twenty elephants). The expression "pyrrhic victory," meaning a victory gained at a cost greater than the rewards, originated from the Battle of Asculum in 279 B.C.E., when Pyrrhus narrowly defeated the Roman army. Although the Romans' old enemies, the Samnites, joined Pyrrhus, most of Rome's other allies remained loyal to the city. In 275 B.C.E., the Romans defeated him at Beneventum. Pyrrhus's misfortunes continued in his attacks on Sicily, where, after initial victories, he was held off by the powerful forces of the Carthaginians. In 274 B.C.E., Pyrrhus returned to Epirus and from there managed to conquer most of Greece and Macedon. He was killed at the city of Argos, supposedly by a pot that a woman threw out of a window, hitting him in the head. Strangely, this is a common trope in ancient literature. As a means of denigrating the memory of warriors, stories are told of their deaths caused by women throwing household goods from higher stories of buildings (for a similar story, see the Book of Judges 9:50–54 in the Old Testament). So it is unlikely that this is how Pyrrhus actually died. In 272 B.C.E., the war came to an end when the Romans laid siege to Tarentum. This victory gave Rome complete control of southern Italy (Pallotino 1991: 137).

The Punic War and Expansion

At the same time that Rome emerged as a world power, the city of Carthage (in Tunisia) had reached a similar status. Carthage was founded in the Iron Age by Phoenicians from the city of Tyre (in modern Lebanon). The Phoenicians were sea merchants with a long naval tradition. They spoke a Semitic language known as Phoenician, through which the alphabet was introduced into Greek (itself the basis of today's alphabet). Phoenician language inscriptions that are written in Latin script are referred to as Punic.

Carthage and Rome had long been allies, seeing common enemies in the Etruscans, the Greeks, and King Pyrrhus. But after Rome had conquered the southernmost sections of Italy, the Mediterranean Sea became a contested arena. Sicily, which allowed easy access to both Italy and North Africa, became the first contested ground (Pallotino 1991: 141).

The First Punic War. From 264 B.C.E. to 241 B.C.E., Rome and Carthage fought on the island of Sicily. Initially, the war on Sicily had nothing to do with either of these great cities (Craword 1982: 55; Grant 1978: 95). The Sicilian city of Syracuse had hired Greek mercenaries (the Mammertines) to fight for them. But after a disagreement about pay, the Mammertines seized the city of Messana (modern Messina) on the northeastern tip of the island (Caven 1980: 82). Syracuse responded with force and the Mammertines responded by pleading for help, first from the Carthaginians and then from the Romans. Rome was divided as to whether it should assist. According to Polybius, the Senate did not vote to attack, but the assembly did. Rome did invade, however: Sicily was located too strategically to allow the Carthaginians to gain control of it (Caven 1980: 15).

The Romans' arrival at Sicily was met with some successes. The early victories led to an alliance with Hiero of Syracuse (Grant 1978: 95), and soon Rome dominated most of Sicily. But the Romans did not control the seas, a vital area when battling for control of an island. In contrast, naval forces had been a

Phoenician strength since at least the late Bronze Age (and probably earlier). Rome had never developed as a sea power. This was in great part because of its geographical location; it was an inland city without a seaport, and Rome's growth throughout Italy had not required extensive naval powers. Polybius claims that Rome rectified the situation by building a navy of ships modeled after a wrecked Carthaginian vessel that had been captured. After a rocky start, Rome eventually gained the upper hand at sea, possibly through an innovation on the ship design. Added to Roman ships was the *corvus* (the crow), which was a drawbridge with an iron spike at the end. A Roman ship would come alongside a Carthaginian ship and drop the drawbridge onto it. The iron spike would hold the Carthaginian ship to the side of the Roman ship and allow Roman soldiers to board the enemy ship and defeat them from inside. This grappling technique took away the Carthaginian naval advantage and allowed Rome to use its hand-to-hand fighting skills at sea (Ferril 1988: 53; Grant 1978: 96).

In 241 B.C.E., Carthage was forced to withdraw from Sicily, make peace with Rome, and pay a large indemnity. Shortly thereafter, Rome altered the terms of the agreement by taking control of Sardinia as well. Both Sicily and Sardinia were treated as territories by Rome. These territories were taxed and ruled directly by Rome, a significant departure from the treaty-building model Rome had used to bring mainland Italy under its control (Crawford 1988: 28; Grant 1978: 99).

The Second Punic War.   In the aftermath of the Roman defeat of Carthage, rebellions broke out among Carthage's Spanish territories. These rebellions brought Hamilcar Barca (a Carthaginian general) to Spain, along with his son, Hannibal. Carthage fought numerous wars in this region, losing Hamilcar along the way. In what modern scholars call the Treaty of Ebro, Hamilcar's successor, Hasdrubal, promised Rome that Carthaginian forces would not cross the Ebro River, although it was probably a unilateral statement on Hasdrubal's behalf and not a bilateral agreement per se (Caven 1980: 82; Grant 1978: 115).

When Hasdrubal was assassinated in 221 B.C.E., the Carthaginian army declared Hannibal their leader. Hannibal, one of history's most brilliant military tacticians, led the Carthaginian army against Rome in the Second Punic War, which lasted from 218 B.C.E. to 202 B.C.E. The conflict ignited over the town of Saguntum, south of the Ebro River. The Romans claimed Saguntum as a protectorate (although the exact nature of the relationship is debated), so when Hannibal attacked the city, on the grounds that Saguntum was a security threat to Carthaginian holdings, it was tantamount to a declaration of war against Rome (Caven 1980: 88–89; Ferril 1998: 54; Grant 1978: 115). No one is certain if Hannibal intended this act as an invitation for war with Rome, but when Saguntum fell to Carthage in 218 B.C.E., Rome and Carthage became enemies again.

Hannibal decided to attack Italy directly. The logical route would have been through the Mediterranean Sea, but because Rome had become the preemi-

Hannibal and his soldiers crossing the Alps, with elephants. (Library of Congress)

nent naval power, this would have meant devastation for the Carthaginian forces. So a land route was necessary and Hannibal's legendary crossing of the Alps was the solution. The exact route Hannibal followed has been obscured by time, but it is most probable that he and his massive forces traveled along the Spanish coast, moved north along the Rhone River, and then went over the Alps and into Italy (Caven 1980: 119; Grant 1978: 116). Rome sent an army to cut off Hannibal's forces at the Rhone River, but in a strategic misstep they arrived too late and missed the Carthaginian army.

When Hannibal came out of the Alps, he gained the support of the Gauls, whom the Romans had recently defeated. Indeed, the Po Valley was an area of weakness for Roman security, and Hannibal marshaled new allies there, rebuilding the army that had decreased through the arduous journey (Crawford 1982: 56; Grant 1978: 116). In 218 B.C.E., Hannibal defeated Roman armies at the Ticino and Trebbia Rivers. While Rome recalled troops from around the empire, Hannibal moved his forces through an unguarded corridor toward central Italy. At Lake Trasimene in 217 B.C.E., Hannibal ambushed and defeated a Roman army. The Romans changed strategy with the election of Quintus Fabius as dictator. Now the Roman armies avoided head-to-head conflict with

Scipio Africanus

Born in 236 B.C.E., Scipio was one of Rome's greatest military minds, never having lost a battle. He is most famous for his defeat of Hannibal at the Battle of Zama in 202 B.C.E. The title *Africanus* was bestowed upon him for his victories in Africa. The battle strategies Scipio employed were so effective that General Patton is said to have employed strategies based on Scipio's in World War II. Scipio was also known as a lover of all things Greek. At this stage in Roman history, this was an unusual attitude, one that was used against Scipio by his enemies in the Roman Senate. But for the most part, Scipio was extremely popular with the Roman public and his own soldiers had a near-mystical devotion to him.

Hannibal's army, preferring to keep Roman forces in upper areas to engage in small raids against Hannibal (Ferril 1988: 54; Grant 1978: 118). Such tactics were known as "Fabian tactics," which, in modern vocabulary, refers to tactics of delay and harassment. But this was unpopular with the Roman populace (Caven 1980: 129), and in 216 B.C.E., Rome engaged Hannibal head-on at the Battle of Cannae. This was a stunning defeat for Rome, in which possibly 70,000 Roman men lost their lives, severely diminishing the Roman military. The defeat also led to the abandonment of numerous Roman allies, including the Samnites, Syracuse, Philip V of Macedon, and numerous individual cities throughout Italy (Caven 1980: 141).

The weakness in Hannibal's strategy was that he was cut off from Carthage, unable to reinforce his army, and therefore unable to protect his holdings (Caven 1980: 149). After nine years, Hannibal's brother's army (in Spain) set out to help in Italy. But this Carthaginian force was destroyed by the Roman general Scipio. This victory led to Scipio's election as consul and to his subsequent journey to Africa to attack Carthage directly. Now with Rome as the aggressor, Carthage was forced to recall Hannibal to Africa, where his forces were defeated by Scipio's in 202 B.C.E. at the Battle of Zama. Henceforth, Scipio became known as Scipio Africanus, for his conquest of Africa (Crawford 1982: 61). (See sidebar above.)

The Roman terms of surrender were brought to Carthage by Hannibal, who accepted the harsh conditions. In addition to a yearly payment to Rome, Carthage lost all holdings outside of Africa and was forbidden to wage war outside of Africa. Rome took over Spanish holdings in Spain (although numerous rebellions made this a difficult region to administer). Within Africa itself, Carthage could go to war—with Rome's permission. Hannibal gave up his military role to concentrate on domestic management and Carthage's economic success grew again. Rome, uncomfortable with Hannibal's continued presence, demanded he be handed over. Hannibal refused and fled eastward until 182 B.C.E., when he poisoned himself to avoid capture.

The Third Punic War.   The third and last Punic War (151–146 B.C.E.) led to the complete destruction of Carthage. The North African city and its remaining holdings had continued to prosper economically (Grant 1978: 143). But considerable enmity was still felt toward Carthage in Rome. Politicians, most notably Cato the Elder, insisted that Rome's safety could not be guaranteed until Carthage was razed (Crawford 1982: 93; Grant 1978: 144). Public opinion favored a military end to Carthage. In 151 B.C.E., Rome had its ally, Numidia (in Africa), manufacture a crisis to force Carthage to attack, thereby breaking its treaty obligations (Crawford 1982: 93; Grant 1978: 144). Rome, declaring this to be a breaking of the previous agreement, declared war on Carthage. In 146 B.C.E., Carthage was destroyed completely. All of the surviving citizens became slaves, and the North African lands became a Roman province (Grant 1978: 144).

The Conquest of the East.   Throughout the Punic Wars, Rome was also involved in military affairs in the Greek and Near Eastern worlds (Errington 1971: 102, 131). During this time, Rome fully encountered the Hellenized world and began to assimilate Greece into the newly expanding Roman Empire. Even though Rome traditionally had been somewhat involved in Greek affairs, it had always been reluctant to engage Greece fully (Errington 1971: 7). It was during the First Illyrian War (229 B.C.E.–228 B.C.E.) that Rome's expansion began to include Greece (Crawford 1982: 62). The war, according to Polybius, began in a setting of state-supported (or at least not discouraged) piracy. The Illyrians, a people who lived east of the Adriatic Sea from Rome, had long engaged in piracy against ships traveling in that vicinity. According to Polybius, this piracy reached its pinnacle while under Queen Teuta of the Illyrians. When the Romans protested the piracy, the Roman ambassador was killed. At this, Rome declared war against Illyria. Rome easily defeated Illyria and left much of Queen Teuta's kingdom under the control of a Greek named Demetrius of Pharos. Furthermore, restrictions were placed on sailing in this region and a heavy tribute was imposed (Scullard 1961: 190).

In 220 B.C.E., the Second Illyrian War broke out—this time against Rome's former ally, Demetrius. There were several factors involved in initiating war once again. At the time, the Romans claimed that Demetrius's destruction of Greek cities and acts of piracy went against the treaties reached after the First Illyrian War (Crawford 1982: 63). Certainly, in this, Rome was gaining the support of Greek public opinion. Crawford (1982: 63) has also suggested that, with the second Punic War imminent, the Romans wanted to shore up their eastern flank against Carthage. Whatever the motivations, Rome quickly forced Demetrius to flee.

Demetrius fled to Philip V of Macedon. By this time, the Second Punic War was well under way. Demetrius convinced Philip (according to Polybius) to join sides with Carthage against Rome. Certainly, Philip V had been made uneasy by Rome's ability to intervene in political affairs in Illyria, and he desired to limit Rome's powers. So after the Roman defeat at Cannae, Philip V allied himself with Hannibal. But when the tide turned against Carthage in 205 B.C.E.,

Philip V removed himself from the alliance and formed a treaty with Rome (Scullard 1961: 219).

Livy and Polybius disagree on exactly when and how conflict arose again between Rome and Macedon. The likeliest course of events is that when Macedon began moving against Rhodes, the island asked Rome for help. Claiming that Philip V and Antiochus III (of Syria) were conspiring about dominance over Egypt, Rhodes was able to convince Rome that Philip was in a position to become too powerful. Consequently, in 200 B.C.E., Rome attacked Macedonia. Under the direction of General Gaius Flaminius, Rome managed to defeat Philip in 197 B.C.E. at the Battle of Cynoscephalae.

At first, Rome left the Greek city-states to their own devices (Gruen 1968: 78; Rawson 1988: 52; Scullard 1961: 219). At the Isthmean Games in 196 B.C.E., the same general who led Rome to victory against Macedon—Flaminius—declared all Greek cities free. However, the Greek cities proved themselves unable to manage their internal affairs without conflict and Rome soon returned, intervening (Grant 1978: 134–138). Antiochus III of Syria, who had amassed a large empire in the Near East while Rome was fighting Carthage, attacked Greece in 192 B.C.E. Rome, with the help of Carthage, and was able to defeat Antiochus in 190 B.C.E. at Magnesia. Rome gave much of Antiochus's empire to Pergamum, the city that had initially requested Roman help against Antiochus.

Between 171 B.C.E. and 168 B.C.E. the Romans went to war against Philip V's son, Perseus. His defeat in 168 B.C.E. led to the dissolution of Macedon into four republics (Grant 1978: 140). The tax imposed on these Macedonian republics was very high—so high, in fact, that all Roman citizens were exempted from taxes at the time (Scullard 1961: 297–298), a fact that led to revolt in 149 B.C.E. Rome easily crushed this revolt and re-formed the four separate republics into one larger Macedonia. Another revolt was crushed in 146 B.C.E. This second revolt led to the total destruction of the city of Corinth (Grant 1978: 143; Scullard 1961: 305). Rome had gained a new empire to the east, and in 133 B.C.E., King Attalus II of Pergamum willed all of the territory gained from Antiochus III to Rome. The Roman republic now controlled territory from Spain to Syria and from Africa to the Alps.

Fall of the Republic

Rome's now huge empire and immense wealth caused a number of problems that eventually led to the collapse of the republic and the concentration of political power in the hands of a single individual—the emperor. The gulf between rich and poor had grown tremendously (Grant 1978: 151). Wealth flowed into the capital in huge amounts, but only to a small group of families. Furthermore, because senators were restricted in the kinds of commerce in which they could engage, the ruling families were no longer necessarily the wealthy families. Land was often confiscated from the poor to grant it to military personnel (a group that had become quite powerful). Much of the tax burden rested on Italians outside of Rome, who lacked many of the rights of Roman citizens. Various military threats further demonstrated the incapacity of the Roman republic to deal with problems both inside and outside of Rome.

Up to this point, this chapter has dealt mostly with Rome's expansion and external affairs; however, the fall of the republic is deeply rooted in the internal affairs of the government of Rome.

The Land Crisis.   As Rome's territories had grown, the wealthy in Rome had gained massive fortunes. Much of this wealth was converted into landholdings, with the wealthy buying huge estates throughout Italy (Stockton 1979: 7). This amassing of land into elite hands undermined the traditional Mediterranean economy, which was based on small-scale subsistence farming and pastoralism (Crawford 1982: 103; Crawford 1988: 33; Grant 1978: 162). Large cities, especially Rome, depended on food imported from the countryside, and created much more profitable venues for the sales of the cash crops produced by these huge farms, which were often run by absentee landlords. This meant that the rural, landless poor had increasingly little access to staple foods. The situation worsened with the return of Roman soldiers to Italy. Many small farmers were evicted from their lands so that the returning soldier could be provided with a farm for his own family. The rural poor, forced off their land with no access to the basic necessities of life, moved into urban centers (Grant 1978: 165). Two brothers, Tiberius and Gaius Gracchus, attempted to solve these problems. Their efforts eventually led to the breakdown of the republican system.

The Gracchi came from a very prominent family (Stockton 1979: 23). Their father was a governor of Spain, and their mother was the famous Cornelia, daughter of Scipio Africanus. Tiberius, who was elected tribune in 133 B.C.E., was married to the daughter of Appius Claudius (see the sidebar on page 72). Tiberius approached the problem of the landless poor by looking to long-ignored laws that limited the amount of land that could be owned by one family. By resurrecting these laws, Tiberius ensured that the surplus land held by the aristocracy would be given up and redistributed among the poor (Crawford 1982: 109; Crawford 1988: 33–34; Grant 1978: 169; Starr 1953: 53). Whereas the Senate refused these measures, Tiberius enacted the legislation through the Plebeian assembly. Technically either assembly could pass legislation without agreement from the other, but traditionally this was not practiced (Crawford 1982: 109–110; Grant 1978: 170). The only way the Senate could prevent this legislation was if another tribune vetoed the legislation. One of the ten tribunes did attempt to veto, but Tiberius had the man deposed. The legislation was passed and a commission consisting of Appius Claudius and the Gracchi was created. Tiberius attempted to be elected tribune for a second year, but while the Senate debated whether this breach of custom was legal, Tiberius was killed by a mob that opposed his reforms.

Tiberius's brother, Gaius, became tribune in 123 B.C.E. and had similar goals. Not only did Gaius want to enact land reforms, he also wanted to reform prices and the military and establish new colonies (Grant 1978: 174). Most revolutionary was his desire to offer the vote to non-Roman Italians. But this also weakened his support from the urban poor, whose power to vote was one of their means of political force (Grant 1978: 175). Riots broke out, martial law was declared, and a price was put on Gaius's head by Opimius, the consul at

Appius Claudius Caecus

Known as "The Blind" because of his blindness in old age, Appius Claudius Caecus was a famous censor of Rome. Classical sources tell us that he extended membership of the Senate to rich citizens of the lower classes and to the sons of freedmen. This new list of senators drawn up by Appius caused considerable controversy in Rome. It is difficult to know how much of a populist Appius really was and how much is the bombast of ancient historians, such as Livy. It is very likely, however, that Appius increased taxes, with the intention of facilitating his public works projects, the two most famous being the *aqua Appia* (the first major aqueduct in the city of Rome) and the Via Appia (a paved road from Rome to Capua). During the time of Appius Claudius Caecus, Rome began incorporating numerous Greek traditions, such as the public worship of war gods and the use of coinage. Whether any of these innovations can be ascribed to Claudius is unclear. Toward the end of his days, he vehemently opposed peace with Pyrrhus. Classical sources preserve many writings attributed to him, including aphorisms, and Cicero wrote that Appius Claudius Caecus was a great orator.

the time (121 B.C.E.). During these riots, senators killed many of Gaius's supporters. Gaius, once cornered, had his slave kill him rather than be captured, and more than 3,000 other Gaius supporters were executed. So the reform attempts of the Gracchi met with failure, but the brothers became martyrs of Rome and symbols of political virtue.

The Rise of the Military. The immediate legacy of the Gracchi and the attempts at land reform was the death of the consensus-style leadership that had been so successful in the early years of the republic (Ferril 1988: 57; Grant 1978: 176; Starr 1953: 53). It was replaced by the rise of party politics, the domination of the Roman government by the Senate, and the rise to power of generals whose armies were more loyal to them than to the state of Rome. The land issue was somewhat resolved by the expansion of Rome into the Po and Rhone valleys (because so much new land was acquired). But war in Africa was to further the internal strife of the republic.

War (112 B.C.E.–105 B.C.E.) with the Numidian king Jugurtha in Africa found Rome divided as to how to proceed with the battle (Crawford 1982: 125). The political conflict within Rome reached its apex when a Roman army surrendered to Jugurtha. While various investigations of the Senate were launched, a non-noble named Marius was elected consul, to better run the campaign against Jugurtha. This was a tremendous blow to the power of the Senate, which traditionally had been responsible for the conduct of war (Ferril 1988: 57). The monumental step that Marius enacted was to allow almost any male to join the army. That is to say, a man no longer needed property to become a soldier, he only needed to be recorded in the census (see chapter 7). This led to a professionalization of the military, because the ranks had become filled with the landless poor lacking otherwise gainful employment. When war was over, these men had no home to return to, leaving Marius in control of a very powerful force. Within two years, Marius's professional army, trained in new tactics, had defeated Jugurtha.

A new threat from Germanic tribes in the north put further pressure on the Roman army. In 105 B.C.E., a Roman army was defeated by these tribesmen at Orange. This emergency set the stage for Marius's unprecedented five consecutive elections to the position of consul (in total, Marius was consul for seven years) to deal with this emergency for Rome's northern holdings (Ferril 1988: 57; Grant 1978: 179). The military under Marius was generally successful and by 101 B.C.E., the threat from the Germanic tribes ended (Grant 1978: 179). From 104 B.C.E. to 99 B.C.E. Marius also quelled a slave revolt in Sicily, which broke out when a planned release of illegally imprisoned slaves was repealed.

The Social War and the Rise of Sulla.   Rome enjoyed nearly a decade of relative peace, which was broken in 91 B.C.E. The tribune, Marcus Livius Drusus, brought forward legislation that would give various rights to Italian non-Romans, including the right of citizenship (Ferril 1988: 58). Drusus was killed by elements in Rome who opposed Italian emancipation.

The murder of Drusus led to a coalition of Italian cities, according to Livy. They formed an embassy that went to Rome to voice their complaints. When the Senate refused to hear them, the Italians declared war on Rome. This was the beginning of the Social War (the Latin word *socii* means "allies"), a civil war within Italy that lasted two years. Rome brought the conflict to an end by making a number of concessions. Most important of these was that citizenship was granted to any revolting city that laid down its weapons and to any individual who quit fighting and came before the praetor in Rome.

On the heels of the Social War arose a new figure—Lucius Cornelius Sulla. In 88 B.C.E. he was elected tribune and gained control of the army. A threat had arisen from King Mithradates of Pontus, who had invaded Roman territory and massacred a large number of Romans. Sulla was to take the army to battle Mithradates, but was challenged by supporters of the seventy-year-old Marius, who believed that Marius should lead the battle against Mithradates. Riots between supporters of Marius and supporters of Sulla broke out and Sulla fled the city. Once out of Rome, Sulla gathered his army and returned, burning the city and killing the supporters of Marius. Although Marius himself escaped, Sulla cemented his power in Rome and then left with the army to battle Mithradates.

While Sulla was battling the forces of Mithradates, Marius returned to Rome with his own army. By stopping supplies from entering Rome, Marius forced Rome to surrender to him. Once in Rome, Marius killed numerous political opponents and was elected consul for the seventh time (83 B.C.E.). But Marius died only a few days after gaining the office, and Lucius Cinna (the consul who had called Marius back in the first place) gained control of Rome.

At the same time, Sulla made a treaty with Mithradates and returned to Rome with his well-trained and experienced army. In 82 B.C.E., Sulla fought a Samnite army at the walls of Rome in what has come to be known as the Battle of the Colline Gate. Sulla, victorious, executed about 6,000 Samnites and took control of Rome. Appointed dictator, Sulla began eradicating his political opponents. Through proscriptions, Sulla seized the income of many wealthy individuals in Rome, according to Strabo. Proscriptions were lists of names of individuals deemed public enemies. They could be hunted down and killed for a reward and all of their property could be seized by the state. Furthermore, any sons of a man on the list would lose their citizenship. In further attempts to gain income, Sulla destroyed and looted Samnite territories and raised tribute from other towns. Sulla also strengthened the Senate by decreeing that it had sole power over the military (Ferril 1988: 58–59). Numerous other constitutional reforms were undertaken to prevent the dissolution of Rome into civil war (Grant 1978: 189). In 80 B.C.E., Sulla retired his dictatorship and wrote his memoirs, but left the Roman republic divided and embittered. The end of the republic was dominated by the struggles among powerful men seeking to gain sole control of Rome.

The Last Years of the Republic. The relative stability of the republic had been completely destroyed by Sulla's reign. A series of powerful individuals, leading the army and controlling various factions in Rome, attempted to gain sole control of the republic (le Glay et al. 2001: 113). The first of these ambitious individuals to appear after the resignation of Sulla was Pompey the Great (Gaius Pompeius). Pompey had proven himself a skilled military man under Sulla in the wars against Mithradates. After Sulla died, he was given command of a force to do battle with an anti-Sullan governor in Spain. While Pompey was victorious in Spain, another general, Lucullus, was gaining victories against Mithradates, who had come into contest with Rome again, this time in Bithynia. Although Lucullus was victorious against Mithradates (who was forced to return to Pontus), he lost control of his army and was forced to give his leadership to Pompey (Heichelheim and Yeo 1962: 208). By undercutting the successes of another general, Pompey had gained control of more military power. Back in Rome, Marcus Licinius Crassus, who had been an ally of Sulla and was one of the wealthiest men of the city, was furthering his political power and allied himself with Pompey.

The alliance of Crassus and Pompey led to the eventual end of the slave revolt led by Spartacus (73 B.C.E.–71 B.C.E.). Memorialized in Stanley Kubrick's film, *Spartacus,* the revolt of Spartacus was a massively destructive event. Spartacus was a Thracian gladiator who escaped with some of his fellow gladiators from his training camp in Capua and was joined by escaped slaves from all over the empire. What made Spartacus's force so powerful was that it consisted of well-trained warriors. Many of the slaves were soldiers who had been defeated and captured from enemy forces, and many had been trained as gladiators. This was an awesome army, and under Spartacus they terrorized Italy for two years. Moving along the Apennines, they looted towns, with the eventual goal of moving north and out of Roman territory. Eventually the forces of Crassus were able to defeat them, and Pompey's forces mopped up the remaining rebels.

Crassus and Pompey were elected consuls in 70 B.C.E., even though Pompey was technically not eligible for the office (he was too young and had not held the required offices). Under these two men, many of the constitutional reforms of Sulla were reversed (Heichelheim and Yeo 1962: 210). In 67 B.C.E. Pompey was granted an army with the mandate to wipe out piracy in the Mediterranean. Amazingly, this feat was accomplished in about three months. After this, Pompey went to battle with Mithradates. This oft-reappearing foe of Rome's was eventually forced into suicide in 63 B.C.E. After defeating Mithradates, Pompey conquered the lands of the Near East—Syria, Judaea, and Mesopotamia. The inclusion of these lands within the

A sculpted portrait of Pompey. (Library of Congress)

Roman sphere of influence gave Rome command of most of the Mediterranean. This stability facilitated trade and travel throughout the region.

While Pompey was carving out an empire in the east, Crassus had allied himself with another figure—Julius Caesar. Caesar, a supporter of Marius, had become quite popular by throwing games at Aedile in 65 B.C.E. Caesar and Crassus worked together in the political life of Rome in many ventures, including a land reform bill. Cicero, the great orator, helped defeat this bill and came to be an unofficial leader of more conservative forces (Heichelheim and Yeo 1962: 221). Despite this, Caesar became a popular figure in Roman political life. In 63 B.C.E. he became *pontifex maximus,* and in 61 B.C.E. he went to Spain as governor. While in Spain, Caesar attempted to run for consul, but Cato the Elder and others blocked him on the grounds that the candidate had to be physically present in Rome. So Caesar returned to Rome in 60 B.C.E., ran for the consulship, and won.

When Pompey returned to Rome in 62 B.C.E., he found a city embroiled in controversy. The Catiline conspiracy (see the sidebar on page 76) had recently been resolved, cementing the powers of conservative forces in the Senate. Pompey had expected that he could easily gain recognition for his eastern settlements and gain veterans' benefits for his troops. The Senate, composed of many old enemies, including Lucullus, rebuffed him (Heichelheim and Yeo 1962: 221). So Pompey looked to Crassus and Caesar to see that his demands were met. These three men agreed to work together in what became known

The Catiline Conspiracy

The Catiline controversy is a very well-documented event in Roman history. The writings of Cicero and Sallust have left detailed accounts of the attempts of one individual to start a revolution in Rome. Catiline was a patrician with political aspirations who lost the election for consulship to Cicero in 63 B.C.E. Catiline had promised to cancel debts and was possibly supported by Julius Caesar, but lost the election again in 62. After this, Catiline gave up on the political process and began planning for revolution. Cicero marshaled evidence against him and when Catiline left Rome, Cicero presented the evidence to the Senate. The Senate arrested and executed Catiline's co-conspirators and sent troops out to kill Catiline. They succeeded in this in 62 B.C.E.

(erroneously) as the First Triumvirate. The relationship was cemented when Caesar's only child, Julia, married Pompey.

The three men managed to achieve much. Pompey's demands were met and Caesar gained command of a military for campaigns into Gaul (which were made famous through his own writings). In 55 B.C.E., Caesar managed to set up a Roman presence as far away as Britain and defeated the Gauls at the Battle of Alesia in 52 B.C.E. During this time, however, the alliance of the First Triumvirate was breaking down (Taylor 1949: 141). In 64 B.C.E., Julia died, an event that broke the familial connection between Caesar and Pompey. And in 63 B.C.E., Crassus died attempting to attack the Parthians. Crassus's death left Rome divided into factions supporting either Caesar or Pompey (Taylor 1949: 141). Pompey's factions gained the upper hand politically in 49 B.C.E., when the Senate declared martial law against Caesar, and Caesar's tribunes (Marc Antony and Quintus Cassius) were forced to flee (Taylor 1949: 160).

In response, Caesar, with his large army, attacked Pompey's forces and easily defeated them. It was Caesar's legendary "Crossing of the Rubicon" in 49 B.C.E. that plunged Rome into civil war. Pompey fled to Greece, and Caesar returned to Rome, where he pardoned his opposition. Against Pompey, he sent seven legions to Greece, where Pompey's larger forces were surprised by a winter attack. In 48 B.C.E., at Pharsalus, Caesar's forces defeated Pompey's. Pompey fled to Egypt, but was killed there. In Egypt, Ptolemy XIII was fighting his sister Cleopatra VII for control over the land of the Nile. Ptolemy, in an attempt to win Rome's backing, cut off Pompey's head and presented it to Caesar when he arrived in Egypt. Caesar, however, sided with Cleopatra, and installed her as ruler of Egypt.

In 47 B.C.E., Caesar returned to Rome (after his famous dalliance with Cleopatra) and began reorganizing the Roman state. In 44 B.C.E. he appointed himself *dictator perptuus* (dictator for life), fundamentally altering Roman government forever. His power, which seemed that it could grow even more absolute, became a source of concern for the Senate. So on March 15, 44 B.C.E. (the Ides of March), he was killed by a group of senators, who stabbed him repeatedly.

Augustus visiting Cleopatra in her chamber. (Library of Congress)

Rome, however, was not impressed with this assassination. Marc Antony managed to prevent the annulment of Caesar's acts, while mobs burned down the Senate house. Caesar's heir, Octavian, gained the backing of the senators who had been involved in the conspiracy against Caesar. Individuals such as Cicero supported Octavian simply because Octavian was an alternative to Marc Antony (Stockton 1988: 127). Eventually, however, Octavian joined forces with Marc Antony and his ally, Lepidus—forming the Second Triumvirate. The Second Triumvirate moved back to Rome, where they punished many of their enemies, including Cicero.

The Second Triumvirate divided the empire among themselves: Octavian took the west, Antony took the east, and Lepidus took Africa. Octavian and Antony began careful maneuvers to cement their power. Antony attacked the Parthians and cemented his military power. He married Octavian's sister, Octavia. Together, Antony and Octavian made a treaty in Misenum (39 B.C.E.) with Pompey's son, who controlled Sicily and Sardinia. Octavian cemented his power by allowing his brilliant general, Agrippa, to attack and defeat Pompey's son and gain other important military victories. Octavian also entangled himself further in Roman nobility by divorcing his wife (Scribonia) on the day she bore his daughter, Julia. He married a noblewoman, Livia Drusilla, forcing Livia to divorce her husband, with whom she had had two children.

The uneasy partnership of Antony and Octavian began to fall apart when

Antony married Cleopatra (who had been Caesar's mistress) in 37 B.C.E. This marriage was not legally recognized because Antony was still married to Octavian's sister, and polygamy was not allowed in Roman law. Octavian began campaigning in Rome against Cleopatra, and Antony divorced Octavia in 35 B.C.E. In 34 B.C.E., Antony declared Cleopatra and her heirs the rulers of Egypt. Following this, Octavian announced that Antony had declared Cleopatra's son (Caesarion) as Caesar's true heir, and with the support of Rome, Octavian declared war on Antony. In 31 B.C.E., at the Battle of Actium, Octavian's forces were victorious. Antony and Cleopatra, their forces having surrendered, fled to Alexandria. Octavian's forces defeated Antony and Cleopatra's remaining forces in 30 B.C.E. in Alexandria, where two of history's most romantic figures took their own lives. With this, the Roman republic was replaced with the Roman Empire.

THE ROMAN EMPIRE

The wars of the final days of the republic had left Rome impoverished and the entire Mediterranean unstable. Octavian was seen as the man who could bring peace and prosperity back to Rome and her provinces. And in this he was successful. But at the same time what was left of the republican form of government was destroyed.

The Principate

Octavian returned to Rome in 29 B.C.E. after reorganizing the eastern provinces that had been devastated in the wars of the previous years. At this time Octavian had tremendous power and controlled the military. He was extremely popular in Rome, and his victory over Egypt, which now supplied free grain to Rome, certainly aided this popularity. The Battle of Actium had left him in near-complete control, but he lacked a constitutional position. Calling himself "Emperor Caesar Augustus, Son of a God" (referring to his adoptive relationship to the now-deified Julius Caesar), he claimed to have restored the republic, but at the same time he had amassed near-absolute governing authority. It was Octavian's consistent use of republican terminology and public dedication to republican principles that made his power palatable to the citizens of Rome (Grant 1978: 248). He never took on the grandiose titles that Julius Caesar had used, nor did he take the position of dictator (Ferril 1988: 65).

In 27 B.C.E., Octavian, in an infamous speech to the Senate, turned over his powers. This announcement had been carefully staged, and his supporters protested his resignation, claiming that Rome could not survive without Octavian. Octavian's response was theatrically reluctant, and he agreed to act as consul for ten years, overseeing the provinces of Egypt, Spain, Syria, and Gaul. Because these were the provinces where most of Rome's legions were based, Octavian had control of the military. In response to Octavian's "generous" sacrifice of power, the Senate bestowed upon him the name Augustus, which means "revered one." From this point on, Octavian was referred to as Augustus. Even though Augustus's control was complete, he had learned from the example of the murder of Julius Caesar (his adopted father) that he required the support of the Senate to retain control. Referring to these acts in 27 B.C.E. as "The First Settlement," Augustus claimed to have restored the republic. In fact, he had gained powers that at one time had been held by numerous offices and brought an effective end to republican government.

With these powers, Augustus left Rome for Gaul and Spain. He remained on the periphery of the empire until 24 B.C.E. From 27 to 24 B.C.E., Augustus accomplished military victories in Spain (the Cantabrian Wars), although he was not a particularly brilliant military tactician. He wrote his autobiography at this time, but it did not survive. The best records from this period are the writings of Dio Cassius. After falling almost fatally sick, Augustus apparently shifted his strategy for leadership. In 23 B.C.E. he resigned his consulship. He gained the position of *tribunicia potestas* (tribune of the people) for life and gained *imperium maius* (power greater than all others). By virtue of his imperium maius, Augustus was de facto leader of the Roman Empire.

In 19 B.C.E., Augustus once again shifted the nature of his powers, having officially received consular powers for life. Scholars have debated the reasons for these periodic strategy changes (Stockton 1988: 128). Were they attempts to combat problems or were they opposition to Augustus? Or did they represent the growth and development of Augustus's understandings of proper governance? Whatever the case, after 19 B.C.E., Augustus was in a position where his political power was no longer questioned.

The Succession.   What was in doubt was who would take over supreme power after Augustus's death. The powers that Augustus had accumulated in his office were not hereditary, but neither was there a system of succession in place, as his position had been created on an essentially ad hoc basis (Grant 1978: 253). So although it was not constitutionally binding, Augustus made certain to indicate whom he would designate as his heir.

The first individual who would be heir to the throne was Marcellus, nephew of Augustus. Augustus himself lacked a son, although his second wife, Livia, had sons from a previous marriage. But Augustus wanted an heir from his own bloodline (the Julian bloodline). His first wife had a daughter named Julia, so Augustus had Marcellus and Julia marry (25 B.C.E.). This seemed like a clear statement of intent that Marcellus was the favored heir (Stockton 1988: 137).

However, in 23 B.C.E., when Augustus thought he was dying, he handed his signet ring (the symbol of his power) over to his longtime friend Agrippa, not to Marcellus (Stockton 1988: 138). Perhaps a power struggle would have ensued had Marcellus not died that same year. Agrippa had been a close friend and general to Augustus for many years and was the military intelligence behind him. In 21 B.C.E., Augustus had his widowed daughter Julia married to Agrippa. They had five children, and Augustus adopted the three sons. By 12 B.C.E., Agrippa's powers were fast approaching those of Augustus, when Agrippa died unexpectedly of illness.

At this time, Agrippa's sons (adopted by Augustus) were too young to rule. So Augustus turned to Livia's sons from her previous marriage (see sidebar

Livia

The third wife of Augustus, Livia is portrayed in classical sources as a schem-ing woman, willing to do anything to give her sons a step up in life. She mar-ried Octavian in 38 B.C.E., after her first husband granted her a divorce at the request of Augustus. It is written (and may represent widespread belief at the time) that the high number of Augustus's heirs who died prematurely could be attributed to her. She was accused, by classical authors, of having killed those who competed with her sons to become heir. The fact that her eldest son, Tiberius, eventually did become emperor furthered the plausibility of this story to the ancient writers. Modern scholars tend to believe, however, that this depiction of Livia is more representative of classical literary topoi than of historical fact. It is widely considered more plausible that she had nothing to do with the deaths of Agrippa and Marcellus. On a more positive note, the classical writers considered her to have been virtuous in her tolerance of Au-gustus's numerous indiscretions. Although it is said that she was the great love of Augustus's life, it did not stop his philandering. This is particularly ironic given the fact that Augustus banished both his daughter and grand-daughter for immorality and banished Ovid for his immoral poetry.

above). The eldest of these sons, Tiberius, was forced to divorce his wife and marry the once-again-widowed Julia. Tiberius married Julia in 11 B.C.E., but be-cause he was very attached to his now ex-wife, Tiberius was quite bitter. By 6 B.C.E., Agrippa's sons, Lucius and Gaius, had entered public office but had proven themselves to be unworthy heirs. Augustus attempted to rein in their power by elevating Tiberius above them. Tiberius refused, left Julia, and exiled himself to Rhodes. However, by 4 C.E. Lucius and Gaius were both dead.

There were now three viable candidates for Augustus's heir: Tiberius, Agrippa's surviving son Agrippa Postumus, and Augustus's great-nephew Germanicus. All three candidates were adopted by Augustus in 4 C.E. Soon enough, Agrippa Postumus proved to be too volatile and was permanently ex-iled. This left Tiberius and Germanicus as the two possible candidates, with Germanicus the only Julian. When Tiberius adopted Germanicus, the problem was solved.

When Augustus died in 14 C.E., the office of emperor had become firmly es-tablished, but the method of succession had not been entrenched. Without a mechanism in place for providing incontestable succession, the identity of the next emperor would always be insecure. But the continued existence of the of-fice itself was secure and would remain so for more than 300 years. The ac-counts of Augustus's death (from illness) tell that he admitted to the performa-tive aspects of his creation of the imperial office and that he asked those present to applaud for him as he departed the comedy of life. This is likely apocryphal, but Augustus died having inaugurated a new political system for Rome.

Table 4.3   The Julio-Claudian Emperors

Name	Regnal Years
Augustus	31 B.C.E.–14 C.E.
Tiberius	14 C.E.–37 C.E.
Caligula	37 C.E.–41 C.E.
Claudius	41 C.E.–54 C.E.
Nero	54 C.E.– 68 C.E.

The Emperors

With the death of Augustus, the imperial period can truly be said to have begun. From this point in Roman history until the death of Constantine, the story of Rome cannot be told without reference to the personalities of the emperors (see Table 4.3).

The Julio-Claudians.   Because Tiberius already shared a great deal of the powers of Augustus, his transition to emperor was a given (Garzetti 1974: 3; Goodman and Sherwood 1997: 47). The transition itself was not particularly smooth. Whereas Augustus's feigned reticence to accept power had endeared him to the Senate, the same approach by Tiberius simply annoyed that political body (Ferril 1988: 68). Also problematic was that the legions used the death of Augustus as an excuse to revolt for higher payment. Such revolts were quickly quelled by Germanicus. Tiberius was not well liked, but he ruled from 14 C.E. to 37 C.E. His bad reputation is due to the writer Tacitus, who portrayed him in a shockingly negative fashion. Initially Tiberius attempted to allow the Senate freedom of action, but he became frustrated by their lack of ambition. Toward the end of his reign, Tiberius had become increasingly paranoid about treason, and numerous treason trials engulfed Rome (Garzetti 1974: 43–49). Eventually Tiberius withdrew to the island of Capri, where he spent his final ten years. Various rumors of his homosexuality and pederasty on the island circulated, but these were typical allegations against unpopular public figures, so it is difficult to evaluate their veracity. When he died in 37 C.E., he was remembered as having been extremely unpopular.

As with Augustus, dynastic succession under Tiberius was complicated. Germanicus (Tiberius's adopted son) and Germanicus's son Drusus were the two major generals under Tiberius. Fighting the Germans beyond the Rhine, Germanicus fought three substantial campaigns (Garzetti 1974: 33–38). After these, he campaigned in the east, where he met his end in 19 C.E. (Garzetti 1974: 42). His son Drusus also met an untimely end (23 C.E.), meaning that the two most likely heirs died before Tiberius. Scholars are divided as to whether the death of Drusus was really caused by his wife Livilla, poisoning him for her lover Sejanus, who was head of the Praetorian Guard (Garzetti 1974: 57). However, Sejanus was retroactively accused of many crimes when he asked to marry Livilla two years after Drusus's death, a request that Tiberius refused. Sejanus ordered the widow of Germanicus and her sons killed, accusing them of attempting to seize the throne. While Tiberius was on Capri, Sejanus became the virtual ruler of Rome (Garzetti 1974: 55). But this came to an end when Sejanus plotted against Tiberius's named heir, Gaius (Caligula). Sejanus and all of his supporters were killed. When Tiberius died, his only heir was Caligula, who took the throne, becoming one of Rome's most notorious emperors.

Caligula reigned from 37 C.E. to 41 C.E. The son of Germanicus, he went to live with Tiberius at Capri when the plot led by Sejanus against him was revealed. He became seriously ill shortly after becoming emperor. Whether the illness was physical or psychological is unclear, but his later actions are not those of a well-balanced individual. After killing numerous possible rivals, Caligula depleted the treasury for massive spectacles (such as creating a bridge of ships across the Bay of Naples in 39 C.E.). His favorite racehorse dined with him and was dressed in the garb of emperors. To refill the treasury he raised taxes and auctioned off gladiators. In 39 C.E. he left to conquer Britain, but returned in 40 C.E., having failed. Toward the end of his life, Caligula declared himself a god and was said to have wandered about talking to the god Jupiter and to the moon. His incestuous union with his sister Drusilla was looked upon with contempt. He built a temple to himself and ordered the Jerusalem Temple converted to an imperial temple, but he died before this was carried out. In 41 C.E. he was assassinated at the Palatine Games—an assassination that had widespread support (Garzetti 1974: 101–103).

With Caligula's death, some members of the Senate had hoped for a return to the republican system (Garzetti 1974: 106). But, according to Josephus, when Claudius was discovered hiding behind a curtain of the palace, he was quickly elevated to the emperorship. Claudius was the son of Drusus, but he had some sort of physical disability that embarrassed the imperial family, so he had been kept out of public affairs (Garzetti 1974: 101–103). Claudius reigned from 41 C.E. to 54 C.E., fearing for his life throughout that time. His first actions were to punish those who had conspired against Caligula, and for the rest of his reign he would quickly dispatch anyone who he feared was plotting against him, eventually killing more than 300 people (Garzetti 1974: 108, 114). Claudius is most notable for his successful invasion of Britain and his poor judgment in wives. His third wife, Messalina, was notorious for killing her rivals and her numerous lovers (Salmon 1966: 171). In 48 C.E., she married one of these lovers (while still married to Claudius), an action that led to her execution. Claudius's luck with wives was just as bad with his fourth wife, Agrippina, daughter of Caligula. After having secured the position of heir for her son Nero, Agrippina poisoned her husband, Claudius (Salmon 1966: 17).

Agrippina succeeded in putting her son on the emperor's throne, but that same son eventually had her killed. Nero, who reigned from 54 C.E. to 68 C.E., was one of the most notorious emperors. Along with matricide (Salmon 1966: 178), Nero ordered a boy named Sporus castrated and then married him. Other bizarre behavior included taking a man named Pythagoras as his "husband" and kicking another wife (who was pregnant) to death. Classical sources suggest that he spent evenings wandering the streets assaulting women and stealing from shops. His love of playing the lyre as accompaniment to the singing

Charles Laughton as Nero in *The Sign of the Cross*, 1932. (Bettmann/Corbis)

of songs he had written was also not well received (Garzetti 1974: 157). In 64 C.E., when a fire broke out at the *circus maximus* and engulfed Rome, people accused Nero of starting it. This was unlikely, and although Nero did substantially deplete the treasury through relief measures, the story that he sang a song while watching the fire consume Rome has, despite its improbability, long held great power in historical writings. Nero exacerbated his unpopularity by blaming the fire on Christians and persecuting members of this group (Garzetti 1974: 164). After a number of attempts, Nero was finally overthrown by supporters of a man named Galba who was declared emperor in Spain.

The Flavians.   Galba, who had been crowned emperor in 68 C.E., was over-thrown shortly thereafter. In quick succession, two new emperors came in and out of power. Otho committed suicide when it was clear that Vitelllius's forces would soon overwhelm him. And Vitellius (who was supported only by the German legions) was killed by the supporters of the Flavian family, led by Vespasian.

Vespasian's accession to the throne inaugurated the second great hereditary line of emperors—the Flavians (see Table 4.4). The Flavians came out of the equestrian class and brought back stability from the chaos that had engulfed Rome after the uprising against Nero (Ferril 1988: 70; Goodman and Sherwood 1997: 62). Vespasian's reign from 69 C.E. to 79 C.E. was peaceful and stable. From a political perspective the same could be said for his son Titus's reign (79 C.E.–81 C.E.). However, breaking the stability was the eruption of the volcano Mount Vesuvius, which destroyed Pompeii and Herculaneum. When Titus died unexpectedly, his brother Domitian took the office of emperor and ruled from 81 C.E. to 96 C.E. Domitian was a capable but unpopular ruler (Salmon 1966: 285). He was very afraid of conspiracies against him, and from 93 C.E. until his death, he executed and banished people at will, based on his paranoia. Eventually realizing that they would all be killed, Domitian's wife and numerous high-ranking officials had the emperor killed, ending the Flavian control of Rome (Goodman and Sherwood 1997: 65).

Table 4.4   The Flavian Emperors

Name	*Regnal Years*
Vespasian	69–79
Titus	79–81
Domitian	81–96

The Five Good Emperors.   After the fall of the Flavians, there was a line of five emperors who had orderly successions and generally good relations with the Senate, hence their designation "The Five Good Emperors" (see Table 4.5). Nerva, who reigned from 96 C.E. to 98 C.E., was installed after the assassination of Domitian. When Nerva sensed that the tide was turning against him, he adopted the governor of Upper Germany, Trajan, as his heir (Ferril 1988: 72). The selection of an heir based on skill rather than on bloodline (theoretically) stabilized the succession process (Garzetti 1974: 305). Rather than being killed in a coup, Nerva was allowed to live out his final months in peace and brought an end to the expectations of bloodshed in the transition between emperors. Nerva's successor, Trajan, was the first emperor born in the provinces (Spain) and he reigned from 98 C.E. to 117 C.E. Under Trajan, the Roman Empire grew to its largest extent (Salmon 1966: 274), pushing all the way to the Persian Gulf. Trajan was also an energetic builder. His most impressive monument, Trajan's Column, still stands in Rome but has been adorned by a statue of St. Peter since 1588. While campaigning in the east, Trajan fell ill (Salmon 1966: 290). Some ac-

Portrait of Emperor Trajan, engraved after a sculpted bust. (Pixel That)

counts claim that he named Hadrian his heir when he became ill. Others suggest that after Trajan died, his death was unannounced until letters naming Hadrian as his heir could be engineered. Either way, Hadrian became emperor in 117 C.E. and reigned until 138 C.E. He was quite capable, although he had a rocky start involving the execution of four senators who, it was thought, were intent on overthrowing him (Salmon 1966: 296–297). Hadrian gave up Trajan's eastern conquests (Garzetti 1974: 420) and solidified preexisting borders (Hadrian's Wall between England and Scotland is a remnant of this policy). A lover of Greek culture, Hadrian traveled the empire (Salmon 1966: 301)—probably a wise idea, because he was not well liked in Rome. Before dying, he named as his heir Antoninus Pius, who reigned from 138 C.E. to 161 C.E. Not much is known about Antoninus, who reigned from Rome; he is notable in that his adopted son became one of the most famous emperors (see Table 4.6).

Table 4.5   "The Five Good Emperors"

Name	Regnal Years
Nerva	96–98
Trajan	98–117
Hadrian	117–138
Antoninus Pius	138–161
Marcus Aurelius	161–180

Table 4.6   The Antonine Dynasty

Name	Regnal Years
Antoninus Pius	138–161
Marcus Aurelius with Lucius Verus	161–169
Marcus Aurelius	161–180
Commodus	180–193

Marcus Aurelius became emperor in 161 C.E. but insisted that Lucius Verus be given the same honors. The two reigned together until Verus's death in 169 C.E. Marcus Aurelius continued to reign until 180 C.E. This emperor is most famous for his work *Meditations,* which still survives. Much of Marcus Aurelius's reign was spent at war, first with the Parthians, then with German invaders, then against Cassius, the governor of Syria (who probably mistakenly thought that Marcus Aurelius was dead), and again against the Germans. The empire that had been solidified by Trajan and Hadrian had begun to fall apart. Plague hit Rome in 167 C.E. and lasted for at least ten years. Before dying of illness, Marcus Aurelius named his son Commodus his successor—the first successor linked by heredity in eighty years.

Commodus, Civil War, and the Severans.   Historians consider the period after the death of Marcus Aurelius to be a time of decline for Rome (Ferril 1988: 75). Until this time Rome had been the center of the empire and the center of imperial power. But after the death of Marcus Aurelius, power shifted to the provinces, where centralized control was minimal. Also, the Roman borders were almost continually under attack and were gradually shrinking. Most historians date the beginning of this decline to 180 C.E., the year of Marcus Aurelius's death.

Marcus Aurelius died while campaigning in Germany. He had been accompanied by his son Commodus, whom Marcus Aurelius had been grooming for the position of emperor. At the death of the emperor, Commodus became sole ruler (his father had already made him co-emperor to ease the succession), ushering in a period of collapsing Roman fortune (at least from the imperial perspective). He negotiated a settlement with the German forces the Roman army was fighting at that time and quickly returned to Rome.

Commodus may be best known to modern audiences as the antagonist in the film *Gladiator,* played by Joaquin Phoenix. Commodus reigned from 180 C.E. to 192 C.E., but for the most part he had given up on administering the empire as soon as he had returned to Rome. He let his advisors run the government for him. The energies of Commodus were concentrated more on games, sex, and paranoia. His love of gladiatorial battles was legendary (indeed, numerous tales survive that try to explain why he was so obsessed with this sport). Commodus was very skilled, and he often participated in gladiatorial games by finishing off injured gladiators and killing animals. Although it made him extremely popular with the crowds, it horrified the senators and governing classes (Garzetti 1974: 550). Commodus's sexual appetite was as voracious as his appetite for sports. Contemporary sources claim that he kept 300 young girls and 300 young boys for his sexual enjoyment.

Governing power was mostly in the hands of the advisors of Commodus. The first powerful advisor was Saoterus, who sat with Commodus in the emperor's chariot during Commodus's triumphal procession, receiving numerous kisses from the emperor. Saoterus was killed in 182 C.E., shortly after an attempt was made on Commodus's life by his sister and her nephew. These attacks made Commodus paranoid and he removed himself from governing. While Commodus gorged on sex and sports, his advisor Perennis took over his responsibilities. But in 185, Commodus had Perennis executed, fearing that his advisor had become too powerful. The next powerful advisor was Cleander, a Phrygian slave who had risen through the ranks in the imperial household. Very corrupt, Cleander sold offices and became quite wealthy. This worked against him in 190 when, during a grain shortage, the populace came to believe that Cleander had fixed the prices to make a profit. When an angry mob descended, demanding Cleander's execution, Commodus accommodated them. After the death of Cleander, Commodus demanded that he be deified and be called Hercules, son of Zeus. Commodus, like Hercules, often wore a lion skin and carried a club. When fire destroyed the Temple of Vesta and the Peace Temple, Commodus initiated major rebuilding in the center of Rome. Calling himself the second founder of Rome, he renamed the city Colonia Commodiana. In 192, Commodus sealed his fate when, during a gladiatorial game, he paced in front of the senators brandishing the severed head of an ostrich as a threat. It was well known that he planned to kill the two proconsuls at an upcoming Games (Garzetti 1974: 551). Shortly thereafter, Commodus was assassinated, leading to a civil war.

The first emperor after Commodus was Pertinax, but after 87 days he was killed by the Praetorian Guard. The next emperor, Didius Julianus, reigned only 66 days. This short-lived emperor had gained the office in a bidding war with another man. But in the periphery, the military did not approve of this, and three commanders marched on Rome. The commander from the Danube, Septimius Severus, reached Rome first. Didius Julianus was killed and the Senate proclaimed Septimius Severus emperor, founding the line of Severan emperors (see Table 4.7).

Septimius defeated and killed the other governors who had marched to

Table 4.7   The Severan Emperors

Name	Regnal Years
Septimius Severus	193–211
Caracalla	211–217
Geta	211
Macrinus	217–218
Elagabalus	218–222
Severus	222–235

Rome and purged their supporters from the Senate. He reigned from 193 C.E. to 211 C.E. and regained some of the territory that the empire had previously lost. Septimius sacked the Parthian capital of Ctesiphon and made northern Mesopotamia a province. Septimius died while campaigning in Scotland. He was succeeded in 211 by his two sons, Caracalla and Geta, who were supposed to reign jointly. But Caracalla killed Geta within a year. Caracalla then ruled until 217 B.C.E., when he was killed by an assassin. Caracalla was replaced by a Moor named Macrinus, who reigned until he was assassinated in 218. Macrinus's assassins proclaimed a fourteen-year-old Syrian boy, Elagabalus, as emperor. This boy was also the high priest of the god Elagabalus, and he set up worship of this deity in Rome. His foreign religious practices and attempts to elevate Elagabalus above Jupiter infuriated the Roman population (Cook et al. 1939: 55). Also, Elagabalus's practice of dressing as a transvestite and working as a prostitute raised concerns in Rome. Tales survive describing his requests to be bodily transformed into a woman, but it is hard to separate fact from polemic in the accounts of his sexual practices. Elagabalus, after adopting Alexanius, was assassinated. Alexanius (now Alexander Severus) took the throne and ruled from 221 to 235. He was only thirteen, and the power actually resided with his mother, Mamaea. The two of them were executed by their legions after an unpopular settlement with Germanic invaders in the north.

The Barracks Emperors.   For fifty years after the death of Alexander Severus, the Roman Empire was beset with problems (Christiansen 1995: 150). At least twenty-seven emperors were selected (see Table 4.8), most from the ranks of the military (hence the term *barracks emperors*), and most were killed, often by their own troops. Alongside these twenty-seven emperors were approximately fifty usurpers to the throne. Those emperors raised from within the military ranks were often the biological sons of the previous emperor. The armies frequently supported this kind of transition as it ensured their continual payment. However, frequently enough, the army would turn against its own chosen emperors.

The instability among the military led to an instability of the empire's defenses. Rome's frontiers were besieged from almost every side (the Sahara proved to be an exception). Frontier battles were difficult because frequently the emperor had to return his army to Rome to quell an internal uprising. The Franks and Alamanni (who would later become the French and Germans) at-

Table 4.8   Major "Barracks Emperors"

Name	Regnal Years	Name	Regnal Years
Maximinus I	235–238	Macrianus	260–261
Gordian I	238	Claudius II	268–270
Gordian II	238	Quintillus	270
Balbinus	238	Aurelian	270–275
Pupienus	238	Tacitus	275–276
Gordian III	238–244	Florianus	276
Philip the Arab	244–249	Probus	276–282
Decius Trajan	249–251	Carus	282–283
Trebonianus Gallus	251–253	Numerian	283–284
Aemilian	253	Carausius	286–293
Valerian	253–260	Diocletian	284–305
Gallienus	253–268		

Table 4.9   The Leaders of the Gallic Empire

Name	Regnal Years
Postumus	260–269
Laelianus	269
Marius	269
Victorinus	268–271
Tetricus	271–274

tacked across the Rhine River. The Vandals and Goths attacked across the Danube River. (See sidebar on page 90.) These forces were the first enemy forces to kill a Roman emperor in battle—Decius, in 251 B.C.E. And in the east, the Sassanians' mighty army brought instability and became the first army to capture a Roman emperor in battle (Valerian in 260 B.C.E.). (See sidebar on page 90.)

When news of Valerian's capture was made known, two major provinces broke off from Rome and became independent. The Gallic province, supported by British and Spanish legions, declared independence and set up a capital at Trier. Independence was maintained until 274 (see Table 4.9 for a list of leaders). Similarly, in the east, centered on the city of Palmyra, the Palmyrene province broke away until 274. These provinces were brought back under control by the emperor Aurelian in 274. Aurelian was a general who managed to quell numerous rivals to the throne and reunify Rome. Aurelian was dedicated to the worship of the Unconquered Sun, a popular deity within the army (Ferril 1988: 77). The worship of this deity, in Aurelian's time, became a cultural phenomenon that united the otherwise very separate cultures in the empire. After Aurelius's murder, another six emperors would reign before Diocletian stabilized Rome.

From Diocletian to Constantine.   Diocletian is often painted by Christian historians as a dark and evil emperor, in juxtaposition to Constantine, who inaugurated Christianity as the official religion of the empire. Indeed, Diocletian did bring a revived intolerance for Christianity through edicts in 297, 298, and

Huns, Goths, and Vandals—Who Were the Barbarians?

It can be difficult to keep track of all of the different groups called "barbarians" by the Romans. In general, barbarians were anyone who was not Greek or Roman. However, the more specific use of the term *barbarian* refers to any of the seminomadic tribes who engaged in war with the Romans. Often the individual names of the tribes are derived from their reputed origin. The Huns, who seem to have come from central Asia, eventually dominated the Black Sea region. Their most famous leader was Attila, who, after 451, began attacking Rome. The Goths were a Germanic group who came from near the Vistula River. Goths separated into two groups. The Ostrogoths (eastern Goths) dwelt near the Black Sea from about the fourth century on, and did not have much to do with Rome. The Visigoths (western Goths) sacked Rome in 410. The Vandals were Germanic tribes from the Baltic coast who migrated to the area of modern Hungary and eventually formed a kingdom in North Africa. The Alans were Asiatic tribes pushed into the Roman heartland by the expansion of the Huns and the Goths. Other Germanic tribes included the Alamanni, the Burgundians, and the Suebi.

Sassanians

From 226 C.E. until the seventh century, the Sassanid family ruled the Persian Empire. They came to power by destroying the ruling elite of the Parthian dynasty, but for the most part, they perpetuated Parthian governance and society. The Sassanians were massive builders and can be considered an eastern version of the Roman Empire for their legacy of building and imperial conquest. The major religion of the Sassanids was Zoroastrianism, but other religions did thrive in this environment. The Sassanian Empire was one of the most powerful in history but is frequently overlooked in history books.

304 (Bowder 1978: 12–13), which demanded that all soldiers and administrators offer sacrifice on pain of death (an activity prohibited by the Christian religion). Diocletian, who reigned from 284 to 305, restructured the Roman Empire and the nature of leadership (Christiansen 1995: 162). At a fundamental level, the nature of the emperor's mandate changed under Diocletian. The emperor was no longer the chosen of the people, but rather the chosen of the gods—in particular, Jupiter. The new title that went with this was *dominus* (which means "master") and an emperor's reign was no longer called a *principate* but a *dominate* (Ferril 1998: 79). The origins of the divine right of European

Constantine the Great converting to Christianity at the Battle of Milvian Bridge. (Bettmann/ Corbis)

medieval kings to rule can be found in this philosophy of Diocletian's. Determining that the empire was too large to govern single-handedly (Bowder 1978: 3), Diocletian installed Maximian as Caesar of the west. Furthermore, to ensure a smooth succession, Diocletian and Maximian each adopted a Caesar to assist in governance and to take over after their own deaths. Diocletian chose Maximanius and Maximian chose Constantine (Bowder 1978: 3–5). These four rulers became known as the Tetrarchy. Each ruler ruled from his own palace (none of which were in Rome). Diocletian engaged in massive building projects and reorganized the Roman governmental system. He retired in 305.

The Tetrarchy, which theoretically had been established to ensure a smooth succession, actually prevented a smooth succession (Ferril 1988: 79). From 305 until 324, the empire once again disintegrated into factions, as Constantine, Maximanius, and three other claimants (including a man named Licinius) vied for the throne. Constantine courted the Christian church for popular support. In 312, Constantine and Maximanius met in battle at the Milvian Bridge. According to Eusebius, Constantine had a vision the night before the battle in which he saw a Christian symbol blazing against the sun. So he had all of his army paint this symbol (the *chi-rho*) on their shields and was subsequently successful in the battle. Whatever the truth behind the story of Constantine's conversion to Christianity, this battle left two emperors of Rome—Licinius in the east and Constantine in the west. By 324, Constantine had killed Licinius and taken control of the empire.

Rise of Christianity

The pretext for Constantine's attack on Licinius was Christianity (Bowder 1978: 32). After the Battle of the Milvian Bridge, Licinius and Constantine had shared power over the Roman Empire, and Licinius had been tolerant of Constantine's efforts to Christianize Rome. Sporadic conflicts marred the peace between the two leaders, but for the most part the status quo remained, with power evenly divided between Constantine and Licinius. This changed in 323, when Licinius made the mistake of moving against the Christian factions within the imperial bureaucracy (Bowder 1978: 42). Fearing that all Christians were working on behalf of Constantine, Licinius had some bishops executed and razed some of the churches. This provided Constantine with an excuse to attack Licinius. Constantine soundly defeated Licinius at Hadrianopolis, and then again at Chrysopolis. Eventually Licinius surrendered, on the condition that his life would be spared. But in 325, Constantine broke his promise to allow Licinius to live, and he had his former rival and Licinius's son executed.

For Christianity, the year 324 C.E. marked a turning point. The religion had moved from its origins as a fringe movement in Judaism (see chapter 8) and had become the official religion of the empire. While Licinius still had power, Constantine had been checked in his attempts to exclude non-Christian religions from practice. But with Licinius out of the way, Constantine was able to legislate against paganism. Sacrifice was forbidden, and the treasuries of pagan temples were confiscated. Roman social life was also legislated based on Constantine's Christian principles. Most notably, gladiatorial combat was outlawed. The laws passed by Constantine, infamous for their harsh punishments, directly reflected Christian morality.

Christianity flourished under Constantine's patronage. In 325 C.E. the Council of Nicaea convened at the request of the emperor. Worrying that Christian unity was threatened by theological disagreements, Constantine invited bishops and theologians to meet in order to come to a consensus on the nature of the Trinity. Known as the Arian controversy, the Church had become divided on how to understand the relationship of God, Jesus, and the Holy Spirit in relation to one another. An Alexandrian priest named Arius had brought the controversy to a head by suggesting that God was dominant and that Jesus and the Holy Spirit were subordinate, although at the highest level of creation. The other viewpoint, which would eventually prevail in Christian thought, held that God is one being, but a being that exists in three forms—Father, Son, and Holy Spirit. The end result of the Council of Nicaea was the composition of the Nicaean Creed, which affirms the non-Arian viewpoint, in very ambiguous language. It is intriguing that a Roman emperor would play a role in theological decision making, and goes to show how Christianity had changed from a fringe movement into an organized religion playing a role in government.

Perhaps the most tangible illustration of Christianity's integration into Roman imperial government was the movement of the capital from Rome to Constantinople. In 324 Constantinople was founded atop the existing city of Byzantium. Constantine had spent most of his early years reigning from Trier and spent little time at Rome. The foundation of Constantinople further undermined Rome's status as the center of the empire. Even though Constantine erected fabulous buildings in Rome, his disbanding of the Praetorian Guard brought with it Rome's concomitant loss of status as the imperial city. In 337 Constantine became ill and finally accepted baptism to Christianity. He was buried in Constantinople, much to the horror of the Roman aristocracy, who expected him to be buried in Rome. The historical irony is profound, in that the man who legislated Christianity as the sole religion of Rome was deified by the Senate after his death!

Fall of the Roman Empire

Edward Gibbon's monumental masterpiece, *The Decline and Fall of the Roman Empire,* has indelibly affected scholars of Rome. No discussion of Rome can be complete without a discussion of whether even the title of this work can be considered accurate. Chapter 11 discusses in more detail the nature of this controversy. What follows here, rather, is a description of the basic historical events that bring Roman history to a close. The end date of the Roman Empire is typically understood to be 476, when a barbarian king sat on the throne of the emperor. But many consider the Byzantine civilization and the Holy Roman Empire to be continuations of Roman glory. However one understands the ends of Rome, from a material culture perspective (that is to say, an archaeological perspective), the end of Roman civilization with recognizable links to the Republican and monarchical periods comes in 476.

Constantine left his three sons, Constantine II, Constans, and Constantius II, as rulers of the empire. Constantine II was nominally the leader, but for all practical purposes, the empire was divided into three discrete sections (Bowder 1978: 44). But infighting between the brothers eventually led to Constantius II becoming sole ruler. In 360, Constantius II, feeling that it was too unwieldy to rule the empire alone, elevated his half cousin Julian to a position of power. The two of them eventually feuded over power, but Constantius II died before much came of the conflict. Julian, now Caesar of the west, attempted to reduce the prominence of Christianity and return Rome to paganism (Cameron and Garnsey 1998: 44). For this Julian is often called "The Apostate." Julian died while campaigning against the Persians, and Jovian was named as his successor. Jovian, however, did not live to return to Constantinople and no heir was immediately apparent (Cameron and Garnsey 1998: 113).

Valentinian I, a military officer, was appointed emperor. Shortly thereafter he appointed his younger brother as *augustus* of the east. The House of Valentinian ruled over a Christian Roman Empire, divided between east and west, from 364 to 392. Battles against barbarian forces eventually led to the death of the House of Valentinian. In their place rose the House of Theodosian, which ruled amid various struggles until 455. Although Theodosius I had strengthened the office of emperor, this strength lasted only until his death in 395. His two sons continued the office of emperor, but actual power shifted to advisors. In addition, the capital of Roman government was moved to Ravenna in 404. This city was in a very defensible position—in the middle of a marsh in northern Italy.

The loss of prestige for the city of Rome was furthered by its sack in 410. The commander of the Roman army, Stilicho, had entered into an agreement with Alaric the Visigoth in 407. Alaric was hired to move his barbarian army against Illyrium to bring the area under Roman control in return for a substantial payment. However, after this deal was brokered, other barbarian groups attacked Gaul and the governorship of Britain was usurped. The attack on Illyrium had to be called off, and Alaric was not paid. In response, Alaric sacked Rome. Although the actual destruction was not great, the sack of Rome was certainly demoralizing. It also illustrated one of the growing weaknesses of the Roman Empire. The Roman military had become dependent on barbarian military forces that were not loyal to Rome (Ferril 1986). Local barbarian warlords had also become more powerful, and attacks on Roman holdings were not uncommon.

Nine more emperors ruled after the last of the Theodosian-supported rulers (Valentinian III). At this point, the empire was permanently divided between east and west. From 455 on, the eastern empire is better known as the Byzantine Empire. The western empire held on for about twenty years, plagued by barbarian attacks, until finally, in 476, the barbarian king Odovacer became king of the empire. At this point, imperial history comes to an end. No more emperors are presented as leaders of Rome. The power of the western Roman Empire passed completely into the hands of German chieftains.

BIBLIOGRAPHY

Adkins, Lesley, and Roy Adkins. 1994. *Handbook to Life in Ancient Rome.* Oxford: Oxford University Press.

Alföldy, Géza. 1985. *The Social History of Rome.* Baltimore: Johns Hopkins University Press.

Astin, A. E., et al. (eds.). *The Cambridge Ancient History,* Volume 8, *Rome and the Mediterranean to 133 B.C.* London: Cambridge University Press.

Beard, Mary, and Michael Crawford. 1984. *Rome in the Late Republic.* Ithaca: Cornell University Press.

Bloch, Raymond. 1960. *The Origins of Rome.* London: Thames & Hudson.

Bowder, Diana. 1978. *The Age of Constantine and Julian.* New York: Barnes & Noble.

Bowman, Alan, et al. (eds.). 2000. *The Cambridge Ancient History,* Volume 10, *The Augustan Empire, 43 B.C.–A.D. 69.* London: Cambridge University Press.

Bradford, Ernle. 1981. *Hannibal.* New York: Barnes & Noble.

Brown, Peter. 1971. *The World of Late Antiquity, A.D. 150–750.* London: Thames & Hudson.

Bury, John. 1928. *The Invasion of Europe by the Barbarians.* London: Macmillan and Co.

Cameron, Avril, and Peter Garnsey (eds.). 1998. *The Cambridge Ancient History,* Volume 13, *The Late Empire, A.D. 337–425.* London: Cambridge University Press.

Cameron, Avril, Bryan Ward-Perkins, and Michael Whitby (eds.). 2001. *The Cambridge Ancient History,* Volume 14, *Late Antiquity: Empire and Successors, A.D. 425–600.* London: Cambridge University Press.

Caven, Brian. 1980. *The Punic Wars.* New York: Barnes & Noble.

Christiansen, Erik. 1995. *A History of Rome: From Town to Empire and Empire to Town.* Aarchus, Denmark: Aarchus University Publishers.

Cook, S. A., et al. (eds.). 1939. *The Cambridge Ancient History,* Volume 11, *The Imperial Peace, A.D. 70–192.* London: Cambridge University Press.

Cornell, Tim. 1995. *The Beginnings of Rome.* New York: Routledge.

Cornell, Tim, and John Matthews. 1982. *Atlas of the Roman World.* New York: Facts on File.

Crawford, Michael. 1982. *The Roman Republic.* Cambridge: Harvard University Press.

———. 1988. "Early Rome and Italy," pp. 9–38 in *The Oxford Illustrated History of the Roman World.* John Boardman, Jasper Griffin, and Oswyn Murray (eds.). Oxford: Oxford University Press.

Crook, J. A., et al. (eds.). *The Cambridge Ancient History, Volume 9, The Last Age of the Roman Republic, 146–43 B.C.* London: Cambridge University Press.

Dorey, Thomas, and Donald Dudley. 1972. *Rome against Carthage.* Garden City: Doubleday.

Dudley, Donald. 1960. *The Civilization of Rome.* New York: New American Library.

Errington, Robert. 1971. *The Dawn of Empire: Rome's Rise to World Power.* London: Hamish Hamilton.

Ferril, Arthur. 1986. *The Fall of the Roman Empire: A Military Explanation.* London: Thames & Hudson.

———. 1988. "Historical Summary of Rome," pp. 45–85 in *Civilization of the Ancient Mediterranean: Greece and Rome.* Michael Grant and Rachel Kitzinger (eds.). New York: Charles Scribner's Sons.

Garnsey, Peter, and Richard Saller. 1982. *The Early Principate.* Oxford: Oxford University Press.

Garzetti, A. 1974. *From Tiberius to the Antonines.* J. R. Foster (trans.). London: Methuen.

Gjerstad, Einar. 1962. *Legends and Facts of Early Rome.* Lund, Sweden: C.W.K. Gleerup.

Goodman, Martin, and Jane Sherwood. 1997. *The Roman World 44 B.C.–A.D. 180.* New York: Routledge.

Grant, Michael. 1978. *History of Rome.* New York: Charles Scribner's Sons.

Gruen, Erich. 1968. *Roman Politics and the Criminal Courts, 149–78 B.C.* Cambridge: Harvard University Press.

Hadas, Moses. 1956. *A History of Rome.* New York: Garden City Press.

Harris, William. 1971. *Rome in Etruria and Umbria.* Oxford: Clarendon Press.

———. 1979. *War and Imperialism in Republican Rome, 327–70 B.C.* Oxford: Clarendon Press.

Hart, B. H. Liddell. 1994 [1926]. *Scipio Africanus: Greater Than Napoleon.* New York: Da Capo Press.

Heichelheim, Fritz, and Cedric Yeo. 1962. *A History of the Roman People.* Englewood Cliffs: Prentice-Hall.

Heurgon, Jacques. 1973. *The Rise of Rome to 264 B.C.* James Willis (trans.). Berkeley: University of California Press.

Holmes, Rice. 1923. *The Roman Republic.* 3 vols. Oxford: Clarendon Press.

Jones, A. H. M. 1964. *The Later Roman Empire, 294–602.* Oxford: Clarendon Press.

le Glay, Marcel, Jean-Louis Voisin, and Yann le Bohec. 2001. *A History of Rome*. 2nd ed. Antonia Nevill (trans.). Malden: Blackwell.

Lintott, Andrew. 1988. "Roman Historians," pp. 226–242 in *The Oxford Illustrated History of the Roman World*. John Boardman, Jasper Griffin, and Oswyn Murray (eds.). Oxford: Oxford University Press.

Luttwak, Edward. 1976. *The Grand Strategy of the Roman Empire*. Baltimore: Johns Hopkins University Press.

MacMullen, Ramsay. 1966. *Enemies of the Roman Order: Treason, Unrest, and Alienation in the Empire*. Cambridge: Harvard University Press.

———. 1976. *Roman Government's Response to Crisis, A.D. 235–337*. New Haven: Yale University Press.

Marsh, Frank Burr. 1963. *A History of the Roman World from 146 to 30 B.C.* 3rd ed. London: Methuen.

Mommsen, Theodor. 1871. *History of Rome*. 4 vols. New York: Scribner.

Ogilvie, R. M. 1976. *Early Rome and the Etruscans*. Atlantic Highlands: Humanities Press.

Pallotino, Massimo. 1991. *A History of Earliest Italy*. Martin Ryle and Kate Soper (trans.). Ann Arbor: University of Michigan Press.

Rawson, Elizabeth. 1988. "The Expansion of Rome," pp. 39–59 in *The Oxford Illustrated History of the Roman World*. John Boardman, Jasper Griffin, and Oswyn Murray (eds.). Oxford: Oxford University Press.

Richardson, J. S. 1980. "The Ownership of Roman Land: Tiberius Gracchus and the Italians." *Journal of Roman Studies* 70.

Salmon, Edward. 1966. *A History of the Roman World from 30 B.C. to A.D. 138*. 5th ed. London: Methuen.

———. 1969. *Roman Colonisation*. Ithaca: Cornell University Press.

———. 1983. *The Making of Roman Italy*. Ithaca: Cornell University Press.

Scarre, Chris. 1995. *Chronicle of the Roman Emperors*. New York: Thames & Hudson.

Scullard, H. H. 1961. *A History of the Roman World 753 to 146 B.C.* London: Methuen.

———. 1976. *From the Gracchi to Nero*. 4th ed. London: Methuen.

Seager, Robin (ed.). 1969. *The Crisis of the Roman Republic*. New York: Barnes & Noble.

Sherwin-White, Adrian. 1984. *Roman Foreign Policy in the Greek East*. Norman: University of Oklahoma Press.

Smith, Richard. 1955. *The Failure of the Roman Republic*. Cambridge: Cambridge University Press.

Starr, Chester. 1953. *The Emergence of Rome*. Ithaca: Cornell University Press.

Stockton, David. 1979. *The Gracchi*. Oxford: Clarendon Press.

———. 1988. "The Founding of the Empire," pp. 121–149 in *The Oxford Illustrated History of the Roman World*. John Boardman, Jasper Griffin, and Oswyn Murray (eds.). Oxford: Oxford University Press.

Syme, Sir Ronald. 1939. *The Roman Revolution*. Oxford: Oxford University Press.

Taylor, Lily Ross. 1949. *Party Politics in the Age of Caesar*. Berkeley: University of California Press.

Walbank, Frank, A. E. Astin, M. W. Frederiksen, and R. M. Ogilvie (eds.). 1989. *The Cambridge Ancient History*, Volume 7, Part 2, *The Rise of Rome to 220 B.C.* London: Cambridge University Press.

V CHAPTER 5
Economics

Many economic aspects of modern life are taken for granted today in North America and Europe. Very few people are actually involved in primary food production; most people do not harvest their own crops or butcher their own meat (except on a very small scale). Likewise, people do not produce their own clothes, and even fewer actually create the fabric used in clothes. This disassociation with primary production is a hallmark of the industrialized world. To understand ancient Roman economy, it is necessary first to understand this major difference between modern industrialized life and ancient Roman life. Other than the very wealthy, most Roman households were very involved in the day-to-day production of food and clothing. There were markets where goods could be bought and sold, but they certainly did not play as important a role in supplying a family with their needs as stores do today. This chapter describes some of the major elements of the Roman economy. For a general overview of the controversies relating to the study of Roman economy, read the appropriate section in chapter 11.

AGRICULTURAL AND SUBSISTENCE ACTIVITIES

The basis of the Roman economy was agriculture (Hopkins 1988: 753). The vast majority of people living within the Roman sphere of influence gained their livelihood through small-scale subsistence farming (Finley 1973: 139). Their economic interactions with the rest of society were relatively limited. They produced what they needed, when they needed, on their own. The number of agricultural workers within the classical world has been a controversial topic. Some scholars have argued that almost every nonelite Roman engaged in some sort of agriculture. Others have argued that a significant proportion of agricultural production was done on a massive scale on massive estates, freeing most other Romans from these obligations. Unfortunately, there is not enough evidence to say either way. We do, however, know a lot about the actual practice of farming in Roman times, and that is the subject of the remainder of this section.

Landholding and Types of Farmsteads

Ownership and control of land are central issues in understanding agricultural economy. Who owns the land and who has rights to it are important, but also usually very complicated, issues. Landownership usually involves a hierarchy of rights to land use, and it is frequently not possible to say that one individual owns land outright. Usually no one has complete rights over a piece of real estate. The individual landowner was frequently obligated to the state in return for the right to own the land; in the period of the republic these obligations included military service. On the other hand, even the emperors did not have full control over land, because they had to deal with laws and customs protecting the rights of individual landowners. Real estate ownership issues are much more complicated than ownership issues involving moveable property, which can be owned outright. What follows is a discussion of the major Roman types of landownership, but it is important to remember that the categories discussed here were not as clear-cut in actual practice.

The Family Farm.   The ideal form of Roman landownership was the small family farm. In later times, the Romans believed that all of their ancestors had farmed small plots of land (Shelton 1988: 152). These early Romans had owned their land, and it was the hard work of their forefathers that had led Rome to such success (Shelton 1988: 153). In reality, it is unlikely that the earliest Roman settlements consisted of independent, self-sufficient, single-family farm dwellings. Nonetheless, this was a powerful myth and became the norm in the early Republican period. The *pater familias* of the farmstead was obligated to fight in the military, a difficult burden for the farm (Stockton 1979: 9). Because the farm probably operated only slightly above the subsistence level, the loss of one productive member during important agricultural periods was significant. Small family farms were just as economically unstable in the ancient world as they are today. Subsistence farmers were at the mercy of the weather, price fluctuations, and a variety of other variables beyond their control.

Ager Publicus.   The *ager publicus* was public land, farmland owned by the state, and the subject of much controversy in the late Republican period. The Roman state gained this land during the conquest of Italy by confiscating it from those cities that resisted Roman advances (Stockton 1979: 11). Much of this land was assigned to colonies. Some of it was doled out to individuals. By about the middle of the second century B.C.E., however, much of this land was distributed to wealthy landowners who already had large estates. When Roman forces took over new areas, they incorporated the preexisting landownership schemes into the Roman administration. Because of this, there was great variation in local landownership practices in the empire. But the land that was annexed as ager publicus was administered in an entirely Roman fashion. Agricultural production was geared toward producing a surplus—enough for the city dwellers in the nearby colony and the Roman army stationed in that region.

Latifundia.   *Latifundia* were huge corporate agricultural estates run with the purpose of making a profit. Owners of these kinds of land began to dominate Roman agriculture, gradually buying out the small landholders (Pallotino 1991: 130; Rees 1987: 484). Larger farms were better equipped to deal with uncertainty in an economic activity revolving around considerable insecurity

(Stockton 1979: 13). These small landholders moved to the city and became the urban poor, because the larger landholders did not normally hire these ex-farmers to work the newly purchased land (Rees 1987: 484). Instead, latifundia were worked by massive amounts of slave labor.

Tenants and Sharecroppers. Eventually, large landholders found that large slave-based work teams were not economically viable. Even though slaves were not paid wages, they were expensive, because all of their needs had to be met by the farm owner. So these large corporate farmers began to rent out land to smaller farmers. The larger farms were divided into smaller units. Some of these units were rented out to tenants. The tenant was obliged to pay a yearly fee and/or was compelled to work on the renter's farm. A system similar to sharecropping was also used in certain circumstances. These types of land-holding relationships became prominent in about the second century C.E. (Stockton 1979: 15). They lasted well into the medieval period, and some have argued that they formed the basis of European feudalism and manorialism.

Methods of Farming

Farming methods throughout the empire were related to and dependent upon the climate of the area being farmed. It is useful to think of Roman farming as either dry farming or moist farming, depending on the amount of precipitation in the particular region (Rees 1987: 481). Farming practices varied considerably throughout the empire, having developed from local traditions, predating the Romans by centuries (Rees 1987: 482). Some broad generalizations can be made, and will be explored in the section that follows.

Dry-farming techniques were essential in areas with a Mediterranean climate (see chapter 2). Farmers working in this type of climate were forced to cope with, before all other problems, issues of water management. There was substantial precipitation in Mediterranean climates, but it was unpredictable. Terracing techniques of water conservation were important (these are discussed in detail in chapter 2). Agriculturalists in the Mediterranean typically farmed according to a two-year system, in which fields were left fallow for one year at a time and generally used every other year (but see White 1970: 47). Seed was sown sometime between October and December, and harvesting took place in June or July. The tools used by Roman farmers were relatively simple. Plowing was done with a tool called a light ard. Hoes and sickles were also used. In general, Roman agricultural tools consisted of iron heads with wooden handles (Rees 1987: 489).

Moist farming, typical of northern Europe, was much less work-intensive than dry farming and had more predictable yields. This kind of farming involved the use of agricultural tools that were different from those used for dry farming. During Roman times, farmers used harvesting machines called the *vallus* or *carpentum* in these regions (Rees 1987: 498). There were lighter and heavier versions of this machine, but all were pushed by draft animals. We know about these machines not because they have survived archaeologically, but because they are depicted in Roman art and described by Pliny. Another

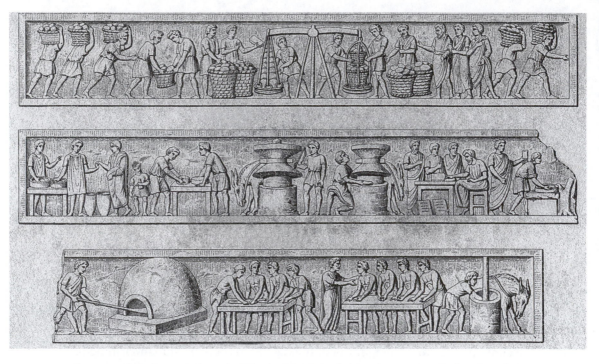

Engravings based on reliefs on the "Tomb of the Baker" show the process of baking bread in ancient Rome. (Pixel That)

tool used in Roman moist farming was the wheeled plow. This tool had two small wheels, attached to an iron spade that could be pushed along the soil, making plowing easier on the farmer's back (Rees 1987: 498).

Types of Crops

Most Roman farms engaged in mixed agriculture, meaning that a variety of different crops were grown. Cereals (such as wheat and barley) were very important in subsistence agriculture and formed the basis of the Roman diet. Olives and grapes were successful cash crops. Growing these vine-based crops could not support a family, but because olive oil and wine were always in high demand in the cities, farmers who grew these crops could be confident that they could sell their produce. Vine-based agriculture was a significant investment of time and resources, because it takes years for planted vines to become agriculturally productive. Fruit, nuts, vegetables, and figs were also important Roman crops.

Animal Husbandry

Animal husbandry was usually integrated with agriculture on small subsistence farms, but some scholars have argued that it was divorced from agriculture on the larger estates. Animals were an important part of all Roman farms and fulfilled a number of roles (Rees 1987: 486). The manure produced by animals was used as an important source of fertilizer (White 1970: 125). Roman writers observed that for the larger estates it was difficult to acquire sufficient amounts of fertilizer (White 1970: 144). The massive strength of draft animals also assisted in agricultural labor.

But animals were also useful sources of products for consumption (see White 1970: 272–231 for a slightly different understanding). Cattle were very important in Italy. There was a large demand for meat in Rome and dairy products were always desired. Hides and bones were important resources for other industries. Sheep were also used for dairy production and meat, but wool was their most valuable contribution. Pigs and other animals played various roles as well.

Shepherds were an important part of agro-pastoralism. In Roman literature, shepherds are described in very romantic terms. But generally, Romans seem to have disliked the duties of the shepherd, and usually shepherding chores became a slave's responsibility. The shepherd would wander with the sheep, protecting and assisting them. Thieves were one of the primary enemies of the shepherd, who often spent days at a time away from the settlement.

CRAFT SPECIALIZATION AND PRODUCTION

Related to issues of agriculture were issues regarding craft specialization. Because not all people were involved in food production, those who were had to produce a significant surplus in order for everyone to be fed. Craft specialization is an important archaeological concept. A craft specialist is an individual who has a particular knowledge of and access to the necessary equipment for a specific kind of production. The presence of craft specialists in a society implies some kind of division of labor, because not everybody can produce all things. In other words, each individual has a specific occupation or job. In Roman times there was a high degree of craft specialization. This was especially true of urban dwellers, who had a much larger pool of occupational choices. Based on the occupations recorded in Roman tombstone epithets, there were at least 200 jobs in which Romans could engage, and there were likely many more possibilities that have not been recorded (Hopkins 1988: 772). Most of the return from working these jobs probably went to purchasing food or fulfilling other primary needs (rent, clothes, etc.). People were trained in specific fields to produce specific goods. By creating a surplus of these goods (more than the individual producer could use), the craft specialist could exchange the surplus for other specialized goods. Trading specialized products was also the mechanism by which the specialist would gain food and other products necessary for survival. What follows is a discussion of particular kinds of specialist activity in which the Romans engaged.

Mining and Quarrying

The Romans required resources on a tremendous scale—a scale previously unknown in the ancient Mediterranean. Therefore, mining and quarrying were extremely important aspects of industrial production. Some modern scholars have even suggested that in terms of scale, these occupations were second only

The quarry at Carrara, Italy, has provided fine white marble since ancient times. (Library of Congress)

to agriculture (Adkins and Adkins 1994: 330). Much archaeological evidence for mining exists; however, there are several problems with using this kind of data. The most important problem is that it is often very difficult to date mining sites. If a mine was not exhausted in Roman times, it probably remained in use until well after the Roman period. Also, because the process of mining is so destructive, Roman evidence often does not survive. Another problem with archaeological investigation of mining is that the most common sources of ore and stone were aboveground surface deposits. After such resources are fully exploited, nothing remains, so it is difficult to get an accurate sense of the degree of mining in any period before record-keeping procedures were employed.

Mining and quarrying techniques remained fairly similar throughout Roman history. In general, aboveground resources were exploited as much as possible. When veins of precious ores ran out above ground, miners would follow the deposits underground. Vertical shafts were cut straight down into the ground to gain access to these deposits (Woods 1987: 613). Aboveground resources were gathered in a number of ways. Large amounts of water were sometimes used to wash away the debris or soil-covering deposits (Healy 1988: 783). The stone or ore itself would often be subject to extremes of heat (through fire) and cold (through water) to produce cracks and separate the material from the deposit. Preexisting cracks in the rock were similarly used. Tools were wedged into cracks and pressure was exerted to increase the split (Woods 1987: 615).

Miners themselves were usually slaves or convicted criminals (Healy 1988: 788). The job was so unpleasant and dangerous that freedmen were unlikely to willingly engage in it. The organization of mining within the Roman world is not exactly clear. In the imperial period, it seems that there were state-run mining operations used to supply the building projects of the empire (Healy 1988: 787–788). But for the most part, local stone was used in building projects to reduce transportation expenses. Private (but wealthy) individuals or groups controlled these operations. Mining seems to have been contracted out by the state to various organizations (Healy 1988: 788). Evidence for this comes from discoveries of unused ingots of metal that are stamped with the names of mining companies or private individuals. Probably it is most accurate to consider Roman mining and quarrying as industries financed through a combination of public and private organizational strategies.

Metallurgy

Metallurgy was well developed in the Near East and Europe centuries before Roman civilization arose. There are a number of distinct steps in metallurgy, all aimed toward the goal of creating usable objects from metal materials. Metallurgy involves a significant degree of investment in terms of materials, processing, and levels of education. First, ore had to be processed into usable metal. This process involved heating the ore to very high temperatures. To make bronze, tin and copper had to be mixed in a fixed ratio. The Romans gained quite a degree of precision in the composition of alloys like bronze. Usually this kind of processing occurred near the mine. The metal was cast into ingots with the understanding that the ingots would later be melted down by a local craft specialist.

The actual techniques of working metals varied depending on the type of metal used. Gold and silver were both hammered and engraved into desired forms. They could also be melted and cast in molds—especially common for jewelry. Iron was heated and pounded or punched. Bronze was also cast, usually in molds or through what is called the lost-wax method. The lost-wax method (often referred to by its French name *çire perdue*) involved the use of a temporary mold made out of wax. It is very easy to sculpt with wax, which allows for more ornate designs. After the metal poured inside the mold cooled, the wax molds were disposed of. Iron, lead, and copper were also important metals in Roman times.

Woodworking

Carpentry and woodworking were important skills in the Roman world. The Romans used many wooden products. Boats, carts, tools, and furniture (or at least parts of these items) were made of wood. Unfortunately, wood does not survive well, according to the archaeological record. It deteriorates relatively quickly in most archaeological contexts. But from a variety of sources, like artistic and literary descriptions, there is evidence for the kinds of wooden objects used (Liversidge 1976: 155). Many objects were made of wood, and it is likely that the tools used for carving were very similar to those used today (Adkins and Adkins 1994: 329; Liversidge 1976: 159–165). In most parts of the Roman world, wood was a plentiful resource; however, there is some evidence for deforestation in different periods and places.

Pottery and Manufacture

We know about ceramic production from a number of different sources. Archaeologically, the study of production sites (i.e., kilns) can provide information about the methods of manufacture. Examination of the pottery itself can also reveal the methods of production. Further evidence comes from ethnographic analogy, which is the study of how modern potters work their craft. More is said about Roman pottery styles and production in chapter 9.

Textile Production

Textiles were produced in the home and in larger industrial contexts. The processes of manufacture were relatively similar in both contexts (Manning 1987: 598–599). The first step was the collection and preparation of the fiber. Wool was sheared from sheep. Flax and hemp were harvested at certain times of the year and then specially treated for use as fiber (Adkins and Adkins 1994: 327–328; Wild 1976: 168). It is likely that individual homes purchased these raw materials, rather than producing them themselves. The next step was to spin the fiber into a usable form. This could be done at the household level, using techniques and tools that predated the Romans by centuries (Wild 1976: 169). After the fiber was spun, it was woven, similarly possible at the household level, with relatively simple and inexpensive equipment. At this stage, the woven textile was given to specialists for further treatment (Hopkins 1988: 764; Wild 1976: 176). The textile was washed, and then fullers treated the fabric (with earth or urine) to remove the grease, dirt, and animal oils (Hopkins 1988: 764).

Leather was used by the Romans in a number of contexts, not just for clothing. Created from the skins of animals, the animal was first slaughtered and the hide removed. The hide was then treated extensively, involving considerable scraping to remove leftover pieces of flesh, and beating the hide to soften it for easier manipulation (Adkins and Adkins 1994: 329; Waterer 1976: 179). Tanning leather involved soaking it in a particular solution (Waterer 1976: 179).

Usually this was a solution of liquid and tree bark, but it varied regionally (Waterer 1976: 180). After some further finishing treatments, the leather was available for a number of uses.

TRADE

The study of ancient trade can be a difficult task. It is very important (and very difficult) to avoid bringing one's own preconceptions to this subject. Although more is said about the controversies of this subject in chapter 11, a few points are important to bear in mind. The work of the anthropologist Marcel Mauss, exemplified by his work in *The Gift*, has demonstrated that beneath the transfer of goods between people lie important social relationships. These social relationships are particularly important in the study of ancient trade. A great deal of information can be learned, not only about the specifics of trade, but also about the relationships between the people or groups that traded.

An important difference between modern times and Roman times is the relative standing of merchants within the community. Although the ability to make a profit is considered a virtue in many sectors of modern society, it was not a virtue in Roman society. Trading and selling were considered distasteful and not the activities of proper Romans. This was not unique to the Romans—many precapitalist societies shared a similar disregard for selling. It is a unique feature of the modern world that making money is considered morally acceptable rather than socially reprehensible. On the other hand, there is certainly evidence that this did not prevent people from attempting to make a profit.

Shopping in Rome

The degree to which trade was important in ancient economies is a question of great controversy (see chapter 11). But in the city of Rome itself, there is undeniable evidence that trade was conducted. Evidence exists for standardized systems of measurement. Merchants sold their wares as a primary means of making a living. Profit was the goal of these sales—to be certain, there are enough accounts (and complaints) about this in Classical literature. Often merchants were artisans as well. Sometimes homes, shops, and workshops all were connected, and there is evidence that artisans often sold their crafts from shops attached to their workshops. In other situations, however, merchants could act solely as middlemen. These shop own-

Weights and measures found at Pompeii. (Library of Congress)

Storefronts on Fortuna Street, Pompeii. (Library of Congress)

ers were completely divorced from production, much as store clerks in malls are today.

Some areas of the city of Rome were specifically geared toward shopping. The Forum was the major center for shopping throughout much of Roman history (Cowell 1980: 124). Various markets in and around the area were dedicated and renovated by various emperors. The most magnificent was Trajan's Market, which was founded in 114 C.E. This ancient mall had over 150 shops that sold a variety of products (Cowell 1980: 125). The market was right by a river, so that deliveries could be made by water directly to the larger stores. Other sections of Rome also facilitated trade, and certain streets were known for their shops. Probably the most famous was *vicus Tuscas*, which had many different types of wares for sale (Cowell 1980: 126). Some products were sold in areas informally designated for that kind of commodity. For example, the *forum boarium* was where cattle were sold. Undoubtedly, Rome was a world shopping capital, much as London, Paris, New York, and Hong Kong are today.

International Trade

International trade was an important component of Roman society from very early on. Literary sources provide ample descriptions of the kinds of trade that Rome engaged in over long distances. Archaeological evidence is also helpful

An imaginary scene in the Roman Forum. (Pixel That)

in studying long-distance trade. Although the actual products that were traded have often not survived in the archaeological record, the containers in which those products were shipped (e.g., pottery) have been preserved and recovered. Furthermore, the numerous excavated shipwrecks provide even more complete pictures of trade (see sidebar on page 108).

Before the imperial period, international trade was probably relatively informal. Connections between elite families across borders were probably the dominant force behind the earliest Roman trade (Parker 1987: 635). International trade by sea was made safer after Pompey's campaign against piracy, which was conducted explicitly to make sea commerce secure (Parker 1987: 636). In the imperial period, international trade became an important component of the state economy. The city of Rome came to rely on regular imports. Laws revolved around the importation of certain commodities to ensure that their delivery was dependable.

Roman trading networks in the imperial period were quite expansive, from China to Scandinavia (Adkins and Adkins 1994: 194; Parker 1987: 651). Evidence of this comes from the Roman material culture found in both of these regions dating to this time. Especially notable is the large amount of Roman coins discovered in India dating to the imperial period (Adkins and Adkins

Shipwrecks

The many shipwrecks that lie at the bottom of the Mediterranean Sea have provided archaeologists with important evidence for the nature of Roman seafaring and international trade. The study of these ships, which is referred to as underwater archaeology, has become an important subdiscipline within archaeology. There are basically two methods used to study these underwater ships—excavation and reconnaissance. Excavation is quite time consuming, but it is also very rewarding. The sea preserves many types of objects that are not preserved in dry areas, but great care must be taken when moving these artifacts to the surface. Reconnaissance is less destructive, involving observing and recording discovered wrecks, but without removing the ancient remains from their underwater graves. As technology improves, underwater archaeology will prove to be an even more important tool for archaeological work.

1994: 194; Greene 1986: 29). Gold and silver coins were traded, probably based on the value of their metal, rather than on the value invested from imperial authority. In general, the Romans exported goods that had been secondarily produced or had added value. That is to say, the Romans exported to the periphery manufactured goods with the Roman manufacturing, not raw materials. Imports to Rome were mostly raw materials and semimanufactured goods. Grain was the most important import to Rome, so much so that its importation was government regulated (see sidebar on page 109). A substantial proportion of Rome's grain supply came from Egypt. This is not as odd as it may seem; it was probably much easier to transport large quantities of products across the Mediterranean rather than across Italy by land (Greene 1986: 40; Manning 1987: 592). Olive oil and wine were also traded across the Roman world in significant quantities.

There were many individuals who participated in international trade. But the people mostly responsible were the middlemen, who were willing to travel to buy and sell goods in faraway locations. Two types of traders were active in ancient Rome. *Mercatores* were merchants who traded specific goods (Adkins and Adkins 1994: 194; d'Arms 1981: 3; Manning 1987: 590). They were distinguished from negotiators, who were traders of more general kinds of products. Negotiators were representatives of larger organizations, agents of trading companies, or the active members of groups of investors (Adkins and Adkins 1994: 194; d'Arms 1981: 25).

COINS AND MONEY

Coins are one of the richest sources of data for the study of ancient Rome. There are a number of ways in which coins can be used in historical study. The

---

The Grain Dole

One of the benefits of living in the city of Rome was possible access to free wheat. At varying times in Roman history, wheat was offered to the citizens of Rome free of charge. This was a valuable political tool, especially for the emperor, as it preserved his popularity within the city. With grain imports from Egypt well regulated, the citizens of Rome had access to a constant food source. Given the large population of the city and the growing use of the surrounding land for cash crops, the free wheat provided to Romans was very important.

---

first, which assists in the dating of archaeological sites and materials, was discussed in chapter 3. Coins can also be used indirectly as sources of information from an art-historical perspective. Images on coins frequently consisted of pictures of architectural features, showing what buildings may have looked like (Burnett 1991: 31–32). Even more frequently depicted on Roman coins were portraits of important Romans (Burnett 1991: 34–36). Sometimes these portraits attempted to depict features realistically, but most often they are interesting because specific traits of these individuals were purposefully depicted. The artist who designed the coin chose to emphasize specific physical features, either because the person actually looked like that or for propagandistic purposes. This leads to another use of coins in the study of Rome: the use of coins to understand the larger state apparatus from propaganda and economic perspectives (Burnett 1991: 37–41). Finally, a noteworthy use of coins, one that will be explored in this chapter, is for the specific study of the Roman economy. First, the history of coin use in the Roman world will be discussed. Second, what coins can tell us about Roman economy will be explored.

The History of Roman Coins

The use of coins in ancient Rome started slowly. None were used in the regal period, and it was not until later in the republic that a system of coinage was adopted. It was Roman contact with the region of Campania that provided the impetus for the minting of the first bronze coins. Rome's first mint was established in 289 B.C.E. (Greene 1986: 48), minting bronze coins, with a base denomination called the *as*. The *as* was about 1 pound of bronze, and had smaller subdivisions, as low as 1/24 *as*. These coins were too large to be made with a die (the kind of press normally used for coins) and had to be cast, like large, bronze objects (Greene 1986: 48). There were also some less prominent silver and gold coins in circulation at this time.

The next major phase in the history of Roman coinage came in approximately 211 B.C.E. This was around the time of the second Punic War, and the Roman economy was in shambles. It was with the new coinage system at this time that the *denarius*, a silver coin, became the base currency unit. This was

Table 5.1   Major Denominations of Coins from Augustus to Caracalla

Name	Value	Metal
quadrans	1/4 as	bronze
semis	1/2 as	brass
as	base	bronze
dupondius	2 asses	brass
sestertius	4 asses	brass
quinarius	8 asses	brass
denarius	16 asses	silver
aureus	25 denarii	gold

about equal to ten bronze asses. Bronze coins were still more important in everyday usage, but silver had become the new standard of value. Under Augustus, Roman currency underwent another major reorientation (Greene 1986: 49). But the denarius was still the base currency unit (see Table 5.1). This currency system, while undergoing occasional changes based on imperial edicts and the changing value of metal, remained intact until the third century C.E. (see Kent 1987).

What Coins Meant for the Roman Economy

Coins, when they appear in an economy, are a distinct feature. Most items involved in economic transactions have some sort of value that is ascribed from a number of angles. The value of coins is explicitly derived from some sort of economic authority. An institution (normally affiliated with the state) creates the coin in standard, comparable amounts, and makes a declaration as to its value. This institution must have enough authority to influence participants in the economy to accept these values and use the coins as a means of storing and transmitting wealth (Burnett 1991: 10). This does not mean that the values set by these authorities are absolute, but they must be sufficiently grounded in reality to allow the coins to function within the economy. So already the presence of coins informs the historian that the Roman government had enough authority over economic matters to set values and standardize currency.

But what role did coins have in the Roman economy? This question is not as easy to answer as it might appear. It lies at the heart of an important debate on the nature of preindustrial economies (see chapter 11). Coins can fulfill specific roles; Greene suggests three possibilities (Greene 1986: 51). They can make exchange easier. Instead of bartering (in which both parties must have goods that the other party desires), coins allow trade when only the goods of one party are desired. Related to this, coins can act as a standard of value. Even if coins are not physically traded, it is often useful to have a sense of an item's value in relationship to other items. Coins can provide that standard. Also important is the use of coins for storing wealth. Coins (ideally, though never practically) are a stable mechanism for accumulating wealth. For example, it is much more convenient to be paid in coins than in dairy products, because coins will not quickly go bad and lose their value. This means that people who get coins can save them, and use that wealth later. These are some of the theoretical uses of coins, but which of these uses actually happened in Roman times?

Because we know coins existed in Roman times, we can postulate some of the ways that coins were used. Coins were used as a standard of value; written sources give information about the price of goods and services from the denominations of coins. Coins may have been used to store wealth. Numerous coin hoards have been discovered throughout the empire. This does not necessarily reflect wealth storage, but it is the most likely option. Individuals, as part of economic transactions, also used coins. There are anecdotal accounts of people using coins to buy and sell in Roman literature. And, for another example, we know that people paid a *quadran* to get into the baths in Rome. Another important type of evidence is the denomination of coins. If denominations were too large, then only certain individuals and institutions could use them (Burnett 1991: 44–45). In Roman times, however, this was not the case. The denominations reflected a wide variety of values, from negligible values to extremely expensive values (Greene 1986: 52). So, theoretically, everybody could use coins.

But questions of scale need to be considered as well. Just because there were coins, and people used them in a way that is similar to how people use money today, it does not mean that coins functioned exactly the way coins and money do today. It is likely that the Roman use of coins was on a much smaller scale than the use of money today. In the cities, coins were definitely important for trade (Crawford 1970: 45). The same probably cannot be said for rural areas or areas of the empire without strong monetary traditions. Coins were not important in every transaction, and many transactions could occur without any consideration of money. It is important not to equate Roman coins with modern money—the two, although appearing similar, are in fact different in many ways.

BUSINESS AND INVESTMENT

The nature of Roman business and investment can seem very different depending on the account that one reads. It is a controversial topic, and studies on the subject often reflect more about a scholar's personal beliefs than historical reality. These issues are dealt with more fully in chapter 11, but some comments can safely be made here about the nature of Roman business and investment. For the wealthier Romans, those for whom investment was an option, business life revolved around the patrimony and the patrimonial estate (Veyne 1987: 139). It also revolved around increasing (or at least sustaining) the patrimonial estate. Rigid occupational categories were not applied to the Roman pater familias, who could invest in a variety of manners. Unlike modern times, when people can say that they are advertisers or publishers, the professional aspects of Roman life were not as important a means of social identification. Ideally, the occupation of the pater familias was the management of his estate.

Most of these forms of investment revolved around landholding. Land was the basis for most types of investment available to a wealthy Roman (Frier

1980: 21; Parker 1987: 635). Agriculture was by far the most important kind of property-based investment (White 1970: 12). The owner could be directly involved in agricultural production (managing the estate himself or through his slaves) or indirectly involved by renting out the land and profiting from agricultural fees. Nonagricultural land was also important (Frier 1980: 21). Income was derived from renting out domestic property, especially within the cities (Frier 1980: 27). Apartment complexes were owned by wealthy individuals who sought profit through rental fees (Frier 1980: 28). It was also common for rental fees to be gained from other pursuits, such as renting workshop or commercial space. Small businesses like *tavernes* or inns also provided possible investment opportunities.

Publicani and Societas

In the absence of direct government initiatives, the Roman government would auction off contracts to individuals and groups to perform jobs for the state. These kind of projects varied and included diverse tasks such as tax collection and road construction. Auctions were held and contracts were given out to the highest bidder. The individuals who took these contracts were called *publicani*. An organization of men bidding as a group was called a *societas* (Shaw 1988: 816). These were essentially investment groups who put their land down as collateral to gain the right to participate in these profitable enterprises. Although never formally part of the Roman government, these groups became entrenched over time, because an organization that had once held a contract was likely to continue getting contracts.

Moneylenders and Safekeeping

Long before Rome, money lending had become an extremely common practice in the ancient world. But this kind of money lending was very different from the kind of lending services offered at banks today. Normally, private individuals gave loans. Banks as such did not exist, although banks and banking houses are frequently mentioned in scholarly literature. These designations refer more to groups of individual moneylenders in joint ventures or families with long histories of money-lending, rather than to the formal economic institutions of today. Essentially, however, a moneylender could be anybody with enough liquid assets to provide a loan to another individual (Shelton 1988: 140). Money lending was a very profitable enterprise, because interest was charged at exorbitant rates. Theoretically there were government limits on rates of interest, but in practice it was easy to circumvent these regulations. Usually the person who needed the loan was not in a position to negotiate. Loans were also made to larger groups; for example, provincial cities that could not pay their taxes. Tax collectors increased their profit by making loans to people or groups who owed taxes but could not pay them (Shelton 1988: 149). The interest rates in these cases were very high.

Unlike today, when a family might be proud that one of their children had grown up to be a banker, in Roman times this was considered shameful. Although loaning money was very common in Rome, moneylenders were viewed with disdain. Perhaps the most well-known criticisms of moneylenders are found in the New Testament, but similar sentiments are also found in other ancient literature. Often, well-established members of Roman society would hide their money-lending enterprises by hiring an agent to take care of the logistics of the transactions (Shelton 1988: 140).

Other services associated with modern banking were performed in Roman times—especially those related to long-distance trade. Currency exchange was an important service for foreign merchants (Greene 1986: 63; Thompson 1988: 829). Visitors to other cities also normally needed a safe place to store their money or assets, and individuals living in the cities could offer these kind of services (Thompson 1988: 830). There are even some examples of ancient insurance. When a loan was advanced to facilitate a maritime trading expedition, clauses that freed the debtor from repayment if the ship sank could be added to the agreement (Thompson 1988: 834). There is also evidence for home insurance, especially as protection from fires, but not much is known about those agreements.

The Patron-Client Relationship

Arguably, the patron-client relationship was the most important, nonfamilial relationship in Roman society. The relationship formed when a lower-class, less powerful individual (the client) asked a wealthier and more powerful individual (the patron) for patronage. The patron was expected to provide legal and financial assistance to his clients (Shelton 1988: 14). Sometimes a payment (called a *sportula*) was given to the client as well (Ellis 2000: 170). The clients provided political support for the patron, revolving around the election process (Ellis 2000: 170; Shelton 1988: 15). Just as important for the patron was the social capital that came from having a large retinue of clients. Clients were important Roman status symbols, and clients were expected to demonstrate this relationship publicly.

The origins of the patron-client relationship are unknown. In the regal period, this relationship was considered legally binding, meaning that it had been formalized from a very early point in Roman society. Initially only patricians were allowed to be patrons, but during the period of the republic this restriction loosened to allow any wealthy citizen to become a patron. In the imperial period, as elections became less important, the relationship became more of a master-servant relationship. Also, clients became less distinguishable from parasites. *Parasite* here is used in its original sense. Initially, a parasite merely referred to a fellow diner (in Greek times) but came to refer to an individual who acted as a moocher (Faas 2003: 61).

The most regular obligation of the client to the patron was the morning *salutatio* (Ellis 2000: 170–171; Shelton 1988: 16). Early in the morning the client was expected to visit his patron's house and greet him. This was the point of the day at which it was appropriate for the client to ask for assistance. The salutatio was held in the *triclinium* (see chapter 9) of the patron's house (Ellis 2000: 170). The patron would receive clients while seated; where the client sat depended on his status and the favor of the patron.

Patronage was one of the main mechanisms through which the arts were perpetuated in Roman society. Much in the same way that patrons of the arts are understood today, a patron could support an artist or writer if the patron liked the artist's work. Often the patron would make very specific demands of the artist (Blagg 1987: 728). But more important for the patron was the social esteem gained from other upper-class Romans by patronizing the arts. Even better was when the patron was memorialized in the art of the client. Perhaps the most famous patron is the one memorialized in Shakespeare's eighteenth sonnet, which begins, "Shall I compare thee with a summer's day."

TAXATION

Roman taxation was significantly different from modern taxation. Taxes were not paid so that the government could provide infrastructure (Shaw 1988: 824). A Roman taxpayer would never wonder about "his taxes at work" and expect an accounting from the government. Neither were taxes collected as any sort of economic regulating device (Shaw 1988: 809–810). So, for example, taxes collected on imported and exported goods were not really customs dues, because they were not levied as a means of controlling trade. These forms of taxation were simply methods of increasing state revenue. Keeping in mind this role of Roman taxes helps explain Roman tax collection in general. Taxes were not paid only in money, but could also be paid as services or as goods in kind.

In the earliest years of Roman history, only people renting out *ager publicus* (the public lands) paid taxes. But as Rome expanded across Italy, the government increasingly needed revenue to support military activity (Shaw 1988: 810). *Tributum* (tribute) was imposed directly on an individual. The degree of tax owed was decided through the census (Shaw 1988: 811–812). About every five years, a census was taken to evaluate the level of wealth of an individual

A detail from *The Tribute Money* by early Renaissance artist Masaccio shows St. Peter handing over payment to a Roman tax collector. (Sandro Vannini/Corbis)

(and his family) to determine the individual's rank. This was a crucial determination regarding the individual's participation in political life, as well as his military obligations. The Roman ideal was that citizens of Rome should be exempt from paying taxes, except for military obligations, and the major burden of taxes should be held by noncitizens and provincial subjects (Shaw 1988: 811).

Taxation institutions varied through the Roman period. In the period of the republic, revenue was held by the treasury of Saturn (*aerarium Saturni*), which was controlled entirely by the Senate (Shaw 1988: 810). From the time of Augustus on, the treasury of Saturn became more and more just the treasury of the city of Rome (Shaw 1988: 810). The powerful state treasury was the *fiscus* in Rome, associated with numerous provincial *fisci* (Shaw 1988: 810). The fisci represented the emperor's personal wealth, and he had control over it. All the people who ran the fisci were appointed by the emperor and controlled by him.

Tax collection was not a centrally organized system in Roman times. There was a considerable quantity of different kinds of taxes that were levied, known because of the hundreds of different types of taxes listed in papyri from Egypt (Shaw 1988: 810). The specifics were different for each type of tax. In general, the right to collect taxes was auctioned off to the highest bidder. This gave the government a predictable source of income (Shaw 1988: 815). Because the Roman tax base was essentially agrarian, it received amounts of taxes that varied year by year. But through this method of auctioning off tax-collecting rights, Rome received a fixed sum from the tribute collector. This tribute collector had the right to collect taxes at a higher rate than the government required, allowing considerable profit for the collector and encouraging tremendous corruption. Because the tribute collectors, in order to purchase the rights to tax, needed considerable funds and could not be senators, the equestrians became the dominant class involved in tax collection (Shaw 1988: 816).

TRANSPORTATION

In discussing issues of economics, scholars often do not take into account issues of transportation. Yet in many ways transportation is fundamental to economies. The limits of transportation dictate the limits to economic activity. Speed, cost, and accessibility of transportation were all important issues to the ancient economic participants, so it is just as important for modern scholars to consider them. It is easiest to divide Roman transportation into two categories—land transportation and water transportation (Greene 1986: 17). Within these two categories, it is important to distinguish between local and long-distance transportation. Some of the stranger elements of Roman economic life make more sense when the problem of transportation is considered.

Land Transportation

Roads and other kinds of infrastructure are discussed in chapter 9. What is discussed here are the kinds of evidence available for the study of long-distance

Table 5.2 Roman Distance Measurements

Measurement	Metric Equivalent
mille passus (mile)	1,480 m
stadium (maritime)	187.5 m
actus	35.48 m
passus	1.48 m
pes (foot)	29.4 cm
uncia (inch)	2.43 cm

Roman land transportation vehicles and the kinds of land transportation activities that took place. Measurement systems are not discussed in detail, but see Table 5.2 for the most important distance measurements. Local traffic was normally on foot or, if transporting goods, with simple wagons. Travel by foot or by pack animals was most likely the choice of the less well-off members of Roman society. Horses were not used for this kind of transportation in Roman times; they were too expensive. Various kinds of wheeled vehicles were the preferred form of transportation.

In general, there is much less evidence for land transportation vehicles than for water vehicles. Most of the knowledge about this is derived from literary descriptions and art-historical representations. It is very difficult to make technical assessments of the craft based on this kind of information. From Roman art we can see that two- and four-wheeled vehicles were used, powered by draft animals (Greene 1986: 37; Laurence 1999: 123). Literary sources indicate that at a certain point the Romans adopted Celtic technology, but specific evidence is not very strong (Greene 1986: 36). There is a general tendency in Roman scholarship, based on this evidence, to describe the low technological level of Roman wheeled vehicles. Recent reevaluation of some of these long-held technological assumptions (e.g., that Roman vehicles did not have suspension or separate front axles) has shown that they are incorrect (Greene 1986: 38).

Couriers and messengers also traveled along Roman roads. In Republican times, *tabellarii* (couriers) were hired to deliver messages (Adkins and Adkins 1994: 184). Augustus established a state postal system of sorts during his reign (Adkins and Adkins 1994: 184). This system, called the *cursus publicus* (public course), was for military and state personnel only. Officials used it for conveying messages and supplying armies. The basic system was one in which vehicles and animals were stationed in fixed positions along the route. The courier would travel to each point and switch vehicles to facilitate quick transport of the message.

Water Transportation

Water transportation was a much more important form of transportation in Roman times (but see Brunt 1971). Roman ship technology was quite advanced. More than thirty Greek and Latin names for types of ships are known, and many shipwrecks provide information about ancient Roman crafts (Ad-

A busy Roman harbor scene depicted in a fresco from Pompeii. (Mimmo Jodice/Corbis)

kins and Adkins 1994: 186). Roman shipbuilding was unique in that the first step was the construction of the outer shell—the hull (Adkins and Adkins 1994: 186; Greene 1986: 21–24). After the hull was built, the interior of the vessel was added. This is exactly the opposite order of how most ships were built before the Industrial Revolution. Mortise and tenon joints were used to connect the various planks of the ship. Pitch and beeswax were used as caulking for the hull, to keep the ship waterproof. Merchant ships were powered by sails, and had much smaller crews than warships. The typical Roman trading vessel could be anywhere from 12 to 40 m long. Cargo capacities were large. It is known from shipwrecks that four layers of amphorae (see chapter 9) could be stacked within a merchant ship (Greene 1986: 26). This was about

6,000–8,000 pots, and with each pot weighing (when full) about 50 kl, it was quite a large cargo. The speed of these vessels varied depending on the route. Sailing from Italy to Egypt would take about ten days. But sailing the opposite direction, from Egypt to Rome, was much longer, possibly taking up to two months, because the winds blew in the wrong direction (Greene 1986: 28).

The Romans built artificial harbors so that large sailing vessels could be accommodated directly in the ports. Often, though, cargoes were transported to smaller vessels for travel up through the system of rivers that connected the interior of the Roman Empire (Adkins and Adkins 1994: 190; Greene 1986: 31). These vessels were much smaller than seagoing vessels. The technology was also quite a bit simpler, based more on hollowing out large logs than on compound construction. Actual examples of these river-based ships have been found in the Rhine River (Greene 1986: 31). These inland water routes were probably more important transportation systems than the roads for which Rome is so famous, and they certainly were the major routes for conveying cargo.

BIBLIOGRAPHY

Adkins, Lesley, and Roy Adkins. 1994. *Handbook to Life in Ancient Rome.* Oxford: Oxford University Press.

Badian, E. 1972. *Publicans and Sinners.* Ithaca: Cornell University Press.

Blagg, T. F. C. 1987. "Society and the Artist," pp. 717–741 in *The Roman World.* John Wacher (ed.). London: Routledge & Kegan Paul.

Brunt, Peter. 1971. *Italian Manpower.* London: Oxford University Press.

Burford, Alison. 1988. "Crafts and Craftsmen," pp. 367–388 in *Civilization of the Ancient Mediterranean: Greece and Rome.* Michael Grant and Rachel Kitzinger (eds.). New York: Charles Scribner's Sons.

Burnett, Andrew. 1991. *Roman Coins.* Berkeley: University of California Press.

Casson, Lionel. 1974. *Travel in the Ancient World.* London: Allen and Unwin.

———. 1988. "Transportation," pp. 353–366 in *Civilization of the Ancient Mediterranean: Greece and Rome.* Michael Grant and Rachel Kitzinger (eds.). New York: Charles Scribner's Sons.

Charlesworth, Martin. 1926. *Trade Routes and Commerce of the Roman Empire.* Cambridge: Cambridge University Press.

Chevallier, Raymond. 1976. *Roman Roads.* Berkeley: University of California Press.

Crawford, Michael. 1970. "Money and Exchange in the Roman World." *Journal of Roman Studies* 60: 40–48.

d'Arms, John. 1981. *Commerce and Social Standing in Ancient Rome.* Cambridge: Harvard University Press.

Duncan-Jones, Richard. 1977. *The Economy of the Roman Empire: Quantitative Studies.* Cambridge: Cambridge University Press.

———. 1990. *Structure and Scale in the Roman Economy.* Cambridge: Cambridge University Press.

Ellis, Simon. 2000. *Roman Housing.* London: Gerald Duckworth & Co. Ltd.

Faas, Patrick. 2003. *Around the Roman Table.* New York: Palgrave Macmillan.

Finley, Moses. 1973. *The Ancient Economy.* Berkeley: University of California Press.

Frank, Tenney. 1927. *An Economic History of Rome.* Baltimore: Johns Hopkins University.

Frank, Tenney (ed.). 1933–1940. *An Economic Survey of Ancient Rome.* 5 vols. Baltimore: Johns Hopkins University Press.

Frier, Bruce. 1980. *Landlords and Tenants in Imperial Rome.* Princeton: Prnceton University Press.

Garnsey, Peter, Keith Hopkins, and C. R. Whittaker. 1983. *Trade in the Ancient Economy.* Berkeley: University of California Press.

Garnsey, Peter, and C. R. Whittaker. 1983. *Trade and Famine in Classical Antiquity.* Cambridge: Cambridge Philological Society.

Greene, Kevin. 1986. *The Archaeology of the Roman Economy.* Berkeley: University of California Press.

Healy, John. 1978. *Mining and Metallurgy in the Greek and Roman World.* London: Thames & Hudson.

———. 1988. "Mines and Quarries," pp. 779–794 in *Civilization of the Ancient Mediterranean: Greece and Rome.* Michael Grant and Rachel Kitzinger (eds.). New York: Charles Scribner's Sons.

Hopkins, Keith. 1980. "Taxes and Trade in the Roman Empire (200 B.C.–A.D. 400)." *Journal of Roman Studies* 70: 101–125.

———. 1988. "Roman Trade, Industry, and Labor," pp. 753–778 in *Civilization of the Ancient Mediterranean: Greece and Rome.* Michael Grant and Rachel Kitzinger (eds.). New York: Charles Scribner's Sons.

Jones, Arnold. 1974. *The Roman Economy: Studies in Ancient Economic and Administrative History.* Peter Brunt (ed.). Oxford: Blackwell.

Keller, Donald, and David Rupp (eds.). 1983. *Archaeological Survey in the Mediterranean Area.* Oxford: BAR International Series.

Kent, John. 1987. "The Monetary System," pp. 568–585 in *The Roman World.* John Wacher (ed.). London: Routledge & Kegan Paul.

Laurence, Roy. 1999. *The Roads of Roman Italy.* New York: Routledge.

Liversidge, Joan. 1976. "Woodwork," pp. 155–166 in *Roman Crafts.* London: Gerald Duckworth & Co. Ltd.

Manning, W. H. 1987. "Industrial Growth," pp. 586–610 in *The Roman World.* John Wacher (ed.). London: Routledge & Kegan Paul.

Mauss, Marcel. 1990. [1950]. *The Gift.* W. D. Halls (trans.). New York: W.W. Norton.

McWhirr, Alan. 1987. "Transport by Land and Water," pp. 658–670 in *The Roman World.* John Wacher (ed.). London: Routledge & Kegan Paul.

Pallotino, Massimo. 1991. *A History of Earliest Italy.* Martin Ryle and Kate Soper (trans.). Ann Arbor: University of Michigan Press.

Parker, A. J. 1987. "Trade within the Empire and beyond the Frontiers," pp. 635–657 in *The Roman World.* John Wacher (ed.). London: Routledge & Kegan Paul.

Polanyi, Karl. 1957. "The Economy as Instituted Process," pp. 243–269 in *Trade and Market in the Early Empires.* Karl Polanyi, Conrad Arensberg, and Harry Pearson (eds.). Chicago: Henry Regnery Company.

Rees, Sian. 1987. "Agriculture and Horticulture," pp. 481–503 in *The Roman World.* John Wacher (ed.). London: Routledge & Kegan Paul.

Rickman, Geoffrey. 1980. *The Corn Supply of Ancient Rome.* Oxford: Clarendon Press.

Rostovtzeff, Michael. 1957. *Social and Economic History of the Roman Empire.* Oxford: Oxford University Press.

Shaw, Brent. 1988. "Roman Taxation," pp. 809–828 in *Civilization of the Ancient Mediterranean: Greece and Rome.* Michael Grant and Rachel Kitzinger (eds.). New York: Charles Scribner's Sons.

Shelton, JoAnn. 1988. *As the Romans Did.* Oxford: Oxford University Press.

Stockton, David. 1979. *The Gracchi.* Oxford: Clarendon Press.

Strong, Donald, and David Brown. 1976. *Roman Crafts.* London: Duckworth.

Thompson, Wesley. 1988. "Insurance and Banking," pp. 829–836 in *Civilization of the Ancient Mediterranean: Greece and Rome.* Michael Grant and Rachel Kitzinger (eds.). New York: Charles Scribner's Sons.

Veyne, Paul. 1987. "The Roman Empire." In *A History of Private Life,* vol. 1. Philip Ariès and Georges Duby (eds.). Cambridge: Belknap Press.

Waterer, J. W. 1976. "Leatherwork," pp. 179–194 in *Roman Crafts.* Donald Strong and David Brown (eds.). London: Gerald Duckworth & Co. Ltd.

White, Keith. 1967. *Agricultural Implements of the Roman World.* Cambridge: Cambridge University Press.

———. 1970. *Roman Farming.* Ithaca: Cornell University Press.

———. 1975. *Farm Equipment of the Roman World.* Cambridge: Cambridge University Press.

———. 1988. "Farming and Animal Husbandry," pp. 211–245 in *Civilization of the Ancient Mediterranean: Greece and Rome.* Michael Grant and Rachel Kitzinger (eds.). New York: Charles Scribner's Sons.

Whittaker, C. R. (ed.). 1993. *Land, City and Trade in the Roman Empire.* Brookfield: Ashgate Publishing Ltd.

Wild, J. P. 1976. "Textile," pp. 167–178 in *Roman Crafts.* Donald Strong and David Brown (eds.). London: Gerald Duckworth & Co. Ltd.

Woods, Ann. 1987. "Mining," in *The Roman World.* John Wacher (ed.). London: Routledge & Kegan Paul.

VI

CHAPTER 6

Social Organization and Social Structure

INTERNAL ORGANIZATION OF ROMAN CIVILIZATION

Geographic organization and social organization are often thought of as two distinct categories. But in actual practice, these two types of organization, although manifested differently, are closely related. This discussion of Roman social history begins, then, with an acknowledgment of the important role of the physical environment in the way people interacted with one another. Certainly for the Romans, the nature of a person's everyday life was directly related to the particular kind of region or settlement in which they lived. There is a lot of evidence on this subject, archaeological and literary, that can help reconstruct the internal, physical organization of Roman society.

One of the most important recent trends in archaeology is the use of surface surveys to better understand settlement and land-use patterns. Surveying is an archaeological technique that does not involve excavation. Because there is no excavation, survey techniques tend to be much cheaper than traditional excavations, causing negligible damage to the site itself. There are three major types of surveys used in Roman archaeology. Reconnaissance surveys involve archaeologists walking or driving over a set region of space, collecting archaeological samples from the surface of sites, thereby identifying the location and geographic range of ancient settlements. The second type of surface survey involves aerial photography. Photographs taken from the air are examined for information about site distribution, because archaeological remains (especially Roman remains) are often easier to recognize from the air. The third and most recent type of survey involves the use of technology called Geographic Information Systems (GIS), which is a computer-based mapping database technology. The effects of GIS are just beginning to be felt in Roman archaeology. All three of these techniques are changing our understanding of the Roman world. Roman remains are so distinctive that surface surveys can provide consistent and reliable information; however, each project must be evaluated on its own merit (Greene 1986: 98–99). Because there is such a wide variety of information collection techniques, the data from different surface surveys are not always directly comparable. What follows is a discussion of some of the results gained from these techniques; however, with the growing importance of surveying, it should not be surprising if future research leads to much different conclusions.

Types of Settlements

An important component of survey work is establishing a hierarchy of sites. This is less subjective with Roman civilization than with other archaeologically identifiable cultures. It seems that the Romans thought of their settlements in terms of hierarchy, so it is not a modern imposition of hierarchy, but rather a discovery of an ancient hierarchy (Poulter 1987: 388; Woolf 1998: 133). Some of the major categories of settlements are discussed in the sections that follow.

Roman cities have been the focus of the vast majority of Roman scholarship. The sources for cities are much richer than the sources for rural areas, and there has been scholarly interest in the concept of the city since the Victorian period. There has been a general realization in current scholarship that for the ancients, the distinction between urban and rural was not as extreme as it is for modern thinkers. Although the Romans certainly saw a distinction (witnessed through the many writings that glorify rural life), in terms of the average Roman's experience of life, there may not have been as great a distinction. But for the purposes of this discussion, it is nevertheless useful to distinguish between types of cities, because the Romans used distinct settlement strategies with each.

Colonies and Capitals. Perhaps the most intentional and aggressive Roman land-use strategies involved the establishment of colonies. In the Republican period, when Rome first began its expansion, colonies were established to achieve very specific goals (Drinkwater 1987: 361). Populations were imported into areas that were underpopulated to facilitate Roman expansion (Crawford 1982: 73, 106–107). Related to this, colonies were set up near cities that had resisted Roman expansion. Often these cities' lands were confiscated and distributed to the new colonies (Crawford 1982: 43, 46). This strategy undermined local resistance to Roman rule by weakening the productive abilities of the cities. New colonies also allowed the exploitation of local resources for Rome's use (Drinkwater 1987: 361). Colonies were also important components of Roman land-use strategy in imperial times. Each province ideally had a major city that functioned as the capital of that province and was designated as such through a legal decision from Rome (Drinkwater 1987: 372). These capitals were expected to be the major economic, social, and political centers of each province. Roman urban centers had standardized infrastructure and facilities, which helped foster feelings of "Roman-ness" among local populations (Drinkwater 1987: 372). For more on the processes of Romanization, see chapter 11.

Incorporated Cities. Especially in the eastern part of the empire, the Romans had to contend with preexisting urban centers. Much of the Greek world never really adopted Roman infrastructure, and Greek culture was still considered "high culture." For the most part, the Romans simply added their administrative systems on top of the preexisting administrative systems of the Greek cities, and they had little direct influence on settlement types (Levick 1987: 331). There were a few exceptions. Some preexisting eastern cities were designated as capitals (Levick 1987: 332). One innovation, however, was the new prominence of the Roman villa. The coastal cities thrived in Roman times because of the renewed Mediterranean trade (Levick 1987: 332). The situation was very different in the western empire, which had only minimal urbanization when the Romans moved in. Because there were no cities, the Romans could build from scratch (Drinkwater 1987: 363). In the west, "high culture" was Roman culture, not Greek culture, and Rome directly contributed to the rise of western cities (see Drinkwater 1987: 345).

Military Sites.   Roman military sites are best known from the western empire locations. In fact, a general tendency in the scholarship of the western Roman Empire is to concentrate on military history, so there is a somewhat skewed view of the importance of military sites in that region. The features of a Roman military camp or fort were quite standard and are discussed in detail in chap-

Hadrian's Wall, looking east toward Housesteads Fort. (Robert Estall/Corbis)

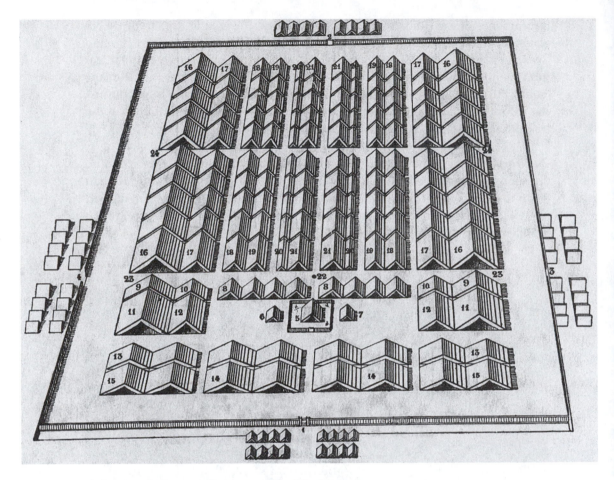

A drawing of a Roman military camp. (Pixel That)

ter 7. But there were also important permanent military settlements in the Roman frontier that should be mentioned. Of importance to Roman conceptions
of the frontier is the concept of the *limes,* the border of Roman control. This
border was conceived as a line, with everything behind the line conjuring up
images of civilization and urban life, and everything beyond the line conjuring
images of barbarians and unsettled societies. Perhaps the best physical example of this Roman sensibility is Hadrian's Wall. But borders in other parts of
the empire have also been identified. Most conspicuous are rows of watchtow-
ers (built of stone and/or timber) that allowed Roman soldiers to guard the
surroundings (Maxfield 1987: 157–164). Forts and garrisons were also important Roman military settlements, and the rate of their establishment corresponded with the expansion of the empire (Drummond and Nelson 1994: 128).
Related to these permanent military settlements were the towns that arose in
adjacent land, filled with individuals whose economic livelihoods were geared
toward servicing the Roman soldiers (Poulter 1987: 388, 394). Because Roman
soldiers could expect consistent and good payment, these subsidiary services
could be supported over the long term (Poulter 1987: 389).

Rural Sites. The most difficult type of site to account for through survey techniques is the rural site. The problems involve primarily issues of definition. Each survey project defines rural sites in different ways (Greene 1986: 71). Even the concept of the villa lacks general agreement (see chapter 9). To make sense of the survey data, one must carefully examine how each survey team defined rural settlements. Rural settlements can encompass anything from a large estate to a small structure in the middle of a field. Yet these rural sites are the least understood from traditional excavations and text study, so their discovery in settlement surveys is extremely important.

Settlement Patterns in Italy

Outside of Rome, extensive surveys of settlement and land-use patterns began after World War II. The postwar reconstruction of Italy brought with it a shift in modern landholding and ownership (Greene 1986: 103). During this transition phase, the British School in Rome set out to gain as much data about rural Roman life as possible before the land was reclaimed for agricultural use (Greene 1986: 103). Since then, surveying has become an increasingly important component of archaeological research in Italy. Although this work is generally geared more toward pre- and post-Roman sites, there is still important work directly related to Roman-Italian land use.

Although the exact patterns of land use differ by topographical and cultural region in Italy, a relatively general pattern has emerged. From about 300 B.C.E. onward, there is a noted decline in Etruscan cities (Greene 1986: 103). These cities were not abandoned, but in rural areas they decreased in size relative to other towns and villages. At the same time, roads appeared throughout Italy, and many new, small sites were founded. These smaller sites proliferated in this early period and became increasingly dense throughout the Republican and early imperial periods (Drummond and Nelson 1994: 6). Roman agricultural sites have been found throughout Italy, indicating a very high level of land use. Toward the end of the Roman period, many of these sites were completely abandoned, and the density of rural occupation decreased significantly (Greene 1986: 109). But the rural population did not move into the former Roman cities, because these locations also experienced a decline in size and population. The villa also disappeared as a settlement unit. The population moved steadily into hill sites, which were easily defended—a response to the lack of stability in medieval times.

These settlement surveys have drastically affected our earlier understanding of Roman society. Previous to the incorporation of survey data, the city was considered the primary organizing principle of Roman civilization. It has now become clear that rural landscapes were dotted with smaller villages and towns, making the role of the city less prominent in the lives of everyday Romans (Greene 1986: 109). Although it is still understood that participation in Roman government required residency in Rome, for the average Roman farmer, economic life was not centered there. Similarly, the density and continuity of land use have proven that there was not as great a distinction between urban settlements and rural settlements in ancient times as there is in the present.

Another innovation in scholarly thought about Roman society is related to our understanding of the Roman landholder. From textual evidence, the process of larger farmsteads swallowing up family farms appears to have dominated Roman economic history (Greene 1986: 109). But survey evidence has shown that this process was limited in geographic scope. Larger farmsteads took over along waterways that facilitated easy transport—land transportation of agricultural goods was prohibitively expensive (Greene 1986: 107). But small, single-family farmsteads remained the norm in inland areas (Drummond and Nelson 1994: 62; Greene 1986: 107). This was all likely related to transportation costs. There would have been no reason to establish a large, agricultural center in an area that was prohibitively far away from major centers and transportation systems.

Outside of Italy: Roman Settlement in Conquered Lands

Outside of Italy proper, Roman settlement and land-use strategies varied, depending on local circumstances. The diverse geographic and environmental features of the various regions had a direct impact on human land use. Local cultures and pre-Roman traditions also had an effect on the Roman incorporation of these lands. It is important to be aware that the different archaeological traditions in each region have also significantly affected our understanding of Roman settlement patterns. Roman archaeology has been of huge interest in Britain for more than 100 years. By contrast, in the Levant, Roman archaeology has been routinely ignored in favor of the examination of earlier civilizations. So some of the regional differences may be due more to different archaeological interests and traditions than to actual ancient differences.

Britain. In Britain, Roman remains have been relatively well examined, in similar proportion to earlier archaeological horizons. Britain has extremely diverse environmental conditions, contained within a relatively small space. But some broad generalizations can be made. There was not much difference between pre-Roman and Roman-period settlement systems (Greene 1986: 126–127). Both before and during Roman times, the region consisted of a dense network of rural sites (Drummond and Nelson 1994: 136). Cities did not play a major role, and likely there was minimal urban-rural distinction. But the Roman presence was not entirely without effect. Interesting observations have been made about land use in proximity to Hadrian's Wall (Breeze 1987: 208). On the Roman side, large, well-planned agricultural estates were prominent (Greene 1986: 126–127). The non-Roman side of the boundary had a less organized and consistent network of agricultural land use (Greene 1986: 126–127). Consequently, the Roman presence in Britain likely facilitated a stable environment for larger agricultural enterprises (Greene 1986: 111).

Spain. Survey research in Spain has demonstrated that the Roman presence in the region had a very large effect on local land use. This was very different from the Roman presence in Britain. With the Roman arrival in Spain, land use increased tremendously, peaking in the second century C.E. (Greene 1986: 115).

Julius Caesar invading Britain. (Library of Congress)

Villas as agricultural estates became very prominent in Spanish settlements until the third century B.C.E. (Greene 1986: 115). From that point on there was a general decline in land use (Poulter 1987: 409). The ups and downs of Spanish agriculture were likely tied directly to the role of Spanish crops (like olives and grapes) in Roman international trade (Greene 1986: 111).

Gaul. Gaul (basically modern France) was affected inconsistently by Roman occupation. The more remote areas were affected less drastically by the more limited Roman presence (Greene 1986: 116). This was true both in terms of actual Roman land use as well as stability against barbarian attacks brought by the Roman military. But for the most part, there was a general tendency for rural settlements to increase with the arrival of the Romans (Greene 1986: 116–117). There were no major cities in Roman Gaul; smaller villages seem to have been the most important centers (Poulter 1987: 398; Woolf 1998: 141). But this is also evidence of less distinction between rural and urban environments in antiquity.

The Aegean Regions. In general, the high urban density of the Greek and Hellenic regions was not drastically changed by the Roman presence (Levick 1987: 331). There is evidence in some regions for some abandonment of Greek settlements in the Roman period (Greene 1986: 134). There was a greater presence of settlements along coastal regions during the Roman period—probably related to the prosperity and stability of Roman maritime trade (Greene 1986: 134–135).

The Near East. From Egypt through the Levant and into Mesopotamia, settlement patterns were relatively unchanged with Roman conquest. However, this impression could have been caused by the relative lack of interest in Roman-period archaeology in these regions (see Kennedy 1987: 273). But for the most part, beginning with the Iron Age, there were relatively consistent land-use strategies until the arrival of Islam. One settlement type that can be considered Roman, however, is the presence of the villa (Greene 1986: 138). Villas were distinctively Roman and were not paralleled in earlier or later settlement systems.

North Africa. North Africa actually should be considered as two distinct geo-cultural areas (Mattingly 1957: 61). The coastal regions are characterized by their Mediterranean climate and have had a long tradition of agricultural productivity (Daniels 1987: 231). The major impact of Rome on settlement strategies on the coast was the increased presence of colonies of Roman veterans (Greene 1986: 133, but see Daniels 1987: 250–252). But the more inland regions, characterized by arid and desert environments, had very different Roman land use from the types of land use that came both before and after. The Roman period was the only period of major agricultural use of this region. Previous to the Roman presence, pastoralism was the major subsistence activity of the arid environments. However, Roman skills in water management facilitated the use of this area for productive agricultural use. It is still quite controversial whether these Roman-period farms represented Roman farmers settling in the region, or whether they represented local people beginning to farm because of the stability created by the Roman presence and the demands of Roman trade (Daniels 1987: 226–227; Greene 1986: 131–132).

Roman soldiers scaling the walls of Carthage, 146 B.C.E. (Library of Congress)

ROMAN POPULATION

There are two basic questions that historical demographers ask about ancient populations. The first is: How many people lived in the population—what was its size? This can be an important problem for the study of Roman society. The size of the citizen population in the Republican period, or the amount of slaves during the imperial period, can drastically affect one's understanding of the past. The second, and related, question is: How long did those people live? Both questions require careful analysis and comparison of fertility and mortality rates. Population movement (immigration and emigration) can also be an important factor in this kind of study. The section that follows details how historical demographers used ancient Roman material, as well as how historical demographers have answered the two questions mentioned above.

Problems in Demographic Estimation

Given the fundamental importance of demographic data in modern society, the lack of data that have survived from the past is striking. Demographic historians have to be very creative in finding and using evidence for this subject. With the rise of Christianity (and the sacrament of baptism), birth dates became important pieces of information, and from that point onward, there are excellent records. Unfortunately, the same cannot be said about Roman-period evidence.

The most obvious kinds of evidence that can be used are surviving Roman census documents. Not much of this evidence has survived, however. There is some information on the total amounts of citizens in Rome during the reigns of Augustus and Claudius. Better evidence comes from Roman-period Egypt, in the form of papyri and ostraca (Bagnall and Frier 1994). Tax records, kept over long periods of time, allow estimates about population size and age. In general, these records from the state administration are useful, but give incomplete glimpses into the ancient populations (Scheidel 2001: 11).

Another important type of evidence comes from funerary inscriptions. Tombstones (or their commemorative equivalents) often give the age at death of the individual. There are quite a few problems with using this kind of data. Parkin suggests a number of ways in which the sampling of funerary monuments is biased (Parkin 1992: 17). Only certain segments of society could afford these kinds of monuments, so there is more evidence about the upper classes (Parkin 1992: 12–13). The very young and the very old are not attested to consistently (Parkin 1992: 7). Given the expectations of high infant mortality, the number of infant commemorative markers is quite small (Parkin 1992: 6). Gender is also problematic because significantly more men were given monuments than women (Parkin 1992: 15–16). Chronological and geographic distributions are also problems, because customs related to death varied throughout time and space (Parkin 1992: 8–11, 13–14).

Likewise, skeletal remains are not as helpful as might be expected. Archaeologists have found many Roman bodies, and paleopathology is an important subdiscipline. But it is not possible to age skeletal remains specifically enough to be useful in demographic studies (Scheidel 2001: 19). But we can learn about nutrition, disease, and other health-related issues from the skeletal remains. This kind of information is important for understanding health-related constraints on the Roman population.

Perhaps the kind of evidence most used in Roman demographic studies is the comparative model. Roman population information is predicted based on analogous population curves and statistical extrapolation. Societies that do not use contraceptive or other birth-control methods are studied in order to understand "natural birth rates" (Parkin 1992: 112). The problem, however, is that these models cannot take into account the specific historical situations in Roman times. It assumes a degree of sameness between modern populations and preindustrial populations.

Despite the difficulties of extrapolating demographic data about the Romans, it is a worthwhile venture. It should be understood that any conclusions reached can be considered only estimates. By taking advantage of all of these kinds of evidence, some useful conclusions can be made. But be aware that any figures given by a Roman demographic scholar should be taken with a grain of salt. Conclusions are never as certain as they may seem when presented in tables and charts containing numbers and equations.

The Population of Rome and Periphery

By combining the types of information above, scholars generally agree that the city of Rome's population, at its peak, was somewhere between 80,000 and 1 million people (Scheidel 2001: 51). These are the figures that are quoted in most treatments, and they are probably accurate. Rome was definitely the largest city in the Mediterranean region at this time. The populations of other large cities (like Alexandria and Carthage) could have ranged anywhere from 300,000 to 100,000 (Scheidel 2001). It is much more difficult to predict population for Italy as a whole. Based on catchment analysis (the study of the amount of people that can be supported by the farmland) and census data, scholars have estimated that there were about 5 million free inhabitants in Italy during the early years of the imperial period (Scheidel 2001: 53). But how many slaves lived in Italy at the same time is still a mystery (Scheidel 2001: 55). Scholars have guessed that there were perhaps another 2 to 3 million slaves, and therefore the total population would have been around 8 million (Scheidel 2001: 56). But this is just educated guesswork. It is easier to predict Egypt's population, because useful census data exist; it was probably about 7 million at that time (Parkin 1992: 65). Extrapolating from this, the Roman Empire had perhaps 50 to 60 million inhabitants as a minimum number, and a maximum number of around 100 million should be considered (Scheidel 2001: 63). None of these figures, however, should be understood as absolute.

Fertility and Mortality Rates

Some general statements about fertility rates and mortality rates can be made. These estimates are based on anecdotal accounts and modern analogy. Fertility rates for the Roman Empire are usually assumed to be analogous to natural birthrates. There are some problems with this, because Roman families used three types of birth control, and natural birthrates are based on societies that did not use any kind of birth control (other than social constraints). The three types of birth control used by Romans were contraceptive techniques (although not very dependable), abortion, and infanticide/exposure (French 1988: 1356). More is said in this chapter about these methods, but they likely did not significantly alter the demographics of Roman fertility.

It is difficult to make generalizations about Roman family size. Scholars suppose that an average Roman woman would have had five pregnancies in her life (Saller 1994: 42). This is an average, however, meaning that some women had more pregnancies, and some would have had fewer (Saller 1994: 42). Note that this number (five) refers to the average number of pregnancies, not to surviving children (Saller 1994: 42). High mortality rates make it difficult to estimate averages for numbers of children who lived to adulthood. There was probably a wide variation in the numbers of surviving children and in the relative sizes of Roman families.

Some comments can be made about Roman mortality. We assume that infant mortality was very high. Likewise, mortality rates were relatively high (although not to the same extent) for young children. If an individual lived past

Ulpian's Life Table

An ancient source used in historical demography is Ulpian's Life Table. Preserved in the *Digest* (a massive collection of Roman legal thought; see chapter 10), Ulpian's Life Table is a series of calculations to determine the taxes on annuities, based on what seem to be predictions of life expectancy. What is controversial about this document is how it can be used in demographic studies. It seems to reflect some Roman interest in predicting how long people tended to live, but what these data are based on is obscure. It may represent a very early attempt at estimating mortality rates, or it may just be a complicated taxation system designed to make the elderly more easily taxable.

the early years of childhood, then the mortality risks decreased considerably (Wiedemann 1989: 16–17). The life expectancy of adults in the ancient world is a controversial issue in historical demographics. Most scholars agree that males had a lower life expectancy than females. Some scholars go even further to suggest that frequently, males must have died at very young ages (in their late twenties and early thirties), because ancient authors frequently discussed female remarriage (Saller 1994: 12–13). This second argument is not very compelling, though, because the disparity in frequency of discussion about male remarriage versus female remarriage tells more about Roman attitudes toward women than about the realities of the situation. And the dangers of childbirth for women should not be underestimated. Pregnancy was a dangerous time in a Roman woman's life. It is difficult to suggest an average life span for either men or women. There is ample evidence to demonstrate that Romans could live quite long lives. Various pieces of indirect evidence argue against the traditionally held notion of thirty years as an average life expectancy. For example, the *cursus honorum* (course of honors) presupposes a much longer life for a Roman man. Other anecdotal evidence hints that someone who died in his or her thirties would be thought to have died young (see sidebar above). On the other hand, being elderly in Roman society was probably not a normal situation, certainly not a situation that someone would have expected (as in modern times).

MARRIAGE AND THE FAMILY

The family was the fundamental organizing principle of Roman society. For most Romans, the family unit was the dominant unit of social interaction and identity formation. Most Romans would have had more to do with their family on a daily basis than with any other group, which makes understanding the family integral to understanding Roman society. There is a wealth of scholarship on this subject. What is remarkable about this scholarship is that most of the evidence used by scholars is very similar. Yet very divergent interpretations of the family are presented based on these same data. This makes studying Roman family life very interesting but also very frustrating.

One of the fundamental disagreements among Roman social historians relates to the degree of affection and love among family members. French scholars have traditionally held that love and affection did not develop until much later in Western history. High infant mortality, and the option of exposing unwanted children, forced parents to take a less loving attitude toward their children. Similarly, scholars have argued that love was possible in marriage, but not probable—marriage was primarily an economic relationship. There are many problems with these notions, however. One of the fundamental problems is how to make sense of Roman literature if love was not an important theme in family life. The prominence of love as a subject in Roman writing (love between husband and wife, parent and child, etc.) does not make sense if this kind of affection did not actually exist. I personally believe that the emotional ties in a Roman family were very strong, and that the more prominent roles of life and death in family situations did not hamper the development of affection.

Another problem for Roman family scholars is how to define the family. Different definitions of family are appropriate depending on the circumstances. In legal contexts, the Roman family involved all members of the household, as well as house and property (Saller 1994: 75). In nonlegal contexts, however, *family* did not include the property, it only referred to the people. Similar problems arise with interpreting the word *domus* (literally, house). The context of use of the word is very important in understanding it. It can refer to the physical house, the entire household including property and people, just the house staff, or a dynastic lineage (Saller 1994: 80–82). *Family* and *house* had different meanings and different connotations; it is misleading to try to pin down an entirely consistent definition of either.

On the other hand, some statements can be made about the constituent members of a family. In regard to a relatively wealthy family, it is possible to reconstruct certain members (given ideal circumstances). The head of the household was the pater familias, the father of the house and the oldest male member. Attached to this male was his wife, who was brought from another male-centered house and incorporated into a new family through marriage. The children of this marriage were also family members. Slaves were considered family members and were the responsibility of the pater familias, although if freed, the slaves were removed (from a legal standpoint) from membership in the family. Deceased ancestors were an important part of the Roman family as well, and in the mental construct of the average Roman, the dead continued to play a role in family life.

Marriage

Marriage was an expected duty of all Roman citizens (Treggiari 1988: 1343; Veyne 1987: 37). Both sexes were expected to marry and produce offspring (Balsdon 1963: 190; Dixon 1992: 62). Marriage was a change in social status in which the bride passed from her father's authority to her husband's. With this, the woman changed families as well, becoming a member of the groom's household. Women should not be seen as completely passive parties in this, however. Consent among all parties was a Roman legal requirement for marriage (Saller 1994: 127; Treggiari 1988: 134). Although parents played a significant role in the choice of partners, it was necessary for both the husband and wife to be willing participants. It was also necessary for both parties to have *connubium*; that is, the legal right to marry each other. Citizenship was required; hence slaves were not allowed to officially marry one another or to marry citizens (Treggiari 1988: 1347). In earlier times patricians and plebeians were not allowed to intermarry, but that restriction was removed early on. Close family members did not have connubium with one another; incest laws were strict in Rome (Treggiari 1988: 1347).

An important question about marriage, and one that is not likely to be answered soon, is that of the age of the partners at marriage. It is generally assumed that in a typical situation, the man was older than the woman. There is sufficient anecdotal evidence to be certain of this, or at least to be certain that the Romans found it very strange when the opposite was the case. But the absolute ages of the individuals are much more difficult to predict. It is often assumed that women could be married as soon as they reached maturity, anywhere in the range of twelve to sixteen years of age (Saller 1994: 26). But just because women *could* be married without negative social pressure does not mean that they actually were. Financial pressure, as well as the availability of a desirable (or suitable from the father's perspective) union certainly played roles (Treggiari 1988: 1340). Some scholars argue that women were usually closer to age twenty at first marriage, with poorer women being among the oldest at first marriage (Saller 1994: 37). A man's age at first marriage was older than the respective woman's, but what the average age was is not known. It was probably conceivable for a man to be married as soon as he became an adult (around age sixteen or seventeen), but he may not have actually gotten married until he had established his own household (Treggiari 1988: 1346).

After deciding that a marriage was appropriate, the father of the bride usually arranged a dowry (but see Dixon 1992: 64). This was a large financial burden, and although not legally required of the bride's father, it was socially expected. It formed the daughter's share of the inheritance or the patrimony but was given into the charge of her husband-to-be. If the marriage were to dissolve, the dowry would normally be returned (or sued for return) to the bride and her family (Treggiari 1988: 1348). But as long as the marriage lasted, the dowry was in the hands of the husband. Wives' rights to property varied. *Manus* referred to the situation in which a woman's property was fully controlled by her husband, but it was not an essential component of marriage (Treggiari 1988: 1344).

No full account of a wedding has survived (Treggiari 1988: 1350). Some have argued that the ceremony was unimportant from a legal perspective and that marriage was a wholly private affair (Veyne 1987: 34). This differs from today, when a marriage involves public declarations in order to make it legal. There were a variety of ritual practices that seem related to weddings, but it is not clear if all were performed at a wedding, or in what combination they were performed. Treggiari suggests that the following events may have occurred at a wedding (Treggiari 1988: 1349–1350): Auspices may have been taken, feasts may have been held, and various public acts (like throwing nuts to the crowd of well-wishers) may have occurred. A procession of the bride to her new home was expected, but rather than the husband carrying her across the threshold, the bride's servants did so. It is important to note that although the wedding lacked legal significance, it probably had very important religious and/or social significance for the couple and their families.

Divorce was possible between Roman couples. Willingness to be married was not just a requirement at the start of the marriage, but also throughout the marriage (Dixon 1992: 81; Treggiari 1991: 32). But scholars are divided as to the rates of divorce in Roman times, and the practicality of the situation. Divorce was likely a luxury of wealthier families. For most of Roman history, both men and women could initiate divorce, but it was usually more complicated if the woman initiated it, because property ownership then became a more difficult issue (Dixon 1992: 81; Treggiari 1988: 34). The children stayed with the father. Remarriage was possible for both widowers and widows and was somewhat expected (Veyne 1987: 75). Both widowers and widows could also engage in relationships without fear of public shunning, a luxury not available to women who had not yet had their first marriage (Veyne 1987: 75).

Polygamy was not acceptable in Roman society. It is possible to form the impression, from reading about the sordid affairs of the imperial families, that polygamy was frequent. For the average Roman it was not, and most would have considered the occasional polygamous actions of an emperor to be distasteful. Affairs and sexual relations with other members of the household were frequent occurrences, however, but for married partners these actions carried a social stigma. Concubinage did occur in Rome, but it had a different connotation. For the Romans, concubinage involved a marriagelike relationship between partners that lacked *connubium* (a legal right to be married). So typically, a concubine was not a second wife, but rather a woman whom the man could not (or was not willing to) marry because of her lower social station (Veyne 1987: 76). Sexual relations were considered adulterous only if a man had relations with a married woman who was not his wife (Fantham et al. 1995: 300). If the woman was not married (even if the man was), it was not considered adultery.

Children

Children were an important aspect of Roman life, and it was considered a citizen's duty to have children (Treggiari 1988: 1327). Fathers were expected to be affectionate and caring toward their children. Education was a responsibility of the father (see chapter 10). The average family had two or three children who survived to adulthood. Childhood was considered a distinct stage in life (Dixon 1992: 102). Infants were infants until they learned to speak (Dixon 1992: 104; French 1988: 1359). Girls were girls until they reached sexual maturity. Boys were men when they reached the age at which they could publicly wear the adult toga (Wiedemann 1989: 143). The actual age at which boys could wear the toga varied among boys.

Unless the couple used some kind of birth control (which would not have been dependable), the woman probably became pregnant soon after marriage. Brent Shaw has argued that there were seasonal spikes in amounts of children born in particular periods that may relate to a fixity of season for marriage (Shaw 2001). Childbirth was a dangerous time for a woman. Premodern medicine could not accommodate the kinds of complications that arose during a pregnancy. On the other hand, for women who could afford a midwife, they could expect a high degree of cultural and emotional support during the process.

Once the child was born, the parents had to decide whether or not to keep the child (Veyne 1987: 9). Exposure was a possibility for the family but was probably not taken lightly (French 1988: 1357). The frequency of exposure (giving up the child) in Roman times is unknown. Some sources suggest that femicide, the killing of girls in preference for boys, was common, but it is impossible to determine whether this was a frequent choice of families (French 1988: 1356). Among the poor, exposure was often an attempt to provide the child with a better life, one with the necessary means of support (Veyne 1987: 9). An exposed child was supposed to be left in a public place and fully clothed so that a family desiring the child could accept it (French 1988: 1356). Children born out of wedlock were considered illegitimate. They did not have the right to take their father's name and took their mother's name instead (Veyne 1987: 11). This treatment was given to children born not only of adulterous affairs but also to children born of unions other than marriage (Veyne 1987: 77–78). A child born out of wedlock had no parental inheritance rights.

The Patrimonial Household

The exposure of children is often considered alongside the power of the pater familias, called the *patria potestas*. This was the absolute power of the pater familias over the other members of his household, including the right to punish family members with death (Saller 1994: 115). The Greeks wrote about this Roman trait with shock (Saller 1994: 102–114). But it is doubtful how frequently a father exercised this authority or how tolerant the state was of such practices (Dixon 1992: 131). The cases that have survived of the pater familias exercising his authority over life and death suggest that it was an abnormal situation.

Without a doubt, however, the pater familias was the supreme power in the household. Greek observers write about grown sons being forced to obey their fathers (Veyne 1987: 27). It is also realistic to assume that there were many situations in which younger boys became the pater familias before reaching maturity because of the early death of the father (Saller 1994: 131). Whatever the actual frequency of these situations was, the pater familias was the oldest living male member of the household, and he exercised authority over it. However, the wife frequently was designated with the authority to run the household. There is also ample evidence to suggest that whereas sole power legally resided with the pater familias, and that the wife had virtually no significant say in matters, all of this was dependent on the temperaments of the two parties involved.

Inheritance and Adoption

Related to the power of the pater familias was control over the patrimony—the family estate. Power over the estate passed between generations through wills. The pater familias declared his intentions in legal documents, which were publicly read upon his death. This was an important event. Wills were judged harshly, and it was important for the person composing the will to follow social norms of respectability and appropriateness (Veyne 1987: 31). Normally, the next oldest male would get the majority of the patrimony and become the next pater familias. If a will did not follow social norms, it could be revoked by the state.

Adoption was a common mechanism to facilitate inheritance to nonbiological kin while preserving the family name (Veyne 1987: 17). Adoption within the imperial family helped ensure proper succession and indicated the favor of the emperor. Males who had living parents could be adopted as well. The benefit to these men was to gain access to a patrimony, especially important for poor families and younger sons.

SOCIAL STRATIFICATION IN ROME

Roman civilization was extremely stratified and hierarchical. Principles of differentiated social position were legislated and codified from the earliest legal materials. In an excellent essay, Saller suggests that Roman society should be looked at in terms of three different social categories (Saller 1988: 550). These categories are order (where membership is formally defined by the state), status (perception of prestige), and class (based on access to the means of production). Related to social stratification is slavery; this topic is discussed later in this chapter.

The Orders

Orders are formally defined categories of people. There were two orders in early Rome—patricians and plebeians. Membership in an order was based entirely on birth. These categories were signified in numerous ways. Most notable was that particular dress was suitable for members of particular orders. For example, patricians were allowed the privilege of wearing a certain kind of shoe.

Patricians. Roman tradition suggests that the *patricii* (patricians) came into existence during the regal period (Mitchell 1990: 2). The early traditions suggest that this order was formed from the original senators chosen by Romulus when he founded Rome. Many scholars have noted a linguistic connection between the word *patrician* and the Latin word for "father" (Cornell 1995: 245, for example). Some have argued that this indicated that patricians produced *patres* (fathers) who were senators (Cornell 1995: 245–246). This may be true; how-

A Roman patrician and his wife, first century C.E. (Mimmo Jodico/Corbis)

ever, it is unlikely that the patricians were the sole ruling class of early Rome. It is likely that very early on, these families took a leading role in city governance (Mitchell 1990: 18). The families had hereditary rights and were connected with the Senate (Mitchell 1990: 17). Membership in the Senate was not exclusive to the patrician order (Cornell 1995: 247). But many patricians were senators and this order wielded much authority over the Senate (Crawford 1982: 32). In addition, patricians held the major religious positions, such as pontiff (Cornell 1995: 251–252; Crawford 1982: 32). Large landholders, the patricians gained their wealth through landownership. From 218 B.C.E. on, senators were banned from engaging in commerce. So they were forced to look to their landholdings even more as a source for the acquisition of wealth.

Modern scholars disagree on when the patrician order became a well-defined social body (Cornell 1995: 252). The classic statement on this issue is by de Sanctis, who suggested in the early twentieth century that the patricians closed their ranks by discouraging intermarriage (de Sanctis 1953). That is to say, they formed themselves into an isolated group by not allowing new membership (except through birth or adoption). By about 450 B.C.E., it had become impossible for a nonpatrician to become a patrician. Even very wealthy nonpatricians were excluded.

Plebeians.   The origin of the plebeian order (or plebs) is obscure although it is well known that the word *pleb* translates to "masses" (Cornell 1995: 256). It is possible to talk about a group known as the plebs early in the republic (Cornell 1995: 256). At that time, the plebs seemed to be a heterogeneous group of underprivileged people. It is also likely that wealthy nonpatricians were members of this group. This group of people (effectively nonpatricians) was excluded from holding senatorial offices and other important positions in city governance. It is the disenfranchised nature of this group that probably lies at the roots of its formation—a formation that is clear in the conflict of the orders.

Conflict of the Orders.   Classical sources viewed Roman society as essentially dimorphic from its inception. The primary difference between individuals was between patricians and plebeians, and most ancient sources describe this as an almost natural difference. Modern scholars think that the issue was much more complex. The division of society into orders developed historically throughout the regal period and the period of the republic in what is often referred to as the Conflict of the Orders.

In 494 B.C.E., a plebeian group withdrew from the city of Rome and took up residence on the Sacred Mount, so tradition tells us. In what became known as "The First Succession," the plebeians formed a governing system to go along with that of the patricians. The exact nature of these offices is described in chapter 7, but it is important to note that this is the point at which the plebs forced their way into Roman governance. Furthermore, demands for laws to be written down led to the composition of the Twelve Tables (see chapter 10).

The motivations for the plebeian succession are not entirely clear. The root causes of the conflict were likely economic in nature (Cornell 1995: 265). The archaeological record of this period suggests that Rome was not prospering economically (Cornell 1995: 266). Minimal public works projects were enacted at this time and fine imported pottery all but vanished (Cornell 1995: 266), indicating a lack of wealth that could be used for prestige activities (activities not directly related to subsistence). It is likely (although not certain) that the plebs were concerned about exploitation through debt-bondage—*nexus* (Cornell 1995: 266; Crawford 1982: 32; Jolowicz 1967: 9). Debt-bondage is an institution that has its roots in ancient Mesopotamia and continues, in some parts of the world, to the present day. A poor farmer, for instance, who lacked capital to purchase seed or other agricultural necessities, would borrow the means of production from a wealthier individual. As collateral, he would leave a member of his household in the charge of the loaner as a guarantee. The person, as collateral, would work in the loan agent's household until the farmer could pay back the debt. At the time of the First Succession, it is probable that this institution was rampant and subject to varying abuses. By forming a plebeian government, the plebs were better able to act against abuses in this system.

The other major problem that was probably dealt with in the First Succession was the land needs of the poor (Cornell 1995: 268; Jolowicz 1967: 8–9). At this time, landholdings of the poor were very small—barely enough for subsistence. And certainly the landholdings were too small to enable the poor landholder to accumulate a surplus as insurance in times of crisis (e.g., poor harvests). Although actual landownership was small, it seems that a great deal of land was designated as public. Individual families could work the public land to supplement their own meek landholdings. However, by the time of the First Succession, apparently, this public land had mostly been annexed by very wealthy landholders—landholders who could afford large staffs of slaves and debt-bonded workers to cultivate the land. It is probable that the plebs demanded more equitable distribution of land at this time (Cornell 1995: 269–270).

Status

Status refers to the perceived prestige of an individual. Normally status is gained through the activities of an individual's life and is not directly based on birth. However, it must be noted that birth into a specific order or class presents individuals with differential access to the kinds of activities that relate to status. In Roman times, status was designated very specifically. People of particular status were described as members of particular groups. Cornell has suggested a more complex understanding of how status was manifested in Rome (Cornell 1995: 258). The terminology used that related to status, according to Cornell, did not represent hard-and-fast groups. Indeed, most of the terminology reflected binary oppositions. In addition, people could be described as members of a number of status groups. In Cornell's perspective, these binary oppositions should be viewed as ranges of status, with the binary oppositions reflecting the most extreme measures of each status relationship (Cornell 1995: 258). The following section deals with some of these Roman status concepts.

Absidui and Proletarii. A fundamental status distinction from the regal period until the reforms of Marius was the distinction between landowners and the propertyless (Crawford 1982: 46). Those who owned property were called *absidui*. Absidui, as landowners, were eligible for military service. The *proletarii* owned no land and were not allowed to perform military service. Within Roman law, proletarii had a lower legal status, probably related to their wealth. For example, proletarii could not act as guarantors for loans to absidui because it was likely that they would not in fact be able to guarantee the loan.

Equites and Pedites. This status group originated in the regal period. Basically knights, *equites* were individuals who could afford the equipment and training for horse-based warfare (Gelzer 1969: 5). However, by the second century B.C.E., this group had withdrawn from military service and had taken on governmental functions (such as tax collection). The basic requirement to become an equite was the ownership of property valued at more than 400,000 sesterces (Gelzer 1969: 10; Jolowicz 1967: 78). On the other side of this status are community members who lacked sufficient funds (in the eyes of the state) to be provided with a horse, hence *pedites*.

Patrons and Clients.   Arguably the most prominent status distinction within Roman society was the distinction between patron and client. A patron was a wealthy individual and held higher status within the community than his client. A client was a subordinate individual who formally asked a patron for assistance. More of this relationship is discussed in chapter 5, but it is important to identify the patron-client relationship as one of Cornell's primary binary social impositions.

SLAVERY

Slavery was an important component of the Roman economy and has received much attention in modern scholarship. It is important, from the outset, to underline the differences between Roman slavery and the slavery that existed in early America. Slavery in Rome was primarily an economic status and as such was changeable. It was not predicated on theories of racial superiority, and it was not confined to one group of people, as it was to African Americans. When considering Roman slavery it is important to try to think of it without reference to slavery in the United States. The two phenomena are not really comparable, other than that the word *slavery* is used to describe both situations.

Who Became Slaves?

In the Roman world, there were many ways one could become a slave. Often people entered into a debt-bondage relationship. Individuals who needed collateral for a loan, or who could not afford to pay back a loan, would enter into the debtor's care (or send a member of the household to the debtor) for an agreed-upon length of time (see chapter 5). Also, children could be sold into slavery if the parents lacked funds or the desire to raise them (Veyne 1987: 55). Another alternative was that the child could be exposed, a process by which the child would be taken away with no payment transaction (Veyne 1987: 52). Less civil means also brought people into slavery. Pirates would sell kidnapped individuals into slavery (Wiedemann 1997: 22). The spoils of war were often human resources—enemy soldiers and civilians were the largest demographic of slaves (Wiedemann 1997: 22). Certain kinds of criminal convictions could also lead to enslavement. And with all of these kinds of slavery, any children born of a slave were themselves slaves (Veyne 1987: 53).

The Purchase of Slaves

Slaves were frequently purchased from slave traders. At a slave market, the slaves were paraded around in the nude, often wearing only placards that listed their attributes. The slaves were auctioned and sold to the highest bidder, although it was also possible to rent slaves for a fixed period. The slave trader, ideally, was supposed to be able to affirm that the slave was not otherwise encumbered or physically unwell (Shelton 1988: 168). Slave markets were found throughout the empire. The island of Delos was a particularly large and infamous slave market, where slaves acquired from Asia were sold.

The Work of Slaves

The kind of work done by slaves depended heavily on the particular slave owner. Household slavery was probably the easiest life for a slave. Numerous occupations were available within a household context. Slaves could be teachers, gardeners, cooks, clothes-makers, barbers, or any other domestic functionary that the householder had need for (Shelton 1988: 170). Within this context, both male and female slaves were also frequently used for the sexual satisfaction of their owners. Slaves could also work almost independently of their owners, running shops or other projects that produced income for their masters. As artisans, slaves could often freely practice their trade (Veyne 1987: 56–57). This made it possible for slaves, in some contexts, to amass large amounts of wealth.

Outside of the home, slaves could work in mines, factories, or on farms. This work was often quite difficult—the worst kind of manual labor, which freedmen had no desire to do themselves. Groups of slaves were often organized under a slave having the position of foreman (Veyne 1987: 55). Towns and cities could also own slaves. These slaves were employed in construction work, such as the maintenance of roads and aqueducts. Cleaning crews consisting of slaves were also used in the cities and in public spaces, such as baths.

Slaves were a very expensive labor force. It was often much cheaper to hire laborers for work than to buy slaves. Slaves were expensive to purchase, but it was also very expensive for the owner to provide and care for the slave. Often, the benefit gained from a slave was the prestige that came with owning a large number of them, rather than an actual production benefit.

The Treatment of Slaves

The treatment of slaves varied radically, depending on the individual slave's owner. A slave could live a prosperous life, and enjoy treatment similar to a family member's if the owner so wished. Marriages between owner and slave were not infrequent. However, slaves were the property of the owner and were treated as such. It is often said that slaves had the same rights as objects within a household. This is not exactly true; it is a mistake based on the conception Romans had of a household, which differed from the conception held today.

Slaves were punished in a number of ways, but punishment depended on the personality of the master (Shelton 1988: 176). Punishment by slave owners was kept in check by the fact that a slave owner would not want to permanently damage his investment. Slaves who committed crimes were punished harshly. In fact, if a slave killed a free man, it was legal to kill all of the slaves within that household (Shelton 1988: 178). Death by crucifixion was a punishment feared by all slaves. Even if not convicted of a crime, slaves were subject to torture in order to elicit testimony from them (Shelton 1988: 178).

Runaway slaves were a problem for the Romans. Branding and slave collars

A scene from the movie *Spartacus*. Laurence Olivier as Crassus talks to defeated slave rebels Spartacus (Kirk Douglas, right) and Antoninus (Tony Curtis). (Pixel That)

were used as means of identifying slaves (Shelton 1988: 180). Particular garments (indicating that a person was a slave) made it difficult for slaves to leave the city unaccompanied by their owners. And any slave who was caught impersonating a freedman was subject to capital punishment. Slave revolt was a concern for Roman citizens (Shelton 1988: 181). In large households, the slave population often greatly outnumbered the free members of the household. Large-scale slave revolts did occur in the Roman world, the most famous of which was led by Spartacus (see chapter 4). Numerous rules existed for the prevention of slave revolts. For example, slaves were not allowed in the military. Contrary to popular belief, slaves did not work the oars of Roman warships. It was understood that a slave did not make a trustworthy soldier.

Slaves could marry one another, but the marriages would not be legally recognized (Treggiari 1988: 1353). This arrangement was called *contubernium*. Children born to slaves were the property of the slave owner. Slaves could save up and buy their freedom, or they could be granted manumission by their owner. In such cases, the relationship shifted from master-owner to patron-client. And often slaves would receive small gifts of money from their owners, called *peculium*.

Freedmen

A slave that had been manumitted by his or her owner was called a freedman (*libertus*). There were many possible reasons an owner might have had for freeing a slave (Treggiari 1969: 11–20). Certainly compassion was a possible motive. Stoic philosophy disapproved of the institution of slavery. And slaves who were in the personal service of their masters and developed personal relationships with them were more likely to be freed. If an owner fell in love with his slave and wanted to marry her, he would have had to free her first. Freed slaves could also be adopted by their masters. Compassion on the part of other freedmen could also have led to manumission; former slaves would sometimes buy the freedom of their friends. Economic motives could also lead to freed slaves. Slaves could save up and purchase their freedom (usually by paying their owner the initial purchase price). If the owner could not afford the slave's upkeep, or if the slave was too old or sick to pay his or her own weight, the owner may have released the slave. Social reasons could also motivate an owner to free his or her slaves. The act of freeing slaves was prestigious, demonstrating both generosity and wealth.

The most common way for slaves to be manumitted was for the master and slave to appear before a magistrate (Watson 1970: 47). The magistrate would perform a ceremony, and the slave was officially freed—able to wear the cap of a freedman (Shelton 1988: 190; Treggiari 1969: 21). Another method of manumission was for the master to provide for it in a will (Treggiari 1969: 27; Watson 1970: 46). Upon the death of the master, the slave was declared freed. The promise of eventual freedom could be a compelling motivation for slaves to be faithful to their masters. Slaves could also be unofficially manumitted. Called *Junian Latins,* these slaves were not legally free, but could live like freedmen (Adkins and Adkins 1994: 342; Watson 1970: 47). The children of Junian Latins, however, were not free, and upon the death of a Junian Latin, his property reverted to the original master (Adkins and Adkins 1994: 342).

Freedmen became citizens of Rome. They could vote but they were prohibited from running for office or joining the senatorial and equestrian orders (but see Treggiari 1969: 52–64). Of course, it was very rare that a freedman would have enough wealth or prestige to run for office or join one of the upper ranks. The children of freedmen, however, were not considered freedmen; they were considered ordinary citizens, with all the rights and privileges of citizens (Treggiari 1969: 227). The granting of citizenship to freedmen was the easiest way for a foreigner to become a Roman citizen.

WOMEN IN ANCIENT ROME

The study of Roman women as a distinct scholarly endeavor is a relatively new subject in Roman studies. What makes the recent advances in the study of Roman women different from what has come before is the incorporation of gender and feminist theory. There is no room in this book to discuss these dynamic and diverse fields of theory, but it is important to be aware that the application of these new theoretical approaches has opened up a new field. How gender is constructed as a concept (in the eyes of both moderns and ancients) and made unstable by a variety of factors such as age and class has been a revolutionary new question. The binary opposition of male-female is no longer seen as a concrete difference, but rather an interaction and process spanning more than these two polar extremes. Roman art and literature are particularly appropriate subjects for these theoretical approaches, and archaeology can help provide information that spans class differences. For the beginner, the vast amount of new literature on women in antiquity can be frustrating because there is just as much excellent scholarship as there is poor scholarship. The discussion that follows includes some of the important themes that have arisen in recent scholarship.

Roles of Women

It would be impossible to describe all of the roles that were available to women in ancient Rome. But an interesting avenue of research is to study the kinds of roles that were glorified in literature and art. But as with all people, it was possible to fill many roles and have many identities. The average modern individual plays various roles throughout a lifetime. It should be assumed that the ancient world had similar levels of complexity regarding the roles women could play.

Mother. One of the primary roles associated with women in Roman times was that of mother. This is not surprising; it is a biological fact of human existence. But what makes this category interesting in Roman times is the centrality of the mother in Roman culture (Balsdon 1963: 203). A woman's virtue was intrinsically linked to her reproductive skills and to her responsibilities as a mother (Dixon 1988: 7). A common notion in scholarship is that women's activities were closely guarded to ensure the paternity of their children, because in antiquity, fatherhood could not be proven scientifically (Balsdon 1963: 197). One of the best sources for these attitudes toward women is mortuary monuments. One of the glowing qualities most often commemorated in funerary inscriptions was the description of the woman as an ideal mother (Fantham et al. 1995: 318).

Wife. Funerary inscriptions also tell much about another role of women— that of wife (Dickison 1988: 1320; Fantham et al. 1995: 1320). Because eulogies tended to describe positive qualities only, the descriptions in ancient eulogies (while not necessarily true of the actual person) were indicative of wider cultural values. The highest virtue that a Roman woman could possess was *pudicitia*, devotion to her husband (Dickison 1988: 1325, Fantham et al. 1995: 225). For all Roman women, with the exception of the vestal virgins, it was expected that they should have a husband. A woman without a husband (unless widowed) was seen as aberrant, and the fringe position of prostitutes within Roman society attests to this (see Krenkl 1988).

Statue of a vestal virgin. (Araldo de Luca/ Corbis)

Religious Participant. There were many roles that women could play in religious life. The Vestal Virgins were among the most powerful cultic officials in Rome, and more is said about them in chapter 7. Likewise, the wife of the *rex sacorum* (the religious official who acted on behalf of the king) played an important role in Roman religious ceremony. There were deities and festivals that were exclusively the purview of women. The *pax deorum* was held twice every year. This was a feast only for married women, held in honor of the goddess Bono Dea.

Views of Women

One of the problems with the study of Roman women is that most of the available evidence has been distorted through male eyes. Almost all of the texts are from a male perspective, and artistic evidence is likely just as phallocentric. This makes it imperative to understand the social beliefs people held about women in order to make use of these sources. If the biases of one's sources are known, there is a much better chance of understanding why a given source says what it does.

Male Guardians. One of the traditional male views of women in Roman times was that they required male guardianship in most of life's stages (Dickison 1988: 1324). Before marriage, women were seen in relation to their fathers, with the father acting as the sole guardian. From the father's house, the normative next step for a Roman woman was marriage and the guardianship of her husband. It certainly seems that in an ideal biography (from a Roman male perspective), a woman was in a man's care at all stages in her life. Even in the absence of a father or husband (through death, for example), there was usually a male who could step in as pater familias, from an ideal perspective. In actual practice, however, the constancy of male guardianship would have differed considerably in every situation.

Women in Myth. The roles of women in the myths of the foundation of Rome are compelling. Consider the story of the Rape of the Sabines (see chapter 3). From this myth, Roman society is cast as initially completely composed of males. These males (in the male-only society) seize and rape a group of women

Queen Boadicea rallying Britons before battling with the Romans. (Library of Congress)

from another city. In antiquity, the emphasis on the rape aspect did not cast the males in a negative light, but rather emphasized the sexual purity and virtue of the female ancestors of the Romans (Fantham et al. 1995: 217). Likewise, the rape of Lucretia (see chapter 4) demonstrates the qualities of a virtuous woman in terms of sexual chastity (Dickison 1988: 1325, Fantham et al. 1995: 225). On the other hand, women are seen very negatively in the story of the sacking of the Capitoline Hill by the Sabines (Fantham et al. 1995: 218). A woman, according to Livy, showed the Sabines a secret route in exchange for payment.

Women in Political Life.   Women were not allowed to vote, nor were they allowed to run for public office. Although they could participate in public gatherings, their direct participation in civic government was barred. This meant that any influence on government activity during the Republican period was indirect, and as such, is very difficult for historians to trace. In the imperial period, the status of women in regard to political life did not change. But historians are better able to trace the effect of some notable women on political life. These women were people who were close to the emperor. Because of the emperor's power, anyone close enough to personally influence him could also influence public life.

Agrippina, wife of Emperor Claudius. Statue, full length, seated, facing right; in Naples Museum. No. 1531.

In Roman literature, the influence of women on male politicians was not looked upon favorably (Dickison 1988: 1325). Women who attempted to act in the public sphere were described as liars, overemotional, and unable to control their desire or temper (Fantham et al. 1995: 367–368). As a means of discrediting a male politician, accusations about the influence of his wife could be levied. Amazingly, this kind of sentiment still persists today, and is commonly part of political discourse—consider the popular-culture image of Hillary Clinton during her husband's presidency.

More prominent in Roman history than the wives of politicians were the mothers of politicians. There was a considerable degree of variation in the in-

Perpetua

An absolutely remarkable document is the diary of a young woman named Vibia Perpetua. She was a wellborn and educated Christian woman who, in 203 C.E., was killed in an amphitheater in Carthage. Perpetua was only 22, and her crime was religious in nature. Although Christianity was not a crime per se in Rome at this time, local governors could use their own discretion in such matters. Often Christian executions were justified through charges of atheism when someone refused to participate in Roman cultic events. Perpetua and four of her housemates were charged with atheism. Her diary provides tremendous insight into the mind of a woman in a situation unthinkable in modernity. The diary records the events of the judicial proceedings and conversations with her father, who begged her to simply recant Christianity and make a Roman sacrifice. Perpetua recorded her feelings and fears about her infant child and about her time in prison. She also recorded four of her dreams in vivid detail. She and her housemates were killed in a public spectacle. They were first attacked by wild beasts but were killed when Roman soldiers slit their throats.

fluence that mothers had over male political actors. On the one hand, there was the influence the mother had as the earliest role model for the child, an influence that should not be ignored, but one that is more difficult to see historically (Dickison 1988: 1323; Dixon 1988: 170). On the other hand, there are the infamous mothers (e.g., Agrippina, mother of Nero) who wielded considerable influence at court (Fantham et al. 1995: 308–313).

The stories about barbarian women provide very interesting insights into Roman conceptions of gender and otherness. Boudicca, who lived c. 26–60 C.E., was the queen of the Iceni tribe, a Celtic tribe in Britain. She led a revolt against the Romans and had many military victories, but was eventually defeated. Queen Zenobia of Palmyra, who lived around 260 C.E., also went to war against Rome, but was eventually defeated. The Roman descriptions of these women are very interesting. Both were described in a virtuous light, and they seem to have commanded the respect of the Romans. On the other hand, there is a very romanticized otherness about these women and their people. That these barbarians would allow themselves to be led by women was more evidence of their savagery (Fantham et al. 1995: 389–390). And, that women in these societies could be described in virtuous terms normally restricted to men further demonstrated the backwardness of Roman civilization.

Women in the Public Sphere

For all who argue for the cultural superiority of the Greeks over the Romans, the position of women in the public sphere is perhaps the best counterargument. In Greek society, women were curtailed from participation in public life to an extreme degree. Although in actual practice it may not have been the case, the ideal Greek woman never left the house. This was certainly not the situation for Roman women, who were allowed a significantly higher degree of civil liberty than most ancient women. Women were a constant presence in Roman public spaces (Balsdon 1963: 201; Fantham et al. 1995: 338). They were not restricted in their ability to move around the city, and they participated in spectacles, baths, and other public activities (Dickison 1988: 1319).

There are also recorded instances of women acting in the public sphere as a collective. One occasion came as a response to sumptuary laws passed in the wake of the second Punic War. The *lex oppia* (opulence laws) limited the amount of gold women were allowed to possess. In 195 B.C.E., women demonstrated in the streets to have this law repealed, and it was (Dickison 1988: 1321). This event is known from the writings of Cato the Elder, who warned about the dire consequences of women who possess too much wealth. There are other examples of women acting as a group. In 309 B.C.E., women were said to have gathered 1,000 pounds of gold to bribe invaders to leave the city. And supposedly, under Emperor Elagabulus, a women's Senate was formed to create a code of female etiquette.

BIBLIOGRAPHY

Adkins, Lesley, and Roy Adkins. 1994. *Handbook to Life in Ancient Rome*. Oxford: Oxford University Press.

Badian, E. 1958. *Foreign Clientelae*. Oxford: Clarendon Press.

Bagnall, Roger, and Bruce Frier. 1994. *The Demography of Roman Egypt*. Cambridge: Cambridge University Press.

Balsdon, J. P. V. D. 1963. *Roman Women*. New York: The John Day Company.

Blagg, T. F. C. 1987. "Society and the Artist," pp. 717–741 in *The Roman World*. John Wacher (ed.). New York: Routledge & Kegan Paul.

Boardman, John, Jasper Griffin, and Oswyn Murray (eds.). 1986. *The Oxford Illustrated History of the Roman World*. Oxford: Oxford University Press.

Breeze, David. 1987. "Britain," pp. 198–222 in *The Roman World*. John Wacher (ed.). New York: Routledge & Kegan Paul.

Brunt, Peter. 1966. "The Roman Mob." *Past and Present* 35: 3–25.

———. 1971a. *Italian Manpower*. London: Oxford University Press.

———. 1971b. *Social Conflicts in the Roman Republic*. London: Chatto & Windus.

Carcopino, Jérôme. 1940. *Daily Life in Ancient Rome*. Henry Rowell (ed.). New Haven: Yale University Press.

Clark, E. G. 1993. *Women in the Ancient World*. Oxford: Oxford University Press.

Cornell, T. J. 1995. *The Beginnings of Rome*. New York: Routledge.

Cowell, F. R. 1980. *Life in Ancient Rome*. New York: Perigee Books.

Crawford, Michael. 1982. *The Roman Republic*. Cambridge: Harvard University Press.

Daniels, Charles. 1987. "Africa," pp. 223–265 in *The Roman World*. John Wacher (ed.). New York: Routledge & Kegan Paul.

d'Arms, John. 1981. *Commerce and Social Standing in Ancient Rome*. Cambridge: Harvard University Press.

de Coulanges, Fustel. 1864. *The Ancient City*. New York: Doubleday Books.

de Sanctis, Gaetano. 1953. *Storia dei Romani*. Firenze: Nuova Italia.

Dickison, Sheila. 1988. "Women in Rome," pp. 1319–1332 in *Civilization of the Ancient*

Mediterranean: Greece and Rome. Michael Grant and Rachel Kitzinger (eds.). New York: Charles Scribner's Sons.

Dixon, Suzanne. 1988. *The Roman Mother.* Norman: University of Oklahoma Press.

———. 1992. *The Roman Family.* Baltimore: Johns Hopkins University Press.

Drinkwater, J. F. 1987. "Urbanization in Italy and the Western Empire," pp. 345–387 in *The Roman World.* John Wacher (ed.). New York: Routledge & Kegan Paul.

Drummond, Steven, and Lynne Nelson. 1994. *The Western Frontiers of Imperial Rome.* London: M.E. Sharpe.

Duff, A. M. 1926. *Freedmen in the Early Roman Empire.* Oxford: Clarendon Press.

Dupont, Florence. 1989. *Daily Life in Ancient Rome.* Christopher Woodall (trans.). Cambridge: Basil Blackwell Ltd.

Fantham, Elaine, Helene Pete Foley, Natalie Boymel Kampen, Sarah B. Pomeroy, and H. A. Shapiro. 1995. *Women in the Classical World: Image & Text.* Oxford: Oxford University Press.

Finley, Moses (ed.). 1960. *Slavery in Classical Antiquity.* Cambridge: Heffer.

French, Valerie. 1988. "Birth Control, Childbirth, and Early Childhood," pp. 1355–1362 in *Civilization of the Ancient Mediterranean: Greece and Rome.* Michael Grant and Rachel Kitzinger (eds.). *Civilization of the Ancient Mediterranean: Greece and Rome.* New York: Charles Scribner's Sons.

Friedländer, Ludwig. 1910. *Roman Life and Manners under the Early Empire.* London: Routledge & Sons, Ltd.

Gelzer, Matthias. 1969. *The Roman Nobility.* Robin Seager (trans.). New York: Barnes & Noble.

Greene, Kevin. 1986. *The Archaeology of the Roman Economy.* Berkeley: University of California Press.

Hallett, Judith. 1988. "Roman Attitudes towards Sex," pp. 1265–1278 in *Civilization of the Ancient Mediterranean: Greece and Rome.* Michael Grant and Rachel Kitzinger (eds.). New York: Charles Scribner's Sons.

Hopkins, Keith. 1978. *Sociological Studies in Roman History I: Conquerors and Slaves.* Cambridge: Cambridge University Press.

———. 1983. *Sociological Studies in Roman History II: Death and Renewal.* Cambridge: Cambridge University Press.

Jolowicz, H. F. 1967. *Historical Introduction to the Study of Roman Law.* Cambridge: Cambridge University Press.

Keller, Donald, and David Rupp (eds.). 1983. *Archaeological Survey in the Mediterranean Area.* Oxford: BAR International Series.

Kennedy, David. 1987. "The East," pp. 266–308 in *The Roman World.* John Wacher (ed.). New York: Routledge & Kegan Paul.

Keppie, Lawrence. 1983. *Colonisation and Veteran Settlement in Italy 47–14 B.C.* London: British School at Rome.

Kleiner, Diana (ed.). 1996. *I Claudia: Women in Ancient Rome.* New Haven: Yale University Art Gallery.

———. 2000. *I Claudia II: Women in Roman Art and Society.* Austin: University of Texas Press.

Krenkl, Werner. 1988. "Prostitution," pp. 1291–1298 in *Civilization of the Ancient Mediterranean: Greece and Rome.* Michael Grant and Rachel Kitzinger (eds.). New York: Charles Scribner's Sons.

Levick, Barbara. 1987. "Urbanization in the Eastern Empire," pp. 329–344 in *The Roman World.* John Wacher (ed.). New York: Routledge & Kegan Paul.

Mattingly, Harold. 1957. *Roman Imperial Civilization.* London: Eduard Arnold (Publishers) Ltd.

Maxfield, Valerie. 1987. "Mainland Europe," pp. 139–197 in *The Roman World.* John Wacher (ed.). New York: Routledge & Kegan Paul.

Mitchell, Richard. 1990. *Patricians and Plebians.* Ithaca: Cornell University Press.

Nicolet, C. 1980. *The World of the Citizen in Republican Rome.* P. S. Falla (trans.). Berkeley: University of California Press.

Parkin, Tim. 1992. *Demography and Roman Society.* Baltimore: Johns Hopkins University Press.

Poulter, Andrew. 1987. "Townships and Villages," pp. 388–410 in *The Roman World.* John Wacher (ed.). New York: Routledge & Kegan Paul.

Raaflaub, Kurt (ed.). 1986. *Social Struggles in Archaic Rome.* Berkeley: University of California Press.

Rawson, Beryl (ed.). 1991. *Marriage, Divorce, and Children in Ancient Rome.* Oxford: Clarendon Press.

Rostovtzeff, Michael. 1957. *Social and Economic History of the Roman Empire.* Oxford: Oxford University Press.

Saller, Richard. 1982. *Personal Patronage under the Early Roman Empire.* Cambridge: Cambridge University Press.

———. 1988. "Roman Class Structures and Relations," pp. 549–574 in *Civilization of the Ancient Mediterranean: Greece and Rome.* Michael Grant and Rachel Kitzinger (eds.). New York: Charles Scribner's Sons.

———. 1994. *Patriarchy, Property and Death in the Roman Family.* Cambridge: Cambridge University Press.

Scheidel, Walter (ed.). 2001. *Debating Roman Demography.* Leiden: Brill.

Shaw, Brent. 2001. "The Seasonal Birthing Cycle of Roman Women," pp. 83–110 in *Debating Roman Demography.* W. Scheidel (ed.). Leiden: Brill.

Shelton, Jo-Ann. 1988. *As the Romans Did.* Oxford: Oxford University Press.

Sherwin-White, Adrian. 1973. *The Roman Citizenship.* 2nd ed. Oxford: Clarendon Press.

Treggiari, Susan. 1969. *Roman Freedmen during the Late Republic.* Oxford: Clarendon Press.

———. 1988. "Roman Marriage," pp. 1343–1354 in *Civilization of the Ancient Mediterranean: Greece and Rome.* Michael Grant and Rachel Kitzinger (eds.). New York: Charles Scribner's Sons.

———. 1991. "Divorce Roman Style: How Frequent Was It?," pp. 31–46 in *Marriage, Divorce, and Children in Ancient Rome.* Beryl Rawson (ed.). Oxford: Clarendon Press.

Veyne, Paul. 1987. *A History of Private Life: From Pagan Rome to Byzantium.* Cambridge: Harvard University Press.

Watson, Alan. 1970. *The Law of the Ancient Romans.* Dallas: Southern Methodist University Press.

Wiedemann, Thomas. 1988. "Slavery," pp. 575–588 in *Civilization of the Ancient Mediterranean: Greece and Rome.* Michael Grant and Rachel Kitzinger (eds.). New York: Charles Scribner's Sons.

———. 1989. *Adults and Children in the Roman Empire.* New Haven: Yale University Press.

———. 1997. *Slavery.* Oxford: Oxford University Press.

Woolf, Greg. 1998. *Becoming Roman.* Cambridge: Cambridge University Press.

Yavetz, Zvi. 1969. *Plebs and Princeps.* London: Oxford University Press.

VII CHAPTER 7
Politics

MONARCHICAL GOVERNMENT

The evidence that can be used to reconstruct the government of the Roman monarchy is meager at best. Archaeological data can reveal the existence of public structures, population and site size, and the spread of material culture. However, this evidence is very open to interpretation. Unlike the multitude of contemporary sources available for the Republican and Imperial periods, there is a lack of historical records contemporary with the period of the monarchy. Much later accounts of the monarchy have survived, but it is often difficult to untangle the historical facts from the blend of mythical accounts and contemporary political polemic.

Romulus, the mythical founder of Rome, is also considered the founder of the monarchical government. Although it is unlikely that this individual actually laid the basis of government in the manner described by the ancient sources, the description of what he was supposed to have established probably provides a reasonably trustworthy account of the monarchy's political structures of (at least toward the end of its existence). The foundation of this government, supposedly established by Romulus, is based on a division of the Roman people into three tribes. Each of these tribes was divided into ten extended families (*curiae*), and further subdivided into families (*gentes*). These tribes and family divisions may not reflect ancient lineages; rather, they may represent a later administrative organization. Whether this division of three tribes existed before Roman government is unknown, but it is likely that the choice of criteria for division was an administrative innovation (Cornell 1995: 114, 117). Other structures that Romulus was thought to have founded were the *comitia curiata* (the assembly of wards) and the Senate (see the section that follows). Certainly, the king and the Senate were the powerful governing bodies of the early monarchy. It is unclear exactly when the comitia curiata actually began to function.

The Senate

Although the Senate lasted throughout Roman history, its functions and powers changed drastically. In the period of the monarchy, the Senate consisted of elders, chosen by the king, to help advise him in matters of government (Staveley 1988: 496). The number of advisors was limited to 100. Tradition suggests that the initial selection of the senators was made by the king, who chose individuals from the families who had supported his rise to the throne (Staveley 1988: 495). The Senate at this time lacked formal ability to legislate; law was the domain of the king. The Senate was more influential in matters of administration.

Comitia Curiata

Another component of monarchical government was the comitia curiata (see below). The exact function of this body during this period is not known, but information about its internal organization does exist. This assembly was composed of ten subdivisions, one representing each of the three tribes, making a total of thirty curiae. It seems that the membership of an individual was based on his birth, but it is not clear how these divisions were originally established (Cornell 1995: 116). The origins of the comitia curiata are obscure and contested. Roman traditions suggest that it was established by Romulus at the inception of the monarchy. Many scholars do not trust these sources and suggest that the comitia curiata was formed toward the end of the monarchical period. Scholars are divided on this issue. Even in the same encyclopedia, *Civilizations of the Ancient Mediterranean*, two scholars (Ferguson and Staveley) offer opposing viewpoints. Comparative study of ancient state formation has shown that when political divisions are justified as representing preexisting lineages, those claims should not be trusted without close investigation. Claims for the antiquity of lineage often cannot be trusted because lineages are such malleable categories. For example, often there is a person in one's family who is not recognized as part of the family tree. Or even more simply, some people take their name from their father's side of the family, some from their mother's side, some from their spouse's side, and still others from somewhere else entirely. It would be hard to imagine trying to piece together a family's heritage if it was recorded only in ancient documents.

The King

The origin of kingship is ascribed to the founding of the city by Romulus, and he is considered by tradition to be the first king. But the exact nature and origin of early kingship has been obscured by time. There is a strong ancient tradition that the king and Senate came into existence together, but the exact nature of the relationship between the two in early times is unclear.

Kingship in Rome was not hereditary (Cornell 1995: 141). That is to say, kingship did not pass from father to son because of the blood connection between the two. However, a king could appoint men to powerful positions—in essence giving them assistance on the road to kingship. Succession at this time was theoretically very orderly. The first step, after the previous king was no longer able to govern, was that the Senate nominated an *interrex* (interim king), who would be the leader of Rome for five days (Ferguson 1988: 649). During these five days, the interrex would choose a king. This choice probably had to be ratified by the comitia curiata (although scholars disagree on this), and the interrex would continue to make suggestions until the curiae affirmed one of his choices.

The king was the head of state and held the office for a life term. He was responsible for the finances of Rome, for lawmaking, and for the armed forces

Romulus on horseback, cheered by a crowd of Romans. (Library of Congress)

(Ferguson 1988: 649). The king was also the religious head of Rome, with various cultic staff reporting to him.

The Reforms of Servius Tullius

Servius Tullius (578–535 B.C.E.) became king through what may have been atypical means. He may have come to power because of the influence of his predecessor, who seemed to have gained the throne through a coup (Staveley 1988: 496). However it was that he came to power, Servius Tullius radically altered the governmental organization and created a framework that would last into the Republican period (Heurgon 1973: 146).

We know of the reforms of Servius Tullius through the writings of Cicero, Livy, and Dionysius, although the accounts are not contemporary with the reforms and do not agree on all of the details. Likely much of what these historians describe came later than Tullius, as their descriptions of the system under Tullius seem very similar to descriptions of the political system during their own time (Heurgon 1973: 149). One must be careful when reading modern scholars' observations; many of them take these accounts completely at face value and basically just paraphrase the ancient accounts.

One of the major reforms was the reorganization of the tribal system (Heurgon 1973: 152–153). Many modern scholars follow the ancient historians, who claim that Servius Tullius divided Roman territories into twenty tribes (Ferguson 1988: 650). This is not likely, since this was well before the period of Roman expansion, when Rome started gaining territory (Cornell 1995: 174). Many of the regions where these twenty tribes supposedly originated were not even controlled by Rome at this time! Most scholars, however, accept that the reform involved the reorganization of Rome into four tribes, each of which consisted of a quarter of the city and some surrounding land (Cornell 1995: 176). No matter how the tribes were divided, it is most important to note that the tribes were reorganized. As Last suggested, this reform altered the very way in which Romans came to identify and organize themselves (Last 1945).

Another major reform that had a lasting effect was the creation of the *comitia centuriata*. Landowners were divided into five classes, based on wealth. Landholders who did not hold enough land were called *proletarri*. Each of these classes was divided into groups of 100 men, hence *centuries*. Fraccaro noticed that these divisions corresponded with the division of the Roman legion (Fraccaro 1931). Note that each of the classes was responsible for providing 1,000 men for military service. This organization lasted into the Republican period.

REPUBLICAN GOVERNMENT

The expulsion of Tarquin (see chapter 4) marked the end of the monarchy and the beginning of the republic. The nomenclature refers to a shift in form of government, but the nature of this transition is unclear. Was it a smooth change from a single leader with a life term to two leaders elected annually? Was there an interim form of government? How rapidly did the change progress? All of these questions are asked and debated by Roman scholars. The foundation for much of the discussion on these issues lies in Polybius's description of the republican government. This foundation is discussed on page 168.

It can be stated for certain that at some point after the expulsion of the monarchy, the leadership of the state was invested in the office of *praetor* (later *consul*), which was held by two individuals, elected for a year's term. The praetors held symbols of leadership that were different from (although related to) the monarch's, but they did have the king's power of *imperium* (the power to command).

Although the powers of the head of state were curtailed with the beginnings of the republic, the powers of the aristocracy grew (Crawford 1988: 19; Walbank et al. 1990: 179). The gradual growth of aristocratic power led to what scholars call the "Conflict of the Orders" (see chapter 6). The conclusion of this conflict led to new powers for various institutions in the political life of Rome (Crawford 1988: 18). The nature of these institutions is described in the sections that follow.

The Senate

When the monarchy was driven out of Rome, the body of elders who advised the king remained in the form of the Senate. Senators were responsible for ad-

A procession of Roman senators, along the side of the Ara Pacis Augustae. (Araldo de Luca/ Corbis)

vising the two consuls (elected annually) on which legislation of the proposals submitted by the consuls should be submitted to the popular assemblies for voting. Although the Senate itself could not pass laws, it strictly controlled which legislation reached the assemblies and was, therefore, one of the most powerful political institutions within the republic (Crawford 1982: 34; Jolowicz 1967: 27; Starr 1953: 21). The Senate could also issue decrees that had "the force of law," if not an actual designation as law (Shelton 1988: 226). The Senate was also responsible for governing the provinces and senators were often sent as governors to the provinces. The Senate usually met at the Forum, in the north-west corner known as the *Curia Hostilia*. However, Senate meetings theoretically could be held in any public place within a certain distance of Rome.

The Senate was composed of men who had once held an elected position as a magistrate (see page 164). At the beginning of the republic, the Senate was limited to 300 men, but by the time of Julius Caesar there were 900. Once the man's term of service came to an end, he became a senator and remained a senator for life, although he could be expelled for misconduct (Cornell 1995: 364; Staveley 1988: 509). So, unlike modern American senators (but much like Canadian senators), Roman senators were nonelected officials serving life terms. These men were not paid for their work as senators, but it was an avenue through which prominent Roman families sought political gain.

Indeed, participation in the Senate was a luxury of the wealthy (see Schatzman 1975 for a description of senatorial wealth). Because one had to have held office to become a senator, it was necessary to have amassed enough wealth to pay for an expensive election campaign (Gelzer 1969: 110). The interests of the Senate corresponded with the interests of the wealthy and well-established families of Rome. But class-based self-interest cannot be seen as the sole motivating force of the Senate. There were senators whose actions in government were based on ideals rather than on personal political achievement (Shelton 1988: 228). And at certain periods, senators would work on behalf of the masses to sway their votes in the assemblies (Shelton 1988: 228). It was especially important to have the support of the assemblies when running for a political position.

The Assemblies

There were two main areas of civic life that were voted upon during the Republican period. Citizens voted on legislation, and they also elected government officials (Shelton 1988: 206). Legislation was never debated or discussed at an assembly, only voted upon. Unlike American representative democracy, in which citizens vote for politicians to represent them at legislative assemblies, the Romans engaged in direct democracy, in which the voters themselves were in attendance at legislative assemblies.

Although the issues could not be discussed at the assembly, often a few days before the assembly was to meet, informal meetings called *contio* were held (Taylor 1966: 2). Anyone could attend these meetings, including foreigners, women, and slaves (although none of these categories of people could vote). Normally a contio was held to familiarize the general public with an issue that was to be voted on, or to introduce the candidates for election (Taylor 1966: 15).

Voting was organized by assembly. Eligible voters met with their assembly outdoors and voted there. In order to vote, the citizen had to physically attend the assembly and, by extension, had to be in Rome. It is difficult to know how many Italian citizens actually made the journey to Rome to vote after they gained the right in the Social War (see chapter 4). Certainly this hampered the voting ability of many citizens who lived outside of the capital. Until 139 B.C.E., votes were cast aloud; after 139 B.C.E., secret ballots were used (Taylor 1966: 15).

There were four different assemblies in the Republican period: the comitia curiata, the comitia centuriata, the comitia tributa, and the concilium plebis. Remember that *comitia* does not have the same meaning as the English word *committee.* It is better translated as "assembly."

Comitia Curiata. Dating from the period of the monarchy, the comitia curiata reflected the ancient tribal divisions of Rome (Crawford 1988: 17). Each of the three tribes was divided into ten wards (curiae). In the Republican period, this assembly ceased to have a practical function. Its role was ceremonial, conferring imperium on some elected officials (Botsford 1909: 189).

Comitia Centuriata. This assembly met in the Campus Martius (Field of Mars). In the period of the monarchy, the comitia centuriata was organized into units of 100 men; this is where the name *centuriata* derives from. But throughout the Republican period, the actual number of members varied greatly. At the Campus Martius, each century had its own meeting enclosure. During the monarchy it was a military assembly, but by the republic it had become a general assembly. There were 373 centuries. As with the *comitia tributa* (assembly of tribes), voters voted as a block, meaning that if the majority of votes within a century were "yes," then that would be considered one "yes" vote and tallied along with the 372 other possible votes (Crawford 1982: 17; Staveley 1988: 489). The division into century was based on age and property value (Heurgon 1973: 147). Because there were fewer centuries of the poorer classes, the wealthier classes could vote as a block against the poor (Crawford 1982: 17; Staveley 1988: 489). At the beginning of the Republican period, this was the major assembly, voting on whether to go to war, electing magistrates, and acting as an appeal court for capital cases (Adkins and Adkins 1994: 39). As the Republican period progressed, more and more power was in the hands of the comitia tributa and the concilium plebis.

Comitia Tributa. This was the assembly of the tribes. The name derives from the division of voters into thirty-five tribes, based on the supposed origins of one's ancestors and/or one's own geographic origin. Voting occurred at the Forum in Rome, with basically the same system as the comitia centuriata, when summoned by a consul, praetor, or tribune. The function of this assembly was to vote for some magistrates, vote on some legislation (legislation put forward by a magistrate), and act as a court of appeal in noncapital cases (Adkins and Adkins 1994: 39).

Concilium Plebis. Structured as thirty-five blocks, like the comitia tributa, the plebeian assembly also met in the Forum, with participation restricted to plebeians (see chapter 6). Established early in the Republican period, after 287 B.C.E., it made decisions that were binding on all citizens, not just plebeians. The actual power of this assembly depended on the mood in the Senate at the time (Heurgon 1973: 194). When the senators supported the concilium plebis, this group could be very influential. But when the group was not favored, the Senate could find ways to restrict its powers.

Magistrates

Magistrate refers to an elected governmental office in Rome (Schiller 1978: 172). Two individuals filled each office—individuals holding the same office were called *collegae* (Schiller 1978: 176). Most of these positions were held for one-year terms. Once an individual had been elected a magistrate for the first time, that citizen was eligible to be a senator, a nonelected position (Shelton 1988: 210).

After 180 B.C.E., the offices for which a citizen was eligible to run were determined by his age and which offices he had previously held (Schiller 1978: 178). This was called the *cursus honorum* (the course of honors). The course of honors (in this usage the word *honors* is best rendered in English as "political offices") was a legalized system, but occasionally an individual would advance ignoring these rules. Pompey's rise to prominence is an example of someone ignoring the cursus honorum (see chapter 4).

The ideal path was that a citizen would have spent at least ten years in a military or judicial position. After this period, he would be eligible to run for the lowest level of office—that of *quaestor,* and, with usually a two-year interval between each office, slowly progress to higher offices. Practically, the upper-level honors were dominated by a select group of powerful Roman families.

Magistrates held one of two types of power in Rome. The upper-level offices held *imperium,* which gave power in a military setting, and the power to enact the death penalty. The comitia curiata theoretically granted imperium, but this was, practically speaking, a symbolic role. Lower-level magistrates held *potestas,* which was the power granted by their specific office.

Quaestors.   This was the lowest level of magistrate, and ideally the first step in the cursus honorum. A man could be elected quaestor at the age of 27 (true of most of the Republican period) and at this time would be able to gain entry into the Senate. The number of quaestors varied along with the size of Rome's external holdings (Schiller 1978: 187). Serving a variety of functions, quaestors were responsible for both public records and the treasury (Adkins and Adkins 1994: 42; Schiller 1978: 187). Outside of Rome, they were responsible for paying the army and administering finances for the governor (Jolowicz 1967: 49).

Aediles.   There were usually four *aediles* at a given time, serving a one-year term. Elected by the comitia tributa, two were plebeians, and two were *curule* (officials with state authority). These individuals were in charge of much of the Roman infrastructure. From the maintenance and building of public works (e.g., aqueducts) to the regulation of weights and measures, the aediles kept the city of Rome running smoothly (Schiller 1978: 186). Until the reign of Augustus, the aediles were also responsible for public games (Schiller 1978: 176). This responsibility placed aediles in a very public setting and provided them with much exposure. Throwing expensive games was a sure way of attracting votes, so even though the position of aedile was not a mandatory position along the cursus honorum, it was a useful political stepping-stone.

Praetors.   At least thirty-nine years of age, praetors were judicial figures. With the initial dissolution of the monarchy, praetors took over responsibilities that had been the king's, including military power (Schiller 1978: 181), although this office later came to be known as consul. As the Republican period progressed, the military responsibilities of the praetors ceased, but they retained the power of imperium. Elected annually by the comitia centuriata, the praetors also issued an edict of law annually (Jolowicz 1967: 46). The number of praetors varied, as did their jurisdiction. For example, the *praetor urbanus* was responsible for law within the city of Rome (Jolowicz 1967: 47). These responsibilities somewhat overlapped with those of the *praetor peregrinus,* who dealt with foreigners (Jolowicz 1967: 47).

Consuls. This is the Roman office after which the American office of president is modeled. The consul was elected for one year. The exact regulations concerning who was eligible for election to this office changed throughout the Republican period. Two consuls served at a time; this acted as a balance and check on their individual authority. Citizens had to be thirty-six years old (later forty-two years old) to be elected consul. Until 150 B.C.E., consuls could not be reelected until a ten-year span had elapsed. After 150 B.C.E., reelection was banned outright, although in fact, many consuls were reelected after this ban. Nominated by the Senate, consuls were elected by comitia centuriata (Jolowicz 1967: 44).

The consul chaired Senate meetings and ensured that the decisions the Senate made were carried through. Primarily, though, the consul was the commander of military forces (Jolowicz 1967: 45; Schiller 1978: 182). In this role, the consul would lead the Roman military on foreign campaigns.

Censors. Censor was the highest position that could be held by a magistrate in a nonemergency situation. The office was held for an eighteen-month period, and was elected by the comitia centuriata (Adkins and Adkins 1994: 43; Jolowicz 1967: 50; Schiller 1978: 183). The specific responsibilities of the censor made it a very powerful position in Rome. The censor registered all citizens, ensuring that they were classified properly for tax and voting purposes (Jolowicz 1967: 50). He was also responsible for commissioning public works and the use of public land (Schiller 1978: 183). As a moral authority in Rome, the censor could expel senators from the Senate (Jolowicz 1967: 50).

Dictator. During a state of emergency, the Senate had the power to nominate a dictator, who acted as supreme commander for six months (Jolowicz 1967: 54), which was the length of time that war was engaged in during a year. The nomination of a dictator did not mean that other magistrates lost their powers. But the dictator did gain complete control over military and judicial matters (Jolowicz 1967: 54). Julius Caesar was the last dictator in Rome (until the twentieth century, at least).

Pro-praetors and Pro-consuls (Promagistrates). In order to cope with the growing size of Rome's territories, Roman government developed the legal concept of prorogation (Staveley 1988: 509). This allowed the powers of a praetor or consul to be extended to another individual for a specific period. It also allowed the pro-praetor (or pro-consul) to act "in the place of" the prae-

Bust of Caesar, Vatican Museum, Rome, Italy. (Corel Corporation)

tor or consul (Ferguson 1988: 652). Usually this extension was made for the purpose of a military campaign. It was an important innovation that allowed the republican form of government to still govern effectively over an ever-increasing territory (Ferguson 1988: 654).

IMPERIAL GOVERNMENT

When Augustus became the first emperor (see chapter 4), the Roman political system underwent another massive transformation. Authority was fully centralized in the figure of the emperor, who was emperor for life. Augustus modernized, clarified, and restructured much of the Roman political system. Through a series of carefully calculated steps, Augustus built upon republican principles to centralize leadership in one personality.

The Emperor

The emperor was the supreme commander of the empire, with authority derived from popular support and most importantly, his complete authority over the military (Campbell 1984: 25; Salmon 1966: 39). In Rome, the emperor's military authority was displayed through the Praetorian Guard. Popular support came from the holding of games, the presiding over of public functions, and a variety of other means. Imperial patronage curried and reinforced popular support. His role as a legislator must not be overlooked, because the emperor was the main source of law. The emperor chose which of his sons would succeed him, and if he had no sons, would designate a successor by adopting him and declaring his adopted son the next emperor.

The Senate

Theoretically, under the empire, the Senate's powers were extended. Its decrees came to have the rule of law behind them and did not require ratification by a popular assembly (Goodman and Sherwood 1997: 94). However, in practice, the powers of the Senate were drastically reduced, beginning with the granting of increased powers to Augustus (Staveley 1988: 524). Augustus reduced the Senate—which had grown to more than 1,000 members—to 600 members. It remained at around this number until the last years of the imperial period. Furthermore, Augustus added a property qualification. Individuals had to possess a certain amount of land before being eligible for senatorial service.

The Senate did retain a certain number of powers. It retained control over the state treasury, and individuals sent by the Senate governed some of the provinces (Goodman and Sherwood 1997: 95). Certain legal proceedings were enacted in the Senate (usually proceedings that involved one of its members or an upper-class family). Various matters of infrastructure were controlled by the Senate, and the occasional foreign embassy was received. But for the most part, the Senate as a body had lost much of its power. Individual senators, however, could gain a great deal of power through their relationship to the emperor (Goodman and Sherwood1997: 96), although depending on the emperor, this was not always a safe venture.

Statue of Augustus Caesar, Vatican Museum, Rome. (Library of Congress)

The emperor, technically, received his power as a gift from the Senate. Although Augustus and the first emperors after him attempted to demonstrate some deference (though only in speech) to the Senate, later emperors lost the sensibility that deference to the Senate was a political necessity. Indeed, as the Senate became increasingly less important as a political body, the disdain of the emperor only grew. Furthermore, the Senate lost much of its influence to the class directly below it (Staveley 1988: 524)—the equine (see chapter 6). More and more, positions that previously had been senatorial jobs went to the equites, further undermining senatorial authority and power.

Magistrates

In the imperial period, the cursus honorum grew even more and the number of magistrates was greatly increased (Bowman et al. 2000: 227). Election to magistrate was no longer a responsibility of the comitia. This body ceased to have an effective function. Rather, the Senate gained control of the power to elect magistrates, many of whom came from senatorial ranks.

Magistrates after Augustus officially shared their power with the emperor. And the emperor had the power to appoint magistrates. This power was fundamental in retaining the emperor's absolute control over the Senate. The institution of the office of city prefect was an important imperial appointment to this end (Staveley 1988: 523). The city prefect had many responsibilities that overlapped with the other magistrates', but its authority superseded all of the other magistrates'. In many ways, these other magistrate offices became more honorific than politically effective.

One of the fundamental developments in the history of governance that occurred during the imperial period was the transference of administrative powers from the hands of elected magistrates to nonelected government officials (Staveley 1988: 523). At this time, a true institutionalized bureaucracy arose. Many of these new, permanent bureaucrats came from the house of the emperor or from the equine class. Although technically the equine class was below the senatorial, this group gained in power through the patronage of the emperor.

The Praetorian Guard

Augustus installed a standing army in the city of Rome itself, which became known as the Praetorian Guard. This guard consisted of nine cohorts of 500 men and acted as the emperor's personal military force. The Praetorian Guard enforced the emperor's will within the city of Rome and was under his direct control (Campbell 1984: 114). Under normal circumstances there were two commanders who wielded considerable power.

THE ADMINISTRATION OF EMPIRE

In Roman studies, nomenclature can be particularly confusing. Caesar is both a name and a title. Rome is both a city and a culture. The word *empire* is another term that has different uses. In the context of Roman studies, *empire* describes two distinct situations. First, it refers to the period of Roman history ruled by an emperor (from the end of Augustus's reign until Oadacer's conquest). Second, it describes a kind of power relationship, in which a center (or core) exercises authority over a periphery. Rome developed these kinds of power relationships (an empire) during the Republican period, so it is correct to say that there was a Roman Empire before the imperial period! This section

An engraving of the Roman Praetorian Guard. (Pixel That)

will deal with the second use of empire and explain how Rome administered areas outside of Rome proper.

The origin, nature, and aims of Roman imperialism are issues of controversy among modern scholars. It is safe to say that after the defeat of the Latin League in 338 B.C.E., Rome took a new position in relation to its neighbors. The Latin cities became *municipia* (municipalities) of Rome. The municipia had different statuses in relation to Rome. Some were fully incorporated into the Roman government and were granted all the rights and obligations of citizenship. However, this was more of a theoretical granting of rights than a practical one. Because all governance took place in Rome, citizens who lived away from Rome were not able to participate in governance as fully. Other municipia did not gain the rights of citizenship, but were still incorporated into Roman governance. The population of the municipia had the right (and was encouraged) to engage in business with Romans as well as to marry them. This was arguably the most effective means the Romans had of ensuring stability and loyalty to Rome. By tying local elites' social and economic welfare to the welfare of greater Rome, it ensured that the local elites would remain loyal.

Another means Rome used to expand into new territory under the republic was through the creation of *coloniae* (colonies). Colonies were cities built by the Romans and settled with people brought from other parts of the empire. These cities were built in astonishingly uniform fashion, mirroring Rome on a smaller scale, but in faraway locations. These "mini-Romes" were usually established in locations of strategic importance, ensuring that Roman values permeated throughout the Mediterranean.

As Roman power expanded beyond Italy, new systems of administration had to be incorporated. Larger territories were divided into provinces. The provinces were placed under the authority of a governor. Governors with the rank of *pro-consul* were elected from the senatorial ranks for a one-year term. During the imperial period, governors could be appointed directly by the emperor, with no fixed-term limit. These governors were called *imperial legates*. A permanent, professional staff did not assist governors. Rather, they brought an entourage, which included assistants, advisors, junior senators, and a military detachment with them to the province. During the imperial period, the equestrian class (now no longer responsible for providing cavalry) would provide fiscal procurators who were responsible for taxation and similar matters in the periphery. Taxation is discussed in more detail in chapter 5. The main responsibilities of the governors were to defend the frontiers and to maintain order within the province.

MILITARY ORGANIZATION

The Roman military has been a subject of great interest to historians. In fact, military history is well recognized as a subset of history in general. What follows is a brief overview of the organization of the Roman military, divided into two discrete periods—the army of the republic and the army of the imperial period. Even though there is evidence for the army of the regal period, it is assumed that there were strong similarities between the regal and republican armies.

The Army of the Republic

The government of the republic was inherently related to the military organization that originated in the regal period. Initially the Roman army consisted of two major groups of men: citizen landholders and auxiliaries (people conquered by the Romans). Individuals were called up to serve for specific battles. So although it was not a standing army, the sheer quantity of battles fought ensured that property owners were called up frequently. However, these property owners could be called up to fulfill different roles in different battles; rank was not held consistently by the drafted soldiers. The organization of the Roman military was ascribed to the innovations of King Servius Tullius (Fraccaro 1931). He is said to have taken a census of the people of Rome, and from that census, military obligations were drawn up. Also, Servius Tullius is credited with introducing the Greek hoplite system into the Roman army (Cornell 1995: 183–186). Associating these innovations with Servius Tullius may, however, just reflect attempts by later Roman historians to identify the origins of institutions.

The ten-year siege of Veii (captured in 396 B.C.E.) is said to have been the impetus for the introduction of payment for soldiers (Grant 1974: 51; Watson 1987: 78). Previously, service had been compelled by the obligations of landownership. During the Veii siege, the length of campaigning became too great for landholders to be involved and still maintain economic security. The institution of payment allowed longer campaigns and campaigns that extended through the winter. It is arguable whether paying troops was meant to be a permanent feature of the Roman military when it was first brought into practice at Veii. But it certainly became a permanent feature from that point on.

Concomitant with this innovation, the phalanx formation was abolished and replaced with the maniple (Parker 1958: 26–27; Webster 1988: 710). In addition, new weapons and defensive equipment were introduced. The combination of technological and organizational innovations and an army that could campaign for longer periods of time greatly strengthened the Roman military.

The reforms traditionally associated with Marius were reactions to changing social and economic conditions in Rome (Parker 1958: 21–23). Land had increasingly been concentrated in the hands of a few wealthy landholders. The large number of poor landholders were unable to shoulder the military burdens. At the same time, landless, or poor-landed individuals, moved into the city in hopes of finding work. In response to these related situations, service in the military was opened to the poor, greatly extending the manpower base of the Roman army.

At the same time that enlistment was opened to a larger group of men, the terms of enlistment changed. Rather than enlisting for a particular campaign, men enlisted for a certain period. The legions that men joined also started taking on independent identities. Legions gained names and symbols and became recognizable as discrete organizations.

The Army of the Empire

After the Battle of Actium, Augustus controlled a huge and powerful army (see chapter 4). For Augustus, there were two major goals that needed to be met through the military (Anderson 1987: 89). The first was to secure the borders of the now quite vast Roman Empire. The second was to maintain the security of his position as sole leader of Rome. These goals were met by the spread of the military throughout the provinces—keeping the army large enough to enforce order, but small enough so as not to form an effective opposition to his command (Anderson 1987: 89–90). Augustus also further professionalized the army by instituting more regularized reward systems (Anderson 1987: 90). Particularly powerful in creating a stable environment was the institution of land grants (Anderson 1987: 90). Although unpopular with local elites (who lost land as part of this process), land grants gave veterans security and a reason to remain loyal to the status quo.

With the stationing of legions in the provinces, auxiliary forces were better able to organize and were included in campaigns (Grant 1974: 58). The regional nature of these military forces eventually worked against a unified Rome. When centralization broke down, the stronger provincial armies were in a position to raise up their men as contestants for the throne. The period of the barracks emperors (235–284 C.E.) represents the apogee of this trend.

Composition of the Military

It is an oversimplification to suggest that the Roman military structure remained the same from the time of the monarchy until Constantine, but some generalizations can be made. So much has been written on Roman warfare that what follows is just a cursory overview of the important structures.

The Organization of the Legion.   The legion (from the word *legio,* which means "levying") was one of the fundamental organizing principles of the Roman army (Adkins and Adkins 1994: 51). Originally the term *legion* referred to the entire army, but after the fourth century B.C.E., it was used to designate a regiment of infantrymen. The number of legions varied through Rome's history. Each legion had a number, and after the reforms of Marius, many had names or nicknames. The numbers were given based on the order of formation (Adkins and Adkins 1994: 55). Titles were based on several criteria, including the geographic region of combat (for example, the *Parthica* legion fought the Parthians), or were used to describe a quality of that legion (for example, the legion name *Felix* means "lucky").

The members of the legion were supplied by a system established during the regal period. Each tribe was responsible for providing 1,000 men, consisting of ten subdivisions called centuries. The equites class was responsible for providing the cavalry.

Polybius provides information about the makeup of a Roman legion. It must be kept in mind that the legion Polybius described reflects legions as they were during the second Punic War. An ideal legion consisted of 4,000 infantry and 200 cavalry. Before the Marian reforms, these men were divided into thirty maniples, reflecting the wealth of the various members. There were four classes of soldiers (based on their wealth, and therefore on the equipment they owned). In descending order they were the *triarii,* the *principes,* the *hastati,* and the *velites* (cloak-wearers) (Parker 1958: 31). After Marius, the legion was divided into ten cohorts (rather than maniples) and the fourfold class distinction disappeared (Adkins and Adkins 1994: 52). However, the most skilled cohort was always the first, and the skill level decreased from there (Adkins and Adkins 1994: 52; Parker 1958: 31).

In the republic, a legion was under the direct control of a consul, a praetor, or in times of crisis, a dictator. Below this leader each legion had six tribunes (ruling in pairs for two months at a time), who each had ten centurions beneath them (one centurion for each centurie). Each centurion designated a partner—*prior centurion* (Parker 1958: 31). This system was changed under Augustus (Anderson 1987: 94–95). The legions were moved to the direct control of a *princeps* rather than a consul or pro-consul. The six tribunes were placed under the authority of the *legatus legionis* (legion commander). And below the tribunes was the *praefectus castorum* (camp prefect), a senior military man who had once held the position of chief centurion. Below him, the ranks remained very similar to those instituted during the republic.

The Cavalry.   The cavalry consisted of the horse warriors of the legion, and it was a powerful military force. Of varying size throughout the regal and Republican periods, it could be anywhere from 300 to 1,800 members strong. The role played by the cavalry in combat was taken over by the auxiliary forces in the imperial period (Adkins and Adkins 1994: 68). The cavalry consisted solely of members from the equite class, who were wealthy enough to afford the expensive equipment.

The Auxiliaries.   Although the infantry was the backbone of the Roman fighting force, it lacked specialization (Adkins and Adkins 1994: 67–68; Anderson 1987: 100; Bowman et al. 2000: 332). Frequently, forces from the region in which the campaign was being fought (normally groups previously conquered by the Romans) were called up as an added force to assist the Roman army (Grant 1974: 57). Julius Caesar gained most of his victories through the successful use of auxiliaries (Adkins and Adkins 1994: 67). In the period of the empire, these forces were used to great effectiveness. And at this time, they were used in place of the cavalry for horse-based combat (Adkins and Adkins 1994: 68).

The Navy.   Rome was late to develop a naval tradition. Because of its inland position, a strong navy was not central to an effective defense of the city. It was not until the first Punic War that Rome was forced to create a large navy. Once it gained a navy, Rome did not sustain its sea forces in the way it sustained its ground forces. Rather, navies were built in response to specific situations (Starr 1953: 36). The objectives of the Roman navy were threefold. First, the navy was responsible for controlling the seas during a battle—particularly important in the Punic Wars and the civil wars. Second, international commerce could be threatened by piracy, so the policing of waters was an important role. Third, the navy moved people and goods around the empire.

Ships were divided into fleets. Under the republic these fleets were overseen by senators; under the empire they were the responsibility of prefects. Prefects also commanded naval bases and outposts. Squadron commanders led the ships at sea, and each ship had a captain who reported to that squadron commander. Sailors were considered low-class soldiers. The Hollywood image of ships powered by slave labor is probably inaccurate. It seems that most sailors enlisted of their own free will but came from the lower ranks of society.

The Urban Forces.   Under Augustus, the city of Rome was fortified by a number of entities. The most powerful of these was the Praetorian Guard (see page 164). Similarly, Augustus established a personal bodyguard consisting of German soldiers known as the *Germani corporis custodes*. The city also had a varying number of cohorts with varying amounts of soldiers dedicated to keeping the peace within Rome. There were also a number of cohorts dedicated to fire-fighting, known as *vigiles*.

ROMAN WARFARE

Rome is often characterized as a militaristic society. Indeed, the governing system and social order of Rome seem to have evolved out of the need for military organization. The art of war under the Romans reached high levels of strength and efficiency. The strategies and tactics of the Roman military and the Roman generals have provided inspiration and ideas for many later generals, and until very recently, the study of Roman warfare was an important part of an American military education. Much has been written on the art of war in Rome. The following provides a basic orientation to this subject.

Tactics

War in the Roman period was based on principles that were very different from warfare after the Industrial Revolution. Indeed, to a modern witness, Roman warfare would have seemed very orderly. Under ideal circumstances, battle would take place in an open area. The combatants would line up against one another and rush to attack in the center. One of the strengths of the Roman army was that it was very ordered and disciplined. The Romans would create three lines (one behind the other) lengthwise to the opposition. The lines would advance one at a time, fight, and then retire. When the first line would retire (and regroup), the second would move up to take its place, and so on, until a victor was decided. However, this was the ideal situation and the underlying principle. Actual battles were much more chaotic and complicated, also involving cavalry attacks and other special forces. Indeed, the enemies of Rome did not always operate under the same principles, and Roman battle tactics developed in response.

Hoplites. Hoplite warfare originated in Greece and was a means of warfare in which a tight line of infantrymen made up the major thrust of the attack. These men would line up in a phalanx so that their armor would overlap and attack the enemy in a series of attack lines (Watson 1987: 76). Although providing a very powerful attack, battle in a phalanx position is not maneuverable and is easily routed by forces who do not attack in a tight formation.

Maniples. To make the phalanx more maneuverable, at the time of the siege of Veii, the hoplites were divided into smaller groups called maniples (Watson 1987: 86). These troops were also equipped with javelins to attack the opposition from a distance. In essence, the defensive nature of a phalanx tactic was replaced with a very offensive one. In fact, though, the defensive capabilities of a maniple were not great. One of the major weaknesses of the maniple system was the front line. Between each maniple was a gap (equally as wide as a maniple). This provided a space for enemy troops to move through and attack the interior of the army before the first assault was finished. This led to the innovation, under Marius, of the cohort system.

Cohort. Marius brought the cohort system into full effect in the Roman military (Watson 1987: 86). However, this was not an entirely original innovation. According to Polybius, Scipio Africanus used the cohort system to defeat Hannibal (see chapter 4). The cohort system solved the problem inherent in the maniple system by increasing the number of men in the combat unit. By increasing the number of men, the gap in the front lines between the units decreased, forcing enemy combatants to engage the front line directly. This was an effective strategy, combining the defensive strength of phalanx tactics with the mobility of the maniples.

Siege Warfare. The siege of cities was another important component of Roman warfare. In the Mediterranean, cities were often built on raised ground and walled. Rome used two basic strategies to break the city and gain control: attrition and the building of siege equipment. Both of these techniques were used at the site of the most infamous Roman siege—Masada in Israel (see sidebar on page 172). By encircling a city, the Roman army prevented the movement of supplies. Eventually a city would be forced to surrender, after having run out of food and possibly even water. Ramps would be built that would lead directly up to the city wall. These ramps were used to bring battering rams up to the city wall. They were constructed by infantrymen who held up their shields and marched in a tortoise formation, which protected them from attacks from the city walls (Parker 1958: 15). When a breach was made in the wall, the Roman army managed to gain entrance to the city and finish off the enemy combatants. Sometimes, instead of a rampart, the Roman forces would create a double line of earthworks to keep troops in the city, and to prevent reinforcements from entering the city. Towers were also built, from which archers could fire projectiles over the city walls.

Weapons

Weapons and armor, before the army was professionalized, were the property of the individual soldier, and brought by him to battle (see Adkins and Adkins 1994: 81–89 for more detailed descriptions of the following weapons and armor). The type of weapon and armor used by the individual reflected his position in the military. The triarii were equipped with long spears and wore full armor. The principes were also fully armored but carried javelins. Also wearing armor were the hastati, who carried a shield, a sword, and two javelins. The lowest class of soldier, the velites, wore no armor and used a sword, light javelins, and light shields. After the reforms of Marius, all soldiers wore armor and carried a shield and javelin. Normally, the heavy javelin used by the Roman forces was called a *pilum*. It was designed to break on impact. This was of great benefit; once it was thrown, the enemy could not pick up the javelin and throw it back against the Roman troops (Adkins and Adkins 1994: 86).

Beyond the infantry, other weapons were used. Archers used bows and

Masada

An account of the siege of Masada can be found in the writings of Josephus. Archaeological excavations at the site have also shed light on this infamous event. Masada is located in the Judean Desert, close to the Dead Sea, in Israel. The site rises high above the surrounding plain and is not easily accessible. Excavated in 1963 and 1965 by Yigael Yadin, the site is a tourist attraction today. It was the last outpost to fall to the Roman army in the First Jewish Revolt (66–74 C.E.). According to Josephus, Jewish zealots occupied the site in 66 C.E., and maintained control until 73 C.E. The Roman army, under Flavius Silva, brought the Tenth Legion to Masada in 72 C.E. The Romans applied two major strategies against the fortress. First, by encircling the perimeter and setting up camp, they prevented the occupants of Masada from leaving for reinforcements or supplies. The Jewish zealots had supplied themselves well, however, knowing that the Romans would use this strategy. Second, the Romans constructed a huge siege ramp (still present today) to bring siege equipment up to use against the wall. According to Josephus, when a breach was made in the wall, the zealots committed suicide rather than submit to Roman rule.

Masada, Israel; the northern palace. (Nathan Benn/Corbis)

arrows. Usually the bow was a composite bow (wood reinforced by animal horns and sinew). Arrows were made of wood, with iron or bone tips. Crossbowlike devices that could propel bolts or stones at the enemy from a great distance were used. In addition, *ballistae* were used, which were stone-throwing machines that were effective at great distances and against walls. Catapults (called *onagers*) had an even greater range and power than ballistae.

Examples of various weapons and devices of war used by the Romans. (Pixel That)

Naval Warfare

Naval warfare was very different from land combat. The heart of Roman naval combat was the warship (although there were actually a variety of ship types in the Roman fleet). The Roman warship was based on Greek designs and shipbuilding traditions (Adkins and Adkins 1994: 72). Warships were built by first laying out the keel, then adding the hull planks. The hull planks were fitted together with mortise and tenon joints, which kept the planks firm against one another. Frames were added after this to provide strength. There were three major types of warships, *trireme, quadrireme,* and *quinquereme* (Adkins and Adkins 1994: 72). These names likely derived from the number of men who worked each oar—the more men needed, the larger the ship. Warships were propelled mainly by oarsmen during battle; the sails were stowed when in combat.

During the Punic Wars, when Rome was forced to take to the seas for battle, one particular innovation called the *corvus* (crow) gave the Romans an edge over the Carthaginians. The corvus was basically a drawbridge fitted with an iron spike. A Roman ship could pull up next to an enemy vessel and lower the drawbridge (which would be secured with the iron spike) onto it. Roman soldiers could run across the corvus and slaughter the sailors on the enemy vessel. Not only would this disable an enemy vessel, but it also provided another ship for the Roman navy!

Military Life

The duration of service required of conscripts and volunteers varied throughout Roman history. Under Augustus, the typical term was sixteen years; later this was extended to twenty years. Auxiliary forces had longer terms, and Praetorian guards had shorter terms of service. Men between the ages of seventeen and forty-six were eligible for military service (Adkins and Adkins 1994: 76; Webster 1988: 705). Soldiers were forbidden to marry while in the service (Parker 1958: 237–238). Training, according to Josephus, was also a part of everyday life for the soldier. Josephus contrasts this with the armies of other peoples, who trained only before battle. Under the monarchy and the republic, soldiers were not paid for their services. Military service was an obligation for landholding. The long siege at Veii changed this, and soldiers began to receive payment. Beyond the structured payments provided to soldiers, military men expected to share in the booty of any campaigns. Often this was the most significant method of wealth accumulation available to the troops. Later in the imperial period, veterans could expect to receive land grants for services rendered—often in the provinces in which they had served.

Roman Army Camps

Very distinctive to the Roman army was the building of military camps. The custom in the ancient Mediterranean was to billet troops within towns that were close to the arena of battle. However, this meant a great disruption of life for the residents of those towns. Soldiers are not known for reserved behavior when off duty, and towns with billeted troops would often suffer as though they had been besieged. But by not keeping Roman soldiers in the towns, Rome could engage in warfare without unduly disrupting the life of the communities nearby.

To the Romans, order and discipline were virtuous. The layout of a military camp was fairly standard, although it varied over time. It consisted of tents, laid out like a small city, on level ground and in an orderly fashion. There were specific sections designated for equipment and animals. Defenses were laid out around the perimeter, and guards were stationed.

BIBLIOGRAPHY

Abbott, Frank, and Allen Johnson. 1926. *Municipal Administration in the Roman Empire.* Princeton: Princeton University Press.

Adcock, Frank. 1940. *The Roman Art of War under the Republic.* New York: Barnes & Noble.

———. 1959. *Roman Political Ideas and Practice.* Ann Arbor: University of Michigan Press.

Adkins, Lesley, and Roy Adkins. 1994. *Handbook to Life in Ancient Rome.* Oxford: Oxford University Press.

Alföldy, Géza. 1988. *The Social History of Rome.* Baltimore: Johns Hopkins University Press.

Anderson, Alistair. 1987. "The Imperial Army," pp. 89–106 in *The Roman World.* 2 vols. John Wacher (ed.). New York: Routledge & Kegan Paul.

Badian, E. 1958. *Foreign Clientelae.* Oxford: Clarendon Press.

———. 1968. *Roman Imperialism in the Late Republic.* Ithaca: Cornell University Press.

Balsdon, J. 1979. *Romans and Aliens.* Chapel Hill: University of North Carolina Press.

Botsford, George. 1909. *The Roman Assemblies.* New York: Macmillan Company.

Bowman, Alan, Edward Champlin, and Andrew Lintott (eds.). 2000. *The Cambridge Ancient History,* Volume 10, *The Augustan Empire, 43 B.C.–A.D. 69.* London: Cambridge University Press.

Brunt, Peter. 1966. "The Roman Mob." *Past and Present* 35.

———. 1971. *Social Conflicts in the Roman Republic.* London: Chatto & Windus.

Burton, Graham. 1987. "Government and the Provinces," pp. 423–439 in *The Roman World.* 2 vols. John Wacher (ed.). New York: Routledge & Kegan Paul.

Campbell, J. B. 1984. *The Emperor and the Roman Army.* Oxford: Clarendon Press.

Cornell, Tim. 1995. *The Beginnings of Rome.* New York: Routledge.

Cowell, F. R. 1980. *Life in Ancient Rome.* New York: Perigee Books.

Crawford, Michael. 1982. *The Roman Republic.* Cambridge: Harvard University Press.

———. 1988. "Early Rome and Italy," pp. 9–38 in *The Oxford Illustrated History of the Roman World.* John Boardman, Jasper Griffin, and Oswyn Murray (eds.). Oxford: Oxford University Press.

Earl, Donald. 1967. *The Moral and Political Tradition of Rome.* Ithaca: Cornell University Press.

Errington, Robert. 1972. *The Dawn of Empire: The Rome's Rise to World Power.* London: Hamish Hamilton.

Ferguson, John. 1988. "Roman Administration," pp. 649–666 in *Civilization of the Ancient Mediterranean: Greece and Rome.* Michael Grant and Rachel Kitzinger (eds.). New York: Charles Scribner's Sons.

Fraccaro, Plinio. 1931. "La storia dell'antichissimo esercito romano e l'età dell'ordinamento centuriato," pp. 91–97 in *Atti II Congresso nazionale di studi romani* 3.

Friedländer, Ludwig. 1910. *Roman Life and Manners under the Early Empire*. London: Routledge & Sons, Ltd.

Gabba, E. 1976. *Republican Rome, the Army and the Allies*. Berkeley: University of California Press.

Garnsey, Peter. 1970. *Social Status and Legal Privilege in the Roman Empire*. Oxford: Clarendon Press.

Gelzer, Matthias. 1969. *The Roman Nobility*. Robin Seager (trans.). New York: Barnes & Noble.

Goodman, Martin, and Jane Sherwood. 1997. *The Roman World 44 B.C.–A.D. 180*. New York: Routledge.

Grant, Michael. 1974. *The Army of the Caesars*. New York: Charles Scribner's Sons.

Gruen, Erich. 1995. *The Last Generation of the Roman Republic*. Berkeley: University of California Press.

Harris, William. 1979. *War and Imperialism in Republican Rome, 327–70 B.C.* Oxford: Clarendon Press.

Harris, W. V. (ed.). 1984. *The Imperialism of Mid-Republican Rome*. Rome: American Academy in Rome.

Heurgon, Jacques. 1973. *The Rise of Rome to 264 B.C.* James Willis (trans.). Berkeley: University of California Press.

Hill, Herbert. 1952. *The Roman Middle Class in the Republican Period*. Westport: Greenwood Press.

Hopkins, Keith. 1980. "Taxes and Trade in the Roman Empire (200 B.C.–A.D. 400)." *Journal of Roman Studies* 70: 101–125.

Jolowicz, H. F. 1967. *Historical Introduction to the Study of Roman Law*. Cambridge: Cambridge University Press.

Keppie, L. 1984. *The Making of the Roman Army*. Totowa: Barnes & Noble.

Last, H. 1945. "The Servian Reforms." *Journal of Roman Studies* 35: 30–48.

Liebeschutz, J. H. W. G. 1987. "Government and Administration in the Late Empire," pp. 527–547 in *The Roman World*. 2 vols. John Wacher (ed.). New York: Routledge & Kegan Paul.

Lintott, Andrew. 1968. *Violence in Republican Rome*. 2nd ed. London: Oxford University Press.

MacMullen, Ramsay. 1963. *Soldier and Civilian in the Later Roman Empire*. Cambridge: Harvard University Press.

———. 1967. *Enemies of the Roman Order: Treason, Unrest, and Alienation in the Empire*. Cambridge: Harvard University Press.

———. 1974. *Roman Social Relations, 56 B.C. to A.D. 284*. New Haven: Yale University Press.

———. 1976. *Roman Government's Response to Crisis, A.D. 235–337*. New Haven: Yale University Press.

Millar, Fergus. 1977. *The Emperor in the Roman World*. Ithaca: Cornell University Press.

North, John. 1981. "The Development of Roman Imperialism." *Journal of Roman Studies* 71: 1–9.

Parker, Henry William. 1958. *The Roman Legions*. New York: Barnes & Noble.

Purcell, Nicholas. 1988. "The Arts of Government," pp. 150–181 in *The Oxford Illustrated History of the Roman World*. John Boardman, Jasper Griffin, and Oswyn Murray (eds.). Oxford: Oxford University Press.

Raaflaub, Kurt (ed.). 1986. *Social Struggles in Archaic Rome.* Berkeley: University of California Press.

Rodgers, William. 1964 [1937]. *Greek and Roman Naval Warfare.* Annapolis: Naval Institute Press.

Saller, Richard. 1988. "Roman Class Structures and Relations," pp. 549–574 in *Civilization of the Ancient Mediterranean: Greece and Rome.* Michael Grant and Rachel Kitzinger (eds.). NewYork: Charles Scribner's Sons.

Salmon, Edward. 1966. *A History of the Roman World from 30 B.C. to A.D. 138.* 5th ed. London: Methuen.

————. 1969. *Roman Colonisation.* Ithaca: Cornell University Press.

————. 1983. *The Making of Roman Italy.* Ithaca: Cornell University Press.

Schatzman, Israel. 1975. *Senatorial Wealth and Roman Politics.* Bruxelles: Latonus.

Schiller, A. Arthur. 1978. *Roman Law.* New York: Mouton Publishers.

Shelton, Jo-Ann. 1988. *As the Romans Did.* Oxford: Oxford University Press.

Sherwin-White, Adrian. 1984. *Roman Foreign Policy in the Greek East.* Norman: University of Oklahoma Press.

Starr, Chester, Jr. 1953. *Ancient Romans.* New York: Oxford University Press.

Staveley, E. S. 1972. *Greek and Roman Voting and Elections.* Ithaca: Cornell University Press.

Staveley, Stuart. 1988. "Roman Forms of Government," pp. 495–528 in *Civilization of the Ancient Mediterranean: Greece and Rome.* Michael Grant and Rachel Kitzinger (eds.). NewYork: Charles Scribner's Sons.

Syme, Sir Ronald. 1939. *The Roman Revolution.* Oxford: Oxford University Press.

Taylor, Lily Ross. 1949. *Party Politics in the Age of Caesar.* Berkeley: University of California Press.

————. 1966. *Roman Voting Assemblies.* Ann Arbor: University of Michigan Press.

Thompson, E. A. 1952. "Peasant Revolts in Late Roman Gaul and Spain," *Past and Present* 2.

Tomlin, R. S. O. 1987. "The Army of the Late Empire," pp. 107–133 in *The Roman World.* 2 vols. John Wacher (ed.). New York: Routledge & Kegan Paul.

Walbank, Frank, A. E. Astin, M. W. Frederiksen, and R. M. Ogilvie (eds.). 1990. *The Cambridge Ancient History.* Volume 7, Part 2: *The Rise of Rome to 220 B.C.* London: Cambridge University Press.

Warry, John Gibson. 1995. *Warfare in the Classical World: An Illustrated Encyclopedia of Weapons, Warriors and Warfare in the Ancient Civilizations of Greece and Rome.* Norman: University of Oklahoma Press.

Watson, George. 1969. *The Roman Soldier.* London: Thames and Hudson.

————. 1987. "The Army of the Republic," pp. 75–88 in *The Roman World.* 2 vols. John Wacher (ed.). New York: Routledge & Kegan Paul.

Webster, Graham. 1969. *The Roman Imperial Army.* Totowa: Barnes & Noble.

————. 1988. "Wars and Military Science: Rome," pp. 703–721 in *Civilization of the Ancient Mediterranean: Greece and Rome.* Michael Grant and Rachel Kitzinger (eds.). NewYork: Charles Scribner's Sons.

Wirszubski, Chaim. 1960. *Libertas as a Political Idea at Rome.* Cambridge: Cambridge University Press.

Wiseman, Timothy. 1971. *New Men in the Roman Senate.* London: Oxford University Press.

VIII CHAPTER 8
Religion and Ideology

The study of Roman religion has not prospered in modern scholarship. Although much has been written on this subject, not much of it is very good, and some scholars have gone so far as to say that there are no good books in English on Roman religion. One of the reasons for the lack of quality scholarship is that from the standpoint of classicists, Roman religion is greatly overshadowed by Greek religion. So whereas scholars have tended to look admiringly at Greek religion, with its many myths and sophisticated religious literature, they have looked upon Roman religion with scorn and disdain, often describing it as unimaginative and derivative. Roman religion is not usually considered a major contribution to the world's intellectual heritage. But these kinds of claims are difficult to back up when one actually engages with the evidence of Roman religion. And it should be remembered that it was within this theological environment that Christianity originated and Judaism thrived. Many of the major religious institutions that are perceived to have originated in medieval times are, in fact, developments from Roman institutions. There are some bright lights on the horizon of the study of Roman religion. Very recently, some excellent and methodologically sound works have appeared on the subject and hopefully, this trend will continue.

ORIGINS OF ROMAN RELIGION

Investigating early aspects of Roman religion is problematic. Most of the sources for early Roman religion actually come from periods after contact with

The Myth and Ritual School

One of the most important schools of thought in religious studies that has influenced Roman studies is what is known as the "myth and ritual school." This is a school of thought that developed out of Victorian-era comparative folklore/mythology studies, especially the work of Sir James Frazer (most famous for his work *The Golden Bough*). The myth and ritual school sees myth as inherently related to cultic practices and looks to understand mythology by its place in ritual contexts. Although not very prominent today, this was one of the dominant ways of thinking about ancient religion.

The Dead Sea Scrolls

One of the most important archaeological discoveries of all time, the Dead Sea Scrolls are documents written in Hebrew, Aramaic, and Greek that came to light on the black market in 1947. They were first discovered by Bedouin, and other documents later appeared in controlled archaeological excavations. All of these documents came from sites near the Dead Sea, but the principal location was Qumran, where many scholars believe that a group called the Essenes lived (but this is just a hypothesis). The documents are important for many reasons. Some are copies of biblical texts and are actually the earliest preserved biblical manuscripts. These are very important for biblical scholarship, especially as a means of understanding the transmission history of the Bible. But there are also many texts that are unique to Qumran, and as such, are evidence of a religious community not known from other sources.

Greece seriously influenced Roman religion. It is difficult to recognize and understand Roman traditions before the import of the Greek mythological system. This is an area where archaeology should help, but religion is one of the least understandable aspects of human civilization through archaeology. Although it is often easy to recognize temples and cultic activity, it is difficult to understand what was believed and felt by the ancients. In fact, it is an unwritten rule of archaeology that if something that has been discovered cannot be identified, it is simply labeled "cultic."

Numinous Forces and Other Scholarly Inventions

Most accounts of early Roman religion involve some discussion of numinous forces (for example, see Ferguson 1988c: 853). The word *numinous* refers to impersonal forces, usually localized in one particular area. Numinous powers are usually understood as natural forces that are neither good nor bad, but are simply the energy behind everyday phenomena. There is no anthropomorphic element of numina, meaning that they are not imagined as humans, as the Greeks imagined their deities. This is usually perceived as the earliest identifiable stage of Roman religion (North 2000: 15).

Although there is some evidence for Roman belief in the powers inherent in natural things, the idea that Roman religion experienced a phase of belief characterized by this kind of theology is mostly a scholarly fiction. When the comparative study of religion first developed during the Victorian period, it was popular to apply evolutionary-based models to all aspects of study. Until World War II, this was extremely prevalent in the social sciences, and in religious studies was popular even up to the 1970s. The evolutionary model of religion, in its most simplified form, sees religion as beginning with animism; that is, the worship of the powers of nature. This is akin to the numinous forces supposedly worshiped by the ancient Romans (for example, see Bailey 1932).

The next stage in the evolution of religion was seen as the worship of anthropomorphized deities—gods that acted like humans, as in Greek religion. The culmination of the evolution of religion, while not usually stated, is often presupposed to be monotheistic theological systems, like Christianity, Judaism, and Islam.

The descriptions that the earliest types of Roman religion revolved around the worship of numinous forces are mostly based on these notions. These suggestions cannot be completely discounted, but it is important to understand that such ideas are not based on evidence, but on preconceptions. In religious studies in general, evolutionary models of religious development have mostly been discredited. These kinds of theoretical frameworks presuppose that Christianity, Judaism, and Islam are "more advanced" religions. Mixed in with these problems is the more general issue of scholars giving priority to Greek traditions. Therefore, it will be useful now to discuss the ways in which Greek and Roman religions interacted.

Contacts with the Greek Religion

One of the most prominent misconceptions about Roman religion is that it was simply Greek religion with Latin names. This mistake is especially obvious in the study of mythology. Because mythology was never really an important part of Roman religious life (it was important in Roman historical writing, however), the Romans never developed their own set of elaborate myths (Ferguson 1988c: 854). Because of this, it has often been assumed that Roman religion was entirely based on Greek religion, but in fact, only the mythological accounts were integrated in this manner.

The situation is actually much more complex than that. When Greek influence started to become especially prominent in Roman society, there were attempts to equate Roman and Greek gods (Shelton 1988: 367). Consider Jupiter, for example. From early times, Jupiter was the supreme god of the Latin cities and was also associated with some aspects of the weather. The supreme Greek god was Zeus, who also had weather associations. It was not a large conceptual leap for the Romans to associate Zeus and Jupiter with each other, and eventually the two grew to be interchangeable in popular conceptions (Shelton 1988: 367). But what is important to note is that Jupiter was an independent deity, conceived of by the Romans long before Greek contact. Jupiter is not just the Latin name of Zeus. These identifications of one god with another led to a similar association between Roman gods and the myths of the Greeks (Ferguson 1988c: 855). So, in essence, the mythology of Greek gods became the mythology of Roman gods.

Etruscan Elements

Studies in Roman religion usually detail the aspects of Etruscan religion that were preserved in later traditions. Indeed, the importance of Etruscan religion for Roman civilization cannot be overstated. What is problematic is that we know much less about Etruscan religion than Roman religion, so it is important to be careful when reading about this subject to determine why scholars have come to the conclusions that they have. Often the modern scholarly assumptions made about Etruscan religion are based on uncritical readings of Roman accounts of Etruscan religion. This is not methodologically sound, especially because many of the later Roman writers who discussed the Etruscans actually knew very little about them. In ancient times, new concepts were often justified by claiming even older origins for them. Older was better, and more authoritative, and new things (especially religion) were not trusted. So sometimes these authors claimed Etruscan roots just to appear more legitimate.

Most later Roman sources emphasize that Etruscan religion centered on written knowledge and books of wisdom (Ferguson 1988b: 951). Unfortunately, the Etruscan language has yet to be deciphered. Classical authors did preserve Latin translations of fragments of these works, however, and they are important sources of information on Etruscan religion. Especially important for later Roman traditions were Etruscan techniques of divination. It is possible to speak confidently about Etruscan skills in the study of weather-related omens, especially those of thunder and lightning (Ferguson 1988b: 951). But this is not really "religious." The ancient omen readers treated this form of inquiry as more of a science. The discussion on divination in this book can be found in chapter 10.

DOMESTIC RELIGION

It is somewhat arbitrary to separate out religious aspects of domestic life in ancient Rome. But there are many elements of ancient home life that modern people would recognize as religious, rather than just another aspect of daily life. Many day-to-day activities could be considered religious or cultic. The home was an area in which nonvisible forces were at work, and important chores involved pacifying these forces.

Vesta

The most important deity of the household was Vesta, who was the goddess of the hearth. The hearth was central to the life of the family. It provided warmth for the house and fire for cooking food and warming water (Fowler 1922: 73). The hearth was an important life-giving force, and so was Vesta. Every day, offerings were made to her, in the form of salt cakes or other foodstuffs (Ferguson 1988e: 921). Each family member was responsible to make daily supplications to Vesta. Her prominence in Roman state religion should be understood as an extension of this protective household role to the entire state of Rome (see Shelton 1988: 361). Her only known temple was located in the Roman Forum. The vestal virgins were responsible for keeping the fires continuously lit in the temple.

Genius and Juno

The genius was the sacred fertility power held by the pater familias. This was the procreative power of the male household, the power that allowed him to have children (Ferguson 1988e: 921). It was seen as the connecting force between family members and an important link to male ancestors who came before. The major celebration for the genius was held on the birthday of the pater familias. Genii were also associated with specific areas of the house, and eventually with groups of people and cities. The symbol for the genius, if used, was the snake (Ferguson 1988e: 921). The female equivalent of the genius was the *juno*. It played a similar role in domestic cult, but was not considered as important as the genius, especially as a binding force between family members.

Lares

The pater familias was responsible for the upkeep of the *lares*, who were protective deities. They seem to have originated in one of the earliest periods of Roman religion, and it is not certain what their original role was. It is often suggested that these spirits were originally related to agriculture but eventually came to reside in the house (see Ferguson 1988e: 921). There is not much evidence for this, even though the agricultural origin of the lares is stated as fact in numerous books. One of the most important responsibilities of the pater familias was to keep a shrine to the lares, called a *lararium*, in the house, most often in the atrium (Shelton 1988a: 363). Lares outside of the household were thought to dwell on roads, especially at crossroads (Ogilvie 1969: 101).

Household Locations

Many of the divine or semidivine forces that resided within the household were associated with specific locations within the house. These locations were ones of particular danger or need for the family (Fowler 1922). Vesta and her association with the hearth, as well as the hearth's essential power in the house, have already been discussed. Other household locations had similar (although less powerful) protective deities and semidivine creatures. Particularly important locations were areas where food was kept, or liminal areas. Liminal areas are dangerous areas that border two distinct locations. The first of these forces is the one associated with doorways. The god most associated with thresholds and doorways in Roman times was Janus. It is not clear when Janus came to be associated with all thresholds. He was certainly the deity responsible for a gate located at the Roman Forum from early times. Another semidivine force associated with specific household locations was the *penates*. These spirits protected the food storage areas (Ferguson 1988e: 921; Fowler 1911). The penates required daily offerings, usually given to them by throwing food or salt on the fire. These offerings were normally presented at mealtimes. Ideally, some food offerings were left on the tables for these spirits as well (Ogilvie 1969: 102). Images of the penates were kept in the atrium. Also related to household locations was *Termina*, who was associated with property boundaries, especially in rural areas (Fowler 1922: 82). Each boundary stone had its own divine force related to Termina. These forces were worshiped in the *Terminalia* festival, celebrated every February 23 (Perowne 1969: 23).

An engraving of a household shrine found at Pompeii. (Pixel That)

A statue from the Republican period shows a Roman holding busts of his ancestors. (Gianni Dagli Orti/Corbis)

Lemures and Manes

The dead played an important role in Roman domestic life. The dangerous dead were the *lemures,* who were essentially hostile ghosts associated with the house (Fowler 1922: 85). These ghosts were often the ghosts of people who had died at a young age or otherwise unexpectedly. Because of the tragic elements of their death, these "ghosts" were considered dangerous. These haunting spirits could be kept away by performing the proper household rituals. The most important of these rituals were those held every May 9, May 11, and May 13 (Fowler 1969: 106–107).

Dead ancestors also played a role in Roman religious life and as members of the household. The ancestors were benevolent spirits known as *manes.* It seems that only later in Roman religion was each individual seen as having a manes, which was akin to a soul. Prior to this, the manes were the collective spirits of the dead, worshiped communally (Fowler 1922: 85). The most important means of worshiping these forces was through the festivals of *Feralia* and *Parentalia.*

THE ROMAN PANTHEON

The Roman pantheon was never as rigidly formalized as the Greek pantheon. There were many deities in Roman religion, and the worship of these deities was not equally prominent in all locations of the empire. There were, however, two important groups of gods in Roman religions. The earliest, most often called the Archaic Triad, consisted of Jupiter, Mars, and Quirinus. Later, the Capitoline Triad, which consisted of Jupiter, his consort Juno, and Minerva, surpassed this triad in prominence (Ferguson 1988c: 854).

The gods were seen as beings distinct from humanity. Although they could influence the everyday world, they were not assumed to have direct contact with humans in the same manner as Greek gods. Roman gods could be contacted through specific media, most commonly through ritual and divination. These indirect methods of communication allowed humans to influence the gods. Within this general framework, the Romans had many gods. Both temporally and geographically dispersed, the gods of the Romans varied considerably in time and place. It is beyond the scope of this book to detail all of the Roman gods. What follows are brief discussions of some of the more prominent Roman deities.

Jupiter

Jupiter was the supreme god of the Romans and was of considerable importance in Roman religion from earliest times until the rise of Christianity. Jupiter was a god associated with weather, and lightning especially was considered a mark of Jupiter (Adkins and Adkins 1996: 119). Very early on, Jupiter was equated with the Greek god Zeus. Likewise, in other parts of the empire, Jupiter was equated with local supreme gods, such as Amon, in Egypt (Perowne 1969: 17). The study of the many epithets of Jupiter is an area of research unto itself. Books have been written on the hundreds of titles associated with Jupiter, or forms of Jupiter, throughout Roman history. His main temple in

Jupiter in his chariot, yielding a thunderbolt. (Pixel That)

Rome was located on the Aventine Hill. Much is recorded about the cultic practices of this temple, including the interesting restrictions on the *flamines* (chief priests) of this temple (Ferguson 1988e: 911).

Mars

Mars was the Roman god of war and agriculture (Perowne 1969: 19) and was much more important in Roman religion than his Greek counterpart Ares was in Greek life. As the god of war, Mars was offered sacrifices before battles to ask for victory, and after battles in thanks for victories. The Campus Martius, named after Mars, was the field in which the Roman army practiced. As an agricultural deity, Mars is associated with the month of March, and is related to spring and regeneration (Perowne 1969: 19). This season was one for which many festivals were offered in honor of Mars. The Romans associated him with the woodpecker and the wolf (Adkins and Adkins 1996: 141). Much ink has been spilled on the discussion of whether Mars was first an agricultural god and then a war god, or vice versa. Neither side of this debate has been able to offer conclusive arguments. A notable worshiper of Mars was Augustus, who established many temples to this deity.

Quirinus

The third member of the Archaic Triad, Quirinus was a Sabine god who existed long before the founding of Rome (Perowne 1969: 21). Despite the importance of this deity, not much of certainty can be said about Quirinus. Most scholars see some evidence that Quirinus was a war god (Perowne 1969: 21). More concrete is the fact that in later times Quirinus was associated with the divine form of Romulus (see Dumézil 1970). His Sabine origins provide evidence of the importance of this population group in the early formation of Roman civilization.

Juno

Jupiter's consort, Juno, was a member of the Capitoline Triad. She came to be associated with the Greek goddess Hera, and it is likely that this Greek association caused her to be considered the consort of Jupiter. However, her existence independent of Jupiter was quite important, especially for Roman women. From earliest Roman times, Juno was associated with childbirth and marriage (Perowne 1969: 18). The festival *of Matronalia,* in which only women could participate, involved Juno. Another important festival involved husbands giving wives presents. As with Jupiter, Juno had many epithets, and different forms of Juno played different roles throughout Roman society. From the late republic on, she was often referred to as a queen. The Temple of Juno Moneta at Rome was associated with weights and measures, and records of standards for measurement were kept there.

Minerva

The third member of the Capitoline Triad, Minerva was also sometimes seen as the consort of Jupiter (Perowne 1969: 18). She came to be associated with the

Greek goddess Athena, and therefore had some warlike characteristics (Adkins and Adkins 1996: 153). But in Roman religion, Minerva's influence over issues of the mind and intelligence were more important (Perowne 1969: 19). She seems to have originally been the patroness of crafts and the creative arts. Later in Roman times, Minerva came to be prominent for her wisdom and inspirational powers. She eventually surpassed Mars as the most important military deity.

Janus

Janus was the god of beginnings, and as such, his name is usually the first spoken in Roman prayers (Adkins and Adkins 1996: 111). The month January gets its name from this deity. Related to this role, he was also the god of thresholds and doorways, and because of this he was worshiped at both the household and state levels. He was also associated with bridges, and there were at least five shrines to Janus located throughout the city, near bridges. Janus was depicted as a two-faced individual, with one face looking forward and one looking behind.

Saturn

The origins of Saturn are obscure, but he came to play an important role in Roman religion. Some Roman writers claim that Saturn was originally a Greek god, but the reasons for this claim probably stem from the Greek-seeming worship practices used in Saturn's cult. He seems to have been an agricultural deity, and some scholars have argued that the festival of Saturnalia, held in December, was originally related to winter sowing (Adkins and Adkins 1996: 200). His temple was at the foot of the Capitoline Hill. During the Republican period, Saturn's temple functioned as the state treasury.

Vulcan

Vulcan was the Roman god of fire and industry. He was associated with the Greek deity Hephaestus. Vulcan's associations with fire were both destructive and productive. The importance of fire in smelting and metal production explains Vulcan's importance for metalsmiths (Adkins and Adkins 1996: 245). There was an important cult of Vulcan in the town of Ostia. His main festival was the aptly named *Volcanalia*.

Venus

Venus was an important early deity, but unfortunately not much is known of her. She was likely a goddess of fertility and vegetation but was associated with the Greek goddess Aphrodite from very early on (Adkins and Adkins 1996: 232). This association was so strong that she eventually took over the mythology of Aphrodite in its Roman incarnations. At the state level she was important because Aphrodite was the mother of Aeneas, one of the legendary founders of Rome (Adkins and Adkins 1996: 232). Important political figures took her as a patron, including Pompey and Sulla. These traditions have obscured her original role, but this is also characteristic of her popularity in Ro-

A Roman bust of Venus. (Araldo de Luca/Corbis)

man society. Roman women were often depicted as Venus in funerary art as a means of demonstrating their virtue.

Mercury

Mercury was the Roman god of communication and trade. He was associated with the Greek god Hermes, and was frequently depicted wearing a winged hat and shoes. Mercury, while having his own temple in Rome, was never assigned a flamines (Adkins and Adkins 1996: 152), indicating that his worship in Rome never reached levels of substantial importance. But there is evidence for organized worship of Mercury among elites outside of the official state structures (especially among groups of investors). Outside of Italy proper,

Mercury was a very popular deity. According to Julius Caesar, worship of Mercury was prominent in the western empire (Adkins and Adkins 1996: 152).

Diana

Diana was a very popular goddess among Roman women and is often assumed to have originally been Etruscan. She was a hunter and was associated with the woods as well as with the moon (Adkins and Adkins 1996: 60). Diana was a virgin, but also a deity that could be invoked for assistance in childbirth (Adkins and Adkins 1996: 60). Her Greek counterpart was Artemis. But it was her role as a defender of women that made her popular with that demographic. Servius Tullius, it is said, built a temple for her on the Aventine Hill in the regal period.

Ceres

Ceres was a grain goddess in Rome and a popular goddess in Sicily. Very little is known about this deity, who was also associated with nature and regeneration (Adkins and Adkins 1996: 44). She was associated with the Greek goddess Demeter, and had an important cult center in Rome. She was worshiped in a festival that occurred annually from April 12 to April 19. The importance of grain for basic subsistence underscored the importance of Ceres, and imploring her favor was a way for farmers to attempt to gain control over something that they in fact had very little control over.

Foreign Cults

In general, however, the Romans were tolerant of other religious traditions (Ferguson 1988c: 856). This might seem strange given the traditions in Christianity and Judaism of Roman intolerance, and it is an important issue to address. To the Romans, the problem with Judaism and Christianity was that both of these traditions did not allow worship of other deities. Because of this, Christians and Jews were frequently accused of atheism, and for that they could be sentenced to death. However, for the worshipers of other, non-Roman deities, the Romans were usually tolerant as long as the worship remained within the limits of civic taste.

Isis. The cult of Isis was very popular among the elite of Rome. Isis was an Egyptian deity, worshiped in that country from early times. She was both the wife and sister of Osiris, and mother of Horus. In Egyptian myth, Isis was a powerful protective force, and stories of her protecting her infant son Horus were popular. During the Ptolemaic period in Egypt, Isis became an almost universal goddess of feminine power. By the time Isis became popular in Rome, her cult had been greatly influenced by Greek ideas and concepts. Some scholars believe that images of Isis holding Horus as an infant were influential in early Christian images of Mary holding the infant Jesus.

Apollo. Apollo was a Greek god and was always recognized as such in Roman times. He was never associated with a different Roman deity. Apollo was introduced into Rome in the early Republican period but became especially in-

The *Aeneid*

The *Aeneid* is one of the great classics of world literature. It is an epic poem, written in Latin, and composed by Virgil in the years 29 B.C.E.–19 B.C.E. Virgil tells the story of the foundation of Rome (giving credit to Aeneas, a hero from the Trojan War). Using structures and narrative devices similar to those used by Homer, Virgil glorifies the history of Roman civilization, especially the interactions between human and divine, through Rome's past. Written during the reign of Augustus, the *Aeneid* is consistent with the general artistic program under Augustus of celebrating Rome through literature.

fluential under Augustus. This deity's influence in Rome was first felt as a healing god and as an oracle. Apollo was also associated with poetry, and Virgil wrote much about him. There is a rich mythological tradition surrounding Apollo, perhaps enhanced by his relationship to poets.

Bacchus. Bacchus was the Roman version of Dionysus. Knowledge of the worship of Bacchus and the practices of the *Bacchae* is derived from Livy, but it is difficult to untangle truth from fiction. Most of the worshipers of this deity were women. These women would work themselves into ecstatic frenzies, and they ate raw flesh. Livy describes the *Bacchanalia* (the rites of worship of Bacchus) as wild and criminal. Whatever the truth of Livy's accounts, the worship of Bacchus was severely restricted by a decree of the Senate in 186 B.C.E. (North 2000: 64). Because this was a mystery cult, the initiates would not reveal what happened in the worship. This secrecy fed Roman fears that the Bacchae were conspiring against the state, so assembly of the Bacchae was forbidden (but see North 2000: 64). This did not, however, prevent private worship of Bacchus (Turcan 2000: 119).

Mithras. Mithras was a Zoroastrian deity that came to Rome in a mystery cult, with worship reserved exclusively for men. Roman Mithraists were generally men in the military who had served in the east or traders who bought and sold in the same region (Ferguson 1988c: 858). But worship of this deity became very popular beyond this group, at times rivaling Christianity in terms of numbers of worshipers. But the secret and exclusive nature of the cult prevented it from ever playing a prominent role in Roman civic life. Temples to Mithras were built into caves or other underground locations (Turcan 2000: 132). Worship consisted of a communal meal, and the priesthood was hierarchical and formalized (Turcan 2000: 132). Bulls seem to have played a prominent role in Mithraism (Perowne 1969: 102). Mithras took the form of a bull, and there is evidence that bull sacrifice was an important component.

Cybele. In 204 B.C.E., a consultation of the Sibylline Books concluded with the suggestion that the worship of Cybele be brought to Rome from Phrygia. A Ro-

Bacchus, after a relief on a Roman sarcophagus. (Pixel That)

man emissary traveled to Asia Minor and returned with the black stone that became the centerpiece of the worship of Cybele (Perowne 1969: 64). Cybele, also known as *magna mater*, was a goddess of the earth and fertility. But her worship was a bit wilder than Roman manners preferred. We are not certain how much of what was written about these worshipers is true, but it was said that the men castrated themselves and the women slashed their arms (Shelton 1988: 402). Suffice it to say, the Roman government soon restricted the nature of this deity's worship.

Judaism

Roman-period Judaism is a well-studied subject and is a discipline in its own right. Only cursory mention can be made of Judaism in this volume, but there is a considerable amount of scholarly literature on this subject. This is a period of many remarkable moments in Jewish history. On the one hand, it was in the Roman period that the Hebrew Bible (what Christians call the Old Testament) reached its final form, and it is the period of the latest biblical writings. Two important Jewish historians, Josephus and Philo, wrote during Roman times. And two other works, still important today, were completed—the Mishnah and the Talmud. On the other hand, this was also the period in which the Jerusalem Temple was destroyed. This event had a profound effect on the development of Judaism, and it was one of the contributing factors in the rise of the synagogue as the dominant location for worship and for the rise of rabbinic thought as a prominent locus of authority. Much of modern Judaism has its roots in Roman-period Judaism.

Christianity

As with Judaism, Christianity in the Roman period is a subject too large to be dealt with in this volume and is actually a discipline in its own right. Unlike Judaism, Christianity can be said to have begun in Roman times. As a fringe branch of Judaism, Christianity developed in Palestine under Roman rule. Based around the teachings of Jesus, Christianity eventually developed into the official religion of the Roman Empire. The earliest history of the Church is obscure, but most scholars agree that early Christians prepared themselves for the end of the world, which they believed was coming soon. Theological concerns shifted away from eschatology with the teachings of Paul, who spread Christianity beyond Roman Palestine. Paul and his school wrote most of the books in the New Testament in the Greek vernacular of the day, called Koine. Paul's Christianity attracted many adherents, as it was rooted in the venerable traditions of Judaism, but it did not require worshippers to follow Jewish regulations (like keeping kosher or getting circumcised). The great Christian theologian St. Augustine lived in Roman times, and much of his writings reflects a Roman conquest.

THE STATE CULT

This section on state cult, if an ancient Roman had written it, would have been part of chapter 7, the chapter about politics. With a few exceptions, the operation of the state cult was seen as an integral part of Roman governance. These cultic officials were not distinct from other elite members of Roman society and did not require specialized skills or knowledge (Beard 1988: 933). The information and skills were learned after appointment to the position. Cultic officials were elected members of the government, performing a government task.

This government task was the maintenance of the *pax deorum* (Fowler 1911: 169). This was the maintenance of the proper relationship between citizens and their gods, done through *ius divinum* (North 1988b: 982). The gods were mostly ambivalent to humans but very legalistic in their responses. In order to curry divine favor, rituals had to be performed perfectly (North 2000: 45). Any deviation from the prescribed procedure would nullify the ritual, and to gain the gods' favor it would have to be started again (North 1988b: 981; Shelton 1988: 372). The importance of this was so great that the Roman state created an apparatus dedicated to the maintenance of human-divine relationships to ensure the proper carrying out of the ritual and festival procedures (Ogilvie 1969: 100; Shelton 1988: 380). To the Romans, the proof of the efficacy of these procedures came from the continual economic and military success of the Roman Empire (Shelton 1988: 372). Misfortune at this scale was explained by improper cultic acts (Shelton 1988: 391).

The organization of the state cult was based on distinct colleges. These colleges were separate from one another; each had its own internal organization and structure. The duties of the colleges were very specific, with no overlap between the organizations (North 2000: 25). There was also an implicit hierarchy of cultic officials, with some colleges having more perceived importance in Roman life and some individual offices carrying more status (North 2000: 25–26).

The Four Colleges

There were four major colleges of Roman cultic officials that were important enough that they would regularly be consulted by the Senate: the *Pontifices*, the *augurs,* the *sacris faciundis,* and the *epulones.* The Romans themselves saw a distinction between these four colleges and the other colleges, and these four were perceived as the most important in cultic life (Beard 1988: 372). In the Republican period there is much evidence for public discussions of the nature of these institutions (North 2000: 26). An issue of great importance in Roman civic life was the method of determining who would become cultic officials (Beard 1988: 934; North 2000: 26). In the earliest phases, it seemed that the colleges themselves selected new members. But eventually the system of internal selection was modified so that the citizens of Rome voted on membership (North 2000: 27; Shelton 1988: 386). It is interesting to note the prominence of the day-to-day running of these colleges in Roman public debate.

Pontifices.   The *collegium pontificum* was the highest ranking of the Roman colleges. The members (pontiffs) were responsible for the overall maintenance of the state cult (Ogilvie 1969: 107). Festivals and other state-sponsored worship were under the control of these officials. They acted as advisors to the Senate on religious issues and oversaw some matters, including adoption and inheritance (Beard 1988: 935). Rules and regulations involving burials were also included among their responsibilities (Beard 1988: 935). In earliest times, the Pontifices may have had some responsibilities for bridge building, as the name of the organization had some linguistic connection to bridges (Ferguson 1988e: 910; Ogilvie 1969: 107). There were three pontiffs at a given time, and all had to be patricians. But by the end of the republic, the restriction on patrician membership was lifted, and the number of pontiffs increased to sixteen.

The highest-ranking cultic official in Rome was the *pontifex maximus* (Ogilvie 1969: 108). This was the chief pontiff, who also had a supervisory role over the vestal virgins. He was the major public face of the Pontifices, responsible for publishing the decrees of that body. The responsibilities of the pontifex maximus included cultic roles originally held by the king during the regal period. But along with the *rex sacrorum,* the pontifex maximus took over these responsibilities. The pontifex maximus dwelt in an official residence throughout the Republican period. In the empire period, however, the emperors filled this position until the reign of Gratian.

Augurs.   The *augurs* were the state body responsible for asking for and interpreting omens (see chapter 10). The main method for gaining signs was by taking an auspice (or a sign) from the behavior of birds. The movements and activities of birds were one of the major methods used by the Roman gods to make their will known to their human subjects. It was very important to ask for signs before major events (such as a military campaign) to make certain that the gods favored the action (Beard 1988: 935; Ferguson 1988e: 911). Signs could also come unsolicited, and it was the responsibility of the augurs to recognize such signs and report them to the Senate.

Sacris Faciundis.   The major responsibility of this college was to keep and protect the Sibylline oracles (North 2000: 54). If requested by the Senate, this group would consult the Sibylline oracles, but most of the daily activities of

The emperor as pontifex maximus: relief of Augustus as a priest on the Ara Pacis Augustae. (Araldo de Luca/Corbis)

this group were simply maintenance. Usually they were consulted only in emergencies (Ferguson 1988b: 953). The Sibylline oracles were a collection of books that, according to legend, had been acquired during the regal period. The Sibyls were ten female prophets, one of whom tried to sell books of the oracles to King Tarquinius Priscus. The king refused, so the prophet began destroying the nine books. According to legend, when only three books remained, the king broke down and bought the remainder, paying the price she had originally asked for all nine (Ferguson 1988b: 953–954). Thus went the legend of the Sibylline oracles. They remained the preserve of the *sacris faciundus* until they were destroyed in a fire in 83 B.C.E. (Ferguson 1988b: 954).

Epulones. Arguably the least prestigious of the four colleges was the *epulones,* whose main responsibility was to administer feasts and games (Beard

1988: 935). This was the least prestigious college for a citizen attempting to make a name for himself, but it was nonetheless important. And because of the public role of the epulones in game and feast settings, it was a way to make a name for oneself. The number of epulones changed through Roman history. Originally three, then seven, the eventual size of the college was ten.

The Other Colleges

There were other organizations of priests in Rome that did not have such an important role in political life. These other priesthoods did not have as much political power and were less likely to be able to influence the Senate. Nonetheless, these other organizations were considered very important in Roman religious life and were seen as important contributors to the Roman religious community.

Vestal Virgins. One of the most widely written about groups of cultic officials is the vestal virgins. As the name suggests, this organization consisted of women responsible for the public worship of the goddess Vesta. This was the same goddess that was worshiped in every Roman home as the goddess of the hearth, but in the case of the vestal virgins, Vesta was associated with the public hearth. It was important to keep the fires of this hearth burning and to keep Vesta properly supplied to ensure the continued success of Rome (Beard 1988: 935; Shelton 1988: 387).

The members of this order were more set off from regular society than the members of other Roman religious organizations. They lived in an official residence, were materially supported through state funding, and wore clothing that distinguished them from the rest of Roman society (Beard 1988: 934, 936). Originally four and later six women formed the college (Ogilvie 1969: 108). Membership was selected by the pontifex maximus from girls of patrician families, ages six to ten. These girls had to take a vow of chastity and remain virgins for thirty years, after which they were released from service (Beard 1980). After thirty years, the woman could choose whether to continue in service, and it is assumed that most did. The punishment for breaking the chastity vow was death, and there are some gruesome accounts of vestal virgins actually having being killed for breaking their vows. The method of execution was to be buried alive, as it was prohibited to strike a priestess of Vesta (Beard 1988: 935; Ferguson 1988e: 911). But this aspect should not be overemphasized. Membership in this organization was a powerful way for women to take an active role in Roman public life, in a context other than that of wife or mother (Beard 1988: 935).

Flamines. The *flamines* were the cultic officials appointed as leaders of worship for specific deities (Beard 1988: 936). There were ideally fifteen flamines at all times, each regulating the worship of different deities, although only the specifics about the flamines for three deities are known (Ferguson 1988e: 911). They were supervised by the Pontifices, but unlike the pontiffs, the work of a *flamen* was a full-time occupation (Beard 1988: 936; Ogilvie 1969: 109). As such, these priests wore distinctive clothes (including a white conical hat called an apex) and were barred from certain activities (Beard 1988: 936). We know of many of these taboo activities for the flamen of Jupiter, who could not ride horses or wear knots on his body (Ferguson 1988e: 911). We assume that there were similar (and to us, seemingly arbitrary) taboos for the other flamines that marked them off as sacred individuals, but concrete evidence is lacking.

Arval Priests.   The Arval Priests, it has been argued, were the oldest Roman religious organization. They performed cultic acts for the goddess Dea Dia (Fowler 1911: 435). Other activities involved making sacrifices and performing duties that would make the agricultural fields productive. There were a total of twelve of these priests, and the individuals were elected for life. The oldest example of Latin poetry is the *carmen arvale*, which is a song of these priests (Fowler 1922: 78).

Fetiales.   The *fetiales* were responsible for the religious components of relationships with other states and foreign peoples (Ferguson 1988e: 911). These cultic workers were responsible for ratifying treaties and declaring war against other nations. There were twenty members at a given time, and they worked in pairs (Ferguson 1988e: 911). One half of the pair was responsible for carrying the sacred herbs (the *verbenarius*). The other half of the pair (the *pater patratus*) was responsible for the oral pronouncements.

Haruspices.   Strictly speaking, the *haruspices* were never a college per se, but by the time of the imperial period, they were a formal organization that was consulted by both the Senate and the emperor. The haruspices were, like the augurs, responsible for interpreting signs and omens. There were two common methods for this—the examination of the entrails of animals and the observation of meteorological phenomena. Although the Romans considered the haruspices to be experts in Etruscan divination arts, there were, in fact, direct connections between the activities of the haruspices and similar activities in ancient Mesopotamia.

Rex Sacrorum

One of the most important religious functionaries in republican times was the *rex sacrorum*. This cultic position was created to fill in the gap caused by the expulsion of the kings (Beard 1988: 936; Ferguson 1988e: 910; Ogilvie 1969: 109). The king (in the regal period) had been responsible for a variety of religious obligations. After the expulsion of the king, the king's responsibilities were divided up between the pontifex maximus and the rex sacrorum. The rex sacrorum was appointed for life and could not hold other civic positions. He, along with his wife, was responsible for enacting various rituals and sacrifices.

ROMAN RITUALS AND FESTIVALS

Roman religious rituals and festivals were an important component of religious life. Days for these activities were called *feriae*, a term that could indicate public holidays or private celebrations. Every day of the year was designated as either *fasti* or *nefasti* (Ferguson 1988e: 912; Fowler 1911: 2). Fasti days were days on which business could be engaged in (Ferguson 1988e: 909). Nefasti, by contrast, were days on which business could not be conducted because of the solemnity of the religious festival. But feriae were not always fasti or nefasti; it depended on the situation. It was important to be aware of whether a holiday was fasti or nefasti, because the obligation not to work (if nefasti) was a legal one held by all citizens. Otherwise, individuals were not obligated to participate in the festivities.

Lupercalia

This is probably the best known of Roman festivals, as Shakespeare described it in detail in his play *Julius Caesar*. But at the same time, the significance of this celebration is not clear, and numerous ideas about its social role have been offered (North 1988b: 983). The origins of this ritual had been forgotten by the Republican period, and the deity associated with it (Lupercus) was likely a later imposition (Fowler 1969: 311; North 1988b: 984). There were two minor colleges of priests associated with this festival. On February 15 of every year, the *luperci* (as these priests were known) gathered on the Palatine. The ceremony began with the sacrifice of goats and a dog and an offering of cakes prepared by the vestal virgins (Fowler 1969: 311). Two prominent youths then had their foreheads rubbed with blood (Fowler 1969: 311). But the majority of the festival involved the luperci, who, wearing only parts of the recently sacrificed goats, ran through town slapping people with strips of skin cut from the goats (Fowler 1969: 311; North 1988b: 983).

Saturnalia

One of the most important Roman festivals (and the basis of the Christian holiday of Christmas), *Saturnalia* officially occurred on December 17, but in actual practice the celebrations could last until December 25 (Fowler 1969: 268). This roughly coincided with the winter solstice, and the principal focus of the celebration was the god Saturn. The festivities commenced with a sacrifice at the Temple of Saturn, followed by a large public feast (Fowler 1969: 271). At home, celebrants were expected to treat each other well, and slaves expected to be treated like equals for the duration of the celebrations (Fowler 1969: 272; Shelton 1988: 385).

Parentalia

This festival commemorating the dead was an annual event that lasted from February 13 to 21 (Fowler 1969: 306). Quite a bit is known about the actual celebration of this festival from the writings of Ovid. Over the course of this celebration, civic structures were mostly closed, as were temples. In general, although it was a state-sanctioned festival (with the vestal virgins performing some rituals), most of the celebration of parentalia was a private affair (Fowler 1969: 307). Most of the cultic acts of Parentalia were performed at home. But one aspect of this festival involved bringing food to the tombs of the deceased

Metamorphoses

Like the *Aeneid*, *Metamorphoses* was written during the Augustan Age and is a Latin epic poem. But unlike the *Aeneid*, the author of *Metamorphoses*, Ovid, fell out of favor with Augustus and was banished from Rome. The work revolves around the theme of transformation, which is also the meaning of the title. Ovid collected numerous myths from Greece and the ancient Near East and reworked them in *Metamorphoses*. It is excellent literature, although scholars often suggest that the literary quality of the individual sections is variable.

(North 1988a: 997). Family members brought these offerings to the tombs of their ancestors. The last day of the Parentalia festival was marked by a public celebration called *feralia*. On feralia, offerings were brought to the tombs of the deceased in a much more public manner than throughout the earlier days of the festival (Fowler 1969: 308). The next day of the festival was a day for celebration among living family members, culminating in a large meal at home.

Lemuria

Another festival for the dead was *Lemuria*, but the dead of this festival were not the benign past ancestors of Parentalia. During Lemuria, it was the ghosts of the dead who were pacified—ghosts who could haunt the household and cause serious problems for the families (Fowler 1969: 108–109). Not much is known about state activities during this festival, but Ovid has described the private ceremonies. It was conducted over three days, on May 9, 11, and 13 (Fowler 1969: 106–107). The ritual observance of this festival centered on the performance of apotropaic magic by the pater familias at set times. The pater familias made ritualistic gestures, walked backward barefoot, and cast beans for the *lemures* (Fowler 1969: 109; North 1988c: 998). This would hopefully keep the lemures at bay.

THE CULT OF THE EMPEROR

The Roman cult of the emperor is very misunderstood, and its prominence is often overstated in popular accounts of Rome. The Romans never experienced the same level of ruler worship as did other ancient civilizations (such as the Egyptians). In fact, the living emperor was never worshiped as a deity in Rome or Italy. Classical writers used the reactions of emperors toward the concept of deification as a means of indicating approval or disapproval (Fears 1988: 1022). So, if a classical writer stated that an emperor desired worship, it was a way of painting the emperor in a bad light. On the other hand, if the emperor was described as feeling uncomfortable with such an honor, then it served as a means of describing the emperor positively. Likely these accounts had little to do with the realities of the situation.

The cult of the emperor was a cult begun after his death. Emperors were deified after they had passed away. Theoretically, if, during the cremation of the emperor's corpse, the Senate witnessed the rising of the spirit of the emperor, then that emperor was decreed divine, and a mortuary-cultic service system was established (Fears 1988: 1014–1015). Not all emperors were deified, and not all deified emperors were worshiped uniformly across the empire.

The earliest deified emperor was Julius Caesar, his status encouraged by his adopted son Augustus. This was most probably a blatant political act on the part of Augustus, because this made him, by proxy, the son of a god (Fears 1988: 1014; Taylor 1975: 181). Emperor cults were of varying popularity in different areas. In the Near East, these were extremely popular cults (including even the worship of living emperors) because of the long traditions of ruler worship (Taylor 1975: 145–148, 205). A more general emperor cult was the worship of Roma, which was a powerful means of centering religious power in Rome (Shelton 1988: 389; Taylor 1975: 147).

The cult of the emperor was a popular phenomenon. In many ways, the emperor came to be viewed as a mediating force between the people and the gods (Fears 1988: 1020). There were two specific aspects of the imperial cult that are important to mention. As with every pater familias, the emperor had a power called genius (Taylor 1975: 191), which was procreative in nature (Fears 1988: 1015). Likewise, the *numen* of the emperor was a power worshiped by the everyday Roman (Taylor 1975: 182–183). Numen was the power of divinity, and in the case of the emperor, the power was related to his imperium.

ROMAN RELIGIOUS ARCHITECTURE

Roman religious architecture was generally conservative, and many scholars emphasize the Etruscan and Greek influences on Roman temples (Boëthius 1978: 156–157). Temples did not function in ancient Rome as modern religious structures function today. They were not laid out or designed to facilitate the needs of worshipers. Rather, they were designed to fulfill the needs of the deity and to preserve varying levels of purity and sacredness. The colleges of the Pontifices and the augurs officially designated areas as sacred temples. Temples marked off space that was distinct from everyday (profane) life.

Most Roman temples were designed with the same basic principles in mind, and most had some standard features. The entrance to Roman temples tended to be at the top of staircases that led directly into the temple complex. Within the temple, the most important room was the *cella* (Nash 1944: 26). This was the sanctuary of the temple, the major religious space. Within the cella, and usually at the back, was the altar or altars, as well as cult statues representing the deity. Often these items were kept elevated above the rest of the temple floor, on podiums (Adkins and Adkins 1994: 294; Boëthius 1978: 156). Here, offerings were left for the deity and ritual observances were performed. In some later temples (especially those in Roman provincial cities) the number of cellas was increased to three (Adkins and Adkins 1994: 294). These three cellas were symbolic of the Capitoline Triad. Surrounding the entire complex were ornaments of columns (of various types), and terra-cotta facing decorations were

A Roman temple: the Maison Carré, Nîmes, France. (Library of Congress)

applied directly to the walls. Sometimes Roman temple cellas were completely round; the Pantheon was the most famous example of this architectural style (Adkins and Adkins 1994: 296; Nash 1944: 27).

ROMAN DEATH AND BURIAL

For many societies that have been rediscovered through archaeology, there is an inordinately large amount of information about those cultures' beliefs toward the dead. The Egyptians were one such culture, in that archaeologists have examined and investigated the funerary customs of these people in a higher proportion to the living world to such an extent that it has been mistakenly assumed that the Egyptians were obsessed with death. There is an opposite problem with the Romans. There is relatively little Roman writing about death and the afterlife. For an understanding of Roman funerary culture, one is forced to rely almost entirely on the archaeological record. Archaeologists with other regional specialties would be surprised about the lack of knowledge (or interest) in Roman attitudes toward the dead on the part of Roman scholars. What follows is an overview of the available data and some of the more prominent interpretations of those same data.

The Afterlife

There are a number of problems reconstructing what the Romans believed happened to a person after death. The major problem is a problem of sources—

Roman descriptions are sorely lacking. Those descriptions that are available, especially in Golden Age poetry, are very problematic. They tend to reflect the tripartite afterlife that was imagined by the Greeks (North 1988a: 999). These three main areas in Greek thought concerning where the dead dwelt were the Elysian Fields, Limbo, and Hades. All of these places appear in Roman literature, but they may be just literary references or conventions, not reflecting actual Roman beliefs in the afterlife. Toynbee has demonstrated, however, that the Romans certainly believed in the survival of the individual in some form after death (1971: 38).

Another method that scholars have used to attempt to reconstruct Roman attitudes toward the afterlife is studying changes in burial strategies. The prominence of cremation in early Roman times (as well as some isolated textual references) has suggested to some scholars that the Romans saw the dead as a collective group, undifferentiated as individuals (North 1988a: 998). A movement toward the use of inhumation indicates a change in these attitudes, since inhumation preserves the body (North 1988a: 998). These arguments are not based on very strong evidence, but they are frequently repeated in the scholarship on ancient Rome. One aspect of Roman belief is certain, however. Some part of the individual survived after death (North 1988a: 1006), whether it survived as an individual or as some sort of collective being. The proof for this lies in the prominent role of festivals honoring the dead in Roman traditions.

Funerals

When a Roman was near death, the close relatives would remain by the person, with the goal of kissing the dying family member and catching his or her last breath (Ferguson 1988e: 922). After the last breath had been taken, the name of the deceased was pronounced and vocal lamentations for the recently departed began (Ferguson 1988e: 922). The body was cleaned, dressed, and stretched out, ideally with the feet facing the door (Ferguson 1988e: 922). The body was left in display like this for a set period. After the time elapsed, the body was processed to another location, outside of the city walls (Ogilvie 1969: 104). There, ceremonies were conducted and the body was either inhumed or cremated (Ogilvie 1969: 104). After this final disposal of the body, the individuals who had shared the household with the deceased were compelled to ritually clean themselves and the house to remove the impurities caused by death.

Cemeteries, Tombs, and Sarcophagi

One of the benefits for archaeologists studying funerary customs is that some of the best finds are made in mortuary contexts. Most archaeology involves sifting through the garbage of the ancients in sites that have been abandoned. But cemeteries almost always consist of purposefully placed items that play the same role today as they did in antiquity. Grave goods (objects interred with the dead) were usually of high quality and were often in very good condition. It is not mere treasure hunting that leads archaeologists to cemeteries. There is much information that can be learned from a society based on its funerary customs. This is the subject of the following discussion.

The James Ossuary

The James Ossuary is an artifact, dating from Roman times, that has been newsworthy recently. An antiquities collector had purchased this ossuary (a funerary container for human skeletal remains) but had not realized its significance until scholars translated the Aramaic inscription on its side. The inscription reads, "James, son of Joseph, brother of Jesus." Controversy erupted soon after the preliminary publication of this find. Was this evidence for the existence of Jesus of Nazareth? Was it a fake? Did it refer to another James, Jesus, and Joseph, not of biblical fame? None of these questions has been answered yet. The box itself certainly dates to Roman times and is authentic. The inscription is more difficult. Scholars are divided on whether the whole inscription is genuine or whether just part of the inscription is authentic and a modern forger added on the mention of Jesus to raise the market value of the ossuary. As of the writing of this book, the Israel Antiquities Authority (IAA) has officially deemed the artifact a forgery; however, the criteria used by the IAA are not universally accepted as accurate without doubt.

Cemeteries. The growth of cemeteries and mortuary deposits through Roman times varied widely, so it is difficult to make overarching statements about cemeteries and cemetery layouts. The common theme, however, is that Roman law forbade the burial of human remains within the city (Nash 1944: 39; Toynbee 1971: 73). So, to investigate funerary remains, archaeologists are forced to look outside of the settlements per se, at associated complexes nearby. The examination of a necropolis can provide much information for archaeologists, but because of space considerations, this discussion is limited to the information that can be gained about funerary customs. For information on how mortuary remains can inform us about demography, see chapter 6.

The easiest cemeteries to recognize are those associated with a specific town. The necropolis of a city could be walled or unwalled, and the organization of the cemetery proper was usually haphazard (Nash 1944: 39). The lack of planning in city cemeteries can be associated both with the unpredictable relative rates of death as well as with the differential needs of the dead, based mostly on class and access to wealth (Toynbee 1971: 74–75). One of the most important examples of Roman cemetery culture is the Street of the Tombs at Pompeii, located just outside the city gates. This remarkable complex is notable not only for its size and preservation but also for the widely varying types of funerary structures in use (Toynbee 1971: 119).

Another important location for burials that followed the laws prohibiting burial within the confines of the city was along the major roads of the Roman world. Especially important was the stretch of the Via Appia near Rome itself. Huge monuments to the dead were erected along the roads, so that the dead were commemorated on a grand scale for the large volume of people traveling to and from Rome.

A less normative location for burials is associated with the Jewish and Christian communities of the Roman Empire. Catacombs refer to belowground burial complexes. They are usually quite large and very winding. Human remains (sometimes in ossuaries and sometimes in sarcophagi) were placed into carved-out niches or benches in the underground complexes. The catacombs were a method of burying large groups of people in close proximity, in much larger numbers than could be accommodated by family tombs (Toynbee 1971: 234–235). Catacombs are best known from the city of Rome itself and from Roman Palestine.

Tombs.   In Roman times there was such a large number of tomb types that it is impossible to detail all of them here. Some of the more important types are mentioned here, as well as some of the important concepts. For the Romans, an important component of the care of human remains was burial. Even cremated bodies were preferably interred in some form or another. This concept lies at the heart of the most basic type of tomb—the simple pit burial (Toynbee 1971: 101). On a slightly more complex scale were unroofed enclosure tombs. In these kinds of tombs, a small area was set off from the rest of the cemetery by walls. Within the walls, the ashes of the deceased were interred, and various mourning rituals took place within the enclosed area (Toynbee 1971: 80). Both

The Street of the Tombs, Pompeii. (Library of Congress)

of these types of inhumations were intended for one person at a time. A mausoleum was a tomb for a single person that was built on a huge scale and was frequently circular in shape (Nash 1944: 41).

Inhumations for more than one person were typically built on a grander scale than the previously mentioned tombs. Family tombs are perhaps the most notable Roman type, in which, as the name suggests, an entire family would be interred within the complex. Larger multiple burial complexes were called *columbaria* (Toynbee 1971: 113–110). A *columbarium* was a large tomb that could accommodate the ashes of literally hundreds of individuals. Normally urns or ossuaries were placed into niches carved into the walls. These were the basic types of multiple individual tombs, but it is important to be aware that there was considerable variation in style, and there were many other types of tombs not mentioned here.

Sarcophagi and Other Mortuary Equipment. Sarcophagi were essentially coffins and were an important component of Roman mortuary culture. It should be noted that both cremated and noncremated remains were placed within sarcophagi. These coffins were made in a variety of materials and with varying levels of care. Wooden sarcophagi have not survived well into modern times, but many of the more elaborate stone sarcophagi have. These stone sarcophagi are frequently covered with beautiful relief art and there are many studies of these items from an art-historical perspective.

Related to sarcophagi are ossuaries and urns that were also used to contain the material remains of the deceased. With these containers, the bodies would have to have been cremated or had only the bones interred due to the small size of the objects. For the less wealthy, simple clay or glass pots could be used as urns (Toynbee 1971: 253). But once again, there were a wide variety of types available to the Romans. Some were very elaborate ceramic, stone, or metal vessels. Some were shaped like houses or altars (Toynbee 1971: 253–255). The most frequent type was those shaped like a simple chest—rectangular in shape with simple decoration.

Also important were tombstones. These tombstones performed essentially the same function as tombstones do today. They marked the location of the burial and indicated some information about the deceased. Even the most common shape of Roman tombstones was similar to that of those found today. They were rectangular and set with the longest axis vertical, and the information was usually carved only on the front (Toynbee 1971: 246–257). The types of information inscribed varied considerably. Often the same information was built directly into tomb buildings, but for less wealthy families a tombstone was a useful means of commemoration.

BIBLIOGRAPHY

Adkins, Lesley, and Roy Adkins. 1994. *Handbook to Life in Ancient Rome.* Oxford: Oxford University Press.

———. 1996. *Dictionary of Roman Religion.* New York: Facts on File.

Bailey, Cyril. 1932. *Phases in the Religion of Ancient Rome.* Westport: Greenwood Press.

Beard, Mary. 1980. "The Sexual Status of Vestal Virgins." *Journal of Roman Studies* 70.

———. 1988. "Roman Priesthoods," pp. 933–940 in *Civilization of the Ancient Mediterranean: Greece and Rome.* Michael Grant and Rachel Kitzinger (eds.). New York: Charles Scribner's Sons.

Beard, Mary, and John North (eds.). 1987. *Pagan Priests.* Ithaca: Cornell University Press.

Beard, Mary, John North, and Simon Price. 1998. *Religions of Rome.* 2 vols. Cambridge: Cambridge University Press.

Boëthius, Axel. 1978. *Etruscan and Early Roman Architecture.* New Haven: Yale University Press.

Dumézil, Georges. 1970. *Archaic Roman Religion.* 2 vols. Philip Krapp (trans.). Chicago: University of Chicago Press.

Fears, J. Rufus. 1988. "Ruler Worship," pp. 1009–1026 in *Civilization of the Ancient Mediterranean: Greece and Rome.* Michael Grant and Rachel Kitzinger (eds.). New York: Charles Scribner's Sons.

Ferguson, John. 1988a. "Classical Religions," pp. 749–765 in *The Roman World.* John Wacher (ed.). New York: Routledge & Kegan Paul.

———. 1988b. "Divine Oracles: Rome," pp. 951–958 in *Civilization of the Ancient Mediterranean: Greece and Rome.* Michael Grant and Rachel Kitzinger (eds.). New York: Charles Scribner's Sons.

———. 1988c. "Divinities," pp. 847–860 in *Civilization of the Ancient Mediterranean: Greece and Rome.* Michael Grant and Rachel Kitzinger (eds.). New York: Charles Scribner's Sons.

———. 1988d. "Magic," pp. 881–885 in *Civilization of the Ancient Mediterranean: Greece and Rome.* Michael Grant and Rachel Kitzinger (eds.). New York: Charles Scribner's Sons.

———. 1988e. "Roman Cults," pp. 909–924 in *Civilization of the Ancient Mediterranean: Greece and Rome.* Michael Grant and Rachel Kitzinger (eds.). New York: Charles Scribner's Sons.

Fowler, William. 1911. *The Religious Experience of the Roman People.* London: Macmillan.

———. 1969. *The Roman Festivals at the Period of the End of the Republic.* 2nd ed. Port Washington: Kennikat Press.

Gardiner, Jane. 1993. *Roman Myths.* Austin: University of Texas Press.

Jones, Richard. 1987. "Burial Customs of Rome and the Provinces," pp. 812–836 in *The Roman World.* John Wacher (ed.). New York: Routledge & Kegan Paul.

Liebeschuetz, John. 1979. *Continuity and Change in Roman Religion.* Oxford: Clarendon Press.

MacMullen, Ramsay. 1981. *Paganism in the Roman Empire.* New Haven: Yale University Press.

Nash, Ernest. 1944. *Roman Towns.* New York: J.J. Augustin Publisher.

North, John. 1976. "Conservatism and Change in Roman Religion." *Papers of the British School at Rome* 44.

———. 1988a. "The Afterlife: Rome," pp. 997–1008 in *Civilization of the Ancient Mediterranean: Greece and Rome.* Michael Grant and Rachel Kitzinger (eds.). New York: Charles Scribner's Sons.

———. 1988b. "Sacrifice and Ritual: Rome," pp. 981–986 in *Civilization of the Ancient Mediterranean: Greece and Rome.* Michael Grant and Rachel Kitzinger (eds.). New York: Charles Scribner's Sons.

———. 2000. *Roman Religion.* Oxford: Oxford University Press.

Ogilvie, R. M. 1969. *The Romans and Their Gods.* London: Chatto & Windus.

Perowne, Stewart. 1969. *Roman Mythology.* New York: Paul Hamlyn.

Rose, H. J. 1948. *Ancient Roman Religion.* New York: Hutchinson's University Library.

Scullard, Howard Hayes. 1981. *Festivals and Ceremonies of the Roman Republic.* Ithaca: Cornell University Press.

Shelton, JoAnn. 1988. *As the Romans Did.* Oxford: Oxford University Press.

Taylor, Lily Ross. 1975. *The Divinity of the Roman Emperor.* Philadelphia: Porcupine Press.

Toynbee, Jocelyn. 1971. *Death and Burial in the Roman World.* Ithaca: Cornell University Press.

Turcan, Robert. 2000. *The Gods of Ancient Rome.* Antonio Nevill (trans.). New York: Routledge.

Ward-Perkins, John. 1981. *Roman Imperial Architecture.* New Haven: Yale University Press.

IX CHAPTER 9
Material Culture

ARCHITECTURAL ACHIEVEMENTS

One of the most recognizable achievements of Roman civilization is the architecture. Probably most people have a vague idea of what Roman architecture looks like (although they may confuse it with Greek architecture), as the visual power of these monuments is so effective. The modern city of Rome still incorporates ancient monuments directly into urban life. And wherever the Romans went, they left Roman-style buildings, which still dot the landscapes of Europe, Africa, and Asia. The monumental size and durable construction of Roman buildings resulted in wide-scale preservation of Roman buildings in modern times. A great deal is known about Roman architecture because so much of it has survived.

It is also lucky that Roman writings about architecture have survived, which means that we can understand what the Romans thought about their buildings. One of the most important sources is *On Architecture*, written by Vitruvius, in the period of the late republic (Ellis 2000: 14). Pliny the Younger also wrote about architecture in two letters (Ellis 2000: 14). *Satyricon* by Petronius is a satire, but because it describes domestic activities (albeit from an exaggerated perspective), it provides important evidence for the use of household space (Ellis 2000: 15).

One of the key concepts to understand about Roman architecture is standardization. The same types of buildings were supposed to look the same and function the same in every city in every province. Think of how recognizable American fast-food restaurants are wherever they are located, and how minimal local variation is. Although the Romans certainly did not operate on the same scale, it is still a useful analogy. Any Roman could, ideally, enter any house and know what the rooms were used for. Likewise, a Roman should have been able to recognize the baths in any city, and expect to find consistent features.

Public Architecture

In the imperial period, public construction was highly organized. Under the supervision of an imperial office devoted to public works, numerous bureaucrats commissioned construction projects (MacDonald 1982: 141). Often private companies were involved, but some areas always remained under the control of the imperial government. So for example, although the imperial

Vitruvius

Vitruvius was an architect and military engineer under Julius Caesar, who wrote extensively during the reign of Augustus. His writings are among the most important sources on Roman architecture and construction techniques. His treatise, *De architectura*, is well preserved and is a valuable resource for modern scholars. Although somewhat dependent on earlier architectural treatises (especially Greek), his work was original and in-depth. Vitruvius believed that architects had to be knowledgeable about all aspects of human life, as architecture affected and was affected by all aspects of life. So his treatise includes discussions of issues that would not be included in architectural manuals today.

government was solely responsible for brick making, private companies were able to construct roads (Packer 1988: 307).

Construction crews worked directly under the supervision of one individual—the architect. For this reason, much of Roman architecture can be attributed to historical individuals—an uncommon kind of knowledge in ancient studies. The craftsmen who worked beneath the architect were organized according to specialized tasks. Often scholars call these organizations "guilds." This is not the best term, because it refers to a historically specific kind of medieval organization, but it is a useful way of thinking about Roman professional organization.

The Walls of Rome.   The construction of the first city wall is attributed to the second-to-last king of Rome, Servius Tullius. Excavations of the Servian wall suggest that it was actually built much earlier. About 7 miles in length, the stone wall surrounded the earliest settlement. But Rome's growth soon spread beyond the confines of this wall. In 271 C.E., Emperor Aurelianus built a new wall to enclose the extended city of Rome (Lanciani 1967: 66). About 12 miles in length, this wall acted as a fortification for the city of Rome well into the nineteenth century. Unfortunately, this has meant that the wall has been continuously renovated, and not much of the actual ancient wall remains.

Fora.   The *fora* were open areas within Roman cities, akin to the *agora* of Greek times (Adkins and Adkins 1994: 134). Used as markets as well as meeting areas for entertainment and religious functions, the forum was the center of the Roman city (Boëthius 1978: 145; Woloch 1983: 40). In fact, in planned cities, the forum lies at the very center, and the rest of the city radiates out from this point (Boëthius 1978: 146). In Roman cities, fora were structured axially, usually surrounded by monumental architecture (Adkins and Adkins 1994: 134; Boëthius 1978: 146). They were often colonnaded as well. Fora at both Casa and Pompeii are extremely well preserved and follow this pattern.

The most famous of these was the *Forum Romanum,* which was the center of Roman religious and commercial life. Legend has it that this was the area designated by Romulus as a meeting center for the Romans. It probably became the central meeting place at some time in the sixth century B.C.E., when the marshes in the region were drained (Woloch 1983: 35). Built on a level, rectangular space at the foot of the Capitoline and Palatine Hills, the Forum Romanum was approximately 520 feet by 150 feet in size. Starting sometime in the second century B.C.E., the Forum Romanum became the meeting place of the various comitia (Boëthius 1978: 48). It was renovated frequently and was gradually surrounded by monumental architecture. Some of the more important monuments associated with this forum are the Black Stone, the Arch of Titus, the Temple of Venus, and the Severan Arch.

Basilicas. The word *basilica* has many connotations. In the strictest sense (and the sense in which it is used here) a basilica is a particular kind of building. The basilica is defined by particular architectural characteristics. The most important is the peristyle—an open central space (Boëthius 1978: 149). The peristyle of a basilica is roofed. On the other side of the columns that line each side are four aisles (called ambulatories). Basilicas were often attached to fora and used as public structures. Merchants could conduct business within if the weather was not suitable for outdoor trade (Woloch 1983: 45). They were frequently used as temples and in later times were important in Christian architecture.

Baths. An important aspect of Roman life was the public bath (see also chapter 10). Baths originated in the Greek world and are still found in modern-day Turkey. By the first century C.E., baths were found in every major Roman city, usually near the forum. Roman baths had consistent architectural features (Woloch 1983: 70). Each had a changing room (*apodyterium*). The bathrooms were organized according to temperature (Adkins and Adkins 1994: 138). There was an unheated room with a cold-water basin (*frigidarium*). Of middle-temperature range was the *tepidarium,* which was indirectly heated, and as the name suggests, provided tepid water. The hottest room was the *caladarium,* which had a hot pool and water basins. Frequently associated with baths were *palaestra,* which were essentially exercise yards (Adkins and Adkins 1994: 138; Boëthius 1978: 197).

Entertainment Complexes. Spectacle, the viewing of entertainment, was an important part of Roman social life (see chapter 10). Distinct types of public architecture were used for distinct kinds of entertainments, and these architectural types are very identifiable. For many modern people, Roman entertainment complexes are the most recognizable type of Roman architecture.

A Roman chariot-racing arena was called a circus. The most famous of these is the *Circus Maximus,* located in Rome. A circus typically consisted of two parallel sides, with one end enclosed in a semicircle. The other side held starting gates, ideally twelve (Adkins and Adkins 1994: 141). In the center of the com-

The Roman theater in Orange, France. (Library of Congress)

plex was the raceway, divided into two tracks by a long barrier (Boëthius 1978: 198). Audience members sat on either side of the circus.

Theaters were semicircular structures in which dramatic performances were staged. Roman theaters, while inherently derived from Greek theater architecture, were novel in a number of ways. Unlike Greek theaters, Roman theaters were not cut out of the hillside but were entirely freestanding architectural units (Adkins and Adkins 1994: 140; Woloch 1983: 58). This contributed to the isolated and closed-off feeling of Roman theaters; the Roman theater was separate from the rest of the world. Also adding to this feeling was the back wall of the stage (the *scaenae frons*), which rose to the full height of the theater, as did the sidewalls (Adkins and Adkins 1994: 140; Woloch 1983: 60). Smaller theaters were roofed as well (Woloch 1983: 61). The seats of the theaters were sectioned off according to social rank (Boëthius 1978: 202). The best seats in the house were the two balconies over the *cavea* (orchestra pit), in which the emperor and his retinue, as well as the vestal virgins, could sit. Rome did not have a permanent theater until 58 B.C.E., when Aemilius Scaurus built one of wood that seated about 80,000 people (Boëthius 1978: 202–203). In 55 B.C.E., Pompey had a theater built in stone (Boëthius 1978: 205–206). Later, Augustus built the Theater of Marcellus as a memorial to his dead nephew.

Amphitheaters should be distinguished from theaters, both structurally and functionally. Amphitheaters were oval (sometimes circular) in shape and were the site of spectacles like gladiatorial combat. Almost every Roman city had an amphitheater, but many of the older Greek cities did not. Unlike theaters, amphitheaters were an entirely Roman innovation. The first amphitheaters were made of wood and were located outside of Rome, in Campania (Woloch 1983: 64). Usually amphitheaters were situated on the outskirts of the city, unlike most public architecture, which was more central (Woloch 1983: 66). The center of the amphitheater was called the arena, where the spectacle took place. Awnings separated the audiences from the arena, protecting them from the violence below.

Infrastructure and Aqueducts

Among the greatest achievements of Roman civilization was the infrastructure. No civilization prior to Rome had been as skilled at building roads or supplying the urban population with its basic needs. The combination of skilled planning and advanced engineering talents facilitated Rome's development. Transportation and water management were high priorities for the Romans and were important contributions to the enduring nature of Roman civilization.

Roads and Streets. Urban streets were very narrow in Rome, often no more than alleyways cramped between towering insulae and gigantic monuments (Cowell 1980: 15; Chevallier 1976: 67). By the time of the later republic, most of the streets were made of stone or volcanic rock; previously the city streets had been dirt or gravel (Cowell 1980: 15; Chevallier 1976: 71). After the great fire of 64 C.E., Nero is said to have widened the streets considerably (Cowell 1980: 16; Chevallier 1976: 72). But two centuries later, Juvenal complained about the narrow streets of the city of Rome. Roads in cities founded later in Roman history (such as those in colonies) tended to be wider and followed a more regular plan (Carcopino 1940: 45).

"All roads lead to Rome" is the famous maxim, and, as maxims go, it is fairly accurate. From Rome, it was very easy to travel throughout Italy. The Via Aurelia led north along the western coast, and the Via Salaria linked up with that same road after traveling through the Italian interior (Chevallier 1976: 67). Both the Via Flaminia and the Via Salaria led north from Rome to the east coast (Chevallier 1976: 67). One could move straight to the east coast from Rome on the Via Tiburtina (Chevallier 1976: 67). The Via Casilino led south to the west coast. But perhaps most famous was the Via Appia, which, for 650 km, headed southeast to the Mediterranean coast (Chevallier 1976: 67). Once out of Rome, funerary monuments lined the Via Appia as tributes to the wealthy dead. Milestones were set along these roads that indicated distances. The network of roads linked people in other cities to Rome, both in the ability to travel to Rome and in a feeling of connectedness to Rome (see Laurence 1999).

Roads were built through a combination of public and private organizations. Although the Roman government (usually a consul or censor) decided what roads needed to be built, state officials contracted out the construction to private organizations that managed the work. The distinction between public and private becomes confusing because these "private" organizations frequently used armies and Roman military crews (Chevallier 1976: 84–85). The money for the construction of roads also came from a combination of public

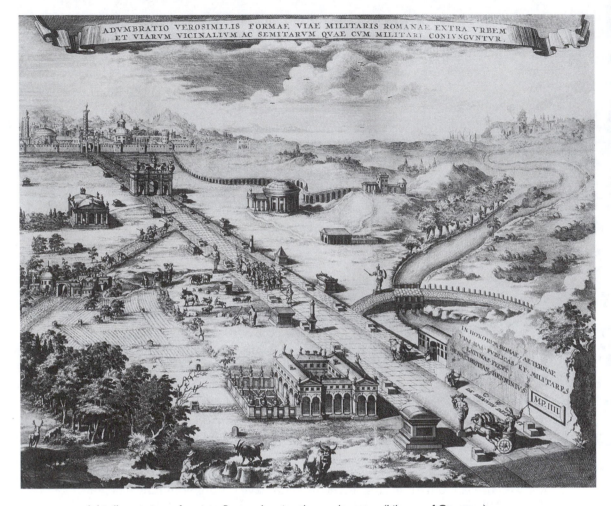

ADVMBRATIO VEROSIMILIS FORMAE VIAE MILITARIS ROMANAE EXTRA VRBEM
ET VIARVM VICINALIVM AC SEMITARVM QVAE CVM MILITARI CONIVNGVNTVR

A bird's-eye view of ancient Rome, showing the road system. (Library of Congress)

and private sources. Although the Roman government frequently paid a substantial portion of the cost, private individuals, especially the people who actually used the road, contributed to the fund (Laurence 1999: 46). In the earlier periods of expansion, Roman roads were built one at a time. But beginning with the Flavian emperors, entire networks of roads were planned and constructed in tandem (Carcopino 1940: 51; Laurence 1999: 47–48).

Roads in the countryside were constructed mostly from locally available materials. Construction began by digging a large roadbed, in the best circumstances about 15 feet wide and 3 feet deep (Chevallier 1976: 83). The bed was filled with very tightly compacted stone and gravel. Above this, a layer of sand or some other soft material was added. The pavement was placed on top of this softer material and consisted of a variety of materials. Sometimes gravel was used; other times, stones were cut to fit one another and firmly placed without mortar, as the street surface. From very early on, the Romans were aware of the importance of draining water from the roads (Chevallier 1976:

83). Because water can create a number of problems if not removed, a variety of drainage systems (dependent on the type of construction) were used to remove water and lengthen the life of the road.

Bridges. Because bridges were built to be very strong in order to support the heavy traffic, they tended to survive in the archaeological record. Roman bridges were especially well built and some are still in use today! Bridges were used over rivers and in certain dryland areas that were too hilly or depressed to allow for an even road to be built. There were three major types of bridges employed by the Romans: wooden bridges, pontoon bridges, and stone bridges (Adkins and Adkins 1994: 180–182). Each of the different kinds of bridges was based on different technological and engineering principles.

Wooden bridges were probably the earliest type of bridge built by Roman engineers. The bases of these bridges were composed of many wooden poles sunk into the bottom of the river (Adkins and Adkins 1994: 180; Boëthius 1978: 94). Looking directly down upon one of these bridge bases, one would see what looked like a bed of nails. Flat pieces of timber were then laid across the tops of these wooden poles. Because the top levels of the poles would have been even with one another, the wooden beams laid on top created a flat surface. The sheer volume of poles beneath the planks made the bridge relatively stable.

Pontoon bridges were a more temporary transportation solution. The basic concept of a pontoon bridge was to lay boats side by side across a river (Adkins and Adkins 1994: 180). Although the boats were side by side, people could move from boat to boat, leading from one bank of the river to the next. This kind of bridge was used only as a temporary means of moving across rivers, and usually only in military contexts. A notable pontoon bridge was that created by Emperor Caligula in 39 C.E.

Stone bridges were the strongest type of bridge, but they also required a considerable labor and material investment. Roman stone bridges are distinct because of the use of arches as the major source of support. The first stone bridge on the Tiber was built in 142 B.C.E. (Cowell 1980: 15). But these were not the only kinds of bridges used by the Romans, and often these technologies were used in combination with one another, especially in areas like marshlands, where variable techniques were more appropriate (e.g., wooden poles were used as the base, but limestone paving stones were used as the platform). And in some places where the river was too wide, ferries were used.

Water Management. Bringing water to a city as populous as Rome was a difficult venture, even with the abundant quantities of water nearby. Note, however, that in most parts of the empire, water was gathered directly by individuals from rivers and lakes, or through wells dug into the ground (Adkins and Adkins 1994: 135; Woloch 1983: 72). In the larger cities, however, this was impossible, so mechanisms for transporting large quantities of water were needed. The Roman solution to this problem was the aqueduct.

The initial impetus for building aqueducts in a city was the need to supply large and consistent amounts of water to the baths (Adkins and Adkins 1994:

The Pont du Gard, Nîmes, France: an aquaduct constructed during the time of Agrippina. (Library of Congress)

135). Surprisingly, the other uses of aqueducts were secondary. Since it is very difficult to block an aqueduct once it is built, these secondary uses of aqueducts (like public fountains and private water supplies) were actually mechanisms for draining water (Adkins and Adkins 1994: 136). An aqueduct began at a water source outside of the city and ran downhill to the highest point of the city, usually the center. The tunnels ran as close to the ground (ideally underground) as possible (Adkins and Adkins 1994: 135). The volcanic material around Rome (*tufa*) was quite easy to dig through, making underground tunnels very easy to construct. Sometimes, if the topographical levels varied between the water source and the city, pipes were used to siphon water uphill (Adkins and Adkins 1994: 136). Shafts were installed along the length of the aqueduct to allow repair crews to inspect and fix the aqueducts on a regular basis (Adkins and Adkins 1994: 136).

Sanitation.   Given the high degree of technological and architectural skill held by the Romans, it is surprising how unimportant sanitation was in Rome. The Romans did not connect poor sanitation and disease in the way we do today. Indeed, the impetus for sanitation and waste removal was based on aesthetic rather than health reasons. At the domestic level, cesspits were the major component of waste management technology. In apartment complexes, these cesspits were often connected through piping.

Public latrines were also an established feature of Roman cities throughout the empire. Very easily identifiable when visiting a site, a Roman public washroom consisted of benches (often set in a U shape) with holes. Various channels were cut into the stone, and water basins were in place throughout the room.

Hypocausts

The Romans were able to provide central heating for some of the public buildings and houses through hypocausts. This system of heating was remarkably simple and sophisticated at the same time. In the basement of the structure, a fire was lit when heat was desired. The heat from the fire would rise and fill the rest of the building. The movement of the heat was controlled by openings in the floor and hollowed-out walls, forcing heat to specified areas.

The stone benches were heated by a hypocaust system. Throughout Rome, urinal pots were also set up on street corners. The contents of these pots were kept for use in textile manufacturing.

Construction

When visiting a Roman archaeological site, one of the striking features one sees is the quantity of structures that have been preserved. The Romans were so skilled at building that not only do their monuments survive to the present, but everyday buildings have survived as well. Advances in architecture, engineering, and construction are some of the most important contributions that the Romans made to Western civilization, so it is worth looking at these aspects of Roman life in depth.

Surveying. An important aspect of engineering is surveying, at which the Romans were very skilled. Upon the founding of a new town the axes of the town were marked according to careful astronomical observations (Adkins and Adkins 1994: 131; Woloch 1983: 11). There is disagreement among scholars about the nature of these observations, but certainly the stars functioned as useful fixed points for measuring large spaces. The lines of the walls of the city were marked by plowing their outline into the dirt (Woloch 1983: 12). Land surveyors were called *agrimensores* (Adkins and Adkins 1994: 150). They used a *groma*, which was an instrument used for sighting land (Boyd 1988: 1697). The functional components were two arms, crossed at right angles (Adkins and Adkins 1994: 150). When the groma was set into the ground, it was possible to sight accurate square or rectangular land plots (Boyd 1988: 1697). Rural land was also surveyed and distributed on the principle of the quadrant (Boyd 1988: 1697). The surveyors would trace out the grid on the ground and divide that area into four sections by marking the two axes. The remaining space was then divided into 100 segments (*centuriae*), taking into account preexisting roads and topography. The surveyors would then allocate the land to colonists, based on a lottery system.

Building Techniques. Modern scholars know the details of Roman building techniques very well. There are a large number of treatments of the subject, with varying levels of complexity. Some of the major principles deserve a men-

The Arch

The quintessential Roman architectural feature was the arch. But it is inaccurate to suggest that it was the Romans who invented the arch, because there is evidence for arches in much earlier architecture in the Levant and Mesopotamia. The principle behind the arch is relatively straightforward. Arches, by definition, are a means of spanning an open area without using a single, flat block. The arch can hold much greater weight than the single block (usually called a lintel) because the downward weight of the arch's components and the materials set above the arch are redirected upward by the material on the side of the arch. In essence, the arch creates an upward-moving pressure rather than a downward-moving pressure. There are many different types of arches, and the Romans used many types of arches in their buildings.

tion here. The earliest Roman construction was simple, and like most of Bronze Age Europe, the dominant architectural style in early Roman periods was the wattle-and-daub hut (Boëthius 1978: 34; Packer 1988: 299). *Wattle* refers to a wall built of interlocking branches. Daub is the mud mix that is plastered over the wooden frame. These houses typically had a thatched roof and mud floors. Also used in the regal period were mud-brick structures with wooden roofs and ceramic tiles (Boëthius 1978: 34–35, Packer 1988: 299).

The Romans are actually best remembered for their skills in building with more permanent materials, such as stone. Construction in stone was based on the principle of cutting even-sized, rectangular stone blocks. The cut stones were lain in regular courses, although the exact design of the courses varied considerably. The Romans did not invent this technique; it can be found in much earlier Greek architecture. But it was certainly one of the more important methods of construction.

Roman architecture advanced beyond anything that had come before in the ancient world with the integration of concrete and arches (Boëthius 1978: 144). Concrete allowed roofed buildings to reach unparalleled sizes and extremely high shapes (MacDonald 1982: 153). Concrete was cheap and easy to form into the shape of arches. And arches were strong enough to allow monumental-sized roofs to survive.

Building Materials.   Rome had access to what was, until that time, unsurpassed quantity and variety of building materials. Not only was Italy wealthy in natural resources, but the expansion of the empire also gave access to tremendous amounts of new materials. Wood was also an important material in Roman construction. Especially in the apartment complexes, wood was used in the frames of larger structures (MacDonald 1982: 147–148). Some of the smaller architectural components were ceramic (MacDonald 1982: 150). Pipes within houses were frequently made of clay, and roof tiles were also ceramic.

Similarly, bronze and other metals were used as components of larger architectural features (MacDonald 1982: 146–147).

But stone was the most important material in Roman construction (Packer 1988: 300). The wide use of stone is one of the primary reasons that so many Roman remains are preserved today. Quarried from many locations, the major drawback of using stone was that it was difficult to transport. From about 50 B.C.E. onward, local stone (called *tufa*) was employed (Packer 1988: 300). After about 100 C.E., travertine (a type of limestone formed in hot springs) was used in construction (Boëthius 1978: 139; Packer 1988: 301). Travertine had to be brought from far away.

Marble, probably the material most associated with Roman construction, was used widely beginning in the first century B.C.E. (Packer 1988: 300). The closest source of white marble was the Colony of Luna (Packer 1988: 301; Wilson 1986: 368). Marble was sent from Luna to Rome over water (Packer 1988: 301). Colored marble was sent to Rome from all over the empire, often at great expense (Packer 1988: 301). Marble was quarried in the shape of rectangular blocks, which could then be used for either architectural construction or sculpture. Often, though, marble simply served as the façade for what were mostly concrete-based structures.

Concrete is often cited as a Roman invention. This is not technically true; there are much earlier examples of concrete use. But it is accurate to state that during Roman times, concrete took on a much more prominent role in construction contexts. Beginning with the reign of Nero, concrete was used in all kinds of building contexts, not just utilitarian contexts (Ling 1988a: 1677). Concrete, in ancient contexts, is a substance composed of mortar and larger aggregates (Packer 1988: 302; Ward-Perkins 1977: 65–66). Roman mortar was typically made by combining lime and volcanic sand (Wilson 1986: 364). These components distinctly set Roman concrete apart from earlier types of concrete, as both are well suited for this kind of use (Ward-Perkins 1977: 68). When water was added to this combination, the new substance would harden, creating a very strong but malleable building material. It would take the form of whatever mold surrounded it, making it cheaper and quicker to use than stone (MacDonald 1982: 154). Usually this concrete was faced with another material, and some scholars have suggested that the facing was the stronger structural component. This is incorrect; the concrete, after hardening, was the strongest component (Wilson 1986: 364). The facing was merely decorative or aesthetic.

Monumental Architecture

Monumental architecture is architecture built on a larger scale than most other buildings. Usually monumental architecture does not have just a functional purpose but is also deeply symbolic and meaningful. The Romans were great builders, and some of these buildings are particularly noteworthy. It would be impossible to describe all of the major Roman monuments, so a few that are particularly illustrative of Roman monumental architecture in general are presented here.

Column Types

Many have read about Aeolic, Doric, Tuscan, Ionic, Corinthian, and Composite orders, or capitals. These terms refer to styles of columns, and the names reflect the areas in which the styles supposedly originated. All but the Composite style originated before the Roman period, but all were used in Roman architecture.

The Colosseum.   More properly referred to as the Flavian Amphitheater, the Colosseum is one of the world's most recognizable ancient monuments, on a par with the Pyramid of Khufu or the Great Wall of China. We do not know the identity of the architect of this massive structure, although many scholars have made educated guesses. We do know that it was endowed by the emperor Vespasian and inaugurated by Titus in 80 C.E. The inauguration ceremony lasted for 100 days, during which more than 5,000 wild animals were slaughtered. It was spectacle of immense proportions. In a valley between the Palatine and Esqualine Hills, a lake that had been part of Nero's Golden House was drained to accommodate this large structure (Ward-Perkins 1981: 67). More than 157 feet high, the Colosseum consists of four primary levels (Ward-Perkins 1981: 68). The first floor has Doric columns, the second has Ionic columns, the third has Corinthian columns, and the fourth is one long, continuous wall. Integrated into this fourth level were poles that held up an awning that roofed the Colosseum, protecting spectators from the weather. Spectators sat on hard stone bleachers; blankets and cushions could be rented to make viewing more comfortable. Although we do not know if there was an entrance fee, we do know that food and souvenirs were sold in the galleries on the first floor.

The Pantheon.   Technically, the Pantheon should have been discussed in chapter 8 because it is a temple. But the sheer magnitude of the structure and its prominent place in the history of architecture make it worthy of discussion in an architectural context. The Pantheon was a temple built to all of the gods, and as such was a departure from the norms of Roman temple architecture (MacDonald 1982: 111; Wilson 1986: 386–388). It was built from 118 to 125 C.E. by the emperor Hadrian, but the name of Hadrian's predecessor, Marcus Agrippa, is still carved on the Pantheon. We assume that Marcus Agrippa constructed an earlier (and much smaller) version of the Pantheon (Ward-Perkins 1981: 111). The size of the Pantheon is what makes it truly spectacular. The diameter of the large domed roof is over 40 m, and it was the largest roofed building until the twentieth century (Wilson 1986: 386). The dome weighed more than 5,000 tonnes and was composed of arches made of concrete. The walls that supported this gigantic dome were more than 7 m thick. The lower sections were constructed of travertine and the upper were concrete (Ward-

Interior of the Pantheon, Rome, showing the coffered dome and the oculus. (Library of Congress)

Perkins 1981: 114). The inside feels like a wide-open space. This effect was purposely planned (MacDonald 1982: 115; Ward-Perkins 1981: 116). The interior walls are constructed of many niches, which add to the feeling of vastness.

Hadrian's Wall.   Built by Hadrian (as can be guessed from the name) between 122 C.E. and 128 C.E., Hadrian's Wall is about 120 km long. It is composed of rubble and concrete, faced with stone, and follows the topography of the land. Ditches were dug both in front of and behind the wall. A steep bank behind the wall also allowed the sentries to see for long distances. This wall marks the boundaries of the Roman Empire in Britain, roughly separating Britain and Scotland. In antiquity this wall did not act as a defensive fortification. Rather, it was a vantage point from which to watch the northern tribes, as well as a border checkpoint allowing unarmed northerners to come and go. It represented a massive investment of manpower, around 11,500 men.

Hadrian's Villa.   Another important building commissioned by Hadrian was the villa named after him, built in Tivoli, near Rome. Hadrian's Villa was constructed from 125 to 135 C.E. It is an interesting blend of a variety of architec-

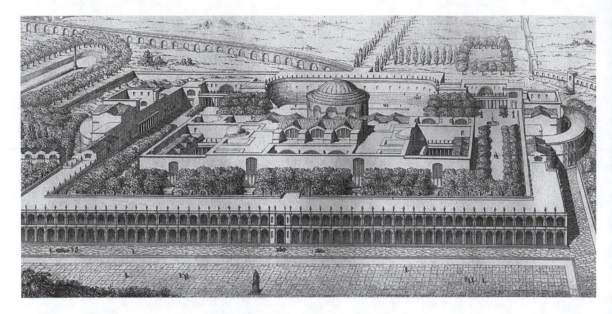

A reconstructed view of the Baths of Caracalla, Rome. (Pixel That)

tural styles. Some of the sections of the complex were named after various places that Hadrian had visited (Ramage and Ramage 1996: 184). So, for example, there was a section named the *Accademia* after the school in Athens founded by Plato. This villa was actually a unique fusion of many architectural traditions, which was unusual in Roman times.

Baths of Caracalla.   Also known as *thermae Antoniniane,* the Baths of Caracalla were remarkably large. The complex was over 11 hectares in area, and had cisterns that could hold 80,000 cubic meters of water. The *caladarium* (heated room) was domed, and itself was as large as the Pantheon. Almost 2,000 people could bathe there at one time. Constructed in 211 C.E., the baths were used until 537 C.E. Throughout their use, entrance was relatively inexpensive, making them accessible to all.

Nero's Golden House.   The *domus aurea* was a monumental palace built by Nero after the Great Fire of Rome. Nero annexed fire-devastated land in order to build this structure, and it may have been this act that led to the rumors that the emperor started the fire (Ellis 2000: 55). Essentially, the Golden House was in the style of a country estate but was located in the center of the city. The centerpiece of the complex was a large artificial lake, which later became the site of the Colosseum (Ward-Perkins 1981: 61). It was a striking structure not just for its size (Nero's contemporaries were appalled by what they considered a waste of space), but also for its many breaks with Roman architectural traditions (Boëthius 1960: 96–97, 128). For example, the octagonal rooms in the Golden House were a radical departure from the rectangular rooms typical of Roman buildings (Wilson 1986: 379).

Domitian's Palace.   Before this palace was built, the eastern half of the Palatine Hill (about 440,000 square feet) was leveled (Ellis 2000: 56). Once this was accomplished, marble from Egypt and Libya was imported, and construction was led by the architect Rabirius (Ward-Perkins 1981: 78, 80). The palace was grouped into two main sets of buildings. The *domus Flavia* was the official area, where matters of statecraft were engaged in (MacDonald 1982: 49; Ward-Perkins 1981: 80–82). The *domus Augustana* was the private residence of the royal family (MacDonald 1982: 49; Ward-Perkins 1981: 82–83). Although only rubble remains of the palace today, descriptions of it are preserved in the poetry of Statius.

Trajan's Column.   To commemorate Trajan's military victories, the Senate commissioned Trajan's column, erected in Trajan's forum. A large column, 100 feet high (30 m) and made of twenty-eight blocks of marble, it was faced with a frieze depicting the two Darian wars fought by Trajan (Ward-Perkins 1981: 87; Wilson 1986: 383). The images on the higher portion of the column were not meant to be read from the ground, but from the upper stories of surrounding buildings (but see Ward-Perkins 1981: 87). Inside the column is a spiral staircase that leads to the top. The base of the column was a funerary chamber for

Narrative relief sculpture on the Column of Trajan, showing episodes from the Dacian War. (Alinari Archives/Corbis)

Trajan. The column still stands today, but the statue of Trajan that was once atop the column was replaced by a statue of St. Peter in 1588.

Domestic Architecture

The homes in which ancient Romans lived are a fascinating subject, and there is much excellent scholarship on this subject. Not only does the study of ancient household architecture provide insight into the daily life of the average Roman, it can also tell us a lot about Roman social relationships and identities. Andrew Wallace-Hadrill has made some very important arguments about the centrality of the Roman house and domestic space in the social relationships of the ancient Romans (see Wallace-Hadrill 1994). To simplify his argument considerably, Wallace-Hadrill suggested that the house was designed and decorated as a way of communicating status and identity to the rest of the community (Wallace-Hadrill 1994). Where one lived, as well as how one lived, was a primary means of situating oneself within the larger structure of Roman society. There is much evidence for Wallace-Hadrill's interpretations. For example, in the discussion that follows, the reader will note that the reception and dining facilities in Roman houses were located at the back of the house. Guests had to traverse the entire household to reach the receiving area (Zanker 1998: 13). Along the way, these visitors were shown the entire household, which communicated messages about the owners and residents. It is possible that uninvited guests could often see far into the house from the street and view messages about the status of the house's owner. However, scholars vehemently disagree on the degree and nature of privacy in the Roman home. Some of the written accounts suggest that guards were posted at doors to help keep the residence separate from the rest of the city (Cowell 1980: 20).

Elite Homes.   Elite homes—the homes of the wealthy and higher classes—underwent many changes in style over the course of Roman history. Although individual houses were unique, it is often possible to talk about "ideal types" of houses. Indeed, although houses had generally regularized divisions of space, there was a considerable degree of difference in terms of size and luxuriousness. An ideal type of household is a hypothetical house that incorporates all possible features of a house in all of the right combinations of layout and size. Because of the rich archaeological and written record of Roman elite housing, scholars have been able to identify ideal types of houses in different periods. The house was referred to as the *domus,* although it should be noted that this word can also be used to describe buildings with a public function.

In the period of the republic (at least from about the third century B.C.E., although possibly earlier), the ideal elite house of a Roman was the atrium house (Ellis 2000: 26). Although there are many variations of the atrium house, some underlying principles have been identified by modern scholars. The name of this type of house is derived from the central feature of the structure— the atrium. In a Roman house, the atrium was square or rectangular, and it was located in the center of the building. In the earliest houses, this was the location of the family hearth, but later homes lacked this feature. Most of the

The House of the Faun in Pompeii

One of the most amazing examples of an elite Roman home is the structure known as the House of the Faun, found in Pompeii. Excavations at this house began in 1830 by the German Archaeological Institute. These archaeologists erroneously named the structure "The House of the Faun" because of the statue of a satyr found in the atrium of the house. It is also known as "The House of Goethe," because excavations on the structure began while the son of the famous poet was visiting the site. The house, while inhabited during the final days of Pompeii, preserved the styles of the period of its initial construction in the second century B.C.E. The walls are decorated in the First style, long out of fashion by the time of the house's destruction. The mosaics of the house are well preserved. At the entrance, the Latin word for "welcome" was tiled. But more remarkable was the amazing mosaic depicting the battle between Alexander the Great and Darius, found in the *exedra* of the house. One of the most fabulous Roman mosaics ever discovered, this mosaic suited the large and majestic home now known as "The House of the Faun."

atrium was roofed over, but the very center was left open. Directly beneath this opening, and embedded in the floor of the building, was a small pool called an *impluvium*. The impluvium was where rainwater collected as it entered the atrium through the opening in the roof directly above. The atrium ideally was the center of the household, with other rooms surrounding it on all sides. The main household entrance (the *vestibulum*) led to the entrance hall (the *fauces*), which led directly to the atrium (Boëthius 1978: 185; Ellis 2000: 27). The main reception room of the house, the *tablinum*, was found at the other end of the atrium (Ellis 2000: 27). The tablinum was flanked on both sides by rooms called *alae*, and both the tablinum and the alae were open to the atrium (Ellis 2000: 27). Another important room in the atrium house was the dining room. The dining room was called the *triclinium*, after the dining couches ideally found within. Most scholars stress the importance of the axial nature of private homes. By this they mean that, within the layout of the house, there was a straight line from the vestibule, through the fauces and atrium, culminating in the tablinum. Scholars used to believe that this kind of house was found only in Italy, but recent excavations have demonstrated that there may be some atrium-style houses in the western provinces (Ellis 2000: 28–31). In the east, no houses have been found so far that can confidently be described as atrium houses (Ellis 2000: 28). But remember, it is often very difficult to identify specific rooms from archaeological evidence, so these kinds of reports have to be carefully evaluated.

Gradually supplanting the atrium-style house as the most popular in Rome was the peristyle house (Elllis 2000: 31). This style of architecture was related to Greek styles, but scholars are divided about the exact relationship between

The peristyle courtyard of the House of the Two Brothers, Pompeii. (Richard T. Nowitz/Corbis)

Greek and Roman peristyle architecture (Cowell 1980: 19; Ellis 2000: 34–35). This ideal type of house has also been found throughout the western provinces, but each province developed its own unique interpretations of peristyle architecture. The term *peristyle* refers to a particular room of the house. The peristyle was an area enclosed on four sides (but still open-air), often centering on a garden. Columns surrounded the interior of the enclosure. Some scholars have seen similarities between these columns and monumental architecture in the public areas of the city. Related to the peristyle was the *oecus,* which was a dining and reception area adjacent to the peristyle (Ellis 2000: 35–37). In Rome, older atrium-style houses were not usually demolished and replaced by peristyle houses. Rather, a peristyle was added to the garden of an already-standing atrium house (Ellis 2000: 32). But throughout the period of the empire, the peristyle was *the* elite type of house (Ellis 2000: 41).

Apartment Complexes. We assume that most of the population of ancient Rome lived in apartment or tenement homes, rather than atrium or peristyle houses. Unfortunately, there is not as much archaeological evidence for this as one would hope. These buildings tended to be made out of much poorer materials (Frier 1980: 3) and have not survived archaeologically in many sites. The major exception is the port of Ostia, where there is direct evidence for this kind

An Advertisement for an Apartment Rental

Rental notices that had been painted on the walls of buildings in Pompeii have been found. One is presented here in translated form, taken from Shelton's anthology (Shelton 1988). The notice reads:

The Arrius Pollio Apartment Complex
owned by Gnaeus Allius Nigidius Maius
FOR RENT from July 1
streetfront shops with counterspace,
luxurius second-story apartments,
and a townhouse.
Prospective renters, please make arrangements
with primus, slave of Gnaeus Allius Nigidius Maius.

There are a number of interesting features about this rental ad. It shows that apartment complexes had proper names, and could be owned by an individual. There are sections with different functions available for rent, including commercial space and domestic space. Note, too, the prominent role of the slave in the business transaction.

of habitation (Boëthius 1978: 183; Ellis 2000: 73). Between archaeology and ancient writings, it has been possible to reconstruct (somewhat) the architecture of the less-privileged ancient Romans.

These apartments were part of three- or four-story buildings. Before Augustus legislated height limitations, some of them reached heights of eight or nine stories (Cowell 1980: 19). Often these apartment complexes took up entire blocks. In these situations, the blocks are called *insulae*. According to Cowell, in 350 C.E., Rome had 44,173 insulae, as opposed to 1,782 private houses (Cowell 1980: 21). The disparity between these numbers (although they are not as exact as Cowell argues) shows that the apartment complex was the dominant living quarters in Rome. Sometimes the inhabitants of the apartment complex would buy the entire floor on which they lived, but most often they would simply lease the space from a landlord.

The most common type of apartment found at Ostia is the *cenaculum* (Ellis 2000: 73; Frier 1980: 6). This kind of apartment would take up an entire floor of a building. The residents entered through a shared staircase, into a long hallway called a *medianum* (McKay 1988: 1378). The medianum ran the entire length of the apartment and was the primary entrance for the three to five other rooms in the complex (Ellis 2000: 74; Frier 1980: 5). The medianum was also the room with windows to the outside, and these windows provided air and light to the other rooms in the residence (Ellis 2000: 74). It is easy to imagine how stuffy it could become, especially in the hot Mediterranean climate. The room farthest from the staircase entrance was the dining and reception room (Ellis 2000: 74). But it should be mentioned that it is not as easy to determine room functions in apartments as it is in elite houses (Ellis 2000: 73–74).

Related to the apartment complexes, and sometimes incorporated into the insulae, were store residences. These were areas that functioned both as a store and as a residence (Ellis 2000: 78). Although there were many shops that did not function as a residence, it is important to remember that commercial and domestic spaces were not as sharply differentiated in ancient Rome as they are in North America and Europe today. Many shopkeepers (or shop workers) lived in their place of business. Most frequently, a store residence was formed from a two-room apartment (Ellis 2000: 78). The front room (the room that opened into the street) was the main commercial space, where people bought and sold goods and services (Ellis 2000: 78). The other room (either behind or above the shop room) could function as residence, storage area, workshop, or any combination of these (Ellis 2000: 78).

Villas.   Another kind of house often found within the urban environment was the villa. Most commonly, however, villas were associated with rural sites and it is likely that when they were incorporated into urban environments, they represented a conscious attempt to capture rural life (Boëthius 1978: 195). The *villa urbana* was a kind of house modeled after opulent country homes. These urban households attempted to capture elements of Greek and learned culture within the decor of the house and to create a luxurious living environment (Zanker 1998: 17, 136). Villas could be found within the city (villa urbana), on the outskirts of the city (*villa suburbana*), on the coast (*villa maritimae*), and in the countryside (*villa rustica*) (Adkins and Adkins 1994: 148).

There were many varieties and styles of villas, and it is difficult to precisely define a villa in the same way that other household types can be defined (Adkins and Adkins 1994: 148; Ellis 2000: 13). Commonly employed in the identification and definition of villas is the concept of Romanization, in which the architecture and décor have closer ties to Rome than those of the local architectural culture (Ellis 2000: 54). But there are many problems with using this concept; see chapter 11 for more on the debate about Romanization. In general, the Italian villa consisted of the *pars urbana,* which was the structure in which the owner lived; the *pars rustica,* which were the farmhouses used by the agricultural workers; as well as various storage buildings (Ellis 2000: 13–14).

Villas of many architectural styles have been identified both archaeologically and through art-historical sources. There were very small villas, called cottage villas, which consisted of a small rectangular building. There were also larger types of villas. Peristyle villas were architecturally consistent with peristyle houses in the city (Boëthius 1978: 192). Basilica farmhouses were a later innovation in the western provinces, defined by the two post rows running through the center of the main building. Courtyard villas had an inconsistent number of buildings constructed around a central courtyard (Adkins and Adkins 1994: 149). Other than the villas built entirely for the luxury of the owner, such as those along the seacoast and within the city, the villa was part of a larger farming complex. But even as parts of a farming complex, the villa lifestyle was associated with luxury.

URBAN PLANNING

The study of ancient urban planning can be very helpful in reconstructing the way space and relationships were viewed in the past. The layout of the city usually reflects how elite members understand the relationships of the various components of city life. In North American urban planning, there is generally a tendency to separate residential, industrial, and commercial spaces. Likewise, within the modern city, these zones are further subdivided by class divisions. Usually it is obvious which are the wealthy parts of town and which are the less privileged. Historians and archaeologists of Roman civilization are very lucky that there is evidence for Roman urban planning in a variety of temporal and geographic contexts. What follows is a discussion of urban planning, first in the city of Rome, and second outside of Rome. Keep in mind the points made in chapter 6 about settlement patterns.

Rome

Construction in Rome lacked an overall scheme like that employed in the construction of colonies (Boëthius 1960: 33). The massive public works projects for which Rome is so well known were built on a case-by-case basis. The rationale behind the earliest urban planning of the city of Rome has been lost, although scholars often assume it was based on Greek and Etruscan principles of how a city should look (Adkins and Adkins 1994: 131). The earliest writings tell us that Rome consisted of four major subdivisions, or urban zones. These zones were the *suburbana, esquilina, collina,* and *palatina* (Cowell 1980: 13). Augustus later reorganized the city into fourteen regions (Cowell 1980: 15).

This is not entirely consistent with what we know of Etruscan town planning, but then again, the information about Etruscan town planning is contradictory. On the one hand, Vitruvius tells us that the Etruscans built towns on a regular plan. According to Vitruvius, this plan consisted of three main streets, with three main gates. On the other hand, the Etruscan cities of Veii and Vetulonia, which have been excavated, bear no resemblance to Vitruvius's description (Boëthius 1978: 65). These cities appear to have developed haphazardly (Adkins and Adkins 1994: 131; Boëthius 1978: 65) in what some scholars call an Islamic city model, but this chapter will refer to it as a segmentary town model. In a segmentary town, the city is not planned according to even distributions of space and overarching strategies, but it is still ordered. The ordering comes from the social relationships of the various kin groups that inhabit the city. Kinship and relationships, not city planners, determine where houses are built and what the urban layout looks like. Other early cities bear a closer resemblance to Greek urban centers (Wilson 1986: 363). The city of Marzabotto has an identifiable, rectangular grid (Boëthius 1978: 69; Ellis 2000: 24). It seems very similar to earlier Greek cities, which used an urban planning model that scholars call *orthogonal.*

What all of these early cities have in common is that they are defined by the topography of the area (Boëthius 1960: 36). Rather than altering the environment, early Roman and Etruscan cities used the natural landscape as a guiding force. Indeed, the environment played an important role in urban planning throughout Roman history. Disasters and destructions provided moments for the transformation of the urban landscape on a grander scale. After the sack of Rome by the Gauls (387 B.C.E.), the city was rebuilt without much consideration for planning. Especially in residential areas, reconstruction was a free-for-all. For the most part, buildings were constructed on vacant lots, without regard for previous ownership or suitability of location.

After the Great Fire of 62 C.E., only four of the fourteen regions survived, allowing for massive rebuilding projects. Indeed, it was natural disaster that allowed the city to be rebuilt and modernized. This is probably at the heart of the accusations leveled at Nero after the fire. The emperor was accused of starting the fire to make room for massive building projects. Although the accusation was false, it demonstrated the real problem of space in the city of Rome.

Empire

Outside of the city of Rome, there were varying degrees of urban planning, depending on the circumstances of each particular city. It is obvious that many cities were not directly planned. Ostia, for example, had the same kind of haphazard development as earlier cities (Boëthius 1978: 181–183). The planning principle apparent for those cities that were planned was the conscious attempt to integrate them directly into the fabric of Roman civic life. The Romans made very conscious decisions in regard to the establishment of new towns or the methods of incorporating preexisting towns into the empire.

Preexisting towns incorporated into the empire could not be extensively reorganized without massive destruction. So overall urban plans were not used in this process. But Roman construction projects were still an important part of the process of incorporating these cities. Constructing Roman public and civic buildings in these newly conquered cities was a powerful means of directly tying the inhabitants of these cities to Roman lifestyles. The construction of buildings that were distinctly Roman helped make these cities Roman. So, although it was not urban planning per se, these kinds of construction projects were powerful means of reinforcing Roman civic identity in areas that lacked Roman civic traditions.

Colonies were cities or towns established by the Romans in a location where no settlement previously existed. Under the republic, during the period of expansion, colonies were founded in areas of weaker Roman power to shore up power in that region. Similar principles were enacted under the empire. Colonies were founded where no previous settlement existed. The principles of the urban planning were based on the same principles that underlay Roman military camps (Adkins and Adkins 1994: 131). The colony, ideally, was square-shaped and surrounded by fortifications. Within the square, the city was divided into quadrants (Adkins and Adkins 1994: 131–132). Two main roads divided the city into these quadrants; the streets were perpendicular, ideally meeting in the center of the city. Within each quadrant, roads ran parallel to the two main streets, creating blocks usually called insulae (Boëthius 1978: 183). Ideally, each insula was equipped with a public fountain that supplied running water. Civic structures were located in the center of the colony; however, those buildings related to entertainment (for example, theaters and amphitheaters) were placed on the outskirts of the settlement (Adkins and Adkins 1994: 131).

POTTERY

Ceramic artifacts are among the most frequent finds at any Roman archaeological site. Ceramics are objects made of clay that have been shaped and then fired in a kiln (a pottery oven). A ceramic object can be broken, but the pieces (called *sherds*) do not decompose like other materials. Only bone, depending on the alkali levels of the soil, can appear in more frequent quantities. This makes the study of Roman pottery important in any study of Roman material culture. Pottery and ceramics are virtually indestructible in the archaeological record.

Pottery Classification Methods

Classification of pottery is an important part of any archaeological investigation. In order to be useful, classification must be based on consistent categories. The kinds of questions asked about the pottery must be the same. This allows useful comparison of pottery from different sites. These comparisons usually involve analysis of form, ware, decoration, and production techniques. The section that follows describes the methods archaeologists use to study Roman pottery, and it will familiarize the reader with the basic terminology used in ceramics scholarship.

Form. The form of the vessel is its shape. There are standardized terms that refer to specific parts of the pot and that are used frequently in pottery analysis. Since most excavated pottery is found broken, archaeologists often initially categorize the finds based on these terms for pot parts. Sections of the pot that have identifiable features are considered diagnostic. A skilled ceramicist can recognize a pot based on a single diagnostic sherd.

The basic components of ceramic vessels are usually referred to using the following terminology. Most frequently found are body sherds. These are sherds that come from the side of the vessel but do not have any identifiable, morphological features (although they may be decorated). More important archaeologically are the diagnostic sections of the vessel. The base refers to the bottom of the vessel and is usually quite easy to identify. Usually the base is also classified according to its shape (such as flat or ring-shaped). On the other end of the pot is the mouth—the opening of the vessel. The edge of the vessel's mouth is called the lip. This is easy to remember; just like a face, the mouth is surrounded by lip. Immediately beneath the lip is the rim, which is often quite distinctly shaped. Technically the lip and rim are separate parts of the vessel, but more often than not the terms are used interchangeably. Other diagnostic parts of pottery are handles and spouts. These basic terms are used in most treatments of Roman pottery.

It is also important to know how to describe the overall shape of the vessel. The most important overall distinction is whether the vessel is open or closed. Open vessels have a mouth at least 50 percent of the size of the maximum diameter of the vessel. Closed vessels are those whose mouth is less than 50 percent the size of the maximum diameter. For example, a modern Coke™ bottle is a closed vessel, but a modern kitchen bowl is an open vessel.

Ware.   Ware (also called fabric or paste) is the material the pot is made of. It always includes clay, and it often includes other elements used as temper (a strengthening component). Temper can be sand, dung, chaff, or any number of materials. There are a number of significant classifications that can be made based on ware. Generally, however, most Roman pottery is divided into coarse or fine ware. Coarse ware often feels very rough to the touch and is very porous, because larger nonclay elements were not removed when the clay was initially mixed with water (levigation). The pottery is porous because some of these nonclay elements burned away completely in the heat of the kiln, leaving only a hole or pockmark. On the other hand, fine ware does not have many inclusions, feels smooth, and looks quite well made. There are many other categories, but these two are the most important for non–pottery specialists.

Decoration.   Decoration describes how the outside of the vessel has been manipulated for aesthetic reasons. If the outside has been manipulated for functional reasons, the decoration is better referred to as surface treatment. Because it is often difficult to determine why a potter chose to make the vessel in a particular way, it can be hard to determine whether *surface treatment* or *decoration* is the better term to use. The term *decoration* will be used for simplicity's sake.

There are many ways to describe the decoration of the vessel. *Appliqué* is any part of the vessel that was constructed separately and then attached to the vessel just before firing. *Paint* is just what it seems it would be—a painted decoration on the vessel. *Slip* is similar, but the "paint" used is made out of a thin layer of wet clay. *Wash* is a kind of slip, but much thinner. It is so thin, in fact, that you can see the original clay beneath the wash. There are many other terms that can be used, but most of them are quite self-evident, and one can understand them when encountering them.

Production Techniques.   Understanding exactly how a vessel was made is an important part of classification. It is assumed that most types of pottery were formed similarly. The clay is chosen and mixed with water and temper until it is in a moldable state. The vessel is then shaped. There are many ways of doing this. Most Roman pottery was shaped on a wheel. The potter shaped the vessel while moving the platform it was set upon (the wheel) very quickly. This same technique is used today. But there were many other techniques used in the ancient world. After its shaping, the clay has usually become hard (usually called *leather hard* because it is tough but still somewhat malleable like leather). The pot is then fired in a kiln. The kind of kiln used and the temperature of the oven substantially affect the pot. This is the typical technique assumed in pottery production. Ceramicists are interested in the minor variations in this procedure and classify the pots accordingly.

Major Categories of Roman Pottery

All of the techniques of ceramic study just listed go into the process of classifying and studying Roman pottery. Form, ware, decoration, and production technique are the major criteria for creating ceramic typologies. Since the nineteenth century, Roman ceramic studies have progressed so much that basic categories of Roman ceramics have been established and are used consistently in Roman studies. What follows is a description of the most important categories of Roman ceramics, especially those categories that are considered to be a given in Roman scholarship. This should provide enough background to read (and understand) more technical works on Roman pottery.

Fine Wares. One of the primary divisions scholars use when studying Roman pottery is the distinction between fine ware and coarse ware. Although this may seem like a subjective distinction (and technically it is), in actual practice the difference is very obvious. Fine ware is pottery of high quality, usually highly fired, thin-walled, and often covered with a slip. There are a few important subtypes of Roman fine ware that are important to be familiar with.

Campanian ware is one of the earliest types of Roman fine ware (Greene 1986: 158). Campanian ware (which is named after its location of production) is derived from Greek and Near Eastern forms. Notable for its reddish slip, this ware occurs in many forms. Chronologically, Campanian ware lasted from about 200 B.C.E. until the beginning of the common era (Hayes 1997: 37). This category of pottery is subdivided into three major phases: Campana A, Campana B, and Campana C (Hayes 1997: 37–39). Campana A is the earliest form and Campana C is the latest. Although related to each other, each subgroup of Campanian ware is easily distinguished from the others.

Perhaps the most typically Roman fine ware is *terra sigillata* ware. This pottery has a glossy red surface (created by the red slip). The pottery is usually quite thin-walled. There were many forms of terra sigillata pottery; the principal forms were cups and bowls (suitable for fluids), plates of various sizes, and bowls with molded designs (Greene 1986: 159; Hayes 1997: 43–44). It is assumed that terra sigillata pottery often represented attempts to render more expensive forms of metal vessels in clay (Hayes 1997: 42). The term for representing one item in another medium is *skewomorph.* Terra sigillata pottery is often also called *Arretine* pottery, because there was a large production center (which exported throughout the Roman world) in Arretium, but technically not all terra sigillata pottery is Arretine ware (Hayes 1997: 42). This was also the term used in ancient texts to describe this kind of pottery. Terra sigillata pottery has been widely studied. The earliest studies are by Dragendorff and Oswald and Pryce, but much has been learned since these scholars established the initial groundwork.

Related to terra sigillata ware is *African red slip* ware, most of which was produced in North Africa, rather than in Italy (Hayes 1997: 59). These forms appear later than terra sigillata, and their categorization is based on region of production. Hayes (1980) has established the major framework used by scholars; however, he acknowledges that more excavations and studies are needed. Hayes's major categories are fourfold (Hayes 1997: 59). Terra sigillata African A and D were produced in Carthage, with D a later variation of A (Hayes 1997: 59). Terra sigillata African B was not actually made in Africa, but rather in the south of France (Hayes 1997: 62). Terra sigillata African C originated in Tunisia (Hayes 1997: 59). The basic forms of all of these categories of red slip pottery are similar to terra sigillata.

Relief ware is a more general term for fine ware pottery with relief decorations. These are very distinctive kinds of ceramics. *Knidian* relief ware (dating from 70 C.E. to 250 C.E.) is mold-made (Hayes 1997: 70). The forms are very interesting and include ornamental jugs, zoomorphic jugs, and phallus-shaped vessels (Hayes 1997: 72–73). *Corinthian* relief ware (dating roughly to the third century C.E.) tend to be small, straight-sided bowls (Hayes 1997: 73). On the walls of the vessels are reliefs of various figural images (Hayes 1997: 73).

Coarse Wares.   Coarse wares are not as easy to study as fine wares. There are a number of reasons for this. First, there is not as much secondary literature on coarse wares because they are not as aesthetically pleasing as fine wares. The forms and materials are, generally speaking, of lower quality and are less likely to interest art historians (who tend to study these materials). Second, because coarse ware was more functional than stylish, it did not change as rapidly or consistently as fine ware (Greene 1992: 31). It is much more difficult to make chronological distinctions in regard to coarse ware. Third, coarse ware varied considerably at the local level (Greene 1992: 31–32). So even if someone is an expert in Roman coarse ware at Pompeii, that scholar has to relearn the corpus for Roman Britain.

There are a few major types of coarse ware that are important to become familiar with. One of the major categories is *buff* ware (Hayes 1997: 75). This kind of pottery is made of clay fired to a cream color (hence the name *buff*). It is usually very porous, meaning that the vessels, when filled with liquid, sweat considerably. Buff ware is, counterintuitively, very good for serving liquids, because it helps cool down the liquid. I have done some experimental archaeology with Egyptian pottery and found that porous vessels actually cool off liquids quite well. When this kind of pottery was transported, a resin (often of bitumen) could be added to seal the liquid inside and stop it from sweating (Hayes 1997: 75–76).

Another important group of coarse ware ceramics is vessels used in food preparation. Cooking pots usually have rounded bottoms, sometimes with small handles near the rim (Hayes 1997: 76). These handles were used to fix the pot above a fire or to tie a lid on top, not to carry the vessel (Hayes 1997: 76). Pompeiian red ware are types of cooking vessels that usually have flat bottoms. They are named Pompeiian red ware not because they were found at Pompeii, but because the clay was the same color as the wall plaster in some Pompeiian houses (Hayes 1997: 78). Also used in Roman food preparation was the *mortarium*. Mortaria are large, flat bowls used for grinding food. Ridges or slits in the interior of the vessel would help grind or husk food, when the food was rubbed or pounded inside the mortarium. These vessels have very thick walls, making them easy to hold. They were probably mass produced in molds (Hayes 1997: 80), because from an aesthetic point of view, the quality of these vessels is never very high.

Amphorae. *Amphorae* are not easily described as either fine or coarse ware. In a sense, they straddle those two categories and are usually considered a separate category of pottery. These vessels are descendants of Syro-Palestinian vessels, dating from as far back as the middle Bronze Age. The clay of amphorae is yellowish, brown, or red. Amphorae are large-capacity vessels with a pointed base. In Roman times, they usually had two handles (Hayes 1997: 27), but in other periods, four- and three-handled forms were also known. The shape of these vessels is designed for maritime transport. Excavations of numerous shipwrecks and various artistic representations (especially earlier Egyptian tomb reliefs) show that the vessels were stacked vertically, in layers on top of one another within the ship. The pointed bottom allowed the vessels to be jammed between the necks of the vessels below, making the whole shipping area quite secure (Hayes 1997: 27). Essentially locked together, the amphorae would not break or shift with the rolling of the sea. The high number of amphorae that are found intact within excavated shipwrecks attests to the success of this strategy.

ROMAN ART

Roman art has been an important subject within Roman studies for a long time. The study of Roman art is a discipline in its own right and only some comment can be made here. No matter what kind of background one has in art history, it is probably easy to recognize Roman art or references to it. There is something very powerful and distinctive about Roman art that makes it (or its influences) easy to identify. This quality makes Roman art very powerful. Even centuries later it is still possible to understand and be influenced by Roman artistry, even though the culture is long gone.

Painting

Paintings from Rome are very important in the wider field of art-historical study because of the large volume preserved (Charles-Picard 1968: 8). Compared with the relative paucity of surviving Greek examples of painting, Roman painting is the major source of our understanding (other than literary descriptions) of Classical painting (Ling 1991b: 5). This art form is usually considered in two major categories. The first is painting on moving tablets (Ling 1988a: 1771; Ling 1991b: 1). The second is painting directly on walls (Ling 1988a: 1771). Because of the nature of preservation, the wall paintings in the Vesuvian cities have been studied in the greatest detail. Also well studied are tomb wall paintings from the beginning of Roman civilization. The first category, movable painting, has not been preserved to nearly the same extent as wall painting, and as such, it is treated in far less detail in the secondary literature. Because wall painting was related to architecture, the forms of wall painting are discussed in more detail in the section titled "Decoration" on page 241 of this chapter.

The techniques and materials used for Roman painting depended on the type of painting. In the first category of Roman art, the paint was applied directly to a wooden (or sometimes stone) plaque (Charles-Picard 1968: 47). Wall art involved painting directly upon a layer of plaster stucco that had been directly applied to the wall (Pratt 1976: 227). The paint itself was derived from natural sources (Pratt 1976: 224). Minerals provided pigments for earth colors (i.e., browns and dark reds). Vegetable and animal sources provided other colors (Pratt 1976: 224). Worth mentioning is the famous purple dye, well associated with Roman royalty, that came initially from Phoenicia. Purple dye was derived from murex shells that were found off the coast of modern-day Lebanon.

Many themes were explored in Roman painting. One of the most important was portraiture. Roman portraiture was quite striking in its attention to realism. Roman portraits can be eerie to view, because one is truly looking at the image of a person from centuries ago. This was a unique feature in the ancient world, because most ancient art attempted to portray ideal visions of the human form (e.g., strength, youth, beauty) or very schematized aspects of the individual. But in Roman portraits, even the wrinkles were painted in close detail. This attempt to faithfully reproduce the image of an individual is called *veristic* style, from the word *veritas,* which means "truth" (Strong 1976: 44).

Landscapes were also an important component of Roman painting (Ling 1991b: 142). At times realistic and at times whimsical, landscape paintings brought the tranquillity of the natural world to the interior of Roman structures (Charles-Picard 1968: 98; Ling 1991b: 143). Similarly, mythological scenes or images of daily life were important themes in Roman painting (Charles-Pi-

Faiyum Mummy Portraits

Roman portraiture is recognized as technically advanced, detail oriented, and concerned with capturing a realistic image of the subject. Roman portraiture and painting techniques merged with Egyptian burial customs in the form of the Faiyum mummy masks. These masks served the same basic function in Egyptian mortuary customs as did the more traditional mummy masks (most notably the golden headpiece of Tutankhamun). But rather than having been sculpted, these masks were made in the form of portraits on wooden panels or on linen. They are called Faiyum portraits because William Flinders Petrie first discovered them in this region of Egypt. Since then, this style of funerary mask has been found in many other parts of Egypt. These mummy portraits illustrate the unique fusion of Roman and local culture in Roman-period Egypt.

card 1968: 98; Ling 1991b: 101). These paintings were often very lush, and all tended to be romanticized representations rather than realistic depictions—exactly the opposite of the intentions behind portraiture.

Mosaics

Mosaic is an art form, incorporated directly into architecture, that archaeologically survives much better than wall painting. The reason for this is that the primary components of a mosaic are the pieces of stone that make up the design. Even if the mosaic was broken or damaged, skilled restorers frequently could put it back together again, almost like a jigsaw puzzle. When traveling in the Mediterranean, if one visits a Roman archaeological site, one is bound to see a mosaic reconstructed by archaeologists. This is true of floor mosaics; pre-

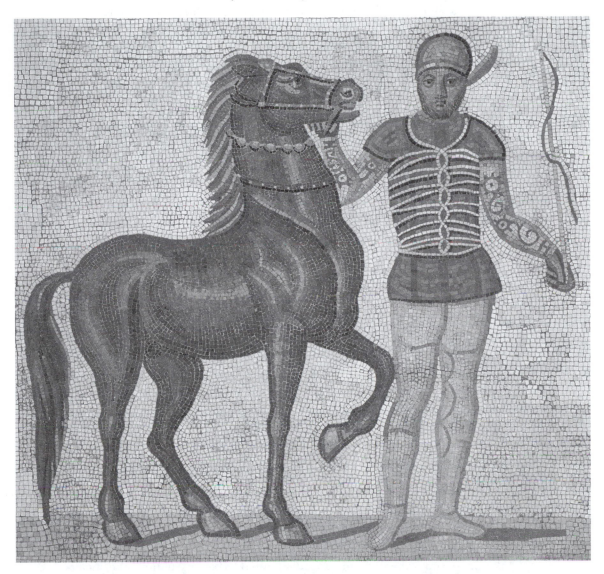

A Roman mosaic depicting a charioteer and his horse. (Araldo de Luca/Corbis)

served wall mosaics are much rarer (although there are exceptions; the Vesuvian wall mosaics have survived virtually intact).

Roman mosaics developed out of Hellenistic traditions of art in this medium (Charles-Picard 1968: 97). But the Romans really took the art of mosaic crafting to a higher level by attempting to create designs specifically for this medium, rather than simply reinterpreting artwork previously conceived of as a painting (Strong 1976: 236). By the empire period, mosaics were quite popular, but they also had become mass produced and of lower quality (Strong 1976: 236).

There were a variety of types of mosaics, based on the different construction techniques. Both Vitruvius and Pliny record the methods ancient artists used to create this kind of artwork. The most well-known kinds of mosaics are those composed of *tesserae*, small stone cubes (Neal 1976: 241). But there are other kinds of mosaics as well. *Signinum* consist of colored mortar and chunks of stone and other materials (Strong 1976: 101). *Opus sectile* are mosaics that use large pieces of stone that are cut in different shapes from one another and are assembled to form the design (Neal 1976: 241).

Mosaics had numerous kinds of designs. Often scholars divide mosaics into two major categories—black and white mosaics and polychrome mosaics (Strong 1976: 101). Certainly the most common kind of mosaics were those that depicted simple geometric images or designs. Unlike Hellenistic mosaics, the geometric or abstract designs lacked a focal point. There were also nongeometric images. Mythic themes were often employed, especially myths appropriate to the type of room (Ling 1991b: 136; Strong 1976: 236). So, for example, water scenes were often found in baths. Human figures were also depicted. However, these figures were not historic individuals, but rather personifications of cities, seasons, months, and other abstract concepts. In the western provinces, scenes taken from daily life—appropriate to the kind of activities that took place in the particular room—were also employed.

Sculpture

Numerous examples of Roman sculpture have survived to the present, and clearly sculpture was a vibrant form of art in Roman times. The subject of Roman sculpture is usually explored alongside Greek sculpture. The relationship of Roman sculpture to Greek sculpture traditions is particularly problematic. The earliest examples of Roman sculpture seem more related to Etruscan artistic styles; funerary masks are especially indicative of this (Bonanno 1983: 82; Ramage and Ramage 1996: 40). But when, in the Republican period, Rome began to expand into Greek regions, Greek artistic influence became very strong (Brilliant 1974: 200). Much of this influence came directly from the Greeks, because Greek artists were brought to the city of Rome. By the imperial period, Greek styles and types of sculpture predominated, but the subject matter had become very Roman. In the provinces, a similar phenomenon occurred in that Roman subjects were sculpted in local styles and materials (Strong 1976: 217).

Like Greek sculpture, Roman sculpture tended to be very naturalistic, meaning that the Roman artists attempted to render the sculpture to look like the

The *Ara Pacis Augustae*

One of the most important pieces of Roman sculpture that illustrate how scholarly categories are not always so clear-cut is the masterpiece *Ara Pacis Augustae* (the Altar of Augustan Peace). This was a monumental version of an altar, probably based on Greek models in a much smaller scale. The reliefs associated with the altar carry a novel kind of imperial image. It is an example of historical relief sculpture, commemorating a procession and sacrifice that actually took place in 13 B.C.E. The altar was atop a stepped platform, surrounded by screens. On the east and west sides were doorways, and associated with the doors were panels sculpted with reliefs of mythological scenes.

subject in form (Strong 1976: 44). Sculptures were made in many materials (Brilliant 1988: 1729). Stone and marble sculptures are the best-known types of Roman statuary in modern times, but this is probably because stone lasts so long in the archaeological record. In fact, many Roman statues in modern museums did not come from archaeological excavations; Roman statues were of such a high quality that they were kept for centuries.

Roman sculpture was created for many reasons and fulfilled many artistic roles. Scholars generally divide Roman sculpture into three categories: commemorative, funerary, and religious (Bonanno 1983: 70–71), but these categories should be considered very loose classifications. Commemorative art tends to be reflected in portraits (Strong 1976: 44). Busts (sculptures of an individual from the shoulders up), statues in the round (statues of an individual's entire body), and equestrian statues (individuals riding horses) are the most common types of commemorative works. Religious sculpture can come in many forms. Cult statues are statues of deities, religious figures, or personified forces. Sculptural decoration is also an important component of religious sculpture traditions. In funerary contexts, sculptured sarcophagi were important in Roman elite funerary culture, even within the context of a tradition of cremation.

Glass

Glassmaking was not a Roman invention, although this mistake is made in many museum displays. Glass had already been manufactured for centuries in Mesopotamia and Egypt. The Romans initially used Hellenistic glassmaking techniques, and after glass blowing was invented in Syria in the first century B.C.E., this technique was also incorporated (Price 1976: 114). By about 100 C.E., blowing glass became the dominant method of manufacturing within the Roman Empire (Price 1976: 111). This new technology allowed glass to be made cheaply and quickly, enabling mass production and shipping throughout the empire.

Glass was very widespread in the Roman world and was used in a variety of contexts. In architectural contexts, glass was used in windows and as a means of decoration. Glass was used for tableware, especially as drinking implements. Luxury items in glass are also attested to. Cameo glasses were very common. This was a kind of decorative art in which two layers of different colored glass (frequently white on blue) were pressed together (Price 1976: 123). The top layer was carved, leaving a design in relief in the color of the lower layer. Cage glasses were later luxury items (Price 1976: 123). These looked like modern drinking glasses, except that the outer layer of glass was carved in what looked like a cage or net design.

Gems

Gems were an important category of Roman art. Gems could be embedded in settings to make jewelry. Of more interest to scholars are those gems that were engraved (called *intaglios*). Roman gems are based on Greek and Etruscan styles (Henig 1983: 153). But unlike Greek and Etruscan scholarship on gems (which is quite advanced), scholarship on Roman gems has only just begun (Spiers 1992: 73). Much of the problem with the study of Roman gems comes from the fact that gems were remarkably similar throughout the duration of Roman history and across the many lands under Roman dominion (Spiers 1992: 75; but see Henig 1974: 43). So it has been impossible to create useful chronological and typological categories for Roman gems. A variety of factors have constrained the development of the study of this artifact category. For example, there is a large temporal gap in the study of Roman gems, because various sumptuary laws limited their use in the early Republican period. More problematic is the fact that most Roman gems do not come from controlled archaeological investigations. They are more frequently purchased illicitly, and there are quite a few in the hands of private collectors (for more on the controversies of collecting, see chapter 11).

Scholars study Roman gems in terms of certain stylistic criteria, often divorced from chronology and geography. These criteria include engraving style, iconography, and any settings in which the gems were placed (Spiers 1992: 76). Often these settings are much easier to date or to place in historical context than are gems on their own. The type and shape of gemstone are also important criteria for study. Gems in Roman times were frequently made of types of quartz, including carnelian, chalcedony, agate, and sardonyx (Spiers 1992: 5). Jaspers, especially red, green, and yellow jaspers, became popular from the second century C.E. in Rome (Spiers 1992: 5). Garnet was also frequently used for gems (Spiers 1992: 5).

ARTIFACTS FROM DAILY LIFE

Roman scholars are very lucky because they have three very good sources of information on artifacts from Roman daily life. Archaeologically, the Vesuvian cities have been particularly good sources of information. The eruption of Vesuvius was so sudden that many objects were left just as they were used every day. This kind of deposition is very unusual because most archaeological finds are the purposefully discarded remains of the ancient world. From an art-historical perspective, there is a rich tradition of visual depiction of everyday life. And especially with the prominence of veristic styles, this information can be very helpful. Textually, because of the encyclopedic tendencies of Roman writers, there are very good written accounts of everyday life.

Household Artifacts

It may be somewhat misleading to include only one section on household decoration, because there were so many different types of houses, and because class and taste were important carriers of difference. But some general comments can nonetheless be made if these problems are kept in mind. Especially in terms of technology and style, household artifacts reflected the values of Roman society. So some standardization was present; just keep in mind that in general, the discussion that follows centers on elite households.

Furniture. The Roman household was furnished but certainly not to the extent that North American and European homes are furnished today. Furniture was extremely expensive relative to other products available in Rome, and space was limited (Cowell 1980: 24–25). So even the wealthy were more likely to concentrate on acquiring better-quality furniture than on greater numbers of furniture (Cowell 1980: 24). As was discussed in the first section of this chapter, Roman homes had rooms that were, at least ideally, divided according to function. Sometimes the furniture of specific rooms reflected these divisions. But consider your own house as an analogy. You might have rooms that are designated for particular functions (dining room, bedroom, etc.), and have appropriate furniture (dining table, beds, etc.), but in actual daily practice a wide variety of activities take place in the rooms. The same was likely true for the Romans. So do not consider these distinctions about rooms and furniture as hard-and-fast rules about how Romans behaved in the home. Rather, consider them in terms of underlying principles that may or may not have been followed by the residents.

The atrium of the house was an ever-changing space that fulfilled a variety of functions and housed a wide variety of furniture. But it is also the easiest space to recognize archaeologically because of its distinct architectural features. There are at least ten examples of Pompeiian homes in which chests were found in the atrium (Ellis 2000: 146). In addition, some Pompeiian atriums contained pottery that was quite large and normally associated with storage (Ellis 2000: 146–147). It is likely that the atrium was used as a storage area, as well as an area of the house in which domestic tasks were performed, because of the open space and open roof (Ellis 2000: 147). Also found in atriums were marble tables called *cartibulum* (Ellis 2000: 146).

Most often associated with the furniture kept within the house was the *triclinium*, named after the couches typically associated with the room. This was the main dining and reception room of the household. In elite houses, diners would recline on couches to eat meals rather than sitting upright (although this was considered a luxury even in Rome and may have been the ideal rather than the typical method of eating). Three couches were placed in a semicircle, probably fitting about seven or eight diners (Ellis 2000: 148). The diners would recline with their heads toward the center of the circle and their feet toward the walls (Ellis 2000: 148). Tables were very small and close to the ground (Ellis 2000: 148). Usually courses were served one at a time, so the small serving space was not a hindrance to dining. But there were no large dining tables such as the kind that would be found in a house today. Sometimes cupboards were placed in the triclinium, in which serving equipment was probably stored, although this is not known for certain (Ellis 2000: 152).

Although it may seem odd to modern readers, beds were not found in great quantities in the Roman household. Slaves were unlikely to have beds, and even children were not necessarily provided with them. Although beds did not survive particularly well in the archaeological record, educated guesses can be made about where they would have been placed in some homes. The basis for this is the of mosaics in rooms assumed to be bedrooms. If the bedroom had a mosaic, there was frequently an undecorated, rectangular segment of the mosaic placed along the rear wall (Ellis 2000: 156). It is assumed that the reason this part of the mosaic lacked decoration was that it would have been covered by furniture.

Kitchens are also difficult to identify archaeologically, a fact that has led scholars to suggest that Roman homes often did not have kitchens, and that food was either eaten cold or acquired from local taverns (Ellis 2000: 159). If a kitchen is identifiable archaeologically, the furniture is usually of two types. The first is the oven and related cooking equipment (Ellis 2000: 158). The second is the domestic shrine or cultic equipment, which seemed to be placed in the same area as food preparation (Ellis 2000: 158).

There were also types of furniture not specific to particular rooms. Chairs were not common in Roman houses in the way that they are today. Wealthier homes did have chairs, and these would have been offered to guests out of respect or used by the higher-status household members (Cowell 1980: 24–25). Folding stools would have been used more frequently due to their ease of storage, mobility, and inexpensive price (Cowell 1980: 25). Portable wooden screens were also used in the household to subdivide space on a more temporary basis than walls (Ellis 2000: 147).

Lighting. The most important source of light for Roman homes was the sun. Windows were strategically located throughout the house to give access to sunlight. This made lighting quite uneven, not only from room to room, but also within individual rooms. But after the sun went down, it was, of course, a useless source of light. Oil lamps were one means of lighting the home (Cowell 1980: 28). Found all over the Roman Empire, oil lamps are instantly recognizable. They are ceramic and seem to be typologically based on the oil lamps used in the Near East from as long ago as the early Bronze Age. There are more luxurious versions of oil lamps, made out of different kinds of metal, but the ceramic lamps are the type found most frequently in excavations. Oil was poured into the lamp, and a wick was inserted. The oil burned slowly, giving off a soft glowing light. These lamps were placed on tables and stands throughout the Roman home. Oil was very expensive, however, so these lamps would not have been used in the poorer homes without consideration of the cost (Cowell 1980: 28). Similarly, braziers were used to burn charcoal, not only for light, but also to heat the home (Cowell 1980: 26). Remember, though, that all of these technologies involving fire were not as easy to use in the ancient world as they would be in modern times. Without matches, creating a fire was a very time-consuming task; there were likely some fires burning all day in order to facilitate the nightly lighting of lamps.

Decoration.   Wall paintings and mosaics dominated decoration in Roman homes. Although these types of art were discussed earlier, it is important to mention the ways in which Roman artists integrated art directly into the architecture of Roman homes. The basic classification of this integration was established in the nineteenth century by August Mau. His terminology has become the basis for modern discussions. Frequently, when one reads scholarship about Roman art, Mau's terms are used, without explanation. So Mau's typology of Pompeiian interior decoration will be described next, in order to provide enough background to study the subject further. These categories roughly correspond with changes in Pompeiian domestic architecture as well.

Mau's typology is roughly chronological and is relatively easy to monitor, because the name of each style is given a number corresponding to the order of its appearance. First style (also known as Incrustation style) of interior decoration involved the painting of artificial architectural features onto the walls of buildings (Wilson 1986: 363). For example, blocks of stone were created in plaster relief to imitate real blocks of stone. There is no figural art; the emphasis is on the irregularities of the wall.

Around 70 B.C.E. a new style became prominent. Second style (also known as Architectural style) incorporated landscape art in the center of the viewing space. The landscape tended to be very idyllic; the term *sacro-idyllic* is often used as the primary description (Ling 1991b: 145–146; Wilson 1986: 372). A shrine or column is usually found in the center of the landscape with various individuals surrounding the architectural feature. Surrounding the landscape, the entire wall is divided into three sections (Charles-Picard 1968: 50). There is a wide central panel (in which the landscape image is placed) and two smaller panels on either side. Architectural effects within these panels are created entirely through painting, creating the illusion of architectural features where none are apparent (see Ling 1988a).

The illusion of architectural features disappeared in the Third style (sometimes called Ornate style). Lasting from about 10 B.C.E. to 50 C.E., Third style divided the wall into three sections horizontally (Wilson 1986: 377). Architectural features were completely subordinate to the decorative scheme (Charles-Picard 1968: 58). The impression one gets from looking at a Third-style wall is that of a large palace with framed pictures hanging on the wall (Ling 1988a). Mythological paintings were placed in the center (Wilson 1986: 377).

Fourth style (Intricate style) attempted to create the illusion of larger amounts of space within the enclosed room (Wilson 1986: 378). Extravagant architectural details were painted; such details, in many cases, would not have been possible had they been constructed rather than painted (Wilson 1986: 378). So although architectural features became important once again, they were no longer realistic architectural features. This was the most commonly attested style at Pompeii, as it was the type in vogue at the time of Pompeii's destruction.

Clothing and Hygiene

There are three major sources of information—literature, art, and archaeological artifacts—that archaeologists have used to reconstruct the personal appearances of everyday Romans (Bonfante and Jaunzems 1988: 1385). Roman literature describes clothing, appropriate methods of use, the kinds of adornment worn by people, and the types of steps taken for personal hygiene. Roman art provides graphic illustration of the same topics. Archaeological evidence is not as useful in terms of clothing, as textiles do not preserve well over time. But artifacts relating to personal hygiene are found in archaeological contexts; museums have actual ancient hygiene tools (for example, combs and razors) on display in their collections.

Clothing. Roman clothing did not vary substantially throughout Roman history. Indeed, there is a remarkable conservatism in Roman dress that spans the Republican and imperial periods (Adkins and Adkins 1994: 344). Although it is possible to make some observations about changing styles, these changes are in the details; the overall nature of Roman clothing was relatively consistent. Clothing also reflected some of the same attitudes that Romans had toward architecture, in terms of standardization (Bonfante and Jaunzems 1988: 1401). Clothing was not a statement of individuality in Roman times; it did not (for the most part) reflect personal tastes and preferences (Bonfante and Jaunzems 1988: 1401). Rather, clothing was functional and standardized. Particular clothes were appropriate for certain people in certain situations (Bonfante and Jaunzems 1988: 1401). Deviation from these norms was not acceptable in Roman society. Clothing directly indicated one's social status and occupation. Although this may be somewhat true of today's fashion (we have clothes that are appropriate for formal occasions, for work, and for the gym), there is still a degree of choice in fashion today that was not available to the ancient Roman.

Textiles in the Republican period were manufactured at home (Bonfante and Jaunzems 1988: 1401; Cowell 1980: 68). Although this continued to some extent in the imperial period, textile factories came into existence at that time as well (Bonfante and Jaunzems 1988: 1402). The most common fabrics were wool and flax, and most fabrics were white in color (Cowell 1980: 68). Most garments were created from one large piece of fabric, rectangular or oval in shape (Cowell 1980: 68). More elaborate garments could involve stitching more than one piece of fabric together (Bonfante and Jaunzems 1988: 1401). Clothes represented a considerable investment of time and resources, and as such were a very valuable commodity. In Roman literature, it is common to encounter instances in which gifts of clothing were given. This kind of gift was very valuable, and even if the clothes were previously used, they were considered a very fine gift (Cowell 1980: 75). Clothes were not washed at home, because most homes lacked the necessary amount of water (Cowell 1980: 69). There were individuals within the city who specialized in laundering.

Although there was not as great a difference between men's and women's clothing in Rome as there is today (Adkins and Adkins 1994: 344), it is nonetheless possible to distinguish between men's and women's fashions. Certainly literary sources comment on some styles that made men appear effeminate and other styles deemed inappropriate for "proper" ladies. So gender roles were expressed in Roman clothing.

The most important component of the Roman clothing ensemble was the tunic (Adkins and Adkins 1994: 345). For men, the tunic ideally fell just below the knees (Cowell 1980: 71). For women, the tunic reached to the feet (Cowell 1980: 71). A belt, normally just a rope tied around the waist, could adjust the length of the tunic (Adkins and Adkins 1994: 345). Although there were more elaborate tunics with sleeves, most simple tunics were sleeveless. The sides of the tunic were open, allowing for great freedom of arm movement (Bonfante and Jaunzems 1988: 1403).

Most notably Roman was the toga. Togas became a formal style of dress toward the end of the imperial period (Cowell 1980: 72). Wearing a toga was a right restricted to Roman citizens (Bonfante and Jaunzems 1988: 1406). Togas were basically heavy garments made of white wool (Adkins and Adkins 1994: 344). There were a variety of methods of wrapping the toga; these methods varied with time. Early on, the toga was worn as the sole piece of clothing; later it became more appropriate to wear a toga over a tunic (Adkins and Adkins 1994: 344).

Clothing bore designs indicating the status of males. Generally these decorations took the form of purple stripes that ran vertically down from the shoulder; the wider the stripe, the higher the status (Bonfante and Jaunzems 1988: 1402–1403). Children also wore stripes on their tunics, but as a marker of age, not of rank (Bonfante and Jaunzems 1988: 1402). The color of garments was also indicative of status or setting. For example, emperors wore purple togas, and mourners wore black togas to funerals (Bonfante and Jaunzems 1988: 1402). Charioteers wore tunics that were the color of their particular order (Adkins and Adkins 1994: 345).

Romans also saw a difference between undergarments and overgarments (Bonfante and Jaunzems 1988: 1403). Undergarments for men could consist of lighter tunics or loincloths. It was inappropriate for Roman men not to wear undergarments, especially men in professions in which whatever was beneath their overgarments may have been exposed publicly. Women had a variety of undergarment options, including leather or linen brassieres, called *strophium,* which bound the breasts (Bonfante and Jaunzems 1988: 1404). Outerwear included various types of shoes, sandals, or boots (Adkins and Adkins 1994: 345). Men did not cover their heads, but married women were expected to do so when out in public (Cowell 1980: 73). Cloaks were also worn over the regular ensemble, depending on the weather (Cowell 1980: 74).

Personal Hygiene.   Hygiene and grooming were very important to the Romans. There is a lot of evidence (more so than for most ancient cultures) for the methods and styles of hygiene. Women wore makeup and perfumes. They plucked their eyebrows and removed unwanted hair by rubbing the area with pumice stones (Cowell 1980: 64). Men kept their beards until Scipio Africanus made it fashionable for men to be clean-shaven (Cowell 1980: 66). Shaving was considered too difficult a task for men to do themselves, so a barber or slave would have to assist (Cowell 1980: 67). Hairstyles in general varied with changing tastes (Cowell 1980: 65). There is much evidence, especially from art-historical recordings, for different hairstyles. Perhaps the best-known type of Roman hairstyle was what is known today as a "Caesar cut," although this was not the name of this style in antiquity. Dental care was just as important as hair care; white teeth were the expected norm of the upper classes (Cowell 1980: 64). Bathing was perhaps the most important element of personal hygiene, but more is said on that topic in chapter 10.

Personal Adornment.   Jewelry is an extensively studied subject. Only passing comment is made on it here, as it is so well covered in popular works. An important type of jewelry was called the *fibula.* This was the pin used to fasten tunics and togas, and was a common component of ancient European and Mediterranean material culture traditions. It was worn by both sexes. Men would wear brooches and possibly rings. Women wore more types of jewelry. In addition to the types listed as worn by men, Roman women wore earrings, necklaces, bracelets, bands, and hair accessories.

BIBLIOGRAPHY

Adkins, Lesley, and Roy Adkins. 1994. *Handbook to Life in Ancient Rome.* Oxford: Oxford University Press.

Boëthius, Axel. 1960. *The Golden House of Nero.* Ann Arbor: University of Michigan Press.

———. 1978. *Etruscan and Early Roman Architecture.* New Haven: Yale University Press.

Bonanno, Anthony. 1983. "Sculpture." In *A Handbook of Roman Art.* M. Henig (ed.). Ithaca: Cornell University Press.

Bonfante, Larissa, and Eva Jaunzems. 1988. "Clothing and Ornament," pp. 1385–1416 in *Civilization of the Ancient Mediterranean: Greece and Rome.* Michael Grant and Rachel Kitzinger (eds.). New York: Charles Scribner's Sons.

Boyd, Thomas. 1988. "Urban Planning," pp. 1691–1700 in *Civilization of the Ancient Mediterranean: Greece and Rome.* Michael Grant and Rachel Kitzinger (eds.). New York: Charles Scribner's Sons.

Brendel, O. 1979. *Prolegomena to the Study of Roman Art.* New Haven: Yale University Press.

Brilliant, Richard. 1974. *Roman Art.* London: Reader's Union.

———. 1988. "Roman Sculpture and Gems," pp. 1727–1748 in *Civilization of the Ancient*

Mediterranean: Greece and Rome. Michael Grant and Rachel Kitzinger (eds.). New York: Charles Scribner's Sons.

Brown, David. 1976. "Pottery," pp. 75–92 in *Roman Crafts*. Donald Strong and David Brown. London: Duckworth.

Carcopino, Jérôme. 1940. *Daily Life in Ancient Rome*. Henry Rowell (ed.). New Haven: Yale University Press.

Casson, Lionel. 1974. *Travel in the Ancient World*. London: Allen and Unwin.

———. 1988. "Transportation," pp. 353–366 in *Civilization of the Ancient Mediterranean: Greece and Rome*. Michael Grant and Rachel Kitzinger (eds.). New York: Charles Scribner's Sons.

Charles-Picard, Gilbert. 1966. *Living Architecture: Roman*. London: Oldbourne.

———. 1968. *Roman Painting*. Greenwich: New York Graphic Society.

Charleston, Robert. 1955. *Roman Pottery*. London: Faber and Faber.

Chevallier, Raymond. 1976. *Roman Roads*. Berkeley: University of California Press.

Cowell, F. R. 1980. *Life in Ancient Rome*. New York: Perigee Books.

Dilke, Oswald. 1971. *The Roman Land Surveyors: An Introduction to the Agrimensores*. Newton Abbot: David and Charles.

Dragendorff, Hans. 1948. *Arretinische Reliefkermaik mit Beschreibung der Sammlung Tübingen*. Reutlingen: Gryphius-Verlag.

Dupont, Florence. 1989. *Daily Life in Ancient Rome*. Christopher Woodall (trans.). Cambridge: Basil Blackwell Ltd.

Ellis, Simon. 2000. *Roman Housing*. London: Gerald Duckworth & Co. Ltd.

Fagan, Garret. 1999. *Bathing in Public in the Roman World*. Ann Arbor: University of Michigan Press.

Friedländer, Ludwig. 1910. *Roman Life and Manners under the Early Empire*. London: Routledge & Sons, Ltd.

Frier, Bruce. 1980. *Landlords and Tenants in Imperial Rome*. Princeton: Princeton University Press.

Greene, Kevin. 1986. *The Archaeology of the Roman Economy*. Berkeley: University of California Press.

———. 1992. *Roman Pottery*. Berkeley: University of California Press.

Grimal, Pierre. 1983. *Roman Cities*. G. Michael Woloch (trans.). Madison: University of Wisconsin Press.

Hannestad, Niels. 1986. *Roman Art and Imperial Policy*. Aarhus: Aarhus University Press.

Hayes, John W. 1980. *Late Roman Pottery with Supplement*. London: British School at Rome.

———. 1997. *Handbook of Mediterranean Roman Pottery*. London: British Museum Press.

Healy, John. 1978. *Mining and Metallurgy in the Greek and Roman World*. London: Thames & Hudson.

Henig, Martin. 1974. *A Corpus of Roman Engraved Gemstones from British Sites*. Oxford: British Archaeological Reports.

———. 1983. "The Luxury Arts: Decorative Metalwork, Engraved Gems, and Jewelry." In *A Handbook of Roman Art*. M. Henig (ed.). Ithaca: Cornell University Press.

Higgins, Reynold. 1966. *Greek and Roman Jewelry*. Berkeley: University of California Press.

Humphrey, John. 1986. *Roman Circuses: Arenas for Chariot Racing*. Berkeley: University of California Press.

———. 1988. "Roman Games," pp. 1153–1166 in *Civilization of the Ancient Mediterranean: Greece and Rome*. Michael Grant and Rachel Kitzinger (eds.). New York: Charles Scribner's Sons.

Jashemski, W. F. 1979. *The Gardens of Pompeii, Herculaneum and the Villas Destroyed by Vesuvius.* New York: Caratzas Brothers.

Keppie, Lawrence. 1983. *Colonisation and Veteran Settlement in Italy 47–14 B.C.* London: British School at Rome.

Kraus, Theodore. 1975. *Pompeii and Herculaneum: The Living Cities of the Dead.* New York: H.N. Abrams.

Lanciani, Rudolfo. 1967. *The Ruins and Excavations of Ancient Rome.* New York: Benjamin Bloom.

Landels, John. 1978. *Engineering in the Ancient World.* London: Chatto & Windus.

———. 1988. "Engineering," pp. 323–352 in *Civilization of the Ancient Mediterranean: Greece and Rome.* Michael Grant and Rachel Kitzinger (eds.). New York: Charles Scribner's Sons.

Laurence, Roy. 1999. *The Roads of Roman Italy.* New York: Routledge.

Ling, Roger. 1988a. "Roman Architecture," pp. 1671–1690 in *Civilization of the Ancient Mediterranean: Greece and Rome.* Michael Grant and Rachel Kitzinger (eds.). New York: Charles Scribner's Sons.

———. 1988b. "Roman Painting and Mosaic," pp. 1771–1794 in *Civilization of the Ancient Mediterranean: Greece and Rome.* Michael Grant and Rachel Kitzinger (eds.). New York: Charles Scribner's Sons.

———. 1991a. "The Arts of Living," pp. 308–337 in *The Oxford Illustrated History of the Roman World.* John Boardman, Jasper Griffin, and Oswyn Murray (eds.). Oxford: Oxford University Press.

———. 1991b. *Roman Painting.* Cambridge: Cambridge University Press.

MacDonald, William. 1976. *The Pantheon.* Cambridge: Harvard University Press.

———. 1982. *The Architecture of the Roman Empire I.* New Haven: Yale University Press.

Matthews, John. 1986. "Roman Life and Society," pp. 338–360 in *The Oxford Illustrated History of the Roman World.* John Boardman, Jasper Griffin, and Oswyn Murray (eds.). Oxford: Oxford University Press.

Mau, August. 1982 [1902]. *Pompeii: Its Life and Art.* F. W. Kelsey (trans.). 2nd ed. New York: Caratzas Brothers.

McKay, Alexander. 1975. *Houses, Villas and Palaces in the Roman World.* Ithaca: Cornell University Press.

———. 1988. "Houses," pp. 1363–1384 in *Civilization of the Ancient Mediterranean: Greece and Rome.* Michael Grant and Rachel Kitzinger (eds.). New York: Charles Scribner's Sons.

McWhirr, Alan. 1987. "Transport by Land and Water," pp. 658–670 in *The Roman World.* 2 vols. John Wacher (ed.). New York: Routledge & Kegan Paul.

Meiggs, Russel. 1973. *Roman Ostia.* 2nd ed. Oxford: Clarendon Press.

Neal, David. 1976. "Floor Mosaics," pp. 241–252 in *Roman Crafts.* London: Gerald Duckworth & Co. Ltd.

Oswald, Felix, and T. Davies Pryce. 1920. *An Introduction to the Study of Terra Sigillata Treated from a Chronological Standpoint.* London: Longmans, Green, and Co.

Packer, James. 1988. "Roman Building Techniques," pp. 299–322 in *Civilization of the Ancient Mediterranean: Greece and Rome.* Michael Grant and Rachel Kitzinger (eds.). New York: Charles Scribner's Sons.

Peacock, D. P. S., and D. F. Williams. 1986. *Amphorae and the Roman Economy: An Introductory Guide.* London: Longman.

Percival, John. 1975. *The Roman Villa: An Historical Introduction.* Berkeley: University of California Press.

Poulter, Andrew. 1987. "Townships and Villages," pp. 388–411 in *The Roman World*. 2 vols. John Wacher (ed.). New York: Routledge & Kegan Paul.

Pratt, Pamela. 1976. "Wall Painting," pp. 223–230 in *Roman Crafts*. London: Gerald Duckworth & Co. Ltd.

Price, Jennifer. 1976. "Glass," pp. 111–126 in *Roman Crafts*. London: Gerald Duckworth & Co. Ltd.

Ramage, Nancy, and Andrew Ramage. 1996. *Roman Art*. Englewood Cliffs, NJ: Prentice Hall.

Richter, G. 1966. *The Furniture of the Greeks, Etruscans, and Romans*. London: Phaidon.

Saller, Richard. 1994. *Patriarchy, Property and Death in the Roman Family*. Cambridge: Cambridge University Press.

Salmon, Edward. 1969. *Roman Colonisation*. Ithaca: Cornell University Press.

Shelton, Jo-Ann. 1988. *As the Romans Did*. Oxford: Oxford University Press.

Spiers, Jeffrey. 1992. *Ancient Gems and Finger Rings*. Malibu: J. Paul Getty Museum.

Strong, Donald. 1961. *Roman Imperial Sculpture*. London: A. Tiranti.

———. 1966. *Greek and Roman Gold and Silver Plate*. Ithaca: Cornell University Press.

———. 1976. *Roman Art*. New York: Penguin Books.

Strong, Donald, and David Brown. 1976. *Roman Crafts*. London: Duckworth.

Veyne, Paul (ed.). 1987. *A History of Private Life: From Pagan Rome to Byzantium*. Arthur Goldhammer (trans.). Cambridge: Harvard University Press.

Wallace-Hadrill, Andrew. 1994. *Houses and Society in Pompeii and Herculaneum*. Princeton: Princeton University Press.

Ward-Perkins, John. 1977. *Roman Architecture*. New York: Electa/Rizzoli.

———. 1981. *Roman Imperial Architecture*. New Haven: Yale University Press.

Wilson, R. J. A. 1986. "Roman Art and Architecture," pp. 361–400 in *The Oxford Illustrated History of the Roman World*. John Boardman, Jasper Griffin, and Oswyn Murray (eds.). Oxford: Oxford University Press.

Woloch, G. Michael. 1983. *Roman Cities*. Madison: University of Wisconsin Press.

Zanker, Paul. 1998. *Pompeii: Public and Private Life*. Deborah Schneider (trans.). Cambridge: Cambridge University Press.

X CHAPTER 10
Intellectual Accomplishments

A common theme will become apparent in this chapter: the claim that the Romans were relatively impoverished in comparison with the Greeks in terms of intellectual accomplishment. This belief is widely held by classicists (especially by those who specialize in Greece) but it is not accurate. Although it is easy to disparage the Roman intellectual heritage when comparing gladiators with Plato, it is more difficult to justify this attitude toward Rome when its cultural achievements are considered. If the Romans really were as intellectually deprived as scholars often suggest, how did they build the Pantheon? And how did they manage an empire of such incredible size and diversity for so long?

Roman intellectual accomplishments have to be considered on their own terms. It is true that in terms of science and philosophy, the Romans borrowed heavily from the Greeks. But at the same time, Romans adapted and used Greek concepts in very distinct ways. The Romans were much more pragmatic—intellectual thought was put into actual, practical use. The Roman writings that have been preserved do not concentrate on speculative intellectualism in the same ways that preserved Greek writings do. But the Romans were familiar with those Greek traditions and attempted to preserve and disseminate Greek science and philosophy. That should be considered an intellectual accomplishment in and of itself.

ROMAN SCIENCE

Roman science was dominated by scholars who researched and compiled information from other authorities (Stahl 1962). The expert in Roman science was ideally the individual who could compile as many different sources on a subject as possible, and by so doing, gain mastery of that subject himself (Stahl 1962). Although some of these authors (such as Varro and Pliny the Elder) produced massive tomes on these subjects, perhaps the most popular Roman scientific works were handbooks (Potter 1996: 93; Stahl 1962). A book like the one you are reading right now would have been very suitable to Roman scientific tastes. Handbooks and abridgments of larger treatises were common tools for a Roman scholar. Not only did they facilitate reading, but they also lowered the cost of copying and purchasing the volumes (Stahl 1962). These kinds of works were produced for practically all subjects, and this trend should be seen as one of the guiding principles behind Roman science. What follows is a discussion of some of the more prominent aspects of Roman science.

Calendar and Time

The Roman conception of the year changed over the course of Rome's history (the systems of year names used in Rome are discussed in chapter 3). In earliest times the Roman year consisted of ten lunar months (Adkins and Adkins 1994: 337; Fowler 1969: 2). Because ten lunar months do not add up to one full solar year, this calendar eventually became problematic. Even when the amount of lunar months in a year was increased to twelve (probably in the sixth century B.C.E.), a Roman year was still not as long as a solar year (Adkins and Adkins 1994: 337).

The month names that are used today are based on the Roman names. July is named after Julius Caesar and August is named after Augustus. September through December are all named after the months' numerical order in the year. The months had uneven amounts of days, with thirty-one, twenty-nine, or twenty-eight days in each. About every other year, because of the discrepancy with the solar year, an extra twenty-two or twenty-three days were added to February (Adkins and Adkins 1994: 337). This did not reconcile the Roman year with the solar year, however. By the time of Julius Caesar, the Roman year was about three months ahead of the solar year (Adkins and Adkins 1994: 337).

Julius Caesar drastically changed the Roman calendrical system, transforming it into basically the system we use today. Known as the Julian calendar, this newly conceived calendar year was almost exactly the length of a solar year. The modern conception of the year, based on the Gregorian calendar (introduced by Pope Gregory XIII in 1582 C.E.), is virtually the same as the Julian. The major exception is that the Gregorian calendar's system of leap years more accurately compensates for the discrepancy between the solar year and the calendar year.

The system of labeling days was very different from our own. Rather than numbering the days in consecutive order (e.g., the first of July, the second of July, and so on), the Romans numbered the days in relation to three named days (Fowler 1969: 9–10). The first of the month was called *kalendae*, the thirteenth or fifteenth day was called *idus* (ides), and in between was a day that was nine days before idus called *nonae*. The other days in the month were numbered based on their relationship to these other days. The concept of the week initially seems to have reflected a nine-day schedule, as every ninth day was considered a market day (Adkins and Adkins 1994: 338). The seven-day week was eventually adopted in Rome through the influence of Hellenistic astrologers and the religions of Judaism and Christianity.

The day itself was understood as consisting of two distinct periods—night and day (Adkins and Adkins 1994: 338). Each half of the day had exactly twelve hours, but the length of the hours varied based on the season (Adkins and Adkins 1994: 338). The modern abbreviations A.M. and P.M. are actually Roman abbreviations for *ante meridiem* (before the middle of the day) and *post meridiem* (after the middle of the day). To tell the hour, Romans used sundials, shadow clocks, and, especially useful at night, water clocks. There did not seem to be any concern with divisions of time that were smaller than hours (e.g., minutes).

Astronomy and Astrology

Although the Romans are often accused of not having contributed anything to the study of astronomy, this is not true. Some of history's most important astronomers lived in Roman times, although not always under Roman rule. Picking and choosing what is Greek and what is Roman leads to misunderstanding the true connectedness of these two cultures. What is presented here is how astronomy was viewed by the Romans, with no effort made to distinguish between Roman and Greek accomplishments. Although certain astronomical theories may have been Greek in origin, the fact is that the Romans likely held these beliefs, and it is worthwhile to know what the Romans understood.

Until Copernicus, perhaps the most influential astronomer was Ptolemy. He lived from 100 to 178 C.E. in Egypt. Ptolemy was not the first astronomer to describe an astronomical system in which the earth was the center of the universe with the sun, moon, and planets revolving around it. But Ptolemy's theoretical explanation of this situation, based on careful observation and synthesis of previous astronomical works, made it the standard within the Roman (and later the Islamic) world. In general, Ptolemy's writings were far more sophisticated than the general Roman understanding of the earth's place in the cosmos.

Particularly important in Roman times were the practical applications of astronomy. Many professions required individuals to be well versed in astronomy. Surveyors' equipment included astronomical manuals (Potter 1996: 94). Roman urban planning was based on astronomical models (Potter 1996:: 94). The sky was divided into quadrants, like the city, and the cardinal lines of the sky (*cardo* and *decamunus*) bore the same names as the main roads in Roman towns (Potter 1996: 93). Similarly, sailors and marine travelers used the stars for orientation. And farmers used astronomy to assist in their planning around agricultural cycles.

Another practical application of astronomy was astrology. Astrology, as most are aware, was the science of predicting events on earth based on the movements of the stars. The Romans inherited their astrological traditions from both the Etruscans and the Greeks, but the oldest source for astrological learning was ancient Mesopotamia. The Mesopotamian roots of astrology were so well acknowledged in Roman times that astrologers were often called *Chaldei*, which is a term better used to describe a distinct group of people from the region near the Mesopotamian city of Babylon. Astrology became very influential in Rome in the Republican period, when Greek cities were incorporated into Rome (Potter 1996: 96). Greek astrologers moved to Rome and produced important works. A notable astrologer was Posidonius, a Stoic, who lived from about 135 B.C.E. to 50 B.C.E. He produced five books on astrology and demonstrated the compatibility of astrology and Stoic philosophy (Potter 1996: 96). In general, astrology was quite popular with the Romans until the period of the Christian emperors.

A fifteenth-century book depicts crowned Greek astronomer Ptolemy and his Renaissance translator Regiomontanus. (Library of Congress)

Divination

Divination, the art of predicting the future based on observations and ritual practices, was an important Roman science. Some might cringe at categorizing divination as a science, but for the ancients this was appropriate. From the earliest evidence of divination (in Mesopotamia), it is clear that ancient divination was based on careful and rigorous observations of the natural world and historical events. It was not a charlatan's art; it was a legitimate attempt by the ancients to understand the connection among various elements of the world.

But the religious basis of divination should not be neglected. For many diviners, these arts were a primary medium of contact between gods and humans. The various divinatory practices allowed humans to find out the will of the gods and to gain messages from the gods. Sometimes humans initiated this kind of communication, when diviners performed in a ritual to ask the gods a question. Other times, the gods initiated the communication system by sending messages in the form of signs, which it was the responsibility of the diviners to interpret. What follows are brief discussions of the major kinds of Roman divination other than astrology.

Haruspices. The *haruspices* in Roman times were diviners who studied particular phenomena in order to understand the will of the gods. The term *haruspex* refers to diviners who used any number of techniques. Only the most prominent will be mentioned here. These traditions in Rome stem originally from the omen literature of Mesopotamia and may have been transmitted to the Romans through Etruscan culture. There were direct connections between these Mesopotamian arts and the Roman arts of the haruspex. Hepatoscopy, the study of animal entrails, was another science that originated in Mesopotamia and lasted through the Roman period. The trained diviner learned the will of the gods through the examination of a slaughtered animal's entrails (in Mesopotamia the liver was the most important organ for this information). This may seem horrifying to a modern reader, but it is important to remember that slaughtering animals was a daily activity in the Roman world. There was not the same kind of disassociation with food production in the ancient world as there is now, so the slaughtering of an animal would not have been shocking to a Roman. Related to hepatoscopy was the study of unusual natural phenomena—deformed births, strange growths, or anything that in modern times would be found in a Ripley's Believe It or Not® museum. These phenomena were signals from the gods and were deeply meaningful. Weather phenomena were similarly important; thunder and lightning were usually bad omens (Potter 1996: 93). Especially given Jupiter's connection to thunder and lightning, these weather omens were of primary importance.

Augury. Augury was a method for learning whether the gods approved of certain actions (like battles) before they were begun (Ferguson 1988b: 911). This involved the careful observation of the habits of birds, referred to as "taking the auspices." Although the Greeks knew this kind of divination, the Romans transformed augury into a rigorous science. Roman augurs followed

Aelius Aristides

Born in 117 C.E., Aelius Aristides is known from his autobiography, *The Sacred Tales*. He was a man plagued by illnesses that first struck him in about 142 C.E. These illnesses were debilitating (although some scholars have called Aristides a hypochondriac). Whatever the nature of his illnesses, they were very real to him. *The Sacred Tales* recount his healing, granted by the god Asclepius. Asclepius communicated to Aristides through dreams, giving him advice on methods of healing. These methods involved fasting, vomiting, and various types of physical shock using extremes of temperature. Asclepius also commanded Aristides to record the advice-bearing dreams, which he did in his autobiography.

very careful rules in performing the rituals and receiving answers to questions. The system was too complicated for the general public, and eventually a college was established. Augurs were elected for life, and were responsible not only for asking questions of the gods, but also for watching for unsolicited messages from the gods.

Dreams and Dream Incubation. Divination through dreams was probably the most accessible kind of divination available to the average Roman. Everyone dreams, so theoretically everyone was able to receive messages from the gods. But not everyone was able to interpret these dreams; for that, experts were consulted. An easier alternative to consulting an expert was consulting a dream interpretation book. These books listed possible topics in dreams and what those topics symbolized. These kinds of books are still available today and many are indirectly based on Roman writings. Dreams could also be incubated, meaning that an individual could attempt to attract a dream addressing certain kinds of information through certain ritual activities. This was especially useful for sick people, who would sleep in a sacred location in order to gain a cure. The most famous of these sacred, dream-related areas was associated with the god Asclepius. Dreams were also important divinatory mechanisms in Jewish and Christian traditions; there are many preserved dream accounts from both communities.

Natural Sciences

It is difficult to discuss Roman scientific inquiry into the natural world in detail. It is often stated that the Romans were not very interested in the natural sciences, or that they never achieved the level of knowledge that the Greeks were able to achieve. These kinds of claims overstate the situation, and in fact, there is evidence for the work of some Roman scientists. The problem is that the work of these scientists has not been preserved in written accounts.

Physics was a subject of great importance to the Romans. The most obvious manifestations of this interest are the massive feats of engineering and technology that would have been impossible without some knowledge of physics. True, this is applied science, but that does not make it any less rigorous or accomplished than theoretical science. For those people who put theoretical science on a higher level, though, there are Roman examples even of this, particularly among the Epicureans. Lucretius's poem, *De Rerum Natura,* is a poem about atomic theory (Potter 1996: 92). In verse, Lucretius expounded on the basic constituent elements of the natural world and commented about quantum mechanics.

Similarly, the biological and geographical sciences were also of interest to the Romans. Perhaps the best-known example of this kind of literature is the encyclopedia written by Pliny the Elder, called *Natural History.* In this thirty-seven-volume work, Pliny has compiled Greek and Latin learning on subjects such as zoology, botany, mineralogy, astronomy, mathematical geography, and topographical geography. The work relies heavily on Greek sources, but its popularity in Rome was surely indicative of Roman interests in the more theoretical aspects of the natural sciences.

The Study of History

More Greek historical writing has survived to the present day than Roman historical writing (Lintott 1988: 226), and because of this, classicists tend to devote more energy to the study of Greek historiography. But the study of history by the Romans was remarkable and innovative. Roman history writing's goals were different from those of modern, scholarly history writing, but this does not mean that Roman history writing was inferior. History writing was not meant to be an objective, dispassionate account of the past. On the contrary, the study of history by the Romans was intended to glorify and preserve the memory of Rome, as well as to provide lessons and practical instruction for future readers based on the actions of past figures (Mellor 1988: 1554). Because of this, Roman history often takes on moralizing tones that are inappropriate in modern history writing (Mellor 1988: 1541). But the goal of compiling history, for the Romans, was to provide lessons for the readers. There are two general types of Roman history writing: the narrative of historical events associated with Rome and the writing of biographies and autobiographies of important people.

The narration of historical events in Roman historical writing usually revolved around the city of Rome, its wars, and its internal politics (Lintott 1986: 236; Mellor 1988: 1543). The glorification of Rome was important, as was the preservation of the memory of Rome (Lintott 1988: 226). But the practical aspect of Roman history writing cannot be ignored. Roman historians did not study history for history's sake. They wrote in order to learn (or provide instruction) from the past (Collingwood 1945: 34). For this reason, the individuals who actually participated in historical events were considered the best history writers (Lintott 1988: 227, 231). Modern history writing discourages this; the modern historian should be objective and uninvolved. But for the Romans,

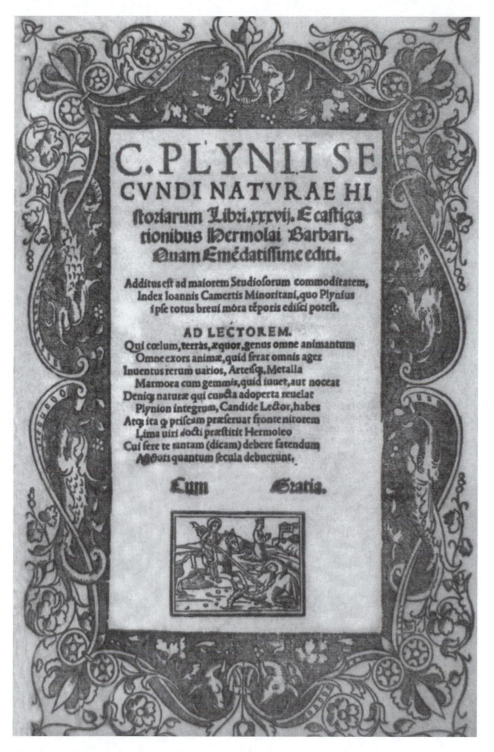

C. PLYNII SE

CVNDI NATVRAE HI

storiarum Libri.xxxvij. E castiga
tionibus Hermolai Barbari.
Quam Emédatissime editi.

Additus est ad maiorem Studiosorum commoditatem,
Index Ioannis Camertis Minoritani, quo Plynius
i pse totus breui mora téporis edisci potest.

AD LECTOREM.

Qui coelum, terràs, æquor, genus omne animantum
Omne exors animæ, quid serat omnis ager
Inuentus rerum uarios, Artesq, Metalla
Marmora cum gemmis, quid iuuet, aut noceat
Deniq naturæ qui cuncta adoperta reuelat
Plynion integrum, Candide Lector, habes
Atq ita q priscam præseruat fronte nitorem
Lima uiri docti præstitit Hermoleo
Cui sere te santam (dicam) debere fatendum
Authori quantum secula debuerunt,

Cum   **Gratia.**

Title page of a 1519 edition of Pliny's *Natural History*. (Library of Congress) people who acted in historically important events could provide the greatest insight and instruction based on their participation. The causes of historical events were particularly important. Understanding why things happened as they did was one of the best means of learning from the past.

Another major theme in Roman historical writing was recounting the stories of great people. Autobiographies were written to justify the individual's own actions to future readers (Lintott 1988: 231; Mellor 1988: 1557). Biographies were written as models for good and bad behavior (Lintott 1988: 23; Mellor 1988: 1554). These biographies were not always glowing praise of past figures. Suetonius compiled imperial biographies, filled with both the achievements and the scandals of the emperors. Plutarch compiled a work that compared the lives of various Roman and Greek individuals to demonstrate particular aspects of humanity.

ROMAN PHILOSOPHY

Roman philosophy has been consistently underrated by later critics. However, it is true that philosophy was not well received in the Republican period. In fact, in 161 B.C.E., the Senate allowed philosophers to be expelled from the city (Shelton 1988: 426). And compared with Greek accomplishments in this area of intellectual activity, Roman accomplishments were less obvious, often based directly upon earlier Greek schools of thought. However, it is important to recognize that the Romans contributed substantially to the history of the discipline of philosophy. Even when using Greek models, Roman philosophers adapted these schools of thought in particularly Roman ways.

Before specific individuals and schools of thought are described, some observations about ancient Roman philosophy in general should be made. For example, to the Roman, philosophy was an important guide to how one should conduct oneself and how one should live. It was more than just an intellectual pursuit; it had direct application to everyday life. Morality and the relationship between humans and gods were important subjects of inquiry. Also of importance to Roman philosophers were the subjects of physics and metaphysics. The very nature of the composition and functioning of the universe was directly tied to "right living" in the Roman mind. Although it might seem unusual to the reader that philosophy and physics should be so connected, that connection is still quite strong today. In the sections that follow, some of the specific schools of thought prominent in Roman times are addressed.

Stoicism

Arguably the most influential philosophical school in Roman times was Stoicism. Founded in Athens by Zeno, the name *Stoic* is derived from the colonnade where Zeno lectured, called the *Stoa*. Originally from Cyprus, Zeno lived from about 333 to 262 B.C.E. He should not be mistaken for the Zeno written about by Aristotle. At the basis of Stoic philosophy was the concept of *logos*, often translated into English as "logic" (Hayes 2002: xx). True knowledge involves understanding logos. All knowledge is a process based on perception by the senses (Hayes 2002: xxvii). These perceptions were then evaluated by the mind, according to Stoic logic. Physics was equally important in the quest for wisdom. Zeno's Stoic school had a distinct view of the makeup of the universe. All things had some sort of bodily substance, and this bodily substance was unified and connected (Shelton 1988: 432). Unlike the Epicureans, Stoics did not believe in atoms, and they did not believe that individual components made up the greater whole (Shelton 1988: 432). Yet the Stoics did believe that at the same time that everything is physically connected, everything is also ever-changing. These basic notions of the physical world lie at the heart of Stoic thought. In addition, ethics, which had as its goal the attainment of happiness, was also important (Shelton 1988: 432).

The popularity of Stoicism in Roman society made sense for a number of reasons. It was possible to study ethics from a Stoic perspective, without studying logic and physics, if the individual was not interested in the latter subjects (Shelton 1988: 431). And indeed, many Romans were not very interested in studies that did not lead to tangible, practical results. Since Stoicism was a very adaptable philosophy, it was easy to pick and choose the parts of the doctrines that were desirable—a particularly Roman approach to philosophy. Many of the specific features of Stoic philosophy were also well suited to Roman values. In general, the Stoics praised discipline and steadfastness as virtuous ways of life (Shelton 1988: 431). The very meaning of the word *stoic* in modern English well suits the Roman Stoic ideals, which also well suits Roman values derived from other areas of life. And because Stoicism did not require withdrawal from public, civic, or familial life, it was easily incorporated into Roman society (Clarke 1956). Stoicism was also more easily compatible with Roman religion (Clarke 1956). The stories of the gods were useful as a means of describing the human condition. But more useful was divination, which allowed the diviner direct access to the rhythms of the world and nature.

Of tremendous importance in Stoic thought was the idea that happiness was best attained by living in harmony with nature (Clarke 1956). However, this was not the kind of harmony with nature, or the simple life, that was espoused by American transcendentalists like Ralph Waldo Emerson. To the Stoics, "nature" meant the material substance that was manifest in all that exists (Shelton 1988: 432). For humans, reason was the embodiment of this concept, and as such, the happy person was the one who lived according to reason. Part of this process was the deprivation of or control over emotion. Remember, in Stoic logic, information is first gained from the senses and then evaluated by the mind. This is the stage when the virtuous individual had the possibility to follow reason and decide not to react emotionally to a situation. Choice was paramount; if you followed Stoic teachings, nothing could affect you unless you allowed it to do so.

Although the exact teachings of Stoicism varied considerably, the foregoing descriptions represent the general gist of the teachings. Although many Romans followed Stoicism, we know about the philosophy through the writings of only a few individuals. Seneca the Younger is an important source on Stoicism, as he wrote so voluminously. Seneca lived from around 4 B.C.E. to 65 C.E.

Engraving from a portrait bust of Marcus Aurelius. (Pixel That)

and argued that it was important to put oneself in difficult situations to test one's ability to endure and apply reason (Shelton 1988: 435). Suicide was an appropriate response to unbearable hardship (Shelton 1988: 435), and Seneca chose this route, killing himself rather than suffer after being implicated in a conspiracy to kill Nero.

Perhaps the most famous Roman Stoic is Marcus Aurelius. Emperor of Rome from 161 to 180 C.E., Marcus Aurelius has gained modern-day popularity with various editions of his *Meditations*. Like *The Art of War* by Sun Tzu, these ancient writings speak vividly to modern readers. People have regarded it as an ancient kind of *Seven Habits of Highly Effective People*. So it is important to be careful about which edition you read, because the commentaries often have more to do with current publishing trends than with Roman civilization. *Meditations* was written while Marcus Aurelius was campaigning against the barbarians and is an eclectic collection of thoughts. He was not particularly representative of Stoics, because in his writings, he appeared quite emotional and was unapologetic for that (Hayes 2002). But his observations were, for the most part, firmly rooted in a Stoic understanding of the world. His writing was also the last major strictly Stoic work, although Stoic philosophy played an important role in later Christian thought.

Epicureanism

Also imported from Athenian tradition was Epicureanism, which, although not as popular in Rome, was still quite important. Epicureans were disciples of Epicurus, who taught in Athens and lived from 341 to 271 B.C.E. Most of our knowledge of him comes from the poet Lucretius, who lived in Rome from 99 to 55 B.C.E. At the outset of this discussion it is important to clarify that the English word *epicure* (meaning a person wholly devoted to sensual pleasure) does not reflect Epicurean thought, but rather the hostile reaction of later writers to Epicurean thought. In many ways, this was actually the opposite of what Epicureans believed.

Sensual pleasure was not real pleasure. Happiness, according to the Epicureans, was attained by becoming free of stress (Shelton 1988: 427). Things that caused sensual pleasure were dangerous because they could lead to pain. Luxury did not increase happiness; it was best to satisfy needs as simply as possible (Clarke 1956: 7; Shelton 1988: 427). Desire, which was related to luxury, was a kind of mental illness (Clarke 1956). Desire for anything—power, wealth, love—would lead to pain eventually (Clarke 1956). True happiness was gained by withdrawing completely from life; marriage and civic participation were not approved of in Epicurean thought (Clarke 1956). Friendship, on the other hand, was healthy and led to increased happiness. Sexual activity was also beneficial, so long as it was unencumbered with obligation (Clarke 1956).

Fear, like desire, was another hindrance to happiness. One of the chief arenas in which fear was created was religion. Humans feared the gods, and this fear led to a loss of happiness. Although the gods did exist, according to the Epicureans, they were remote beings that did not participate in human life in any way (Asmis 1988: 1640). So it was senseless to attempt to involve oneself with the gods through religion. Fear could be vanquished through physics and scientific knowledge (Shelton 1988: 427). To the Epicureans, knowledge of the world made the world a less fearful place. Although the soul did not survive death, the constituent elements of the self—atoms—were eternal (Shelton 1988: 427–428). All things were composed of atoms or void, according to the Epicurean physicists. Death was the process of atoms disassembling from their current state (Shelton 1988: 428).

Much of this philosophy did not fit well with Roman ideals. The idea that civic and familial life should be avoided was anathema to the Romans (Clarke 1956). Civic and familial life were the cornerstones of Roman society. Moreover, the belief that the gods did not participate in human life was also difficult for the average Roman. But even with its lack of fit in normative Roman society, Epicureanism played an important role in the philosophical development of the civilization.

Roman Understandings of Plato

Just as he is today, Plato was regarded as one of the most important philosophical figures in Roman intellectual traditions. A Greek philosopher, Plato lived from 427 B.C.E. to 347 B.C.E. and was one of the most influential figures in human history. This discussion will be limited to Roman additions to the history of Platonic thought.

Plato's contributions are usually seen in terms of three distinct schools, although it should be remembered that these three categories are much more fluid than they may appear in the descriptions that follow. All relate in some way to the institution of the Academy, the school founded by Plato, which survived (with interruptions) in some form or another until the Christian emperors.

Skepticism. Skepticism was the dominant school of thought at the Academy until the rise of Middle Platonism, and even afterward, it continued to be an important tradition in ancient Rome (Meredith 1986: 292). As the name suggests, Skeptics struggled with the impossibilities of human knowledge. Because people experienced the same thing in different ways, absolute truth was an impossible goal. The best approach to knowledge was to reserve judgment and not make truth claims.

Middle Platonism. Middle Platonism was a school of Platonic interpretation that departed substantially from the Skepticism of the Academy. The founder of Middle Platonism was Antiochus, who died in 68 B.C.E. His teachings have not been well preserved, but what is known is that he taught against the Platonic interpretations of the Academy and saw a greater connection between Plato and Aristotle than what was considered acceptable by the Academy (Meredith 1986: 293). Other important thinkers who have been understood in terms of Middle Platonism include Plutarch, Philo of Alexandria, and Albinus. Middle Platonism was never really a coherent, unitary philosophical system, and it is doubtful that these philosophers read one another's works (Meredith 1986: 296).

Neoplatonism. Founded by Plotinus, who died in 270 C.E., neoplatonism was the dominant philosophy of the Roman Empire until the closing of the Academy in 529 C.E. by Justinian. It was a philosophy that attempted to synthesize previous systems, and in so doing criticized Stoicism, Skepticism, and Gnosticism (Meredith 1986: 297). At the base of neoplatonism was experience (Meredith 1986: 297). The individual experienced neoplatonic truths rather than intellectualizing them (Meredith 1986: 297). This is evident from descriptions of Plotinus's personal, ecstatic experiences (Meredith 1986: 298). Also important to neoplatonism was the movement of the individual toward a closer relationship to God. Neoplatonism had a profound influence on Christian thought; St. Augustine's writings were greatly indebted to this tradition.

Gnosticism

The Gnostics were a sect of Christianity with very distinctive philosophical understandings. They were the subject of scorn and attack from other Roman philosophers and are of particular interest to modern audiences. Because of the popularity of Gnosticism in modern, pseudoarchaeological sources, it is especially important to be critical when reading books about them. The term *Gnostic* comes from the Greek word *gnosis,* meaning "knowledge." This knowledge was the knowledge of redemption that humanity gained about the divinity and was held by a specific group of people only. The Gnostics differentiated between the creator and God; they were not one and the same. Of great importance to the study of the Gnostics was the discovery of the Nag Hammadi papyri. Named after the city near where they were found, these papyri have proved to be an important source on the Gnostics from their own perspective. The texts were written in Coptic and include interpretations of canonical scripture as well as unique works.

ROMAN LAW

Roman law was dynamic and complex. It is impossible to give a complete overview of Roman legal practices and philosophy here. Rather, specific themes of importance will be singled out. The evidence for Roman law is quite uneven. There is much information from the later imperial periods, as well as much writing by individuals who were interested in law. On the other hand, there is very little information on how law affected the underprivileged, or what the social basis for law was. The actual practice of law is also not as clear as some scholars suggest.

Modern scholars tend to write glowing accounts of Roman law. It was described as one of humanity's greatest intellectual achievements and was seen

---

Roman Legal Classifications

The Romans had an advanced system of legal classification. To a Roman jurist, there were many different kinds of law, but the primary distinction was between public and private law. This distinction is still present in North American legal systems today. Within this binary division, the law was further understood as being divided into smaller subsections, including criminal law, personal law, property law, and contract law. One of the distinctions within Roman property law that is interesting is the distinction between property that was *res mancipi* or *res nec mancipi* (Jolowicz 1967: 139–141). This was a distinction about the rights an individual had to sell property. Property that was res mancipi could be transferred to another individual only through a very elaborate ceremony (Watson 1988: 618). This kind of property was usually equipment necessary for subsistence and often communally owned, for example, agricultural equipment. By the late Republican period, this ceremony had become anachronistic but was performed anyway (Watson 1988: 618). Property that was res nec mancipi could be alienated in any number of ways, and was not restricted in the same manner (Watson 1988: 618).

as the basis of continental Europe's modern legal system (Watson 1973: 3). One of the key points often suggested by scholars of Rome is that Roman law was the first legal system divorced from religion. Often this is viewed against our most familiar ancient legal source—the Hebrew Bible/Old Testament. The context of the rich legal material found in the Bible is a series of commands given by God. For that very reason, Roman scholars saw Roman law, which was not thought to be divinely inspired, as a step beyond biblical law. Even if this argument could be considered valid (as it is an extreme oversimplification of the biblical material), Rome nonetheless was not the earliest society with laws based in human activities and divorced from the divine. Mesopotamia had a rich legal tradition and survives in many sources. Moreover, in the early years of the Roman republic, the responsibility for the interpretation of law was held by the College of Pontiffs—a religious institution! Roman law was not the clear break with the past that many Roman scholars claim. When reading accounts of Roman law, be careful to separate the author's enthusiasm for the subject from the considerable data available for its study.

Sources of Roman Law

It was previously mentioned that the source of Roman law was not religion. Given that this is the case, where did the authority to create law come from in Roman society? Who created law in Rome? These are complex questions and important ones since they stand at the very heart of Roman legal philosophy. The sources of Roman law changed throughout Rome's long history. Custom certainly played a part in Roman law (Jolowicz 1967: 99; Shelton 1988: 248; Watson 1988: 608). Especially in the governing of the provinces, common law could not be ignored. But unlike North American legal systems, custom was not the dominant legal force in Rome. Rather, law came from people who specialized in the subject through activities such as issuing edicts, compiling legal writings, or trying court cases (Watson 1988: 609). Some of the more important sources are listed in the sections that follow.

The Twelve Tables. A demand made by the plebs during the Conflict of the Orders (see chapter 6) was that laws be written down (Jolowicz 1967: 11). In 451 B.C.E., according to ancient sources, ten patricians (called the *decemviri*) were commissioned to record a series of laws (Jolowicz 1967: 11). These laws came to be known as The Twelve Tables. Tablets were set up in the Forum so that all could read these laws (but see Schiller 1978: 146–147). The Gauls destroyed the original tablets in 390 B.C.E., but their contents were preserved in numerous copies (although no complete edition exists today). Even after their destruction by the Gauls, these laws were perceived as the basis of subsequent Roman law (Jolowicz 1967: 106). An important part of Roman education was the study of these original Twelve Tables or editions of them (Jolowicz 1967: 106; Schiller 1978: 148).

Because a complete edition of the laws is not available, it is impossible to be certain about their contents and format (Cornell 1995: 278). Many scholars have attempted to reconstruct the order of the laws and their overall format, but these attempts can only be considered interpretations (see Schiller 1978:

149–151). The form in which the laws survive is often puzzling. Without context, the fragments of the laws are often very strange and difficult to understand. Sometimes the law was in the form of an "if-then" statement (Cornell 1995: 279; Jolowicz 1967: 107). Other times it was in the form of prohibitive statements ("you shall not") (Cornell 1995: 279).

Scholars have been able to identify some of the issues dealt with by the laws (Cornell 1995: 280–292). Regulations on treatment of slaves and debt-slaves was a theme (see chapter 6). Family law was also included, giving the husband the same rights over his wife as over his children. At the same time, obligations and the rights of other family members were also listed. Regulations on the obligations between individuals of different status were also included (see chapter 6 for a discussion of status).

Edicts.   Legal edicts tended not to be long lists of rules and regulations in the Roman world. Rather, the form of a legal edict was a statement of intent (Jolowicz 1967: 95). The author would attempt to convey a general statement of principle. In the Republican period, the praetors would issue edicts that would stand during their year-long term in office (Watson 1988: 609). By the imperial period, praetorial edicts were no longer an important component. The comitia tributa became more responsible for the issuing of legal edicts (Watson 1988: 610). Any edict issued by the emperor was, of course, binding (Watson 1988: 611). By 230 C.E., the Senate had become the dominant source of legal edicts (Jolowicz 1967: 372–373).

Independent Legal Writing.   One of the most compelling components of Roman law was the primary position of legal intellectuals, who worked within the legal system without a formally state-recognized position. These people were called jurists. From the reign of Augustus on, jurists were the most prominent authorities on law in Rome (Schiller 1978: 273; Watson 1988: 610). They did not have a formal position, nor were they paid for their services (Watson 1988: 609). However, remuneration for their services came in the form of political support gained from helping a wide array of people, because jurists were frequently aspiring politicians (Adkins and Adkins 1994: 47). The jurists produced voluminous amounts of writing and discrete schools of thought arose. Perhaps the most famous of these works is *Institutes* by Gaius (Schiller 1978: 43). This is a book that survived almost completely and was the structural basis for the Justinian Code (Watson 1970: 17). It is an elementary sourcebook, consisting of four sections, detailing different aspects of the law, and was written in the second century C.E. Its contemporaries did not cite this book, nor do contemporary jurists mention Gaius (Jolowicz 1967: 396). It was not until 426 C.E. that Gaius was granted *ius respondendi*, which was the right to give a legal opinion, a right bestowed on prominent jurists (Jolowicz 1967: 92; Schiller 1978: 276).

Legal Practices

The actual practice of law in Rome is not completely clear. The records tend to illustrate the legal mechanisms in place for the wealthy and from the perspec-

An eighteenth-century print of a Roman magistrate ("pretore"). (Stapleton Collection/Corbis)

tive of those heavily interested in the law. There is not much information on how an everyday person encountered Rome's legal apparatus.

There seem to have been two major types of legal action that could be taken by a Roman. One was the drawing up of forms (*legis actio*), which involved the writing of complex legal documents that properly fit into traditional formulas (Jolowicz 1967: 87; Watson 1988: 612). The document's consistency with tradition was one of the primary criteria for evaluating its merit (but, see Watson 1988: 612). The second kind of legal action was the drawing up of a formal claim, which the plaintiff attempted to prove against the defendant (Watson 1988: 613).

Courts existed in numerous forms in Rome. In the Republican period, magistrates were responsible for trying cases (Adkins and Adkins 1994: 47). At some point in the second century B.C.E., permanent courts were established (Adkins and Adkins 1994: 47). Often these courts were dedicated to specific kinds of legal issues, such as inheritance or property cases (Adkins and Adkins 1994: 47). The Senate held power over criminal cases (Adkins and Adkins 1994: 47). In the Roman provinces, legal issues were tried by the governor, who toured the province under his control (Adkins and Adkins 1994: 42).

LITERATURE

The literature of the Romans is one of that civilization's great contributions to world heritage. The Romans produced beautiful and innovative works of prose and poetry. Often Roman literature is unfairly maligned by scholars who put primacy on Greek writing, but much of Latin literature is of the highest quality. In terms of the study of Roman civilization, literature receives the most attention, because the study of classics revolves around the study of those ancient writings. Because of the huge amount of scholarship that has been created through the study of Roman literature (which began in the Roman period!) it would be impossible to survey it here. Rather, the following is a sketch outline of the major periods of Roman literature (as defined by modern scholars). This is only a starting point, but it should help the reader become familiar with the concepts used by scholars of Roman literature.

Formative Period (until approximately 80 B.C.E.)

The earliest Latin literature is heavily dependent on Greek models (Brown 1986: 60). The earliest preserved Latin literature dates from the third century B.C.E. (as did many of the intellectual accomplishments mentioned in this chapter), the period in which Roman contacts with the Greek world were intensifying. Most of the writings from this period have not survived, but later sources describe them. For example, later classical writers discuss Saturnian narrative meter (meter refers to the rhythm of the poem, which, in ancient literature, was based on the number of syllables in the line). But not many examples of Saturnian meter have survived, and scholars disagree on many of its nuances.

What are well preserved are Latin versions of the Greek New Comedy form. Greek New Comedy was roughly equivalent to modern sitcoms; it was stories of stereotyped situations in everyday settings (Arnott 1988: 1485). The characterizations were the major force of the plays (Hunter 1985: 59), which were rigorously structured into five acts separated by choral interludes unrelated to the play (Hunter 1985: 35–36). Between 205 and 184 B.C.E., Plautus wrote twenty comedies in this style. In poetic verse, Plautus still managed to employ colloquial Latin speech and created very engaging characters and settings. Terence wrote plays of this same type slightly later, most revolving around love affairs and ironic situations. The most renowned of these early Latin authors was Ennius, who lived from 239 to 169 B.C.E. Unfortunately his works have not survived. But from later sources we know that he wrote in many genres (Brown 1986: 72). His masterpiece, *Annales*, was an epic detailing the history of Rome, and it was quite well regarded in antiquity (Brown 1986: 73).

The Golden Age (80–14 B.C.E.)

Latin literature reached its highest forms at the end of the republic and the beginnings of the empire. As is true of much of history, periods of great social and political turmoil are often fertile arenas for literary production. At this time, Latin literature began to take on its own forms and to move beyond mere imitation of Greek forms. Writing began to become thought of as a "Roman occupation" (Lyne 1986: 184). And many of the great writers of this period were also statesmen, participating in the construction of society at all levels. Scholars typically divide this period into two subperiods, the Ciceronian period and the Augustan period, both roughly corresponding to the lifetimes of their namesakes.

The Ciceronian period lasted from 80 to 43 B.C.E. It was a time of turmoil and controversy in the city of Rome. The period takes its name from Cicero, one of the most important statesmen in all of history. Cicero was Rome's finest orator, and is often considered to have written in flawless Latin. Much of his abundant body of work survives, including personal letters and masterpieces of Latin rhetoric. But Cicero was not the only skilled writer producing works at this time. This is the period of Lucretius's poem, *De Rerum Natura*, which is poetry stemming from Epicureanism. Catullus innovated styles of poetry that used Greek forms (Nisbet 1986: 114). But what was novel was that Catullus wrote about everyday life in poetic forms (Nisbet 1986: 109). Catullus's most famous poems were those about his mistress, whom he called Lesbia, in order to keep her true identity a secret; she was actually the sister of a very powerful Roman (Nisbet 1986: 111). Other authors from this period are Julius Caesar, Nepos, Publius Syrus, and Sallust.

Cicero

Cicero was one of the major intellectual figures of Roman civilization. Living from 106 B.C.E. to 43 B.C.E., Cicero was a master of many arts, including law, rhetoric, and philosophy. More than 800 of his letters survive, as do numerous examples of other kinds of prose. His writing became a model of prose for later Latin writers, and it is still viewed as some of the most technically superb Latin writing. His philosophical writings were not particularly novel, and according to him, they were more a means of participating in public life after he had been banned from public service. Cicero desired to bring Greek philosophical writing to Rome and attempted to summarize it for the Romans. In his account of philosophy, Cicero purposely avoided taking a stance in regard to the philosophical traditions because he did not want his authority to decide the matter for the reader. Although Cicero's importance in Roman philosophy has been emphasized in earlier chapters of this book, his political contributions should not be ignored. He was an expert statesman and one of Rome's most influential individuals.

Eclogue the First, an eighteenth-century English engraving of the Eclogues of Virgil. (Library of Congress)

The Augustan Age is traditionally considered to have lasted from 43 B.C.E. until 14 C.E. Unlike the Ciceronian period, the Augustan Age was a period of stability and calm. During this time, literature developed in tremendous strides. Much of this literary growth was directly related to the patronage of Emperor Augustus, who purposefully sought to employ artists of all types in service of the state. Augustan art in all media is frequently replete with propagandistic tendencies, but that did not always mean that the art and literature were deficient. In fact, much of this literature was some of the finest ever written. This was the time in which Virgil, one of the world's greatest poets, lived (70–19 B.C.E.). Virgil wrote poetry about a variety of subjects, including nature and farm life. His Epicurean philosophy showed in his writing. He is most famous for his epic poem *The Aeneid*, which he had ordered destroyed upon his death, as he had not been able to complete it to his satisfaction. Augustus did not allow this, and the beautiful poem survives to this day. Horace was another great state-sponsored poet; Augustus was his patron. Likewise, Livy glorified the state of Rome; his large work on the history of Rome consisted of 142 books. Ovid, on the other hand, was an extremely popular writer with the general public, but not with the state. He was exiled in 8 C.E. But before this, Ovid wrote *Metamorphoses*, which recounts much of Greek and Roman mythology. He was also renowned for his work *Ars Amatoria*, which detailed the arts of love.

Silver Age (14 B.C.E. –138 C.E.)

Generally the Silver Age is thought to have marked a decline in Roman literary output. And at one level that is certainly true. At no time in the Silver Age does literature receive as much prominence as it did in the Augustan Age. But the same could be said of many other aspects of Roman life, and the literature of the Silver Age should not be considered inferior to that of the Golden Age. Admittedly, however, there were no masterpieces from this period to rival *Metamorphoses* and *The Aenied*.

In this period, Latin authors no longer wrote in the shadow of Greek authors so much as they wrote in the shadow of the Latin masters of the Augustan Age (Jenkyns 1986: 267–268). This can be seen in some of the developments of the literature of this period. Frequently pointed out is that even in some of the finer-quality works, there is a certain artificiality to the writing (Wheelock 1995: xxxiii). The Roman rhetorical arts certainly influenced literary forms (Russel 1986), which gave the literature a technically superb feel, but a shallow feel nonetheless. Some of the more important writers of this period were Seneca, Martial, Pliny, Tacitus, and Juvenal.

Late Latin (138 C.E.–beyond Rome)

After the Silver Age, it is much more difficult to classify Latin literature in broad terms. The writing of this period covered a long expanse of time, into the medieval period, and as such is difficult to speak of coherently. Scholars are more likely to discuss specific authors than to use broad terms such as those mentioned previously, with some exceptions. One such exception is the use of the designation "Archaising period," which is typically taken as ranging from the mid- to late second century C.E. (Wheelock 1995: xxxiv). Trends at this time included the purposeful use of early Latin and Vulgar Latin (the Latin spoken by the general populace). Fronto and Aulus Gellius are two of the more prominent authors who could be characterized in this way. Another archaising tendency was the rebirth of interest in Greek sophistry (rhetoric), sometimes called the Second Sophistic by classicists. The romance novel became quite popular at this time. These were entertaining adventure stories, featuring pirates, exotic locales, and adventurous situations. Another designation of a time of late Latin literary productivity is the patristic period, which spanned the late second to fifth centuries. The term *patristic* refers to the fact that the writers in this category were early Christian church fathers. Their writings, while heavily influenced by the classics, were Christian in nature and message. The intention was to reach the masses, and because of this, Vulgar Latin was commonly used (Wheelock 1995: xxxiv). Notable is the Latin translation of the Bible, called the Vulgate, produced by St. Jerome at this time. Other famous patristic writers are Tertullian, Ambrose, and Augustine.

Roman Libraries

Libraries were known from the Greek and Hellenistic periods; the library in Alexandria was the most famous. In Rome, libraries were of two types—private and public. Private libraries developed first. Often these libraries, as was the case with the library of Lucullus, were composed of books looted after attacks on Greek cities. Other private libraries, like Cicero's, were created by purchasing books and borrowing books to have them copied. Bookstores were essentially scriptoria, businesses that would copy books for a fee. However, among the elites it was just as common to borrow books and have clerks copy them. Julius Caesar announced the construction of the first public library in Rome in 44 B.C.E. Unfortunately, Caesar was killed before construction could begin. A colleague of his, Asinius Pollio, followed through with Caesar's idea, and after a military campaign in 39 B.C.E., in which he gained enough booty to pay for a library, he founded Rome's first public library. No remains of this library have been preserved. Augustus, in 28 B.C.E., added a library to the Temple of Apollo on the Palatine Hill. This library consisted of two chambers, side by side. One chamber held Latin books and the other held Greek. Niches in the walls held wooden bookshelves that stored the manuscripts. Another important library was the one built by Trajan. Trajan's library also had separate Greek and Latin chambers, but these faced each other, with Trajan's Column (which still stands today) in between. The major innovation of Roman libraries was the space dedicated to reading. Greek libraries were essentially storehouses. But Roman libraries left the center of the rooms open as reading space. There is evidence that individuals could borrow books from the library, but it is not clear to what extent this was allowed.

EDUCATION

Like many components of Roman life, education was a practical matter. Skills and knowledge were taught to children to prepare them for later life. Education was not for the sake of education; not everyone in Rome needed to understand physics. So education in Roman times concentrated on instilling in children the information needed for participation in Roman life. Education first took place in the home and, from the third century B.C.E. on, took place in schools as well.

Home Education

Most of what we know about Roman home education in the earlier periods is derived from the writings of Cato the Elder. Cato was very conservative and argued for a return to the "good old days." Education was one of Cato's interests. Children's education was the responsibility of the pater familias (Wiedemann 1989: 143). In the earliest periods of Roman history, the education given at home was relatively informal. Boys (and, less frequently, girls) learned enough information to conduct simple business transactions (Cowell 1980: 38). This involved some degree of literacy as well as rudimentary mathematics training. The father in the home also taught Roman traditions, laws, and other social information (Wooten 1988: 1109). Boys learned physical skills necessary for military life. Girls accompanied older female household members on their daily routines to learn appropriate domestic skills (Cowell 1980: 39; Wooten 1988: 1110).

Formal Education

Sometime in the third century B.C.E., more formal educational institutions became normative in Rome. Wealthy families could purchase slaves (or hire freedmen) for the job of teaching their children (Shelton 1988: 106). But most Romans chose a less expensive option—sending their children out to a school (Shelton 1988: 107). These schools were privately funded institutions (Shelton 1988: 108), either endowed by wealthy patrons or kept afloat by the sole teacher. Teachers' salaries were very low (Cowell 1980: 41). Some schools were located in rented rooms, in a variety of types of buildings (Cowell 1980: 41). Other schools, to avoid the costs of facilitating a structure, taught outside in open areas (Shelton 1988: 108). The school day began at dawn and normally ended sometime around midday (Cowell 1980: 40; Shelton 1988: 108).

There were three levels of Roman schooling. The lowest level of schooling was open to both boys and girls, and was taught by a *magister* or *litterator* (Cowell 1980: 44; Shelton 1988: 107). Sometime between the ages of ten and twelve, girls would stop their education, but some boys would continue on to the *grammaticus* (Shelton 1988: 107). This level of schooling was mostly in language skills; boys learned writing, speaking, and Greek (Cowell 1980: 44; Shelton 1988: 107). Other topics (such as astronomy) were covered, but they were discussed only to allow the students to better understand literature, not out of a value held for the subject itself. The highest level of schooling was the *rhetor*, to which only the wealthiest boys progressed, at about the age of fifteen (Shelton 1988: 108). This kind of education was geared toward careers in public office through the teaching of rhetoric (Adkins and Adkins 1994: 211; Wooten 1988: 1115).

Rhetoric

Derived from the Greeks, rhetoric (along with literature) was the major goal of a young Roman's education (Clarke 1956). Rhetoric was the art of speaking (but see Kennedy 1972: 3–4), and was a necessary component of education for an individual pursuing a career in public life (such as law or politics). There were five main types of training involved in the study of rhetoric (Wooten 1988: 1114). First, it was necessary to decide what information was appropriate for speaking and what kinds of information needed to be included. Second, the student needed to learn how to structure that information into a coherent whole (Wooten 1988: 1114). Third, stylistic and technical details of composition were elaborated upon (Wooten 1988: 1114). The fourth area of work was learning to memorize the material; a good speaker had to be able to command large amounts of material in his head (Wooten 1988: 1114). And fifth, public speaking techniques were taught; the actual delivery of the speech was just as important as the contents (Wooten 1988: 1114). Other, less directly related subjects were also studied, because a public orator should command a wide variety of information. For example, morality was an important subject, because a good speaker had to have a strong understanding of those issues.

THE ART OF LEISURE

If there was one art that the Romans perfected, it was the art of leisure. Most people are generally familiar with the variety of leisure activities available to the Romans. Leisure is an interesting aspect of society to study, as the values and desires of people are quite apparent in leisure activities. Leisure activities usually reinforce the values of a society and establish norms. Careful study of leisure in any society provides a microcosm of the larger society. For the Romans, this was very apparent. When studying Roman leisure, it is interesting to consider issues of class and gender and how these issues are reflected in various leisure activities. Similarly, leisure activities were often powerful propagandistic mediums; state and emperor were very subtly cast in a positive light. And for the Romans, a society that valued virtue, restraint, and chaste behavior, the kinds of entertainment they chose to engage in seemed to reflect exactly the opposite kinds of values.

Roman attitudes toward leisure were interesting. Roman citizens were not supposed to be participants in performance or athletic activities of any sort. To the Romans, athletics was a functional activity, not the noble pursuit it was to the Greeks (Shelton 1988: 377). Activities that were understood as "entertainment" were considered frivolous (Shelton 1988: 337). Roman citizens had much social pressure preventing their participation. Most performers were slaves, freedmen, or foreigners (Humphrey 1988: 1153). Watching the entertainment was fine, but participating was degrading for any citizen.

Feasting

The image of Rome held by many people doubtless includes some sense of sumptuous and indulgent feasts and banquets. This is not an entirely unfair image of Rome, at least not for one small segment of society. The writings of Martial, Pliny, and Petronius (especially his *Satyricon*) describe these feasts in great, although highly exaggerated, detail. But for most Romans, hosting a banquet was not a feasible economic possibility. The poor had other options available to them. Clubs of various sorts allowed members to participate in feasts (Shelton 1988: 315–316). Likewise, the many taverns in the city provided similar social outlets related to eating (Faas 1994: 41–45).

Ideally every Roman ate two or three meals a day. The Roman equivalent of breakfast was a very small meal, called the *jentaculum,* with the main dish usually a small pancake sometimes dipped in wine (Faas 1994: 38). During the Republican period, the main meal of the day was the midday meal, called the *cena* (Adkins and Adkins 1994: 343; Faas 1994: 40). The evening meal (*vesperna*) was taken just before bed, and was quite light. In the empire, the midday meal was lighter, and the major meal was left for the evening. For the vast majority of Romans, the staple of the diet was wheat-based, usually boiled into a porridge-like mix (Adkins and Adkins 1994: 343).

The elites of Rome, however, engaged in feasting and banqueting on a regular basis. Feasts were large dinner parties; guests brought their own napkins, but the host provided food, wine, and entertainment (Shelton 1988: 317). This could be a remarkable economic burden, but hosting feasts was an important way of building up social capital. People of all social classes and ranks participated in these banquets. Although table manners were not nearly as formal as they are today, the position of individuals around the table was strictly determined by rank (Faas 1994: 58–60). Slaves waited hand and foot on all guests (Faas 1994: 68). The meal began with small appetizers (called *gustatio* or *promulsio*), which consisted of salads, oysters, and especially eggs (Faas 1994: 76, 78). After the appetizers, a drink of wine was provided (Faas 1994: 77). After the wine interlude, the main courses were served—about six or seven (Faas 1994: 77). These were the main dishes and were brought out one at a time. The tables were not large enough to accommodate many dishes, so only one or two dishes could be eaten at once (see chapter 9). These courses consisted of a variety of meats, especially fish, poultry, and pork. A common culinary technique of the Roman chef was to attempt to disguise the food, shaping it into other forms (like a bird) before serving it (Ling 1988: 330). The ingredients were not supposed to be discernible. After these main courses, "second tables" were served (Adkins and Adkins 1994: 343; Faas 1994: 81). This was dessert, consisting of sweetened cakes or fruit. After dessert, the banquet proper began, in which wine consumption was the culinary focus.

The social aspects of feasting were just as important as, if not more than, the food. Entertainment was provided in a number of forms. Sometimes the host would arrange for musicians, dancers, or other performers to entertain guests (Faas 1994: 97–98, 101). Recitations took place at banquets, and learned guests were often invited to present on various subjects (Faas 1994: 96). Guests, especially during the banquet, were expected to discourse on a wide variety of subjects. All the while, slaves would serve the guests and hosts, perfuming them and anointing them with oil.

Bathing

A distinctly Roman leisure activity was to visit the public baths. Ideally, every Roman town had a public bathhouse, in which Romans could relax, bathe, exercise, and socialize. Architecturally, Roman baths were standardized (see chapter 9). These structures were incredibly luxurious yet all classes were able to use the baths. The admission price to the baths was quite low, so in practice, most people really could use the facilities. The normal admission price, when not remitted by an emperor culling favor with the populace, was one *quadran*, the lowest denomination of currency, and next to worthless (the equivalent of a penny nowadays). Both men and women used the facilities. Sometimes

The Roman baths, Bath, England. (Library of Congress)

bathing was in mixed company (this was remembered as particularly notorious under Nero), but normally this was not allowed (Cowell 1980: 145). Women's facilities were next to the men's, and usually smaller in size.

The actual practices at the baths varied by room. Of course, bathing, immersing oneself in water with the goal of cleaning, was the most prominent activity. But other things went on at the baths as well. Impurities were removed from the body by sweating them out. Once the body had perspired enough, a wooden or metal stick (called a *strigilis*) was scraped across the flesh, removing dirt and exfoliating the skin (Cowell 1980: 146). If the bather could afford slaves, the slave would scrape. If the individual was without a slave, he or she would have to do the scraping themselves, or hire an attendant at the bath. Attendants could also be hired to perform other services, including massaging and perfuming the client (Cowell 1980: 146). Slaves were expected to carry the bather's towels and toiletries, but those services could also be purchased from bath attendants (Cowell 1980: 146). Other activities not related to cleaning included a variety of physical activities in the gymnasium. Wrestling was very popular. The less active could relax in the adjoining gardens.

The baths were inherently social, but in a way that was not possible in other centers of Roman social life. At the baths, with one's clothes off, all signs of status and rank were missing as well. This allowed Romans of various classes and wealth to mingle and socialize, without economic-based visual indicators creating the first impression. D. Bruce MacKay has suggested that this was a liminal space; the luxury of the baths and the ethereal feeling of being cleaned in extreme temperature, but at the same time in a tranquil setting, took people out of their everyday lives. The relaxing and harmonious atmosphere conjured up feelings of goodwill not only toward fellow Romans, but to the emperor as well. Because mosaics with rulership themes and the opulence of the structure itself were very subtle forms of imperial propaganda, the baths functioned not just as a place to cleanse oneself, but also as a place where Roman identity was reaffirmed.

Spectacle

Perhaps the most "Roman" of all Roman leisure activities was the viewing of spectacle. Spectacles were held for various purposes. *Ludi* were games held on religious holidays (Adkins and Adkins 1994: 347; Shelton 1988: 332). These religious holidays originated for a number of purposes. Sometimes they were based on older, religious festival days. Other times they honored the gods, perhaps after an important military victory (Adkins and Adkins 1994: 347). The ludi were state-run events, using public money. Aediles were responsible for organizing them, and often paid considerably out of their own pockets in order to curry favor with the public before elections (Shelton 1988: 333). Another occasion for spectacle was a funeral. Private spectacles were funded to honor a recently deceased ancestor. These spectacles were called *munera* and were an Etruscan tradition (Adkins and Adkins 1994: 347). There were a variety of types of spectacles. So much has been written on this topic, and it is so easy to find good information on it, that it will only be cursorily examined here.

Chariot Racing. Chariot racing was extremely popular in the Roman period. This kind of game had a long history—it was an Olympic event in Greek times. In Roman times, chariot racing was a commercial enterprise in which citizens did not participate (Shelton 1988: 350). It was mere entertainment, not a religious demonstration (but see Auget 1994: 122). Chariot drivers were professionals, usually slaves owned by one of the companies (Humphrey 1988: 1156). In Rome there were four chariot-racing companies, called *factio,* that wore either red, white, blue, or green (Shelton 1988: 350). Wealthy businessmen owned these factio; it was an expensive venture (Humphrey 1988: 1156). The owners negotiated rental fees with the aediles, who offered a substantial prize to the winners (Shelton 1988: 350).

The races themselves took place at one of the many circuses, the arenas built specifically for them (see chapter 9). The driver stood in the chariot, with the reins wrapped around his body, which was very dangerous if the chariot crashed (Auget 1994: 129). The chariot was attached to a team of two, four, or six horses (Cowell 1980: 171). The number of competitors racing at one time depended on the size of the circus. The sport was a full-contact sport; drivers purposely crashed into one another and attempted to throw off the other racers (Shelton 1988: 357). The chariot race in the film *Ben Hur* is actually fairly accurate on that account. The audience could also get out of control; a British football type of hooliganism was not unknown in the Roman circuses (Auget 1994: 135–136, 141–142). Betting also took place, and placards with chariot drivers' statistics were available to the audience (Cowell 1980: 172; Humphrey 1988: 1154). Chariot drivers who were successful could become celebrities of great renown within the city of Rome (Cowell 1980: 173; Shelton 1988: 355, 359).

Gladiators. Gladiatorial combat is one of the most compelling topics of ancient Rome. However, the cultural prominence of gladiators in Roman times is not matched by our modern fascination with them. Think of how many films have featured gladiators prominently. This combat originated in Etruscan times and was an important component of munera celebrations (Humphrey 1988: 1159). Controversial among modern Roman scholars is when gladiatorial combat began to be funded in public celebrations. But certainly by the time of Julius Caesar, gladiatorial combat had become a public spectacle (Shelton 1988: 333).

Gladiators were individuals who had been bought by gladiator-training schools (Shelton 1988: 342). They could have been slaves (this was a punishment for unfavored slaves), enemies captured in war, or even impoverished freedmen who sold themselves (Shelton 1988: 342–343). The training schools provided equipment and instruction in a variety of gladiatorial techniques. The school rented out the gladiators for various events. Because of this, not every match was a fight to the death (Shelton 1988: 343). Often gladiators were spared—it would have been too large of a loss in investment if half of your gladiators did not survive the match. It is somewhat of a misconception that the audience determined the fate of the losing gladiator at the end of a match (Grant 1967: 74). The audience would signal their favor with a "thumbs up" or a "thumbs down," but it was the sponsor of the event who made the actual decision (Watson 1967: 74). Eventually gladiators could win their freedom and retire from the arena. Some gladiators achieved a high level of fame, just as chariot drivers did.

Gladiators specialized in the use of certain kinds of equipment and certain fighting techniques. One class of gladiator was the heavily armored gladiators. These gladiators could not move very quickly but had a lot of protection. The *Samnians* (later, after the Samnians were Roman allies, the name was changed) and the *Thracians* were both well armored with helmets and greaves (shin guards) (Grant 1967: 58–59). The *myrmillones* were very heavily armored, with a distinctive fish image on their helmet (Grant 1967: 59–60). There were also lightly armored gladiators who used speed and agility to their advantage. These gladiators learned to use nets and tridents, bows and arrows, or lassoes. Other types of gladiators were the *essedarii*, who drove war chariots (Grant 1967: 62) and the *dimacherii*, who had two swords (Grant 1967: 62). Also noteworthy were the *andabatae*, who wore a helmet that blocked their vision, forcing them to fight blindly (Grant 1967: 61). *Bestiarii* fought wild animals without armor (Auget 1994: 89).

Other Events.   There were other types of spectacles within the Roman world. Large naval battles, called *naumachiae,* were staged on artificial lakes (Adkins and Adkins 1994: 349). Similarly, historic battles or mythological battles were also staged (Grant 1967: 88–91). In these events, people actually died, buildings were destroyed, and ships sank. Also popular were wild animal hunts (Auget 1994: 99). Large numbers of animals were killed this way, and the more exotic the better, as hunts were performed in front of an audience (Adkins and Adkins 1994: 348; Auget 1994: 81). Similarly, animals would be put into arenas to fight each other; for example, lions fighting elephants. Executions were also held in entertainment venues. Convicted criminals would be set, without weapons, against animals or gladiators and killed, to the crowd's amusement (Auget 1994: 93–95). Nero's execution of Christians by feeding them to the lions is a famous example.

Theater, Recitations, and Music

Theater never reached the level of popularity in Rome that it did in Greece. It entered Roman society quite late, considering the popularity of the dramatic arts amongst the Etruscans and the Greeks. When theater began to be performed in Rome, it was mostly in the form of imitations of Greek-style theater. Women were not allowed on stage, so female characters were played by men (Adkins and Adkins 1994: 349). Costumes would differ according to whether the play was a comedy or a tragedy. And it is a subject of contention among modern scholars whether masks were worn on the Roman stage. Companies of actors, consisting of both slaves and freedmen, were organized, and a manager led each company (Arnott 1988: 1488). Although the Romans despised actors as a group, a few popular actors rose to prominence (Humphrey 1988: 1159, Shelton 1988: 337).

More popular for the Romans were the mimes and pantomimes (Humphrey 1988: 1158). Note that in Roman times, mimes had speaking roles and pantomimes did not. Musicians and singers accompanied pantomime performances. In general, pantomime performances celebrated mythological themes and mostly lacked a plot (Humphrey 1988: 1159). The lack of story did not hurt the popularity of pantomimes, because violence, sex, and nudity played very important roles in a pantomime (Shelton 1988: 340). Unlike most Roman theatrical performances, women were allowed on stage for pantomimes. There is one famous story of a female performer who refused to take off her clothes for the crowd at their request (which was the custom of this kind of theater); she was hauled off the stage by the audience.

A less formal type of performance was the recitation. Mostly done in private contexts, a recitation involved reading a piece of literature to an audience. The literature could be a famous poem, for which the performer had prepared a reading. Or it could be an original piece of work, which the artist was presenting for the first time. This kind of activity often occurred in private homes and frequently in tandem with a meal (Shelton 1988: 320). An amusing letter written by Pliny the Younger describes how attending a recitation was not really enjoyable but rather an obligation to suffer through. Recitations were very popular, nonetheless, in the imperial period.

Music was not particularly popular in the city of Rome. Organized concerts and performances were not popular (Cowell 1980: 161). And a free Roman would never have lowered himself or herself to play a musical instrument (Cowell 1980: 159–160). This tendency of the Romans to hold musicians in low esteem should be remembered when considering the rumors that Nero played his harp as Rome burned. This was the pursuit of slaves and professional musicians. Music could be heard in a number of contexts. Street performers were common, and the choral interludes in the theater also provided public music displays (Cowell 1980: 161). Slaves would also perform within the home, especially as after-dinner entertainment. Dancing was not approved of (Cowell 1980: 158). Skilled dancing was discouraged (it might make the dancer look like a professional), although it was taught (Cowell 1980: 158). In the early empire period, dancing had less of a stigma and became a more popular pursuit.

LANGUAGES

One of the primary sources for the study of ancient Rome is the many writings that have survived. This means that the study of ancient languages is extremely important for anyone who wants to thoroughly understand ancient Rome. So much of the evidence comes from these ancient texts that it is difficult to meaningfully study Rome without some knowledge of these languages. Most university programs require specialized study of at least one of the languages used in Roman times, even when students are strictly archaeology or art history majors.

Rome at its height incorporated numerous regions with various languages. Language is one of the primary ways in which communication occurs and through which knowledge is transmitted. Understanding these various languages provides one with greater accessibility to the mindset of the ancient people. To be able to think in the words and language structures that the ancient people used allows a better understanding of them. What follows is a discussion of the languages used in the Roman world and the various ways in which they were recorded.

Latin

The language most associated with the Romans is Latin. The Latin language has had a long history and has been very important in European history. Its use began before the Roman period, and is, in some contexts, still with us today. It has been prominent in a number of different contexts. It was the dominant language of European Christianity until very recently, and is still an important part of many faith traditions. Latin is also used in scientific contexts, as exemplified by taxonomical categories, usually using Latin terminology as a means to cross language boundaries. Until very recently, Latin was an important part of grade-school curriculum, but this has become less common in recent years.

Latin is an Indo-European language. This means that it comes from the family of Indo-European languages, so named because the earliest examples of this language were found in India and Europe. Other Indo-European languages are Sanskrit, Greek, Russian, and English. These languages are all cognate to one another, meaning that they are related to one another but are not derived from one another. Latin is the parent language of the Romance languages, which include Italian, Spanish, and French, and all of these languages are derived from Latin.

Latin is one of the dialects of the Italic branch of the Indo-European family, and its origins are still controversial today. The name *Latin* comes from the name of the group of tribes called *Latini* who lived in the Latium area. Some have suggested that these tribes came from central Europe, but it is difficult to say with certainty where these tribes originated. Whatever the origins, the earliest inscriptions date to the sixth century B.C.E., and the earliest Latin literature dates to the third century B.C.E.

Greek

Although Latin was the language of Rome and its people, Greek played a very important role in Roman society. After the third century B.C.E., when Rome's contact with Greece had grown, Greek played an important role in the intellectual life of Rome. Greek language was studied by schoolchildren (if they got that far in school), and ideally, Roman men were able to read the masterworks of Greek literature. Latin remained subordinate to Greek in the Greek areas of the empire, never supplanting Greek as the dominant spoken language.

Greek is also an Indo-European language, but other than that, it is not related to Latin. Like Latin, Greek is an inflected language, meaning that the form of words is usually more important than word order in a sentence. There are many stages of the Greek language. The earliest certain evidence for Greek language is Linear B, which was first discovered on the island of Crete. In Roman periods, the Greek commonly spoken is called *koine*—this is the language in which the New Testament was written. Attic Greek is the kind of Greek that developed in the fourth century B.C.E. and was the dominant form of literary Greek.

Origins of the Alphabet

Both Greek and Latin use an alphabet derived from the same, earlier alphabet. Indeed, even the alphabet today is based on this alphabet. The earliest evidence for the alphabet comes from Egypt, in the middle kingdom period. Fragments of alphabetic inscriptions have been discovered in the desert, presumably invented by Semitic-speaking miners working for the Egyptians. These Semitic speakers adapted certain forms of Egyptian hieroglyphs into letters and created the alphabet. These earliest discoveries have been announced but have not yet been published, so little should be said about them now. Slightly later discoveries in the Sinai of a similar phenomenon are well published and suggest that this was the probable origin of the alphabet.

The Phoenicians transmitted the alphabet to the Greek world. The Phoenician language was Semitic (see page 281), but it is presumed that contact with Phoenicians led Greek speakers to adopt the alphabet for their own use and to their own language. This is confirmed by the fact that many of the forms of the earliest Greek letters bore a close resemblance to those of Phoenician letters. But later, the scripts diverged considerably. And by adding letters to stand for vowels, Greek innovated beyond Phoenician, which did not have written vowels.

The Latin alphabet is a combination of the Greek version of the alphabet and the Etruscan alphabet. The alphabet did not remain entirely stable throughout Roman history. There were changes in letterforms, and for brief periods, new letters were added. But for the most part, the Latin alphabet remained remarkably stable throughout its long history. Latin used essentially the same alphabet as English, with the exception of there having been no *j, u,* or *w* in Latin.

Both Latin and Greek also have different styles of script depending on the medium used. Generally the kinds of script can be divided into monumental and cursive. Monumental, as the name suggests, is the style of letters used in monumental art, especially when carved into hard materials like stone. Cursive writing is less formal and more suited for writing with ink than for engraving. Another style of writing to be aware of is called uncial, which was a later form of writing. Uncial writing is purposely very easy to read in cursive, as it uses all capital letters, with all the letters rounded. The shapes of letters change over time and can be an important way of dating artifacts if no other dates are given.

Other Languages

There were many other languages that were important in Roman times. Romans did not enforce the use of Latin when they took over a region. However, local elites were encouraged to learn and use Latin, which was essential if they wanted to participate in any form of governance. So Latin gradually spread and became the dominant language in Europe. But it did not usually completely supplant other language traditions. Although the following is not meant to be exhaustive, some of the more important languages are discussed.

Etruscan. Etruscan was the language spoken by the Etruscans (see chapter 4). It was not an Indo-European language, but beyond that, it is difficult to say anything for certain about it. Although we know that there was Etruscan literature (later authors comment on this), none of it has survived to the present. In fact, of the inscriptions in Etruscan that have survived, many are unreadable. Only a few words of Etruscan have been translated. Latin was influenced by Etruscan, but also supplanted it; Etruscan did not survive very long under the Romans.

Aramaic. Aramaic is a Semitic language, with a long history of use and development. It is closely related to Hebrew; in fact, the Hebrew alphabet used today is actually the Aramaic alphabet. Aramaic developed at some time in the second millennium B.C.E., in the Fertile Crescent (the region from modern-day Israel to modern-day Iraq). By about 1000 B.C.E., Aramaic was spoken commonly throughout Mesopotamia, although writing was still primarily in Akkadian. Aramaic became the official language of the Persian Empire, and from this point it spread throughout the Near East. In Roman times, Aramaic was the language spoken in the Levant. Many important Roman-period Ara-

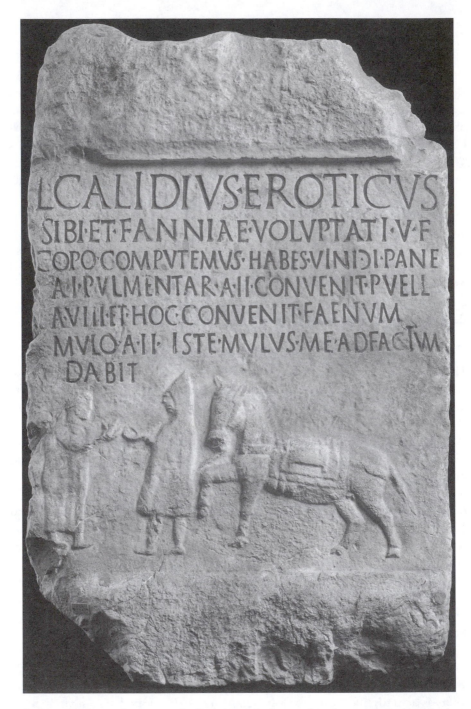

Latin script: Roman funerary stele depicting an innkeeper, found near Isernia. (Araldo de Luca/Corbis)

maic documents have been preserved in Egypt and Israel. It is an essential language for anyone wanting to study Roman-period Palestine, Roman-period Judaism, or Roman-period Christianity.

Phoenician-Punic. Also a Semitic language, Phoenician was the language, spoken by the Phoenicians, through which the alphabet was transmitted to the Greeks. It was an important language for trade and international contact. Punic was the form of Phoenician used in the city of Carthage. Given the important role of Carthage in Roman history, Punic is an important language in Roman studies. There is much inscriptional material preserved in both Phoenician and Punic.

Celtic Languages. The designation *Celtic* refers to a particular Indo-European language family, which has survived as Gaelic, Welsh, and other related languages. There is not much evidence for ancient Celtic languages. The information is primarily secondhand. Celtic words used in Roman inscriptions or on coins are one source of evidence. Another is in the study of ancient names, including place-names and the names of people in Classical literature. Indeed, for anyone wanting to study ancient Celtic traditions, a thorough grounding in Latin is a very important first step.

Writing Materials

Most of Roman writing has not been preserved in its original form, meaning that classical writings are preserved in later copies. Unlike cuneiform tablets, which survive well in the archaeological record, Roman writings were not written on materials that preserve well, except of course, inscriptions. Inscriptions were usually intended to be enduring, and were inscribed into materials that endured well. Other media were not intended to survive in the same way. From the third century B.C.E., the Romans used papyrus from Egypt as paper. Wooden rollers were often attached to the papyrus and were preserved as rolled scrolls. Writing tablets were also used. Sometimes these took the form of thick wood blocks that were hollowed out and filled with wax. Writing was inscribed into the wax. Similarly, in places too remote to be supplied easily with papyrus, leaf tablets were used. Leaf tablets were tablets made of very thin pieces of wood; the wood was malleable and could be bent and formed. Combinations of writing tablets and papyrus were used as the predecessors of modern books. Eight sheets of papyrus were bound together in the middle (making sixteen pages). Covers were created by adding pieces of wood to the front and back. These nonmonumental types of writing are preserved in arid locations, such as Israel and Egypt, but do not survive well in a climate like Rome's.

BIBLIOGRAPHY

Adkins, Lesley, and Roy Adkins. 1994. *Handbook to Life in Ancient Rome.* Oxford: Oxford University Press.

Arnott, Peter. 1988. "Drama," pp. 1477–1503 in *Civilization of the Ancient Mediterranean: Greece and Rome.* Michael Grant and Rachel Kitzinger (eds.). New York: Charles Scribner's Sons.

Asmis, Elizabeth. 1988. "Roman Philosophical Movements," pp. 1637–1652 in *Civiliza-*

tion of the Ancient Mediterranean: Greece and Rome. Michael Grant and Rachel Kitzinger (eds.). New York: Charles Scribner's Sons.

Auget, Roland. 1994. *Cruelty and Civilization: The Roman Games.* New York: Routledge.

Boardman, John, Jasper Griffin, and Oswyn Murray (eds.). 1986. *The Oxford Illustrated History of the Roman World.* Oxford: Oxford University Press.

Borthwick, Edward Kerr. 1988. "Music and Dance," pp. 1505–1523 in *Civilization of the Ancient Mediterranean: Greece and Rome.* Michael Grant and Rachel Kitzinger (eds.). New York: Charles Scribner's Sons.

Bowersock, Glen. 1969. *Greek Sophists in the Roman Empire.* Oxford: Clarendon Press.

Brown, P. G. 1986. "The First Roman Literature," pp. 60–75 in *The Oxford Illustrated History of the Roman World.* John Boardman, Jasper Griffin, and Oswyn Murray (eds.). Oxford: Oxford University Press.

Casson, Lionel. 2001. *Libraries in the Ancient World.* New Haven: Yale University Press.

Clarke, M. L. 1956. *The Roman Mind.* London: Cohen & West Ltd.

Collingwood, R. G. 1945. *The Idea of History.* London: Oxford University Press.

Cornell, Tim. 1995. *The Beginnings of Rome.* New York: Routledge.

Cowell, F. R. 1980. *Life in Ancient Rome.* New York: Perigee Books.

Crook, John. 1977. *Law and Life in Rome.* Ithaca: Cornell University Press.

———. 1995. *Legal Advocacy in the Roman World.* Ithaca: Cornell University Press.

Dilke, Oswald. 1971. *The Roman Land Surveyors: An Introduction to the Agrimensores.* Newton Abbot: David and Charles.

———. 1987. *Mathematics and Measurement.* Berkeley: University of California Press.

Dorey, Thomas (ed.). 1966. *Latin Historians.* London: Routledge & Kegan Paul.

Duckworth, George. 1952. *The Nature of Roman Comedy.* Princeton: Princeton University Press.

Dupont, Florence. 1989. *Daily Life in Ancient Rome.* Christopher Woodall (trans.). Cambridge: Basil Blackwell Ltd.

Earl, Donald. 1967. *The Moral and Political Tradition of Rome.* Ithaca: Cornell University Press.

Faas, Patrick. 1994. *Around the Roman Table.* New York: Palgrave Macmillan.

Fagan, Garret. 1999. *Bathing in Public in the Roman World.* Ann Arbor: University of Michigan Press.

Ferguson, John. 1988a. "Roman Cults," pp. 909–924 in *Civilization of the Ancient Mediterranean: Greece and Rome.* Michael Grant and Rachel Kitzinger (eds.). New York: Charles Scribner's Sons.

———. 1988b. "Divination and Oracles: Rome," pp. 951–958 in *Civilization of the Ancient Mediterranean: Greece and Rome.* Michael Grant and Rachel Kitzinger (eds.). New York: Charles Scribner's Sons.

Fisher, Nicholas. 1988. "Roman Associations, Dinner Parties, and Clubs," pp. 1199–1226 in *Civilization of the Ancient Mediterranean: Greece and Rome.* Michael Grant and Rachel Kitzinger (eds.). New York: Charles Scribner's Sons.

Fowler, W. Ward. 1969. *The Roman Festivals of the Period of the Republic.* 2nd ed. Port Washington: Kennikat Press.

Friedländer, Ludwig. 1910. *Roman Life and Manners under the Early Empire.* London: Routledge & Sons, Ltd.

Grant, Michael. 1967. *Gladiators.* Worcester, MA: The Trinity Press.

Green, Elizabeth. 1988. "Law and the Legal System in the Principate," pp. 440–454 in *The Roman World.* 2 vols. John Wacher (ed.). New York: Routledge & Kegan Paul.

Griffin, Jasper. 1985. *Latin Poets and Roman Life.* London and Chapel Hill: University of North Carolina Press.

Griffin, Miriam. 1986. "Cicero and Rome," pp. 76–100 in *The Oxford Illustrated History of the Roman World*. John Boardman, Jasper Griffin, and Oswyn Murray (eds.). Oxford: Oxford University Press.

Hayes, Gregory. 2002. *Marcus Aurelius, Meditations: A New Translation with an Introduction by Gregory Hayes*. New York: The Modern Library.

Humphrey, John. 1986. *Roman Circuses: Arenas for Chariot Racing*. Berkeley: University of California Press.

———. 1988. "Roman Games," pp. 1153–1166 in *Civilization of the Ancient Mediterranean: Greece and Rome*. Michael Grant and Rachel Kitzinger (eds.). New York: Charles Scribner's Sons.

Hunter, Richard. 1985. *The New Comedy of Greece and Rome*. Cambridge: Cambridge University Press.

Jenkyns, Richard. 1986. "Silver Latin Poetry and the Latin Novel," pp. 267–287 in *The Oxford Illustrated History of the Roman World*. John Boardman, Jasper Griffin, and Oswyn Murray (eds.). Oxford: Oxford University Press.

Jolowicz, H. F. 1967. *Historical Introduction to the Study of Roman Law*. Caambridge: Cambridge University Press.

Kelly, John. 1966. *Roman Litigation*. Oxford: Clarendon Press.

Kennedy, George. 1972. *The Art of Rhetoric in the Roman World*. Princeton, NJ: Princeton University Press.

Laistner, Max. 1963. *The Greater Roman Historians*. Berkeley: University of California Press.

Landels, John. 1988. "Engineering," pp. 323–352 in *Civilization of the Ancient Mediterranean: Greece and Rome*. Michael Grant and Rachel Kitzinger (eds.). New York: Charles Scribner's Sons.

Ling, Roger. 1988. "The Art of Living," pp. 308–337 in *The Oxford Illustrated History of the Roman World*. John Boardman, Jasper Griffin, and Oswyn Murray (eds.). Oxford: Oxford University Press.

Lintott, Andrew. 1988. "Roman Historians," pp. 226–242 in *The Oxford Illustrated History of the Roman World*. John Boardman, Jasper Griffin, and Oswyn Murray (eds.). Oxford: Oxford University Press.

Lyne, R. O. A. M. 1986. "Augustan Poetry and Society," pp. 182–205 in *The Oxford Illustrated History of the Roman World*. John Boardman, Jasper Griffin, and Oswyn Murray (eds.). Oxford: Oxford University Press.

Mellor, Ronald. 1988. "Roman Historiography and Biography," pp. 1541–1562 in *Civilization of the Ancient Mediterranean: Greece and Rome*. Michael Grant and Rachel Kitzinger (eds.). New York: Charles Scribner's Sons.

Meredith, Anthony. 1986. "Later Philosophy," pp. 288–307 in *The Oxford Illustrated History of the Roman World*. John Boardman, Jasper Griffin, and Oswyn Murray (eds.). Oxford: Oxford University Press.

Miller, Patricia Cox. 1994. *Dreams in Late Antiquity*. Princeton, NJ: Princeton University Press.

Nisbet, Robin. 1986. "The Poets of the Late Republic," pp. 101–120 in *The Oxford Illustrated History of the Roman World*. John Boardman, Jasper Griffin, and Oswyn Murray (eds.). Oxford: Oxford University Press.

North, John. 2000. *Roman Religion*. Oxford: Oxford University Press.

Potter, T. W. 1996. "Astronomy in Etruria and Rome," pp. 92–97 in *Astronomy before the Telescope*. Christopher Walker (ed.). London: British Museum Press.

Russel, Donald. 1986. "The Arts of Prose: The Early Empire," pp. 243–266 in *The Oxford*

Illustrated History of the Roman World. John Boardman, Jasper Griffin, and Oswyn Murray (eds.). Oxford: Oxford University Press.

Samuel, Alan. 1988. "Calendars and Time-Telling," pp. 389–396 in *Civilization of the Ancient Mediterranean: Greece and Rome.* Michael Grant and Rachel Kitzinger (eds.). New York: Charles Scribner's Sons.

Schiller, A. Arthur. 1978. *Roman Law.* New York: Mouton Publishers.

Shelton, Jo-Ann. 1988. *As the Romans Did.* Oxford: Oxford University Press.

Stahl, William. 1962. *Roman Science.* Madison: University of Wisconsin Press.

Watson, Alan. 1967. *The Law of Persons in the Later Roman Republic.* Oxford: Clarendon Press.

———. 1970. *The Law of the Ancient Romans.* Dallas: Southern Methodist University Press.

———. 1988. "Roman Law," pp. 607–630 in *Civilization of the Ancient Mediterranean: Greece and Rome.* Michael Grant and Rachel Kitzinger (eds.). New York: Charles Scribner's Sons.

Wheelock, Frederic. 1995. *Wheelock's Latin.* 5th ed. R. A. LaFleur (trans.). New York: HarperCollins.

Wiedemann, Thomas. 1989. *Adults and Children in the Roman Empire.* New Haven: Yale University Press.

———. 1995. *Emperors and Gladiators.* New York: Routledge.

Williams, Gordon. 1968. *Tradition and Originality in Roman Poetry.* Oxford: Clarendon Press.

———. 1988. "Roman Lyric and Elegiac Poetry," pp. 1455–1466 in *Civilization of the Ancient Mediterranean: Greece and Rome.* Michael Grant and Rachel Kitzinger (eds.). New York: Charles Scribner's Sons.

Wooten, Cecil. 1988. "Roman Education and Rhetoric," pp. 1109–1120 in *Civilization of the Ancient Mediterranean: Greece and Rome.* Michael Grant and Rachel Kitzinger (eds.). New York: Charles Scribner's Sons.

PART 3

Current Assessments

XI

Major Controversies and Future Directions in the Study of Roman Civilization

CONTROVERSIES IN ROMAN SCHOLARSHIP

As with all scholarly pursuits, the study of ancient Rome involves many people looking at the issue from many different perspectives. Often it is difficult to reach consensus on important issues in the scholarship of Roman civilization. And it must be remembered that academia is not a democratic pursuit. That is to say, just because a majority of scholars have one opinion does not mean that that opinion is correct. Reading this book should provide one enough of a background in the study of ancient Rome to be able to evaluate various scholarly opinions. What follows is a discussion of some of the major controversies in modern scholarly circles. It is by no means an exhaustive presentation; virtually every aspect of Roman civilization can be viewed from a different perspective! These are just a few of the major controversies.

Origins of Rome

Two different presentations of the origins of Rome have previously been discussed. In chapter 3, mythological stories about the foundation of Rome were explored, and in chapter 4, some of the archaeological and historical evidence related to Roman origins were discussed. In general, scholarly controversy revolves around the basic question of what constitutes a source of information and how those sources should be used. What follows is a discussion of some of the dominant schools of thought within the community of Roman scholars in regard to Roman origins. You may want to refer to chapters 3 and 4 to remind yourself of that evidence.

Theodor Mommsen. The great historian Theodor Mommsen significantly altered scholarly approaches to the foundation of Rome. His notions became the dominant approach used by classicists at the beginning of the twentieth century and are still quite important even today. Mommsen's general approach to the study of early Rome was through the investigation of the myths about Rome's foundation. Mommsen did not believe that the myths or historical accounts were accurate narratives per se. That is to say that Mommsen did not believe that the histories preserved information about actual historical events.

The ruins of ancient Rome depicted in the late eighteenth-century by Piranesi. (Library of Congress)

But for Mommsen, these accounts could nevertheless be useful in reconstructing early Roman history. These myths preserved information about early Roman ethnic composition, about early Roman civic institutions, and about early Roman social structures. So for example, Mommsen saw the story of the rape of the Sabines as nonhistorical, meaning that he did not believe that the event actually occurred. But he suggested that the story reflected the Roman belief that the Sabines were involved in the foundation of Rome. This approach to early Roman history has dominated the field since its initial suggestion and has been a fruitful avenue of research.

Rome and Urbanism.   Most of the scholarly community assumes that the chronologies presented in the ancient sources are roughly accurate. However, a Swedish scholar, Einar Gjerstad, rejected the ancient chronologies in the form in which they have been passed down. Gjerstad, writing after World War II, saw a substantial break in the archaeological remains of Rome that represented a shift from preurban to urban society. It was at the moment of urbanization that Gjerstad placed the foundation of Rome. He suggested that the first king of Rome was Numa Pompilus, and that, in a deliberate act of unification, this first king brought together a number of small villages into a unified political entity—the city of Rome. The argument he made is much more complex than

The Rape of the Sabines. (Bettmann/Corbis)

that; it involves pushing down the chronology of the regal period into the time in which the republic was thought to have been founded.

As the study of urbanism became a prominent topic in the discipline of anthropology, Gjerstad's opinions began to seem less probable. Scholars became less likely to view ancient accounts of a city's foundation as historically accurate. Rather, they began to understand that these stories were purposely simplified accounts. Close reading of foundation accounts suggest much more complicated situations. The German scholar Hermann Müller-Karpe was the first to contrast notions of what he called *Stadtgründung* (city foundation) and Stadtwerdung (city development). Müller-Karpe's view was that Rome developed gradually from one village on the Palatine to the other spurs, gradually becoming a large city.

Indo-European Origins.   The Latin language is an Indo-European language. Scholars, especially around the beginning of the twentieth century, went to great lengths to explain the movement of Indo-European languages from India to Ireland. What spread with these languages? An influential and controversial scholar named Georges Dumézil spent his scholarly career arguing that early Roman practices were infused with an Indo-European social structure. Common to all Indo-European cultures, according to Dumézil, was that society had a tripartite division: rulers and priests, warriors, and producers of goods. Dumézil saw these structural elements as embedded in Roman myth. He never adequately explained the origins of the Indo-European institutions, namely how they arrived in Rome, and why they were perpetuated. His evidence was quite weak, but his prose is quite convincing at first read, and he has been most influential among French scholars. It must be said, however, that attempts at isolating a common Indo-European culture behind each of the civilizations that used an Indo-European language is methodologically unsound and has never been successful. But other scholars using similar arguments have argued that there is evidence from the Late Bronze Age of Indo-European invaders arriving in Italy. But again, these notions are based on outdated models that suggest that cultural change is caused solely by outside influence.

Early Rome in Its Italian Context. The current trend in the study of early Rome is *not* to view the development of Rome as a unique phenomenon. Rather, the development of Roman society should be viewed from its broader Italian context. Scholars such as Giuseppe Micali and Theodor Mommsen suggested this approach long ago, but only recently has that approach come to dominate the field. There has been an increased recognition that the study of other areas contemporaneous with early Rome can shed light on Rome's founding. Archaeology has proved to be the most useful tool for this endeavor. It allows scholars to gain access to evidence that did not survive in classical accounts and likewise is not biased from the perspective of those later classical writers. This is a productive approach to the study of early Rome, and the prominence of Etruscan archaeology in Italy attests to the growing recognition by scholars that it is an important approach to the study of antiquity.

Decline, Fall, or Continuation of Rome? Where did the Roman Empire go? This is a very difficult question. There is no single event that can be singled out as the cause of Rome's end. Numerous ideas have been put forward to explain the incredibly complex reasons why the glory of Rome vanished. No single theory has appealed to a majority of scholars; however, many can be ruled out. Most scholars would argue that there were a number of factors that contributed to the decline of Roman civilization and that no simple answer could ever be valid. This section illustrates some of the more important conceptions about the end of Rome, and those that are most frequently referred to in scholarly literature. You may want to refamiliarize yourself with the historical events mentioned in chapter 4 to better understand where these theories came from.

Edward Gibbon. The single most important work on this topic is *The Decline and Fall of the Roman Empire* by Edward Gibbon. Although much of this magisterial work is out-of-date and problematic, there has never been a historical work that can rival it. As a piece of scholarship, it stood out from the time of its composition. And as prose, the work stands out as a classic of the English language.

Archaeologists excavating the Appian Way near Minturno, 70 miles southeast of Rome, 1956. (Bettmann/Corbis)

Most later readers suggest that Gibbon's main argument for the cause of the fall of Rome was the internal weaknesses caused by the rise of Christianity (especially in terms of military sensibilities) and the barbarian pressures on the frontier. But this is an oversimplification. Gibbon goes to great lengths to describe in detail the various events and circumstances that led to the fall of Rome. The work has to be read in its entirety to get a good sense of Gibbon's understanding. The fall of the Roman Empire seems to be one event in the long, narrative thrust of history. From this perspective, many elements contributed to the fall of Rome, but certainly the rise of Christianity and the barbarian invasions are offered as the most prominent causes in Gibbon's discussions.

Interior of an Etruscan tomb: "The Tomb of the Alcove." (Archivo Iconografico, S.A./Corbis)

Ecological Disaster. There is evidence that the Roman Empire brought significant environmental destruction with it. Both environmental disasters caused by the Romans and climatic changes have been offered as explanations for the end of Roman dominance. Deforestation, for example, went hand-in-hand with Roman expansion. Deforestation increases soil erosion, which leads to poor conditions for farming. The extensive deforestation that went with Roman expansion certainly had an impact, at least at the local level.

Ellsworth Huntington has used the redwood trees in California to make arguments about the collapse of the Roman economy. He has argued that there was a significant climatic change from the fourth to sixth centuries C.E. that would have had an environmental impact. This climatic change was recognizable from the comparison of relative sizes of the tree rings of the California redwoods. In the period that Huntington recognized, the tree rings appear to have been much thinner, indicating a decrease in the amount of rainfall. This decrease in rainfall, according to Huntington, would also have affected the area of the Roman Empire and caused famine and crop failure throughout the Roman world.

Vladimir Simkhovitch made another important ecological argument. Simkhovitch suggested that soil degradation was one of the primary causes for Roman economic collapse. Basing his arguments on textual accounts of Roman agriculture, Simkhovitch stated that although the Romans had advanced agricultural techniques, they did not always practice the most effective types of soil management. This led to the eventual exhaustion of the soil and an inability to grow crops.

Did these environmental problems cause the collapse of Roman civilization? Probably not. The evidence for the widespread effects of these changing conditions is not strong. Environmental problems were a concern throughout the Roman period and seem to have been no worse in the latter years of Roman rule. Certainly environmental issues were matters of life and death for local, small-scale farmers and producers. But in terms of the empire as a whole, these ecological problems do not seem to have been that destructive.

Decay Theories. Sometimes referred to as "seed" or "germ" theories, decay theories about the collapse of Rome are theories that argue that internal structural problems existed within Roman civilization that eventually led to its downfall. These problems could have originated at any point in the history of Roman civilization, so scholars hypothesizing decay theories often do so based on evidence from well before Roman civilization came to an end. Beyond the notion of internal problems, these decay theories, however, bear little or no resemblance to one another.

The reason that ancient Roman writers gave for Rome's decline was loosening moral values. Ammianus Marcellinus, in the fourth century C.E., wrote that greed and luxury had weakened Roman virtue. Salvian, in the fifth century C.E., claimed that the invading barbarians had stronger morality than the Romans who were being attacked. That weak morals should have caused the collapse of Rome is not an accepted type of explanation from a modern perspective. But it is important to be aware of this argument because of its prominence in ancient writings.

One of the more odd theories to have made its way into popular writing is the notion that the Romans died of lead poisoning. Most associated with S. Colum Gilfillan, this theory is based on the fact that ingestion of any kind of lead in certain quantities creates health risks. Since the Roman aristocracy could afford lead pipes in their homes for their water systems, the elites consumed a great deal of lead. The lead poisoned the Roman aristocracy, according to this viewpoint, weakening their minds and bodies, and leading to the eventual death of Roman civilization. There is, however, no evidence for this. The Romans were well aware of the negative effects of lead, and normally used earthenware pipes for their water supply. Although lead can lead to various kinds of illness, nothing in the historical or archaeological record suggests that it had anything to do with the fall of Rome.

It has also been argued that issues of race were an important contribution to the decline of Roman civilization. Whenever scholars bring up race as a category in the study of the ancient world, readers should be extremely cautious about trusting those arguments. More often than not, these modern scholars are projecting their modern notions about race onto the ancients. Modern anthropologists do not widely accept the concept of biological difference in human populations that can be based on race, and in general this concept should be taken with a grain of salt. One of the more shocking theories was put forward by Martin Nilsson, who suggested that rampant interracial breeding in Roman times led to "less Roman" people and that the spirit of "Romanness" was diluted by foreign blood. This argument can be rejected out of hand. A more interesting argument is that made by Tenney Frank. He argued, based on a study of the names on tombstone inscriptions, that greater numbers of non-Romans increasingly entered Roman society, first as slaves, and then after emancipation, as freedmen and citizens. These people, not raised with Roman customs, lacked strong ties to Roman society and hence lacked the motivation to preserve Roman culture. Frank's statistical evidence for this has been disproved completely, and as such his arguments have not stood the test of time. But on the other hand, there probably is something to his notion that Roman hegemony was weakened by the frequency of incorporation of new, lower-class citizens who had no economic stake in Roman society.

This leads to the final decay argument that will be discussed here. Depopulation was an important economic cause for the collapse of Rome, according to some scholars. Arthur Boak argued that a shortage of labor, probably beginning at the end of the second century C.E., eventually led to widespread economic collapse. A decrease in population led not only to a decrease in productive labor, but also to a decrease in military power. As the population shrank, the economic needs of the Roman elite grew, and this burden was shifted onto the decreasing population. Many scholars since Boak have written on this subject and have discovered that there is not much evidence for depopulation on a significant scale, and as such, this theory has been largely abandoned.

Class Conflict.   Another type of explanation for the decline of Rome is rooted in the notion of class conflict. These theories have not been popular in the United States because of their strong association with Marxism. However, theories of decline because of class conflict have been very important in Roman scholarship outside of the United States and should be addressed. Indeed, one of the earliest commentators on the subject, Salvian the Presbyter, wrote in 440 B.C.E. that the Roman Empire was doomed in the west because the tax burden on certain segments of the population was too high to allow these individuals to feel any loyalty to the empire. More recently, Geoffrey de St. Croix has made similar arguments. Evidence comes from the various forms of legislation written at the end of the Roman period that attempted to rein in unfair taxation practices.

Frank Walbank has similarly suggested that most of the Roman population had no access to the wealth of Rome. This prevented the primary producing force from being motivated to produce to capacity. As the empire grew, the primary loci of economic activity moved to provincial areas. In these locations, the producers underproduced, because their primary goal was household subsistence rather than surplus production. This fragmented the Roman economy. Rather than one connected Roman economy, the later Roman economy is more accurately viewed as a series of independent, loosely connected local economies.

One of the most important proponents of class conflict as an explanation for Roman decline was Michael Rostovtzeff. Rostovtzeff argued that the imperial army was itself a class, and that this class was excluded from regular Roman life, yet paradoxically it was responsible for providing and keeping safe the regular Roman life. Soldiers who were stationed in the periphery and were not incorporated into Roman urban life increasingly identified with the rural peasants, who bore the brunt of imperial taxation. The decline of Roman imperial power came with an increasing identification of the army with the rural population.

Military. Most scholars, no matter what they view as the primary cause of the decline of Roman civilization, agree that the barbarian invasions certainly played a part in the fall of Rome. The question, then, is not whether invading forces played a role in Roman decline, but rather why in the fifth and sixth centuries these invasions affected Roman civilization so severely.

Arther Ferrill has made the argument that Rome collapsed because of a shift in emphasis within Rome's military strategy. A number of factors relating to

The sack of Rome. (Pixel That)

the Roman approach to the military changed, which eventually caused Rome to lose its military advantages. After Constantine, according to Ferrill, the Roman military depended more on cavalry and less on infantry. This was necessary to facilitate the use of the army as a personal security force for the emperors. But infantry was a more appropriate attack force against the barbarian hordes. Similarly, the increasing tendency to use barbarian soldiers rather than trained Roman soldiers, although not weakening the army, nevertheless meant that there was no Roman tactical advantage against barbarian foes. These wars became wars between two barbarian armies, and as such, Rome was not guaranteed victory as it was in the early years of the empire.

Ramsay MacMullen made similar arguments. The later Roman army, according to MacMullen, had become less of a military force and more of a bureaucratic force. The Roman army was in charge of many more aspects of provincial administration, especially those related to infrastructure, than it had been before, a fact that weakened the military edge. These soldiers did not live the same regimented lives as soldiers working under Marius and were not nearly as well trained for combat. Edward Luttwack has made a related argument that the frontiers were less militarily secure because the emperors required military security in the heart of Roman territory, a previously unnecessary military expense.

An extremely important contribution to the study of this question came from A. H. M. Jones in his book *The Later Roman Empire, 294–602*. In this volume, one of the themes Jones addressed is not why the western empire fell, but why the eastern empire did not. This is an important approach to the issue of the fall of Rome. This kind of comparison cannot provide certain answers, but it provides useful analogies. So although the two situations were not exactly the same, learning what happened in one situation can suggest new ways of looking at events in the other situation. One of Jones's major conclusions was that the east was strategically less vulnerable than the west. The eastern empire was geographically more secure. Similarly, the east was more populated and more developed. The eastern economy was much stronger than the western economy, so funding the military was not as burdensome. Furthermore, the eastern empire was much more politically secure. It did not suffer from civil wars as the west did, meaning that the military could be used primarily for external security rather than for internal security, and that the east was a more unified political and social body than the west.

"There Was No Fall."   An influential conception that has arisen in twentieth-century scholarship, and has to be dealt with by all Roman scholars, is the suggestion that Rome never fell. In fact, it is often stated that the Roman Empire continued into the tenth century, as did the Byzantine Empire. So rather than looking for causes for the *fall* of Rome, some scholars have suggested that it is more important to look for causes of the *transformation* of Rome into Byzantium. Solomon Katz was the first scholar to argue that Rome's fall was not a major crisis in the history of civilization, and that in fact, many Roman institutions survived long after Rome's political fall—especially law, literature, lan-

guage, and architecture. Peter Brown has also been influential in this line of thought. He has downplayed the role of barbarian invasions and emphasized intellectual and conceptual transformations of Roman civilization into Byzantine civilization. One argument of his that is very compelling is that the shift from Roman to Byzantine civilization represents a shift away from the Mediterranean Sea as the center of international civilization. But the dominant transformation was, of course, the advent of Christianity. Other scholars have made the argument that Christian ways of thinking were not fully compatible with Roman civic virtues. Michael Grant (who should not rightly be included in this category, as he does suggest that Rome fell) has argued that, especially in the writings of St. Augustine, secular and worldly rulers become less important authorities as divine and religious leaders become more important authorities. This marks a radical transformation from previous Roman ideology.

Rome's Relationship to Greece

The relationship between Roman civilization and Greek civilization is quite problematic. Especially problematic is that it is often not perceived as a problem within Roman studies. This issue will not be discussed in much detail here, but there are some aspects of it that the reader should be aware of. It seems that the general impression that people have about Roman and Greek culture is that Roman culture is basically derived from Greek culture. This is especially true of Roman religion, in which it appears that the dominant conception is that the Romans "stole" Greek religion and gave the Greek gods Latin names. The same can be said about attitudes toward Roman science and art. If you continue to study ancient Rome, you will often read that the Romans were "less intelligent" than the Greeks, or that the Romans were a "practical" people and not interested in abstract thought. Two of the most important reasons that people have this impression about Rome and Greece will now be discussed.

First, these attitudes toward Greco-Roman relationships are derived somewhat from ancient sources. In fact, many such ideas can be specifically attributed to the third century B.C.E., when Roman contacts with the Greek world had just become strong. Greek culture was imported directly into Rome at this time, and many of the classical writers (whose works are still preserved) had been born in Greece. Taken alongside a general ancient attitude toward the superiority of Greek culture, our ancient evidence has a skewed presupposition toward the superiority of Greek culture.

Second, the modern study of ancient Rome is intrinsically connected to the modern study of ancient Greece. Most universities' classics departments have specialists in Greek and Roman studies, and often classes or works on ancient history involve only discussion of Greece and Rome together. At the same time that these two ancient cultures are considered in tandem, there are many aspects of the two cultures that are not suitable for comparison. The accidents of literary preservation have preserved writings that are not necessarily comparable. The scale of the civilizations is often not considered, either. Indeed, the way that classical studies has developed as a discipline has made certain that

Greece and Rome are intrinsically linked, but at the same time it has also created a situation in which the relative merits of both cultures are compared. It is quite shocking that scholars still believe that it is appropriate to make value judgments about Roman intellect. Imagine someone trying to compare the intelligence levels of the Mesopotamians with the Mayans. It would be ridiculous. So why continue to do so with Greece and Rome?

Romanization and Imperialism

One of the areas of Roman research that has changed the most drastically over the past twenty years relates to Roman imperialism and Romanization. Earlier scholarship on these subjects has tended to come from one of two perspectives. Roman imperialism was seen as either a positive influence, a force that brought civilization and economic benefits to underdeveloped regions, or, conversely, a vehicle of oppression, suppressing local cultures and voices in favor of the culture of the dominator. Scholars now recognize that the situation was much more complex than either of these ideological poles allowed for. The motivations of Roman imperialism and the effects on local cultures are not simple problems; they are complex sets of issues that need to be explored from a number of perspectives. The next section outlines some of the major controversies, in relation to Roman imperialism, that are manifest in modern scholarship.

Economic Benefits of Roman Imperialism.   This discussion begins with one of the most concrete controversies in studies of Roman imperialism—the economic benefits. This topic is actually much more controversial than it might seem. We are so influenced by our conceptions of nineteenth-century imperialism and the economic benefits for the European imperial powers that it can be difficult to look critically at how imperialism manifested itself in other environments. The economic benefits of imperialism are also often equated with the motivations for imperialism, so it is important to look closely at these issues.

War booty was certainly an economic benefit for Rome and its armies. The defeated powers were forced to pay large indemnities for the cost of war, and conquered cities were thoroughly looted. But this kind of income was only a sporadic one and could not be considered a reliable source of state income. It is unlikely that the economic benefits from the battles themselves were substantial motivating forces at the state level (although the financial rewards for individual participants may have been a compelling motivation).

It has often been assumed that the acquisition of slaves was an important economic consideration of warfare. It certainly cannot be denied that a vast amount of slaves were introduced into the Roman world for precisely this reason. However, scholars have pointed out that there are hints of legislation suggesting that this practice was more a matter of punishing the defeated and dismantling the armies and kinship networks of conquered people than an actual method of resource acquisition.

More stable economic benefits came from the imposition of taxes on conquered people. These taxes became regularized sources of state income. Al-

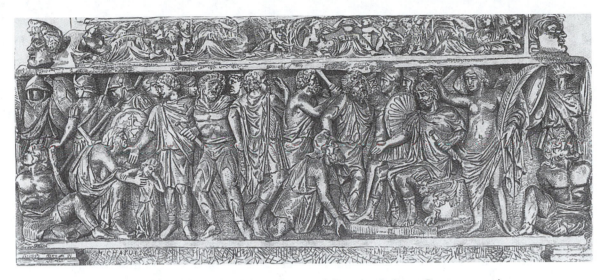

Captives brought before a victorious Roman general. From a relief on a Roman sarcophagus. (Pixel That)

though the amount of taxes collected from the conquered was not stable, the revenue received by the state was, because of the structure of the *publicani* and Roman taxation (see chapter 5). But this was not just an economic benefit; it was an ideological benefit as well. The ability to exempt all Roman citizens from taxation and to force the taxation burden upon provincial populations was a powerful force of state power. But certainly the economic benefits were tangible.

Direct resource extraction was likely an important component of Roman imperialism. Certainly in the early years of expansion in Italy, colonies were purposely established in areas that could provide resources desired by the elite of Rome. Similarly, the incorporation of Egypt into the Roman Empire was characterized by massive grain imports from Egypt to Rome. These imports were extremely valuable to urban populations and certainly became an economic necessity.

Security was an important economic consideration that should not be ignored in a discussion of Roman imperialism. Pompey's eradication of Mediterranean pirates facilitated economic growth on an international scale. Similarly, conquests in western Europe and the policing of the frontiers could not help but increase economic productivity in those regions, and from them, to the empire as a whole. It was much easier to conduct trade if one did not have to worry about running into a barbarian army.

Romanization.   It is doubtful that economic benefits (whatever they may have been) were the sole force behind Roman expansion and imperial development. An important issue, and a lightning rod of discussion in Roman scholarship, is that of Romanization. Many definitions have been given for Romanization. In general, however, it is best to think of Romanization as the process through which non-Romans were integrated into or excluded from Roman society. Be aware that this is a modern scholarly abstraction, which originated in the works of Theodor Mommsen; it is not an ancient concept.

Perhaps the strongest argument for the utility of Romanization as a category of modern scholarship is the homogeneity of Roman material culture. Every area where the Romans expanded has archaeological material that is easily identifiable as Roman. Some scholars have argued that there are significant local variations in the material culture and that the same kind of objects can have different meanings in different contexts. Although both of these statements are true, it is undeniable that the Romans achieved a degree of material culture continuity throughout their empire. It is obvious that an artifact is Roman.

On the other hand, *Romanization* as a concept is often misused. Perhaps the most egregious examples of this are lists of "Roman" traits that have been identified in provincial cultures. Earlier scholars of the Roman periphery would often attempt to identify elements of Roman culture that were "successfully" incorporated into other cultures and those elements that were not successful. This overly simplistic use of the concept of Romanization led to a backlash against it. The best way to understand Romanization is to recognize that the Romans were aggressive in exporting aspects of their culture, but at the same time to understand that this process differed in different times and places. One scholarly method that can be successfully employed in the study of Romanization is postcolonial discourse.

Postcolonial Discourse. Central to both economic and ideological issues surrounding Roman imperialism and Romanization are modern conceptions of how these relationships were constructed. Previous scholarship has tended to emphasize Roman imperialism and culture as monolithic entities and assumed that colonized cultures were likewise monolithic. But the development of discourse analysis has radically altered how issues of empire are viewed and understood. It is now recognized that there is no unified Roman imperialist. Likewise, historians also understand that colonized peoples, such as the Judeans and the Celts, were also not unified entities. There was no simple reaction to imperialism from either side, and different events had different meanings to different people. Discourse analysis involves viewing *empire* not as a fact or an entity, but as a set of relationships and issues. This is important, although it might seem somewhat strange if one has never before encountered postcolonial discourse. But by focusing on issues that appear in situations where there is an empire and a periphery, one can better explore the complexities of those issues.

Another benefit of postcolonial discourse is that it assumes voice and agency (the ability to act) on the part of the colonized. Imperialism is not a one-way stream, with a dominant culture implanting a set of values on a subordinate culture. Rather, it is a process in which all sides (possibly many more than just two sides) affect one another. These ancient people were people with their own lives and cultures, not just automatons who passively gained Roman culture. Think about the literature of the New Testament. These books were written from a distinctly non-Roman voice, and yet they have become some of the most influential writings in history. The Book of Revelation is perhaps the most obvious response to Roman imperialism, but much of Paul's writing discusses how Christians should live within the context of Roman civilization. But remember, imperial discourse is not simply acceptance or resistance of a dominant culture but is the whole series of attitudes, beliefs, and systems of change involved in the interaction of different cultures from uneven levels of power.

At the same time, it is important to recognize that the Roman Empire was very real to the ancients. Some scholars writing from a postcolonial discourse perspective have gone too far, and in trying to illuminate the multifaceted aspects of ancient life have obscured the realities of the ancient situation. Hadrian's Wall really exists and marked a real boundary. Likewise, Roman imperialism was a real historical process; it is only the nature of that process that should be questioned. Indeed, it is important for scholars working from a discourse perspective to have a firm control over the ancient evidence, rather than to make vague, theoretical statements. Ignoring the ancient evidence to support modern generalization simply substitutes one monolithic preconception for another.

Neoclassical vs. Substantivist Economics

Another heated issue in Roman studies and archaeology in general revolves around a basic question: how similar to the modern economy was the ancient economy? This has been a difficult question to answer, especially because most of the sources employed as "proof" for one side or the other are quite ambiguous. This controversy has been driven as much by ideology as it has been by scholarly inquiry. It is important to be aware of this controversy, as most Roman scholars are not particularly explicit about their stance on this issue, but do tend, at the same time, to present dogmatic arguments.

The roots of this controversy can be seen in the writings of Karl Rodbertus, who argued that the basis of the ancient economy was the household—what he called an *oikos* economy (based on the Greek word for "house"). Rodbertus's point was that commerce played only a minimal role in the day-to-day life of the Romans, and that most people got what they needed by making it themselves. Karl Bücher picked up this argument and established an evolutionary model of economic development, a model in which the Roman economy was essentially dominated by self-sufficient households.

Although initially there was much negative criticism against Rodbertus and Bücher, the idea of a household-based economic system was flushed out by the great sociologist Max Weber. Weber was clear in pointing out that language is an important component of an argument and that using modern economic terminology to describe the past is inaccurate. He argued that although some individuals did attempt to make profits in Roman times, such individuals were limited by the state, and that profit-making organizations originated at the household level.

Perhaps the most important early challenge to the argument that the ancient economy differed from the modern economy came from Michael Rostovtzeff, a name that has figured prominently in other discussions of Roman controversies. Rostovtzeff's main contribution to this debate was to claim that there was no meaningful difference between ancient and modern economy. The appearance of difference existed only because of the different scale of economic action. In ancient times, economic activity occurred at much lower levels, and involved much lower quantities than economic activity after the Industrial Revolution.

The most influential figure in this entire debate, however, is Karl Polanyi. His writings took a central position in this discussion, and most scholars take a stance in reference to Polanyi. Polanyi argued that the economy should be viewed as an embedded process, directly integrated into the social structure of the society. People who take this approach are normally referred to as "substantivists." Those who disagree with this approach and see the economy as a distinct sphere of life are often referred to as "formalists." More specifically, formalists who use modern economic models to study the ancient world are often called *neoclassicists,* a term derived from economics, but with a much more specific meaning in that discipline. This is where the argument stands today. There has been no resolution, and for the most part scholars do not explicitly argue about this matter in print anymore. But most scholars who study the ancient economy do so from a formalist or substantivist view, and this should be considered in any further studies of Roman economy and society.

Private Collectors, the Antiquities Market, and Repatriation

Ethical issues about the proper treatment of our cultural heritage have become even more important after the unfortunate tragedies that befell Iraq's museum during the recent U.S. and British military operations in that country. But the illegal sales of antiquities as well as repatriating artifacts back to their original locations have been important issues for years. And even though the United Nations Educational, Scientific, and Cultural Organization (UNESCO) has an official stance on these issues, policy is not always evenly implemented.

The antiquities market and private collecting have been prominent forces in Roman archaeology from its earliest days, and in fact, private ownership was one of the initial arenas in which archaeology developed. In general, most people would assume that the buying and selling of antiquities are morally dubious. Ancient artifacts are part of our common cultural heritage, and they belong in the public sphere. On the other hand, what is more morally difficult is what to do with antiquities that are already in private collections or on the black market. The problem is quite difficult. On the one hand, when private collectors allow scholars to study the artifacts and publish information about them, the collectors are essentially making the artifacts available to the public. This seems like a good compromise. Unfortunately, however, every time information about an ill-gotten antiquity is published in a scholarly journal, the value of antiquities in the market increases and encourages more antiquities trade. This is a real catch-22, and the scholarly community is very divided on

Ruined Library of Celsus, Ephesus, Turkey. (Chris Hellier/Corbis)

the issue. What is worse: never to study antiquities that are already in private collections and lose the information they can provide, or to study the objects at the potential expense of the loss of many more objects over time?

Another issue that has become even more important in the aftermath of the Iraqi museum tragedies is repatriation. Should respected museums like the British Museum, the Louvre, and the Metropolitan Museum of Art be expected to return artifacts from their collections that were gained through unscrupulous or imperialist means? This is another moral question with no easy answers. On the one hand, the loss of a nation's cultural heritage is very sad, especially if that heritage was lost through morally unacceptable behavior. On the other hand, the issue of the Baghdad Museum has shown that artifacts housed in volatile regions can be in grave danger and cannot always be assumed to be protected with the same infrastructure that institutions like the British Museum can provide. And similarly, does modern Italy really have more claim to Roman artifacts than the United States? Although geographically the center of ancient Roman culture, modern Italy bears little resemblance to ancient Rome, and there are many people of Italian descent living in other parts of the world today.

AVENUES FOR FUTURE RESEARCH

The study of Roman civilization is a dynamic discipline. Every generation of the field transforms itself completely. New questions become important, new sources become available, and new approaches to the data are implemented. It is impossible to predict what the future holds for Roman studies. To conclude this book, two new directions in which the field is moving are briefly suggested—they are exemplified by the words *integration* and *synthesis*. One caveat, however: Remember that archaeology is unpredictable. Who knows what may be found tomorrow that will radically change our understanding of Roman civilization?

Integration

The study of ancient Rome should involve integration at different levels—the integration of the large amount of evidence available about Rome and the integration of a variety of disciplines into the field of Roman studies. One of the major problems with Roman studies today is that scholars gain expertise in the interpretation of only one kind of evidence. This is understandable, as it takes years of training to become comfortable working with these data at a scholarly level. But it is unfortunate nonetheless. Archaeological and textual evidence are better served when used in tandem with each other. Volumes written about Rome should involve both kinds of data sets, not just texts *or* archaeology. The field is better served by building on the works of all kinds of scholars, not just those who have done the same type of work before.

Another form of integration that is becoming more prominent in Roman studies and likely will continue to do so is the implementation of advances from other disciplines. The study of Rome has always been multidisciplinary, in that it has incorporated history, archaeology, and art history as interpretive tools. But today, it is important to open up even more and use methods derived from other fields. At the theoretical level, this means integrating the work of scholars in fields such as anthropology, sociology, and philosophy. Roman studies have been particularly bad at involving theory in the interpretation of data. This is mostly because so much data are available for the study of Rome that theory is not needed as desperately as it is for the study of other ancient cultures. But Roman studies can only benefit from a greater exposure to theoretical issues. From a more practical standpoint, the hard sciences also have much to offer to the study of Rome. The earth sciences have already provided valuable tools (e.g., geographic information systems) that have been successfully implemented in Roman archaeology. If these trends continue, it can only be beneficial.

Synthesis

The other main theme in the future of Roman studies is best described as *synthesis.* Roman archaeology especially has been notorious for creating regional syntheses, but not grander scales of synthesis. It is often difficult to compare material from Roman Britain and Roman Africa, even though such comparisons would be of tremendous benefit. The problem, of course, is that synthesis is very difficult. But by creating larger syntheses of the huge amount of available data, the data become more manageable. So much information is now available about Roman civilization that it is no longer possible for a scholar like Theodor Mommsen to control all of the data. But creating synthetic analyses of the data can help manage the huge variety of available material.

One approach that can assist in synthesis is to make sources for study readily available to anyone who is interested in it. The Internet and Web-based data services will be key in the dissemination of new information. There are several reasons why this is so. The Internet removes the geographical barrier of libraries. Do not misunderstand: this author loves libraries and probably always will. But Web-based libraries will make sources available all over the world. So even if one does not live in close proximity to a research institution specializing in Roman studies, it is still possible to have access to the scholarly materials. Another benefit of Web-based publication is that it is far less expensive than publishing a book. Archaeologists are notorious for not publishing final reports of archaeological excavations. Web-based publications allow lower publication costs and quicker dissemination. Related to this, Internet-based forms of data management can be especially useful in the publication of preliminary reports. An exceptional innovator in this kind of information sharing is Ian Hodder, with his Web-based publication of the Neolithic site of Çatal Höyük (http://catal.arch.cam.ac.uk). Hopefully, Roman archaeologists can follow this example of Web-based publication.

BIBLIOGRAPHY

Boak, Arthur. 1955. *Manpower Shortage and the Fall of the Roman Empire in the West.* Ann Arbor: University of Michigan Press.

Brown, Peter. 1971. *The World of Late Antiquity.* London: Thames & Hudson.

Bücher, Karl. 1902. *Arbeit und Rhythmus.* Leipzig: Teubner.

Chambers, Mortimer. 1970. *The Fall of Rome: Can It Be Explained?* 2nd ed. New York: Holt, Rinehart, and Winston.

Cornell, T. J. 1995. *The Beginnings of Rome.* New York: Routledge.

de St. Croix, Geoffrey. 1981. *The Class Struggle in the Ancient Greek World: From the Archaic Age to the Arab Conquests.* Ithaca: Cornell University Press.

Dumézil, Georges. 1948. *L'Héritage indo-européens.* Paris: Gallimard.

————. 1958. *L'Idéologie tripartite des indo-européens.* Brussels: Latomus.

————. 1970. *Archaic Roman Religion.* Phillip Krapp (trans.). 2 vols. Chicago: University of Chicago Press.

Ferrill, Arther. 1986. *The Fall of the Roman Empire: A Military Explanation.* London: Thames & Hudson.

Frank, Tenney. 1915–1916. "Race Mixture in the Roman Empire." *American Historical Review* 21: 689–708.

Gibbon, Edward. 1956. *The History of the Decline and Fall of the Roman Empire.* London: J.M. Dent and Sons.

Gilfillan, S. Colum. 1965. "Roman Culture and Dysgenic Lead Poisoning." *The Mankind Quarterly* 5: 3–20.

Gjerstad, Einar. 1962. *Legends and Facts of Early Roman History.* Lund: C.W.K. Gleerup.

Gordon, Mary. 1924. "The Nationality of Slaves under the Early Roman Empire." *Journal of Roman Studies* 14: 93–111.

Grant, Michael. 1976. *The Fall of the Roman Empire: A Reappraisal.* London: Thomas Nelson and Sons Press.

Harris, William (ed.). 1984. *The Imperialism of Mid-Republican Rome.* Rome: American Academy in Rome.

Huntington, Ellsworth. 1971. "Climatic Change and Agricultural Exhaustion as Elements in the Fall of Rome." *Quarterly Journal of Economics* 85: 173–208.

Jones, A. H. M. 1964. *The Later Roman Empire, 294–602.* Oxford: Clarendon Press.

Katz, Solomon. 1955. *The Decline of Rome and the Rise of Mediaeval Europe.* Ithaca: Cornell University Press.

Luttwack, Edward. 1977. *The Grand Strategy of the Roman Empire: From the First Century A.D. to the Third.* Baltimore: Johns Hopkins University Press.

MacMullen, Ramsay. 1966. *Enemies of the Roman Order: Treason, Unrest, and Alienation in the Empire.* Cambridge: Harvard University Press.

Müller-Karpe, Hermann. 1963. *Zur Stadtwerdung Roms.* Heidelberg: F. H. Kerle.

Nilsson, Martin. 1974. *Imperial Rome.* Chicago: Ares Publishers.

Pallotino, Massimo. 1991. *A History of Earliest Italy.* Martin Ryle and Kate Soper (trans.). Ann Arbor: University of Michigan Press.

Polanyi, Karl, Conrad Arensberg, and Harry Pearson (eds.). 1957. *Trade and Market in the Early Empires.* Chicago: Henry Regnery Company.

Rodbertus, Karl. 1898. *Overproduction and Crisis.* Julia Franklin (trans.). New York: Charles Scribner's Sons.

Rostovtzeff, Michael. 1957. *Social and Economic History of the Roman Empire.* Oxford: Oxford University Press.

Simkhovitch, Vladimir. 1916. "Rome's Fall Reconsidered." *Political Science Quarterly:* 201–243.

Walbank, Frank. 1953. *The Decline of the Roman Empire in the West.* New York: H. Schuman.

Weber, Max. 1968. *Economy and Society.* 2 vols. New York: Bedminster Press.

————. 1988. *The Agrarian Sociology of Ancient Civilizations.* R. I. Frank (trans.). New York: Verso.

Glossary

ABSIDUI: landowners eligible for military service.

ACADEMY: a school of philosophy in Athens founded by Plato that remained important through Roman times.

ACCIUS: a Latin poet; lived from 170 B.C.E.–c. 86 B.C.E.

ACHAEAN LEAGUE: an organization of ten Achaean cities founded in 280 B.C.E. and disbanded in 146 B.C.E.

ACROPOLIS: the upper part of an ancient city; in Latin called an *arx*.

ACTIUM: the site, off the west coast of Greece, where Octavian defeated Antony's fleet in a naval battle.

ACTUS: Roman unit of distance measurement, equivalent to about 35.5 m.

ADELPHI: comedy by Terence, adapted from earlier Greek sources.

AEDILE: the magistrate responsible for the maintenance of Rome's infrastructure.

AEGEAN: the area within the general region of the Aegean Sea roughly equivalent to Greece.

AELIAN: a Stoic and rhetorician who lived in Rome from c. 170 C.E. to 235 C.E.

AELIUS ARISTIDES: wrote an autobiography known as *The Sacred Tales*, which described his attempts to gain a cure from Asclepius.

AENEAS: legendary Trojan leader in the Trojan War; in some accounts considered the founder of Rome.

AENEID: a Latin epic poem written by Virgil celebrating the history of Roman civilization.

AERARIUM: the Roman treasury in the Temple of Saturn.

AFRICAN RED SLIP WARE: form of pottery related to TERRA SIGILLATA ware, but came later and was mostly produced in North Africa.

AGER PUBLICUS: state agricultural land that was assigned to individuals or colonies but frequently held by wealthy investors.

AGORA: the Greek version of the Roman forum.

AGRIMENSORES: land surveyors.

AGRIPPA: an important figure in the establishment and early maintenance of the principate and an important advisor to Augustus.

AGRIPPINA: the daughter of Agrippa and Julia and mother of Caligula who was banished from Rome by Tiberius.

ALAE: rooms in a Roman house, often flanking the TABLINUM and open to the ATRIUM.

ALARIC: Visigothic leader who held Rome for three days in 410 C.E.

ALBA LONGA: one of the oldest Latin cities; may have been the head of the Latin League.

ALEXANDER SEVERUS: emperor from 222 C.E. to 235 C.E.

ALEXANDER THE GREAT: one of the greatest generals in history; conquered most of the Mediterranean and Near East for Macedon, spreading Hellenistic culture to all of the conquered territories.

ALEXANDRIA: city on the northern coast of Egypt, founded by Alexander the Great, and famous for its library.

AMBROSE: patristic writer who lived c. 340 C.E.–397 C.E.

AMBULATORIES: the distinct aisles found in basilicas, but later designated a specific style of church.

AMORES: collection of love poems written by Ovid.

AMPHITHEATERS: oval-shaped structures where spectacles like gladiatorial combat took place and should not be confused with theaters.

AMPHITRUO: a comedy by Plautus.

AMPHORAE: large vessels suitable for maritime trade and transport; found in shipwrecks in large quantities.

ANATOLIA: the designation for the part of Asia Minor roughly equating to the area now known as Turkey.

ANDABATAE: gladiators who wore helmets that blocked their vision.

ANNALES: an epic on the history of Rome by Ennius Quintus.

ANNALS: ancient historical records of important events, but also the proper name for a historical work by Tacitus.

ANNONA: Rome's public grain supply, but the Latin word literally means "harvest."

ANTE MERIDIEM: abbreviated A.M., meaning "before the middle of the day."

ANTHROPOMORPHIC: when something not human is thought of as human in form or crafted into a human form.

ANTIOCHUS: died in 68 B.C.E. and is credited with founding the loose philosophical school of thought known as Middle Platonism.

ANTONINES: the emperors Antoninus Pius, Marcus Aurelius, and Commodus, even though these emperors were not blood relatives.

ANTONINUS PIUS: emperor from 138 C.E.–161 C.E.

ANTONY: the lover of Cleopatra, heir of Julius Caesar and enemy of Octavian.

APEX: the white, conical hat worn by the flamines priests.

APHRODITE: a Greek goddess, later associated with Venus.

APODYTERIUM: the changing room in a bath complex.

APOLLO: Greek god who became very popular in Rome, especially through his connection with poetry.

APOTROPAIC: protective magic, usually performed to keep bad things from happening (as opposed to encouraging good things to happen).

APPIUS CLAUDIUS: the Roman man said to have initiated construction of the Appian Way, the road named after him.

AQUEDUCTS: structures built by the Romans to supply water to the baths, and, by proxy, to the cities.

ARA PACIS: large altar that commemorates the return of Augustus from Gaul.

ARAMAIC: northwest Semitic language, spoken throughout the Near East during the Roman period.

ARCH: an important architectural feature that allows open spaces to be spanned and can hold a considerable weight above.

ARCHAIC: a chronological period, which spans from the seventh century B.C.E. to the beginnings of the classical period.

ARCHAIC TRIAD: group of gods consisting of Jupiter, Mars, and Quirinus.

ARCHAISING PERIOD: period of Latin literature typified by attempts to purposely use Vulgar Latin or earlier forms of the language.

ARCHITECTURAL STYLE: see SECOND STYLE.

ARD: tool used by Roman farmers for plowing.

ARENA: center part of an amphitheater.

ARES: Greek god who came to be associated with Mars.

ARRETINE POTTERY: another name for TERRA SIGILLATA pottery; it is the name more commonly used in ancient texts.

ARTEMIS: Greek goddess who came to be associated with Diana.

ARVAL PRIESTS: priests responsible for the worship of the goddess Dea Dia and for various other activities related to the fertility of the fields.

ARVUM: Latin term for a plowed field.

AS: a unit of Roman currency.

ASCLEPIUS: Greek god that individuals consulted, frequently through dreams, to gain cures and medical assistance.

ASHLAR: kind of masonry, consisting of squared stones laid horizontally.

ATHENA: Greek goddess who came to be associated with Minerva.

ATRIUM: center portion of a house, usually square or rectangular.

ATRIUM HOUSE: type of Roman house, characterized by the centrality of the atrium.

ATTIC: Greek term for stage.

AUGURS: the branch of Roman public religion whose members attempted to understand various communications from the gods, which came in many forms, such as the flight paths of birds.

AUGURY: the science of observing bird behavior to gain omens from the gods.

AUGUSTAN AGE: the literary and artistic period from the death of Caesar until the death of Ovid, and does *not* correspond directly with the reign of Augustus.

AUGUSTUS: title conferred upon Octavian by the Roman Senate; the title came to be used by subsequent rulers of emperors and is the Roman equivalent of the English word *emperor.*

AULUS GELLIUS: author of *Attic Nights.*

AUREUS: a unit of Roman coinage.

AUSPICE: see AUGURY.

AVENTINE: one of the hills of Rome.

BABYLON: ancient Mesopotamian city located in modern Iraq.

BACCHANALIA: rites performed for Dionysus that were banned in Rome in 186 B.C.E.

BACCHIDES: a comedy by Plautus.

BACCHUS: the Roman version of the Greek god Dionysus.

BARBARIAN: the designation used for all non-Greek-speaking peoples.

BARRACKS EMPERORS: from 235 C.E. until 284 C.E., at least twenty-five emperors were selected from within the ranks of the military (hence barracks), normally quickly killed and replaced by a new emperor.

BASE: term used in ceramic analysis to denote the bottom of a vessel.

BASILICA: distinct type of building, characterized by a peristyle with an open central space.

BATHS: public complexes for bathing, found in most Roman cities, and open to all who could afford the inexpensive entrance fees.

BATHS OF CARACALLA: a very large bathing complex (over 11 hectares in area) that was used from 211 C.E. until 537 C.E.

BESTIARII: gladiators who fought wild animals.

BOETHIUS: philosopher and Christian theologian who lived from about 476 C.E. to 524 C.E.

BONA DEA: goddess worshipped exclusively by women and celebrated in a biannual feast called the PAX DEORUM.

BOUDICCA: woman who led a revolt against the Romans in Britain in 61 C.E., also known as Boadicea.

BRUTUS: one of the murderers of Julius Caesar, immortalized as such by Shakespeare.

BUFF WARE: pottery made of clay fired to a cream color.

BUSTS: sculptures of an individual depicting the parts of the body from the shoulders up.

BYZANTIUM: the city of modern-day Istanbul, once the capital of an empire that lasted from 330 C.E. to 1453 C.E.

CAESAR: originally the family name of Julius Caesar; it was assumed by Octavian after his adoption and was subsequently used by other emperors, gaining the title on their accession or upon their appointment as heir.

CAESARION: the nickname for Ptolemy XV, who was a son of Cleopatra and was rumored to have been fathered by Julius Caesar.

CALADARIUM: the hot room in a Roman bath.

CALIGULA: emperor from 41 C.E. to 54 C.E.

CAMENAE: goddesses associated with water.

CAMPANIAN WARE: one of the earliest types of Roman fine ware ceramics and notable for its reddish slip.

CAMPUS MARTIUS: located outside of the city of Rome; the initial meeting place of the Roman army and the comitia centuriata and in English called the Field of Mars.

CAPITAL: an architectural term for the top part of a column.

CAPITOLINE: one of the hills of Rome.

CAPITOLINE TRIAD: group of gods consisting of Jupiter, Juno, and Minerva.

CAPTIVI: a comedy by Plautus.

CARACALLA: emperor from 211 C.E.–217 C.E.

CARDO: one of the cardinal lines of the sky and one of the cardinal lines laid out in land surveying.

CARMEN ARVALE: the oldest surviving example of Latin poetry and a song of the Arval Priests.

CARPENTUM: harvesting machine used in the northern provinces of the Roman Empire.

CARTHAGE: city in modern-day Tunisia, founded in the Iron Age by Phoenician seafarers, which became a huge naval and commercial power and fought with Rome in the Punic Wars.

CARTIBULUM: marble table found in the ATRIUM of a Roman house.

CASSIUS DIO: Roman historian who lived from about 150 C.E. to 235 C.E.

CASTRUM: rectangular, planned Roman military camp.

CATACOMBS: belowground burial complexes, especially associated with the Jewish and Christian communities of Rome.

CATCHMENT ANALYSIS: study of the amount of people who can be supported by the land in a given region.

CATILINE CONSPIRACY: attempted revolution led by Catiline in 63 B.C.E. that was exposed by Cicero.

CATO THE ELDER: Roman moralist, especially noteworthy for his glorified accounts of Rome's past and "good old days" attacks on contemporary Roman society.

CATO THE YOUNGER: a Stoic and vocal opponent of the Triumvirate.

CATULLUS: poet during the Augustan Age who innovated new styles of Latin poetry using Greek forms.

CAUDINE FORKS: site of a Roman defeat to the Samnites in 321 B.C.E.

CAVEA: orchestra pit of a Roman theater.

CELLA: the sanctuary of a temple.

CELTS: group of ancient people who lived in western Europe, spoke a common language, and from whom most of our knowledge comes from Roman sources.

CENA: Roman midday meal.

CENACULUM: apartment that took up the entire floor of a building.

CENSOR: one of the most powerful elected positions in the republic, responsible for registering citizens, keeping censuses of property, and ensuring that senators engaged in moral behavior.

CENSUS: taken every five years as a means of evaluating the wealth of Roman individuals.

CENTUMVIRI: group of men who acted as a jury in some property-related trials in the Republican period.

CENTURIAE: segments of land allocated to colonists, usually by a lottery system.

CENTURIONS: officers in the Roman army, of varying ranks and authorities.

CERES: goddess associated with grain.

CHALDEANS: ancient tribe that lived near Babylon well before Roman times; came to be associated with astrology in classical traditions.

CHALDEI: name used for astrologers in Roman times.

CICERO: lived from 103 B.C.E. to 46 B.C.E.; was a statesman, orator, and writer of unsurpassed talent.

CICERONIAN AGE: term for the literary period roughly contemporaneous with Cicero's life.

CIRCUS: track for chariot racing, semicircular in shape, with a field divided into two sides; spectators sat in stands on either side.

CIRCUS MAXIMUS: the largest and most famous chariot-racing track, located in Rome.

CIRE PERDUE: see LOST WAX.

CISTELLERIA: a Roman comedy by Plautus.

CLAUDIAN: Latin poet who died in 404 C.E.

CLAUDIUS: emperor from 41 C.E. to 54 C.E.

CLEOPATRA VII: commonly considered the last queen of Egypt and romantically linked with Julius Caesar and Marc Antony.

CLIENT: a lower-status individual who was supported, in a variety of ways, by a patron.

CLOACA MAXIMA: the major Roman sewer, first constructed in the regal period and still in use today.

COARSE WARE: cheaper kind of pottery, usually used for utilitarian purposes rather than decorative purposes.

COGNATES: languages or words that are related to one another but not derived from one another.

COLLEGE: not postsecondary school, but rather state organizations of cultic officials.

COLLINA: one of the four major zones of the city of Rome until Augustus reorganized the city.

COLONY: type of Roman city founded by the Romans in newly conquered territories, often settled by veterans.

COLOSSEUM: the large structure (more properly called the Flavian Amphitheater) inaugurated by Titus in 80 C.E. and still one of the most prominent monuments in Rome.

COLUMBARIUM: large tomb that accommodated the remains of hundreds of (usually cremated) individuals.

COMITIA: Latin term for assembly; should not be confused with the modern word *committee.*

COMITIA CENTURIATA: the assembly of centuries, a Republican assembly of 373 centuries (groups of 100 men) who voted on legislation and the election of upper officials.

COMITIA CURIATA: the assembly of wards; each of the three tribes was further divided into ten wards, who voted as a block during the period of the monarchy on approving the king or any other magistrate with imperium.

COMITIA TRIBUTA: the assembly of tribes, this republican assembly functioned like the comitia centuriata but was divided into thirty-five tribes and generally voted on less important issues.

COMITIUM: enclosed building used for assemblies, the most famous located in the forum Romanum.

COMMODUS: emperor from 180 C.E.–192 C.E.

COMPLUVIUM: the open section in the roof of an atrium that leads to the impluvium.

CONCILIUM PLEBIS: structured similarly to the comitia tributa, this assembly consisted only of plebeians.

CONNUBIUM: the legal right of a couple to marry each other.

CONSTANTINE: emperor from 307 C.E. to 337 C.E. who converted the empire to Christianity.

CONSUL: elected military commander.

CONTIO: informal meeting held before an election to inform the general public (patrician and slave, male and female) about an issue.

CONTUBERNIUM: the nonlegal arrangement that allowed slaves to marry one another.

COPTIC: the latest form of the Egyptian language, and also the term generally used for the Christian population living in Egypt.

CORINTHIAN RELIEF WARE: type of fine pottery, dating to the later Roman period, notable for the reliefs molded on the sides.

CORNELIA: daughter of Scipio Africanus and mother of the Gracchi; an influential figure in Roman civic life through her sons and considered a model Roman woman.

CORVUS: developed during the Punic Wars, this was a drawbridge (fitted with an iron spike) that allowed Roman soldiers to board and overwhelm enemy warships.

CRAFT SPECIALIZATION: when an individual has the skills, tools, and resources for one particular occupation and performs that occupation to create a surplus of material or labor that can then be traded for other goods.

CRASSUS: one of the members of the First Triumvirate.

CUBICULUM: the bedroom in a Roman house.

CUPID: son of Venus and Vulcan and a Roman adaptation of the Greek god Eros.

CURIA: the building where the Senate met.

CURIAE: an extended family, of which there were ten in each of the three tribes, during the period of the monarchy.

CURSUS HONORUM: the "course of honors"; after 180 B.C.E., citizens could only be elected to positions in a fixed order, at certain ages, with specific intervals between offices, although some individuals (such as Pompey) were able to ignore these steps.

CURSUS PUBLICUS: Roman military and state transportation network, established by Augustus.

CURULE MAGISTRATES: magistrates (censors, consuls, praetors, and some aediles) with the right to use certain symbols of state authority.

CYBELE: goddess brought to Rome, who was also known as Magna Mater, whose worshippers were notorious for ecstatic behavior.

CYNICISM: type of philosophy that never developed into an established school, but most typified by ascetic beggars who wandered the Roman world.

DEA DIA: goddess whose main worship was performed by the Arval Priests.

DECAMUNUS: one of the cardinal lines of the sky and one of the cardinal lines laid out in land surveying.

DECAY THEORIES: theories that explain the fall of Rome through internal, systemic problems; also known as "germ" or "seed" theories.

DECEMVIRI: groups of ten men formed to perform specific civic functions.

DEMETER: Greek goddess who came to be associated with Ceres.

DENARIUS: a unit of Roman coinage.

DIALOGUE: Greek literary genre, sometimes used in Roman literature, organized around a conversation between individuals.

DIANA: hunter goddess who was invoked for assistance in childbirth.

DICTATOR: supreme commander of Rome, nominated by the Senate for a set period during times of crisis.

DIMACHERII: gladiators who used two swords.

DIOCLETIAN: emperor from 285 C.E.–305 C.E.

DIONYSUS: Greek god worshipped in a mystery cult.

DIS: Roman version of Pluto, the god of the underworld.

DIVINATION: general term for techniques of predicting the future or communicating with the gods.

DOMESTIC RELIGION: religion practiced in the average Roman household, which is usually contrasted with state or official religion.

DOMINATE: from *dominus* (meaning "master"), this is the term used to describe an emperor's reign from Diocletian's reign onward, as opposed to *principate.*

DOMITIAN: emperor from 81 C.E. to 96 C.E.

DOMITIAN'S PALACE: the huge palace built on top of the Palatine Hill.

DOMUS: the word for house that can refer to the physical house, the staff of the house, or a family line.

DOMUS AUREA: Nero's Golden House, a huge imperial estate constructed in the middle of Rome, with an artificial lake as its centerpiece.

DOMUS PUBLICA: the official residence of the pontifex maximus, located in Rome.

DREAM INCUBATION: the practice of purposefully seeking out dreams, often by sleeping in a particular setting.

DUPONDIUS: a unit of Roman coinage.

ECLOGUES: ten pastoral poems by Virgil.

EDICTS: statements of legal intent, issued by Praetors in the Republican period and by the emperor in the imperial period.

EGERIA: type of water nymph that could assist pregnant women.

ELAABALUS: emperor from 218 C.E.–222 C.E.

ELEGY: type of poetry written with a specific meter that was associated with funerals and laments, and in modern times refers only to literature of mourning.

ELYSIAN FIELDS: in Greek and Roman literary traditions, one of the locations where the dead dwelled.

EMPEROR: the office of the leader of Rome during the imperial period.

EMPEROR CULT: the worship of deified, dead emperors, not the worship of living emperors.

EMPIRE: the term for the period of Roman history in which Rome was ruled by an emperor, as well as a more general term for the larger Roman state.

ENNIUS QUINTUS: a Roman poet who lived from 239 B.C.E.–169 B.C.E.

EPHESUS: town in modern Turkey to which Paul wrote his letter to the Ephesians.

EPIC: a literary genre that usually involves accounts of the past involving humans and gods.

EPICUREANISM: an Athenian philosophical tradition that promoted the study of physics and the withdrawal from civic life.

EPICURUS: the founder of Epicureanism.

EPIDICUS: a comedy by Plautus.

EPIGRAPHY: the study of inscriptions.

EPISTLES: the scholarly term for letters or literature written in the form of letters.

EPITHETS: words or phrases describing the attributes of a person, usually associated with their name or titles.

EPULONES: the college of cultic officials responsible for administering feasts and games.

EQUESTRIAN: see EQUITES.

EQUESTRIAN STATUES: statues of individuals mounted on a horse, but not necessarily statues of equestrians.

EQUITES: a status group consisting of property holders who were wealthy enough to afford the equipment for horse-based warfare.

ESQUILINA: one of the four major zones of the city of Rome until Augustus reorganized the city.

ESSEDARII: gladiators who drove chariots.

ESSENES: a particular Jewish sect, infamous from the New Testament, whom most scholars associate with the Dead Sea Scrolls.

ETRUSCANS: the dominant cultural group that lived in central Italy prior to the rise of Roman civilization.

EUNUCHUS: a Roman comedy by Terence based on an earlier play by Menander.

EUSEBIUS: a Christian writer who lived from about 260 C.E. to 340 C.E., and one of the most important sources for early Christianity.

EVANDER: a Greek god, who in some Roman legends was the founder of Rome.

EXEDRA: a recess in the wall of a Roman house.

FACTIO: the four chariot-racing companies in Rome that rented out chariots and drivers for events.

FAIYUM MUMMY PORTRAITS: realistic paintings of human faces, found on mummified bodies in Egypt during the Roman period.

FASCES: an important symbol of power in Rome, consisting of a bundle of rods, and infamous because of its associations with Mussolini's Fascist party (and the source of that party's name).

FASTI: the name of Ovid's poem about the Roman calendar, derived from the same term used to describe days of the year in which business could be conducted.

FAUCES: the main hall of an atrium-style house that connected the VESTIBULUM with the ATRIUM.

FAUSTULUS: the shepherd who supposedly found Romulus and Remus.

FELICITAS: the goddess of luck.

FERALIA: Roman festival for the dead.

FERIAE: a Roman festival day.

FETIALES: the cultic officials in charge of treaties and international relations.

FIBULA: pin for fastening Roman clothing.

FINE WARE: well-made, highly fired pottery.

FIRST SETTLEMENT: in 27 B.C.E., Octavian gained the name Augustus and claimed to have restored the republic, but in fact brought that form of government to an end.

FIRST STYLE: style of wall painting and interior decoration at Pompeii typified by the rendering of artificial architectural features in paint.

FIRST SUCCESSION: the moment when the Plebeians withdrew from Rome and formed an internal governing system.

FISCUS: the private treasury of the emperor.

FLAMINES: the leaders of the cults of particular deities.

FLAVIANS: the emperors Vespasian, Titus, and Domitian.

FLORUS: a Roman historian, whose major work records major events from the earliest times until the time of Augustus.

FOEDUS CASSIANUM: treaty between Rome and the Latin League (493 B.C.E.), which made Rome equal to the league as a whole in terms of dividing spoils of war and gave Rome the sole right to summon the entire league to war.

FORA: the plural form of forum.

FORMATIVE PERIOD: the earliest stage of Latin literature, typically understood as lasting until 80 B.C.E.

FORTUNA: goddess with a temple in the Forum Boarium, associated with good luck.

FORUM: open area, often in the center of the town, used as a public meeting space for a variety of activities.

FORUM BOARIUM: area in Rome where cattle were sold.

FORUM ROMANUM: center of Roman religious and commercial life located at the foot of the Capitoline and Palatine Hills.

FOURTH STYLE: style of wall painting and interior decoration found at Pompeii that depicts fanciful and impossible architectural features.

FRANKS: German tribes who eventually conquered what is now modern France.

FREEDMEN: slaves that have been manumitted.

FRIGIDARIUM: the cold room in a Roman bath.

FRONTO: a prominent orator, especially influential on Cicero.

GAIUS: author of the *Institutes*, an ancient sourcebook on Roman law.

GALBA: emperor from 68 C.E. to 69 C.E.

GALLIC WAR: the name of Julius Caesar's account of the wars of the same name.

GAUL: before 42 B.C.E., this is the designation given to the section of Italy that lies between the Alps and Apennines, but after the conquest of this region by Augustus, Gaul is used to refer to the area of modern France.

GENII: the plural form of the word *genius.*

GENIUS: the spirit that resides within every pater familias that allowed him to procreate and lead the household.

GENIUS AUGUSTI: the manifestation of Augustus's procreative power that was publicly worshipped.

GENIUS LOCI: the term used for a deity when the individual invoking the deity did not know its name.

GENS: a Roman family line, all descended from one male ancestor, and all bearing the same name.

GEOGRAPHIC INFORMATION SYSTEMS: a computer-based mapping database technology, which is becoming very important in archaeological enquiry.

GEORGICS: a poem by Virgil that romanticizes rural life.

GERM THEORIES: theories that explain the fall of Rome through internal, systemic problems, also known as "decay" or "seed" theories.

GERMANIA: the name of the writings of Tacitus on the German tribes.

GERMANICUS: name bestowed on Nero Claudius Drusus for victories over the Germans and held from then on by the Julio-Claudian family.

GERMANY: understood by the Romans to be the area east of the Rhine River and north of the Danube River.

GETA: emperor in 211 C.E.

GIBBON, EDWARD: one of the most influential Roman scholars of all time, famous for his masterpiece, *The Decline and Fall of the Roman Empire.*

GIS: See GEOGRAPHIC INFORMATION SYSTEMS.

GNOSIS: the Greek word for "knowledge."

GNOSTICS: a distinct Christian sect that believed in a creator deity separate from the supreme god.

GOLDEN AGE: a period of Latin literature, traditionally understood as lasting from 80 B.C.E. until 14 B.C.E.

GOLDEN HOUSE: see DOMUS AUREA.

GOTHS: Germanic tribe that settled near the Black Sea.

GRACCHI: two brothers (Tiberius and Gaius) who attempted significant social reforms in the second century B.C.E.

GRAMMATICUS: the level of school attended by boys, beginning around the ages of 10 to 12.

GREEK: an Indo-European language prominent in Roman civilization.

GREEK NEW COMEDY: type of play characterized by stereotyped characters and situations.

GROMA: instrument used in surveying, whose main components consisted of two arms crossed at right angles.

GROMATICI: land surveyors.

GUSTATIO: appetizers at a Roman feast.

GYMNASIUM: Greek sports complex that was also popular in Roman times and often attached to a bath.

HADES: in Greek and Roman literary traditions, one of the locations where the dead dwelled.

HADRIAN: emperor from 117 C.E.–138 C.E.

HADRIAN'S VILLA: villa in Tivoli that incorporated architecture from all over the empire.

HADRIAN'S WALL: the Roman wall in the north of England, erected by Hadrian between 1222 C.E. and 128 C.E., that acted as Rome's border in Britain.

HAMILCAR BARCA: an important Carthaginian general who led the Carthaginian forces in the first Punic War.

HANNIBAL: Carthaginian general who terrorized the Roman countryside during the second Punic War.

HARUSPICES: diviners who studied particular phenomena (such as animal entrails) in order to understand the will of the gods.

HEBREW BIBLE: another name for the books of the Old Testament.

HECYRA: a Roman comedy by Terence.

HELLENISTIC: the term used to describe the Greek culture associated with the conquests of Alexander the Great.

HEPATOSCOPY: the science of studying animal entrails for omens.

HERA: Greek goddess who came to be associated with Juno.

HERCULANEUM: city destroyed when Vesuvius erupted in 70 C.E.

HEROD THE GREAT: king of Judea from 37 B.C.E. until 4 B.C.E., and an important figure in Second Temple Judaism.

HEXAPLA: an edition of the Old Testament consisting of six columns of parallel text from different sources, compiled by Origen.

HIBERNIA: Latin name for Ireland.

HORACE: Roman poet who lived from 65 B.C.E. to 8 B.C.E.

HORTENSIUS: greatest Roman orator until Cicero beat him in trial in 70 B.C.E.

HORUS: Egyptian deity and the son of Isis and Osiris.

HUNS: nomads who are assumed to have originated in central Asia who were fearsome warriors.

HYPOCAUST: system of central heating, created by burning a fire in the basement of a building and allowing the heat to rise through vents or gaps in the floors and walls.

IDES: or idus, the thirteenth or fifteenth day of the month.

IMPERATOR: the title bestowed on a military commander by his troops after a victory, and after Augustus, title assumed by all emperors.

IMPERIUM: Latin word for the political concept of the power to command.

IMPLUVIUM: pool in the middle of a Roman atrium, directly beneath the conubium, that collected rainwater.

INCRUSTATION STYLE: see FIRST STYLE.

INDO-EUROPEAN LANGUAGES: those languages that share common characteristics and possibly a parent language, so named because they are found in India and Europe.

INFLECTED LANGUAGES: languages in which the form of the word is more important than the order of the words in a sentence.

INSTITUTES: a sourcebook on Roman law written by Gaius.

INSULA: literally refers to a city block but in Roman contexts refers to apartment or tenement complexes.

INTAGLIO: engraved gems.

INTERREX: in the regal period, the person appointed to replace the king temporarily upon his death, until the next king was chosen.

INTRICATE STYLE: see FOURTH STYLE.

IRON AGE: period in which the Villanovan culture lived.

ISIS: Egyptian goddess who became quite popular in Rome during the imperial period.

ISLAMIC CITY: see SEGMENTARY CITY.

IUS DIVINUM: the proper relationship between gods and humans.

IUS RESPONDENDI: the right to give a legal opinion.

JANUS: god of thresholds and doorways, commonly depicted with two faces.

JENTACULUM: Roman breakfast, usually just a very small meal.

JEROME: one of the early Christian church fathers, who lived from about 347 C.E. to 420 C.E.

JOSEPHUS: Jewish historian and one of the best sources on Roman-period Judaism.

JUGURTHA: Numidian king who was defeated by Marius in 104 B.C.E.

JULIAN: emperor from 360 C.E. to 363 C.E.

JULIUS CAESAR: brilliant general who became dictator of Rome, but was assassinated in 44 B.C.E.

JUNIAN LATINS: slaves who were unofficially manumitted and allowed to live like freedmen but whose children were still slaves and whose property still belonged to the master.

JUNO: wife of Jupiter, identified with the Greek goddess Hera and also the name for female procreative power.

JUPITER: the supreme god of the Romans, associated with weather.

JURISTS: legal intellectuals who worked in Rome, wrote on issues of law, and participated in legal cases.

JUSTIN: a Roman historian.

JUTURNA: goddess associated with fountains.

JUVENAL: Roman satirical poet.

KALENDAE: the name of the first day of the month.

KNIDIAN RELIEF WARE: mold-made pottery often found in very interesting shapes, dating from 70 C.E. to 250 C.E.

KOINE: the common dialect of Greek and the language of the New Testament.

LACONIUM: the sauna room in a Roman bath.

LARARIUM: the shrine for the household lars, kept in the atrium, which was the responsibility of the pater familias.

LARES: protective household deities, cared for by the pater familias.

LARS: singular form of the word *lares*.

LATE LATIN PERIOD: a broad period of Latin literary output, usually understood as beginning in 138 C.E.

LATIFUNDIA: large agricultural estates, worked by slaves.

LATIN: an Indo-European language and the most prominent language in Rome.

LATIN LEAGUE: association of Latin towns (probably originating in the seventh century B.C.E.) for the joint worship of deities and mutual protection, led by Alba Longa until Rome defeated the city, and made itself a dominant partner (in the foedus Cassianum) until its dissolution in 338 B.C.E..

LATINI: tribes living in Latium before the Roman period.

LATINS: people who lived in Italy between the Tiber River and the Northern Etruscan settlements during the Iron Age; the term later took on a broader meaning.

LATIUM: an area in western Italy between the Apennines and the Tyrrhenian Sea.

LEAF TABLETS: writing tablets made out of very thin sheets of wood.

LEGATI: various officials in Roman provincial governance, including legion commanders, ambassadors, and governors.

LEGIS ACTIO: legal action that involved drawing up forms and legal documents.

LEMURES: hostile ghosts who could be dangerous forces within the household.

LEMURIA: the festival held to satiate the LEMURES.

LEVANT: general geographic term for the regions of land on the east side of the Mediterranean Sea.

LIBATIONS: liquid offerings, usually poured.

LIBERTI: see FREEDMEN.

LICTORS: the attendants who carried the fasces before certain administrative and cultic officials.

LIMBO: in Greek and Roman literary traditions, one of the locations where the dead dwelled.

LIMES: either fortified military roads or permanent borders like Hadrian's Wall.

LIMINAL: describing areas and/or times of transition.

LIMITES: frontier districts.

LINEAR B: earliest certain Greek language, well known from Bronze Age Crete.

LIP: the edge of the mouth of a pot.

LITTERATOR: the lowest level of public schooling, attended by both boys and girls.

LIVIUS ANDRONICUS: Roman playwright also known for his translation of the *Odyssey* into Latin.

LIVY: Roman historian who lived from 59 B.C.E. to 17 C.E., whose work is one of the most important sources of Roman history.

LOST WAX: method of casting metal in which the mold was carved out of wax, which was destroyed after the metal was cooled.

LUCAN: poet who lived from 39 C.E. to 65 C.E.

LUCIAN: an important writer who was born in 115 C.E.

LUCIUS VERUS: coemperor from 161 C.E. to 169 C.E., along with Marcus Aurelius.

LUCRETIUS: an important Stoic who wrote *De Rerum Natura*.

LUDI: games held on religious holidays.

LUPERCALIA: the festival in which the Luperci ran through the streets slapping bystanders with strips of goat-skins.

LUPERCI: the priests in charge of the festival of Lupercalia.

MACRINUS: emperor from 217 C.E. to 218 C.E.

MAGISTER: the lowest level of public schooling, attended by both boys and girls.

MAGISTRATE: an elected official in the Republican period who served in office for one year.

MAGNA MATER: see CYBELE.

MANES: benevolent spirits of dead ancestors.

MANUMISSION: the act of freeing a slave, who, once manumitted, became a freedman.

MANUS: literally means "hand" but is a type of marriage in which the husband gains complete control over the wife's property.

MARCUS AURELIUS: emperor from 161 C.E.–180 C.E.; wrote *Meditations.*

MARIUS: influential Roman general who introduced numerous military reforms and is widely credited with professionalizing the army.

MARS: Roman god of war and agriculture.

MARSIAN WAR: another name for the Social War.

MARTIAL: Roman poet who lived from 40 C.E. to 104 C.E.

MASADA: the site of a Jewish stand against Rome, which was not captured until 73 C.E., well after the Jewish Revolt had been suppressed elsewhere in Roman Palestine.

MATRONALIA: festival in which only women were allowed to participate.

MAU, AUGUST: renowned Roman art historian who identified the four styles of wall paintings at Pompeii still used as categories in scholarship today.

MAUSOLEUM: tomb for a single individual built as a commemorative area.

MAUSS, MARCEL: gifted anthropologist and student (and nephew) of Emile Durkheim, whose study on gift-giving revolutionized the way scholars understand this phenomenon.

MEDIANUM: the long hallway in a Roman apartment complex that functioned both as the primary entrance and the primary source of light.

MENAECHEMI: a Roman comedy by Plautus.

MERCATORES: Roman merchants who traded specific goods.

MERCURY: god associated with communication and trade.

MESOPOTAMIA: the Greek word for the region and civilization that flourished between the Tigris and Euphrates Rivers (basically modern Iraq).

METALLURGY: the art of gaining metal from ore and fashioning that metal into tools and other objects.

METAMORPHOSES: written by Ovid; one of the world's greatest literary achievements, brilliantly connecting Near Eastern and classical traditions through the theme of transformation.

METER: the rhythm of a poem; in classical works it is based on the number of syllables in a line and their respective length.

MIDDLE PLATONISM: a philosophical school of thought founded by Antiochus, which saw connections between the thought of Plato and Aristotle.

MILES GLORIOSUS: a comedy by Plautus.

MILLE PASSUS: Roman distance measurement, equivalent to 1,480 meters.

MINERVA: goddess associated with crafts and creative arts as well as intelligence.

MISHNAH: compilation of rabbinic teaching.

MITHRAS: Zoroastrian god who became very popular in Rome, especially among soldiers and merchants who had traveled to the east.

MITHRIDATIS: king of a small region near the Black Sea who fought with Rome in what are called the Mithraditic Wars.

MOMMSEN, THEODOR: one of the most influential modern Roman scholars.

MONOTHEISM: the belief in and worship of a single supreme deity and the category to which Christianity, Judaism, and Islam all belong.

MORTARIA: large flat bowls that were probably used for grinding and other kinds of food preparation.

MOSTELLARIA: a comedy by Plautus.

MOUTH: the opening of a vessel.

MUNERA: funeral games, a tradition that originated with the Etruscans.

MUNICIPIA: cities in Italy that had many of the rights and obligations of citizens, but lacked the right to vote.

MYRMILLONES: heavily armored gladiators who had a distinctive fish design on their helmets.

MYSTERY RELIGIONS: religions that had restricted memberships and secret practices that emphasized individual cultic participation.

NAG HAMMADI: the site in Egypt of a find of very important Gnostic papyri.

NATURAL BIRTHRATES: birthrates in populations that do not use birth-control techniques, other than social pressures (like prohibitions on premarital sex).

NATURAL HISTORY: the thirty-seven-volume encyclopedia compiled by Pliny the Elder on topics of natural history.

NAUMACHIAE: staged naval battles put on as entertainment for the Roman public.

NEAR EAST: term usually used by scholars to denote the area popularly known as the Middle East.

NECROPOLIS: Greek word for cemetery, used to refer to ancient cemetery complexes.

NEFASTI: days of the year on which business was not supposed to be transacted for religious reasons.

NEGOTIATORES: representatives of large trading companies and investment groups.

NEOPLATONISM: philosophical school of thought that emphasized experience rather than theory.

NEPOS: Roman writer, notable for his biographical works.

NEPTUNE: god associated with water.

NERO: emperor from 54 C.E.–68 C.E.

NERO'S GOLDEN HOUSE: see DOMUS AUREA.

NERVA: emperor from 96–98 C.E.

NEXUS: the institution of debt-slavery, in which a member of the indebted household is given over to the loan granter until the loan can be repaid.

NOBLES: high-status Romans from established families.

NONAE: the day of the month that came nine days before the ides.

NONIUS MARCELLUS: wrote an important encyclopedia of Latin and writings in Latin during the reign of Constantine.

NOVUS HOMO: term used to describe a man who was the first member of his family to be elected consul, which made his family noble.

NUMA POMPILIUS: the legendary second king of Rome.

NUMEN: term used to describe divine power.

NUMINA: impersonal, semidivine forces, usually associated with a particular area or item.

NUMISMATICS: the study of coins.

OCTAVIA: name of the sister of Octavian and wife of Antony, and also the name of the daughter of Claudius and first wife of Nero, about whom a tragedy, named after her, was written.

OCTAVIAN: the man who defeated Antony and Cleopatra and became Augustus, founder of the Principate.

ODOACER: the barbarian who became king of Rome in 476 C.E. and whose ascension is often considered to mark the end of the Roman Empire.

OECUS: the dining area associated with the peristyle in a peristyle house.

OIKOS: the Greek word for house, but often used to describe economies related to household-level production.

OPUS SECTILE: mosaics that consist mainly of large pieces of cut stone, carved to fit together to form one design.

ORACLES: shrines or people through which gods could communicate with humans; the term can also refer to the actual answers given by the gods.

ORATORY: the art of public speech, which was the forum for the practical application of the skill of rhetoric.

ORCHESTRA: the semicircular section in the front of a Roman theater.

ORDERS: formally defined categories of people, of which the most notable in Rome were the PATRICIANS and the PLEBEIANS.

ORIGEN: an early Christian scholar of Alexandria who lived from 185 C.E. to 254 C.E., most known for his work the Hexapla.

ORNATE STYLE: see THIRD STYLE.

ORTHOGONAL: an orderly type of town planning common in Greek cities.

OSCANS: a group of people who lived in Italy and spoke a language related to but distinct from Latin.

OSIRIS: an important Egyptian deity, but in Roman times was more important as the husband of Isis.

OSSUARIES: rectangular boxes in which the bones of the dead were stored.

OSTIA: a port city with well-preserved apartment complexes that have been substantially excavated.

OSTRACA: broken fragments of pottery or stone with writing or drawings on them.

OSTROGOTHS: the eastern Gothic tribes.

OTHO: emperor in 69 C.E.

OVID: one of the greatest Roman poets, author of *Metamorphoses,* who lived from 43 B.C.E. to 17 C.E.

PAGAN: originally meant an inhabitant of a small hamlet, but with the rise of Christianity came to be used to describe people who were not Christians or Jews.

PAGANALIA: celebration, associated with Ceres, celebrating the sowing of crops.

PALAESTRA: an exercise yard, often found associated with bathing complexes in Roman times.

PALATINA: one of the four major zones of the city of Rome until Augustus re-organized the city.

PALATINE: one of the major hills of the city of Rome.

PALEOGRAPHY: the study of ancient writing.

PALEOPATHOLOGY: the study of human health in ancient populations.

PALLADIUS: author of an important treatise on agriculture, one of the primary sources for the study of Roman agriculture.

PALMYRA: an important city built around a rest stop in the Syrian Desert.

PANTHEON: a huge temple in Rome built by Hadrian, dedicated to all of the gods of Rome.

PANTOMIME: theatrical performance, usually of mythological or historical events, involving sex, nudity, and violence.

PAPYRUS: type of paper, made from papyrus reeds found in Egypt.

PARASITE: a fellow diner in Greek society but came to take on the meaning of a "moocher" or "sycophant" in Roman times.

PARENTALIA: festival held to commemorate dead ancestors and provide them with offerings.

PARS RUSTICA: the structures in a villa complex used by agricultural workers and as storage space.

PARS URBANA: the structure in a villa complex that was reserved for the owner's residence.

PASSUS: a unit of Roman distance measurement, equivalent to 1.48 m.

PATER FAMILIAS: the head of a household, ideally the oldest male.

PATER PATRATUS: a fetiales cultic worker responsible for making oral declarations and curses.

PATRIA POTESTAS: the absolute power of the pater familias over the members of his household.

PATRICIANS: an organized group of privileged families, originating in the regal period.

PATRISTICS: the late Latin writings of the early Church fathers.

PATRON: a higher-status individual who supported, in a variety of ways, a client.

PAX DEORUM: feast held twice yearly, in which married women (and only married women) worshipped the goddess Bona Dea.

PECULIUM: a small gift, frequently given by a master to a slave.

PENATES: semidivine forces associated with particular household locations who required daily offerings.

PERISTYLE: a distinct architectural feature, typically consisting of a series of pillars surrounding a set-off area.

PERISTYLE HOUSE: the type of house that eventually overtook the atrium style of house in popularity, characterized by the presence of an attached peristyle.

PERSIANS: the people of what is now known as Iran.

PES: a unit of Roman distance measurement, often called the Roman foot, equivalent to 29.4 cm.

PETRONIUS: author of *Satyricon*.

PHAEDRUS: wrote a collection of fables based on Aesop.

PHARSALI: an epic poem written by Lucan that chronicled the conflict between Pompey and Julius Caesar.

PHILIP OF MACEDON: the man who unified Macedon, paving the way for his son, Alexander the Great, to create an empire.

PHILO OF ALEXANDRIA: an important Jewish writer who died in 45 C.E.

PHOENICIA: the stretch of Lebanon and Syria that the sea-faring Phoenicians called home.

PHOENICIAN: a Semitic language, related to Hebrew, and spoken by the Phoenicians and Carthaginians.

PHORMIO: a comedy written by Terence.

PILUM: the type of javelin used by the hastati princeps.

PLAUTUS: author of numerous comedies who lived from 250 B.C.E. to 184 B.C.E.

PLEBEIANS: a heterogeneous group of underprivileged people in Rome who emerged as an organized group sometime early in the Republican period.

PLEBS: see PLEBEIANS.

PLINY THE ELDER: compiled a thirty-seven-volume encyclopedia called *Natural History*.

PLINY THE YOUNGER: a Roman administrator who died in 113 C.E. and is known to modern scholars because books of his letters have survived.

PLOTINUS: died in 270 C.E. and is credited with founding Neoplatonism.

PLUTARCH: Greek historian whose most famous work, *Moral Lives,* compares and contrasts the biographies of certain Greeks and certain Romans.

PLUTO: the Latin name of the god Hades, of the underworld.

POENULUS: a comedy written by Plautus.

POLIS: the Greek word for "city."

POLYBIUS: Greek historian who came to Rome during Rome's rise as a world power and whose *History* is one of the most important sources on Rome.

POLYTHEISM: the belief in more than one god.

POMPEII: one of the cities destroyed when Vesuvius erupted in 70 C.E.

POMPEIIAN RED WARE: not pottery made at Pompeii, but pottery that is a red color similar to the reds in the wall paintings at Pompeii.

POMPEY: also known as Pompey the Great. Lived from 106 B.C.E.—48 B.C.E. and was a powerful ruler in the later years of the republic.

PONTIFEX MAXIMUS: meaning "chief priest;" a title that was first taken by Augustus and used (even by the Christian emperors) until the reign of Gratian in 383 C.E.

PONTIFICES: state officials in charge of the overall maintenance of Roman religion, usually three in number.

POPULUS: the term used for the citizens of Rome as a collective.

POSIDONUS: a Stoic who lived from 135 B.C.E.–50 B.C.E. and wrote five books on astrology.

POST MERIDIEM: abbreviated P.M., meaning "after the middle of the day."

PRAETORIAN GUARD: the emperor's personal security force, stationed in Rome.

PRAETORS: replaced the king after the monarchy came to an end, and came to take on a judicial role in Roman political life.

PREFECT: the head of a military unit or an upper-level administrator in the Roman government.

PRIAPEA: poems written during the reign of Augustus to celebrate the god Priapus.

PRIAPUS: Greek god adopted into Roman culture, usually appearing as a statue placed in gardens, with a frightening face and large phallus.

PRINCEPS: the name used by Augustus to describe his position as head of the Roman government, and is the word from which principate is derived.

PRINCIPATE: the name generally used to refer to the transition period between the republic and the empire in which Augustus ruled as princeps (first citizen), but can also be used to refer to the period from Augustus until Diocletian.

PRO-CONSUL: see PRO-MAGISTRATES.

PROCURATOR: government official in charge of financial issues.

PROLETARII: the lowest property class of citizens who were not obligated to render military service.

PRO-MAGISTRATES: officials appointed to fulfill the functions of the consul or praetor in place of these officials, usually for military purposes.

PROMULSIO: the appetizers at a Roman feast.

PROPERTIUS: a Roman poet who was associated with Ovid and wrote four books of elegies.

PRO-PRAETOR: see PRO-MAGISTRATES.

PROSCRIPTIONS: under Sulla, men were declared outlaws, listed by name, and could be hunted down and killed for a reward, while the man's sons would lose citizenship and all property was confiscated.

PROSODY: the study of verses in poetry, especially prominent in the study of Greek and Latin.

PROVINCE: an administrative unit of the Roman Empire.

PSEUDOLUS: comedy written by Plautus.

PTOLEMAIC PERIOD: the designation given for the period of history when Egypt was ruled by the house of Ptolemy, the most famous of these rulers being Cleopatra VII.

PTOLEMY: lived in Egypt from 100 C.E.–178 C.E.; was one of the most influential astronomers.

PUBLICANI: private individuals who purchased government contracts at auctions and performed government designated tasks for profit.

PUDICITIA: a kind of virtue a Roman woman could be described as having, best understood as devotion (especially sexual) to her husband.

PUNIC: the name given to the version of the Phoenician language that was spoken and written in Carthage.

PUNIC WARS: the wars that the Romans fought against Carthage during the period of the republic.

PYRRHIC VICTORY: a victory gained at a very high cost.

PYRRHUS: Greek king who went to war with both the Romans and Carthage.

QUADRAN: the lowest denomination of Roman coin.

QUAESTOR: the lowest level of magistrate, whose responsibilities included the administration of public records and administration of the treasury.

QUINARIUS: a unit of Roman coinage.

QUINTILIAN: an important teacher and writer on the subject of rhetoric, who taught important individuals such as Pliny the Younger.

QUIRINAL: one of the hills of Rome.

QUIRINUS: Sabine god and member of the Archaic Triad.

RAVENNA: became the capital of the western Roman Empire under Honorius.

REGAL PERIOD: the first major period of Roman history, deriving its name from the fact that during this period, Rome was ruled by a king.

REGIA: originally the residence of the king of Rome, but in Republican times became the residence of the pontifex maximus.

REGIONES: the administrative unit of the city of Rome, initially four in number, but under Augustus was increased to fourteen.

REMUS: the brother of Romulus, one of the legendary founders of Rome.

REPUBLIC: the second major period of Roman history, so called because of the nature of the Roman government at this time.

RES MANCIPI: property that had restrictions on its sale or alienation.

RES NEC MANCIPI: property that was free to be sold.

REX SACRORUM: the cultic official who took over many of the king's religious roles after the office of king was abolished at the end of the regal period.

RHETOR: the highest level of education available to Roman boys.

RHETORIC: the art of speaking and one of the most important components of a young Roman's education.

ROMA: divine manifestation of the city of Rome.

ROMANCE LANGUAGES: include Italian, Spanish, and French, all languages originally derived from Latin.

ROMULUS: one of the legendary founders of Rome who had a twin brother named Remus, both of whom were suckled by a wolf, according to the stories.

ROMULUS AUGUSTULUS: emperor from 475 B.C.E.–476 C.E.; usually considered the last emperor of the western empire.

ROSTOVTZEFF, MICHAEL: one of the major Roman historians of the early twentieth century.

RUBICON: a river in Italy.

RUDENS: a comedy written by Plautus.

SABINES: group of people who lived north of Rome and probably made up a substantial portion of the Roman population in the regal period.

SACRIS FACIUNDIS: college of cultic officials in charge of the Sybilline Oracles.

SALLUST: Roman historian who lived from 86 B.C.E. to 35 B.C.E.

SALUTATIO: the morning ritual in which a client came to the house of a patron to offer greetings.

SAMNITES: a group of tribes, organized into a loose federation of villages that occupied south-central Italy, who warred intermittently with Rome between 343 B.C.E. and 290 B.C.E.

SARCOPHAGUS: type of coffin used for inhuming the remains of the dead, even if the body had been cremated.

SATIRES: a name of two separate collections, one by Horace, and the other by Juvenal.

SATURN: an important Roman god, probably associated with agriculture, who had a temple on the Capitoline Hill.

SATURNALIA: the Roman festival from which the Christian holiday Christmas is derived.

SATYRICON: a novel, written by Petronius, that did not fully survive, but has a long section describing a feast.

SCAENA: the stage of a Roman theater.

SCAENAE FRONS: the back wall of the stage of a Roman theater.

SCIPIO AFRICANUS: Roman general who defeated Hannibal and conquered North Africa for Rome.

SCRIPTORIA: institutions that copied manuscripts.

SECOND SOPHISTIC: revival of Greek rhetoric in the second century C.E.

SECOND STYLE: style of wall painting and interior decoration found at Pompeii that typically incorporated landscape art into the decorative scheme.

SECOND TABLES: the course of the Roman meal that we think of as dessert.

SECOND TEMPLE PERIOD: the period of Jewish history that ranges from the rebuilding of the temple in Jerusalem until its destruction by the Romans in 70 C.E.

SEED THEORIES: theories that explain the fall of Rome through internal, systemic problems, also known as "germ" or "decay" theories.

SEGMENTARY CITY: type of city also known as an Islamic city that was laid out primarily according to kinship.

SELEUCIDS: one of the ruling dynasties that took over parts of Alexander the Great's kingdom after his death.

SEMIS: a unit of Roman coinage.

SENATE: an important political institution throughout Roman history, the Senate acted in an advisory role first to the kings, then elected officials, and finally the emperor.

SENECA THE YOUNGER: lived from 4 B.C.E. to 65 C.E. and was an important proponent of Stoicism.

SEPTIMIUS SEVERUS: emperor from 193–211 C.E.

SERVIAN WALL: a wall constructed in 378 B.C.E. in the aftermath of the Gallic sack, which surrounded the city proper and still survives in part today.

SERVIUS TULLIUS: one of the early kings of Rome.

SESTERCE: see SESTERTIUS.

SESTERTIUS: a unit of Roman coinage.

SIGNINUM: a type of mosaic made up of colored mortar and large chunks of different kinds of materials.

SILVER AGE: a period of Latin literature, usually understood as ranging from 14 B.C.E. to 138 C.E.

SKEPTICISM: Greek philosophical tradition that struggled with the impossibility of attaining true knowledge.

SKEWOMORPH: the attempt to make an item in one medium look like an item in a different medium (e.g., a ceramic bowl made to look like a metal bowl).

SLIP: a kind of paint, made out of clay, used to decorate ceramics.

SOCIAL WAR: lasted from 90 B.C.E. to 88 B.C.E. when Rome's allies revolted.

SOCIETAS: organizations of investors.

SOCII: the name given to allies of Rome.

SPARTACUS: a slave who led a major slave revolt against Rome from 73 B.C.E. to 71 B.C.E.

SPORTULAE: a payment given to a client by a patron.

STADIUM: a Roman unit of measurement for nautical distances that was equivalent to about 187.5 m.

STATUE-IN-THE-ROUND: statue that is carved on all sides and intended for viewing from 360 degrees.

STATUS: the perceived prestige of an individual that can be signified in many ways.

STICHUS: a comedy written by Plautus.

STOICISM: a Greek philosophical school founded by Zeno that became very popular in Rome.

STOICS: individuals who followed Stoicism.

STRIGILIS: a stick used in a Roman bath to remove dirt from and exfoliate the skin.

STROPHIUM: a Roman brassiere.

SUBURBANA: one of the four major zones of the city of Rome until Augustus reorganized the city.

SYBILLINE ORACLES: a collection of books in the charge of the sacris faciundis, which were based on the knowledge of ten prophets.

TABERNA: chamber opening directly onto the street in a Roman city that was used as commercial or industrial space.

TABLELARII: hired messengers during the Republican period.

TABLINUM: the main reception room of a Roman house, often flanked by ALAE.

TACITUS: historian whose works *Annals* and *Histories* are important sources on Roman history.

TALMUD: collection of rabbinic writings that center on commentary on the Mishnah.

TARQUIN: one of the family names of early Roman kings, traditionally thought to be Etruscan.

TEMPLUM: the area an augur marked off to take an auspice.

TEPIDARIUM: the room in a bath complex with tepid water facilities.

TERENCE: a comedy writer whose works won ancient critical acclaim.

TERMINA: deity associated with property boundaries.

TERMINALIA: the festival devoted to the divine forces in boundaries, celebrated on February 23.

TERRA SIGILLATA: one of the most important types of Roman pottery, easily recognizable because of its glossy red surface.

TERTULLIAN: an early Christian apologist and theologian who lived from 160 C.E. to 225 C.E.

TESSERAE: the small stone cubes used to create a mosaic.

TETRARCHY: the name given to the fourfold ruling system under Diocletian, in which the empire is ruled by four individuals.

TEXTUAL CRITICISM: the study of the transmission of texts, involving examination of differences in various editions, sometimes with the goal of re-creating the original text (although in actual practice this is impossible).

THEATER OF MARCELLUS: the theater in Rome, built by Augustus as a memorial to his nephew Marcellus.

THEATERS: semicircular structures in which dramatic performances were staged; not synonymous with amphitheater.

THEODOSIUS: emperor from 379 C.E.–395 C.E.

THERMAE: a public bath.

THERMAE ANTONINIANE: see BATHS OF CARACALLA.

THIRD STYLE: style of wall painting and interior decoration found at Pompeii that involved dividing the wall into three separate sections.

THRACIANS: group of people and the name of a type of gladiator.

TIBER RIVER: the river that runs through Rome.

TIBERIUS: emperor from 14 C.E. to 37 C.E.

TITUS: emperor from 79 C.E.–81 C.E.

TOGA: the quintessential Roman garment, made out of heavy white wool and wrapped around the body in numerous ways.

TRAJAN: emperor from 98 C.E.–117 C.E.

TRAJAN'S COLUMN: the huge marble column erected to commemorate Trajan's military victories that has friezes all around it, and now has a statue of St. Peter on its top.

TRAVERTINE: a kind of stone used in Roman building, quarried from Tivoli.

TRIBUTE: the payment made by a subordinate state to a dominant state.

TRIBUTUM: tax imposed directly upon an individual.

TRICLINIUM: dining room in a Roman house and also the name of the couches that the Romans dined on within this room.

TRINUMMUS: a comedy by Plautus.

TRISTIA: collection of poems by Ovid.

TRIUMVIRATE: an official board of three.

TUFA: volcanic stone used in concrete and readily available around Rome.

TULLUS HOSTILIUS: the legendary third king of Rome.

TUNIC: the basic component of Roman clothing, worn by both men and women.

TWELVE TABLES: a series of laws, supposedly drawn up in 451 B.C.E., that formed the basis of early Roman law.

UNCIA: a unit of Roman distance measurement, often called the Roman inch, equivalent to 2.43 cm.

UNCIAL: type of Latin cursive using all capital letters so as to be easily read.

VALLUS: harvesting machine used in the northern provinces of the Roman Empire.

VANDALS: Germanic tribe that eventually conquered North Africa.

VECTIGALIA: public revenues and rents.

VENUS: god of fertility and vegetation.

VERBENARIUS: a fetiales priest who carried sacred herbs.

VERISTIC STYLE: a style of art that attempted to depict the subject as accurately and as realistically as possible.

VESPASIAN: emperor from 69 C.E–79 C.E.

VESPERNA: the Roman evening meal, usually taken just before bed.

VESTA: Roman goddess of the hearth, worshipped in every Roman home and cared for by the vestal virgins.

VESTAL VIRGINS: girls who entered service between the ages of six and ten, taking a vow of chastity, to administer the state worship of Vesta.

VESTIBULUM: the main entrance to a Roman house.

VESUVIUS: the volcano that erupted in 70 C.E., covering, among other cities, Pompeii and Herculaneum.

VIA APPIA: also known as the Appian Way, a road built in 312 B.C.E. between Rome and Capua, and named after Appius Claudius; sections of this road can still be visited today.

VICTORIAN PERIOD: the period in which Queen Victoria reigned over Britain, roughly the latter half of the nineteenth century.

VICUS TUSCAS: a famous shopping street in Rome.

VIGILES: Roman firefighters.

VILLA: a term used frequently in scholarly literature on Rome that usually refers to a luxurious country estate.

VILLA MARITIMAE: a villa located by the sea.

VILLA RUSTICA: a country villa.

VILLA SUBURBANA: a villa located on the outskirts of a city.

VILLA URBANA: a villa found within an urban environment.

VILLANOVAN CULTURE: culture that lived in central Italy during the Iron Age.

VINALIA: Roman festival celebrating the harvest of vineyards.

VIRGIL: one of Rome's greatest poets, author of the *Aeneid*.

VITELLIUS: emperor in 69 C.E.

VITRUVIUS: Roman architect who wrote *De Architectura*.

VOLSCI: Italian tribe that spoke a language that was related to but distinct from Latin.

VULCAN: god of smithing and the power of fire.

VULGAR LATIN: vernacular Latin, the form of the Latin language used in everyday speech.

VULGATE: the Latin translation of the Bible, rendered by Jerome.

WASH: a SLIP (paint for ceramic vessel) so thin that the original clay of the pot can be seen beneath.

WATTLE AND DAUB: type of construction material known from Iron Age settlements, consisting of branches and mud.

WHEELOCK'S GRAMMAR: arguably the most used Latin grammar today.

ZAMA: the site of the battle at which Hannibal was defeated by Scipio.

ZENO: the founder of Stoicism.

ZENOBIA: queen of the city of Palmyra who declared independence from Rome until the defeat of her army.

ZEUS: the supreme god of the Greeks, who came to be associated with Jupiter.

ZOOMORPHIC: something that is not an animal, crafted to look like an animal.

ZOROASTRIANISM: the major religion of the Persians, supposedly based on the teachings of Zarathustra.

Chronology

753 B.C.E.	Traditional date of the founding of Rome
753–715	Traditional dates of the reign of Romulus
715–673	Traditional dates of the reign of Numa Pompilius
673–641	Traditional dates of the reign of Tullus Hostilius
641-616	Traditional dates of the reign of Ancus Marcius
616–579	Traditional dates of the reign of Tarquin I
579–534	Traditional dates of the reign of Servius Tullius
534–509	Traditional dates of the reign of Tarquin II (The Proud)
509	King expelled from Rome
508	Treaty between Rome and Carthage
499	Rome defeats the Latin League at the battle of Regillus
493	Treaty between Rome and the Latin League (*foedus Cassianum*)
483–474	First Veientine War
451	The Twelve Tables are drawn up
437–435	Second Veientine War
406–396	Third Veientine War
396	Veii destroyed
390	The sack of Rome by the Gauls
378	Servian Wall built
354	Roman treaty with the Samnites
348	Second treaty between Rome and Carthage
343–341	First Samnite War
340	The Latin War begins
338	Rome defeats and breaks up the Latin League
327–303	Second Samnite War
323	Death of Alexander the Great
321	Roman army surrenders to the Samnites at the Caudine Forks
312	Building of the Via Appia
	Building of the aqua Appia, the first Roman aqueduct
298–290	Third Samnite War
284–272	Pyrrhic Wars
272	Rome gains control of all of southern Italy
264–241	First Punic War
229–228	First Illyrian War
226	Treaty at Ebro River with Carthage
220–219	Second Illyrian War
218–202	Second Punic War

216	Battle of Cannae
215	Sumptuary laws enacted
213	Rome is hit by an earthquake
202	Battle of Zama
200–197	Macedonian War against Philip V
192	Rome is hit by an earthquake
186	Bacchic rites are made illegal
184	Cato the Elder is censor
182	Hannibal poisons himself to avoid Roman capture.
167	Delos declared a free port
151–146	Third Punic War
148	War against Macedonians
	War against Achaeans
146	Corinth is destroyed
144	The Marcian Aqueduct is built
142	First stone bridge over the Tiber River is built
135–132	Slave revolt
133	Tiberius Gracchus is elected tribune and assassinated
123	Gaius Gracchus is elected tribune
121	Gaius Gracchus and supporters are put to death
112–105	War with Jugurtha of Numidia
107	Marius elected consul
105–101	War with German tribes in the north
104–99	Slave revolt in Sicily
91	Marcus Livius Drusus is killed.
90–88	The Social War
89–85	First Mithridatic War
88–82	Civil War in Rome
83–82	Second Mithridatic War
74–63	Third Mithridatic War
73–71	Slave revolt led by Spartacus
67	Pompey rids the Mediterranean of pirates
66–62	Pompey conquers the Near East
63	Catiline Conspiracy
	Cicero is consul
62	Pompey returns to Rome
60	First Triumvirate formed
59	Caesar is consul. Pompey marries Caesar's only daughter, Julia
58–57	Cicero expelled
58–51	Caesar campaigns in Gaul
55–54	Caesar campaigns in Britain
54	Julia dies
53	Crassus killed while campaigning against Parthians
51–50	Cicero is governer of Cilicia
49–45	Civil war in Rome

49	Senate declares martial law against Caesar
	Caesar attacks and defeats Pompey's forces
	Pompey flees Rome
48	Caesar defeats Pompey at Pharsalus
	Pompey is killed in Egypt
47	Caesar is declared dictator for life
46	Cato commits suicide
44	Caesar killed on the Ides of March
44–30	Civil war in Rome
43	Second Triumvirate is formed
40	Second Triumvirate divides up the empire
	Antony marries Octavia
37	Antony marries Cleopatra, though the marriage is not legally recognized
35	Antony divorces Octavia
33	Second Triumvirate dissolved
31	Antony and Cleopatra's forces defeated at Actium
30	Octavian is victorious at Alexandria
	Antony and Cleopatra commit suicide
27	Octavian is given the name Augustus (revered one) by the Senate
26–25	Augustus fights the Cantabrian Wars in Spain
23	Augustus resigns his consulship in exchange for lifelong tribunician powers and imperium maius (power greater than other authorities)
	Marcellus dies
19	Augustus is granted consulship for life
18	Laws regulating marital relations are passed
11	Augustus forces Tiberius to divorce his wife and marry Julia
4 B.C.E.	Herod the Great dies
14 C.E.	Augustus dies one month before his seventy-sixth birthday
14–37	Tiberius reigns as emperor
37–41	Caligula reigns as emperor
41–54	Claudius reigns as emperor
43	Britain invaded
54–68	Nero reigns as emperor
59	Nero has Agrippina (his mother) put to death
60	Boudicca leads rebellion in Britain
61	Nero has Octavia (his ex-wife) put to death
64	The Great Fire of Rome
65	Conspiracy against Nero discovered, conspirators are put to death
66–73	Jewish Revolt in Judea
69	Year of Four Emperors
	Flavian Revolt
69–79	Vespasian rules as emperor
70	Titus destroys Jerusalem and temple

71	Plague and fire in Rome
79	Vesuvius erupts
79–81	Titus reigns as emperor
80	Colosseum inaugurated
81–96	Domitian reigns as emperor
96–98	Nerva reigns as emperor
98–117	Trajan reigns as emperor
117–138	Hadrian reigns as emperor
121	Hadrian commissions Hadrian's Wall
130–134	Bar Kochba Revolt in Palestine
135	Jews banned from Jerusalem
138–161	Antoninus Pius reigns as emperor
161–180	Marcus Aurelius reigns as emperor
167	Rome is hit by plague
168–175	Marcus Aurelius's German war
169	Lucius Verus dies while campaigning with Marcus Aurelius
180–192	Commodus reigns as emperor
182	Saoterus is assassinated
185	Perennis is executed
190	Cleander is executed at the behest of an angry Roman mob
193–197	Civil war ensues after Commodus is assassinated
193–211	Septimius Severus reigns as emperor
211–217	Caracalla rules as emperor
212	All free citizens of Rome are granted citizenship
217–218	Macrinus reigns as emperor
218–222	Elegabalus reigns as emperor
221–235	Alexander Severus rules as emperor
235–284	At least twenty-five "Barracks emperors" rule
250	Christian persecutions
251	Decius becomes the first emperor slain in battle, at Abrittus
260	Valerian is the first emperor captured in battle (by the Sassanians)
260–274	The Gallic and Palmyrene provinces break away from Rome and become independent
270–275	Aurelian, who reunited the empire, reigns as emperor
270	Aurelian builds wall around Rome
284–305	Diocletian rules as emperor
287–296	Britain breaks away
293	Diocletian establishes Tetrarchy
301	Diocletian legislates price controls
303	Christian persecutions
305	Diocletian and Maximian abdicate
312	Battle of the Milvian Bridge
312–324	Constantine controls the western empire and Licinius controls the eastern empire
313	Edict of Milan passed, giving Christians freedom to worship
324–337	Constantine rules as sole emperor

324	Constantinople is founded on the site of Byzantium
325	Licinius and his son are executed
	Council of Nicaea
330	Constantine moves his government to Constantinople
357	Battle of Argentorate
359	Constantinople granted a Senate
361–363	Reign of Julian the Apostate
364–392	House of Valentinian rules Rome
376	Valens permits thousands of Visigoths and Ostrogoths to enter empire
378	Goths defeat Romans at Battle of Adrianople
379–395	Theodosius the Great reigns
391	Paganism banned again
395	Empire divided into east and west
401	Italy invaded by Alaric and Visigoths
402	Ravenna becomes capital
403	Italy invaded by Alaric
406	Germanic tribes invade Gaul
407–408	New Gallic Empire formed
410	Visigoths sack and occupy Rome (for three days)
418	Roman treaty with Visigoths
435	Theodosius II decrees all pagan temples to be converted to Christianity or to be closed
438	Law Code of Theodosius
439	Vandals conquer Roman Africa
451	Romans and Visigoths defeat Attila the Hun
452	Attila the Hun invades, but Pope Leo I persuades him not to enter Rome
455	Rome sacked for two weeks by Vandals
476	Last western emperor deposed; Odoacer takes throne
533	Justinian's Digest is published
609	Pantheon converted to a church
1082	Rome sacked
1349	Earthquake in Rome
1453	Byzantine Empire destroyed by Ottomans
1458–1464	Papacy of Pius II, collector of Roman artifacts
1466	Etruscan tomb opened at Volterra
1468	Pomponio Leto and Roman Academy arrested
1515	Raphael becomes overseer of antiquities in Rome
1527	Charles V sacks Rome
1588–1589	Trajan's Column is restored
1666	French Academy in Rome founded
1703	Earthquake in Rome
1707	Society of Antiquaries founded
1709	Excavations begin at Herculaneum
1727	Accademia Etrusca founded

1738	Renewed excavations at Herculaneum
1740	Pontificia Accademia Romana di Archeologia founded
1748	Excavations at Pompeii begin
1750	Villa of the Papyri discovered at Herculaneum
1753	British Museum in London founded
1776–1788	Edward Gibbon's masterpiece, *The History of the Decline and Fall of the Roman Empire,* is published
1780	Scipio family tomb discovered in Rome
1793	Louvre opened
1794	Gustaf III's Museum of Antiquities opened in Stockholm
1809–1814	French occupation of Rome
1812	Earthquake in Rome
1816	French return antiquities to Rome
1820	Venus de Milo discovered
1837	Pope Gregory XVI founds Museo Gregoriano Etrusco
1853	Villanovan culture discovered and identified
1860	Fiorelli becomes director of Pompeii excavations
1862	First volume of *Corpus Inscriptionum Latinarum* is published
1869	House of Livia discovered in Rome
1870	The Metropolitan Museum of Art is founded in New York
	Museum of Fine Arts founded in Boston
1871–1882	Schliemann excavates Troy
1873	French School in Rome founded
1879	Archaeological Institute of America founded
1895	American Academy in Rome founded
1899	British School at Rome founded
1899	Antonio Mau's *Pompeii—Its Life and Art* is first published (an English translation follows in 1900)
1902	Archaic cemetery discovered in the Forum Romanum
1912	Royal Ontario Museum founded in Toronto
1926	Swedish Institute in Rome founded
1927	Excavations at Herculaneum resume yet again

Sources for Further Study

Abbott, Frank, and Allen Johnson

1926   *Municipal Administration in the Roman Empire.* Princeton: Princeton University Press. (Dense and difficult reading, this book is now out of date but is still one of the most thorough accounts of municipal government and the relationship between Rome and the other cities.)

Adcock, F. E.

1940   *The Roman Art of War under the Republic.* New York: Barnes & Noble, Inc. (Adcock provides a good, general introduction to the Roman military. The writing style is a bit old-fashioned, and the information is slightly out of date. But because it is essentially a collection of lectures, it is quite easy to read.)

Adkins, Lesley, and Roy Adkins

1994   *Handbook to Life in Ancient Rome.* Oxford: Oxford University Press. (An easy-to-use sourcebook on many aspects of Roman daily life that provides information normally not available in one place.)

1996   *Dictionary of Roman Religion.* New York: Facts on File. (This is another good reference tool by Adkins and Adkins. The entries are arranged alphabetically and are trustworthy. The only complaint is that the bibliographies accompanying each entry are relatively sparse.)

Andrae, Bernard

1977   *The Art of Rome.* R. Woolf (trans.). New York: H.N. Abrams. (This is an easy-to-read one-volume overview of Roman art with good illustrations.)

Auget, Roland

1994   *Cruelty and Civilization: The Roman Games.* New York: Routledge University Press. (Auget's book is a good introduction to the Roman games in all their forms. It begins with a discussion of the concept of cruelty in Roman games, and what it reflects about Roman society and modern society.)

Badian, E.

1958   *Foreign Clientelae.* Oxford: Clarendon Press. (Although outdated, this book is still useful as a source on Rome's relationship to client states.)

1968   *Roman Imperialism in the Late Republic.* Ithaca: Cornell University Press. (Arguing against economic motivations for Roman imperialism, Badian analyzes this subject and scholarship on Roman imperialism in general in this volume.)

1972   *Publicans and Sinners.* Ithaca: Cornell University Press. (This is a discussion of the nature of the publicani; the name of the book is derived from the negative image of the publicani in the New Testament.)

Bailey, Cyril
1932   *Phases in the Religion of Ancient Rome.* Westport: Greenwood Press. (This is an important work but is very flawed in its interpretive framework. The major problem is that it presents a unilinear cultural evolutionary model of Roman religion. If the reader can ignore these interpretations, then some of the hard data can still be useful.)

Balsdon, John
1967   *Julius Caesar and Rome.* London: English University Press. (Geared towards the lay reader, this generally follows Gelzer's work, but at a simpler level.)

Beard, Mary
1980   "The Sexual Status of Vestal Virgins." *Journal of Roman Studies* 70. (Very worth reading, this journal article presents an interesting discussion of the vestal virgins and is almost always cited in discussions of this religious group.)

Beard, Mary, and Michael Crawford
1984   *Rome in the Late Republic.* Ithaca: Cornell University Press. (The reader will find a good discussion of the politics of the period in this volume.)

Beard, Mary, and John Henderson
2001   *Classical Art: From Greece to Rome.* Oxford: Oxford University Press. (More than just a descriptive art-historical account, this book provides discussions of sensuality, sexuality, and power in Roman art, as well as more traditional discussions about painting, statuary, and portraiture. Includes a discussion on Greek art as well.)

Beard, Mary, and John North (eds.)
1987   *Pagan Priests.* Ithaca: Cornell University Press. (Articles by different scholars are collected in this volume, all on the subject of pagan priests. Included in the articles are important theoretical discussions about the role of priests in Roman religion and the appropriateness of the use of the term *priest.*)

Beard, Mary, John North, and Simon Price
1998   *Religions of Rome.* 2 vols. Cambridge: Cambridge University Press. (This two-volume collection provides a very good introduction to Roman religion. The first volume presents the history of Roman religion from a chronological perspective. The second volume is an anthology of Roman sources relating to religion.)

Bloch, Raymond
1960   *The Origins of Rome.* London: Thames & Hudson. (Bloch describes the origins of Rome from the perspective of both texts and archaeology. Most important is Bloch's argument that early Roman history should be understood within the context of other events in Italy rather than as an isolated phenomenon.)

Boardman, John (ed.)
1993   *The Oxford History of Classical Art.* Oxford: Oxford University Press. (An edited collection of essays on classical art in a volume meant as a companion to *The Oxford*

History of the Classical World. Directly relating to Roman studies is the chapter on the republic and early empire and the chapter on the late Roman Empire).

Boardman, John, Jasper Griffin, and Oswyn Murray (eds.)
1988 *The Oxford Illustrated History of the Roman World*. Oxford: Oxford University Press. (Contained in this volume is a collection of essays by prominent Romanists on general topics in Roman civilization, but with a very heavy literary emphasis. Those interested in Roman literature would be well advised to start here.)

Boëthius, Axel
1960 *The Golden House of Nero*. Ann Arbor: University of Michigan Press. (This book is not just about Nero's Golden House, although there is a good chapter on it. There are also chapters about Iron Age architecture, domestic architecture, and other topics.)

1978 *Etruscan and Early Roman Architecture*. New Haven: Yale University Press. (Originally published as one volume with Ward-Perkins [1981], this is the only comprehensive book on this subject. The book has been revised in its second edition, with material added after the author's death. The illustrations are very good.)

Bowder, Diana
1978 *The Age of Constantine and Julian*. New York: Barnes & Noble. (The political and religious events of the late Roman Empire are described in detail.)

Bowersock, Glen
1965 *Augustus and the Greek World*. Westport: Greenwood Press. (The adoption and integration of the Greek world into the Roman sphere of influence are the subject of this detailed, text-based study.)

1969 *Greek Sophists in the Roman Empire*. Oxford: Clarendon Press. (Based on a series of lectures, the relationship of Sophistic thought in Rome is well described here. This is probably the best entrance into this subject if the reader wants to approach it from a Roman perspective.)

Bradford, Ernle
1981 *Hannibal*. New York: Barnes & Noble Inc. (Another older volume that has been reissued by Barnes & Noble, this is an easy-to-read account of Hannibal's life, focusing mostly on military affairs. Unfortunately, there is only a brief chapter devoted to Hannibal's life after the Battle of Zama, which was a very interesting time.)

Brendel, O.
1979 *Prolegomena to the Study of Roman Art*. New Haven: Yale University Press. (First published in the *Memoirs of the American Academy at Rome*, because Brendel's essays have been so influential, that they were reprinted. This book is only sparsely illustrated and is not an overview of Roman art. Rather, it tackles questions of what makes art Roman and establishes many of the definitions and questions that are still asked in the field of Roman art history.)

Brilliant, R.
1974 *Roman Art*. London: Phaidon. (There are two distinct sections in Brilliant's

book. The first section [and the largest] is a discussion of various themes of Roman art. The second section provides a chronological analysis of Roman art.)

Brown, Frank

1961   *Roman Architecture.* New York: G. Braziller. (Brown's discussion of Roman architecture is very brief, but because more than half of the book consists of illustrations, it is still a useful treatment on architecture. It is a very easy read and discusses the issue from a chronological perspective.)

Brown, Peter

1971   *The World of Late Antiquity,* A.D. *150–750.* London: Thames & Hudson. (This is a good introduction to the intellectual world of the later Roman Empire and early Byzantine period. Brown's conceptions of this period are very important, especially for scholars of early Christianity.)

Brunt, Peter

1971a *Italian Manpower.* London: Oxford University Press. (This is a thorough examination of Roman census documents.)

1971b *Social Conflicts in the Roman Republic.* London: Chatto & Windus. (Chronologically oriented discussion of various elements of social conflict throughout Roman history. It also includes two background chapters, including one on economics.)

Buckland, W. W.

1975   *A Text-book of Roman Law from Augustus to Justinian.* 3rd ed. Revised by Peter Stein. Cambridge: Cambridge University Press. (Written from the perspective of a lawyer, this very dense and difficult work attempts to list Roman laws, even using legal language. It is thorough but methodologically flawed in its use of sources.)

Burnett, Andrew

1991   *Roman Coins.* Berkeley: University of California Press. (Intended as an introduction for nonspecialists, this book deals with coins in primarily classical and medieval contexts. It is a useful introduction to how archaeologists can use ancient coins to reconstruct the past.)

Campbell, J. B.

1984   *The Emperor and the Roman Army.* Oxford: Clarendon Press. (Not only describing the imperial army, this book discusses in detail the importance of the army for the political support of the emperors, going so far as to argue that the army was the primary force behind the later emperors.)

Camps, William

1969   *An Introduction to Virgil's* Aeneid. London: Oxford University Press. (Specifically geared toward students and first-time Virgil readers, this book provides excellent commentary and discussion on *The Aeneid*.)

Carcopino, Jérôme

1940   *Daily Life in Ancient Rome.* Henry Rowell (ed.). New Haven: Yale University Press. (An overview of Roman life, the first part of the book describes various aspects of Roman social history, such as population, urbanism, family, class, religion, and education. The second part describes a typical day in the life of the average Roman.)

Carson, A. G.
   1978 *Principal Coins of the Romans*. 3 vols. London: British Museum Publications. (Each volume discusses a different period of Roman coinage—the republic, the principate, and the dominate, respectively, and provides ample illustrations and discussion.)

Casson, Lionel
   1974 *Travel in the Ancient World*. London: Allen and Unwin. (Casson discusses the nature of travel in antiquity.)

Caven, Brian
   1980 *The Punic Wars*. New York: Barnes & Noble Inc. (This book provides a comprehensive narrative of many of the events of the Punic Wars. It also provides analysis of the key players and some of the social setting of the wars. The book is chronologically organized, which gives the reader a good sense of the historical flow of the conflict.)

Chambers, Mortimer
   1970 *The Fall of Rome: Can It Be Explained?* 2nd ed. New York: Holt, Rinehart, and Winston. (This is an anthology of the works of important modern scholars on the fall of Rome. It is a good place to begin one's study on this subject, although Kagan's volume [1992] is similar and more up-to-date.)

Charles-Picard, Gilbert
   1966 *Living Architecture: Roman*. London: Oldbourne. (There are useful illustrations and plans in this overview, although some of the plans are missing scales. Charles-Picard singles out some of the most important monuments, but his categorizations are not very helpful.)

   1970 *Roman Painting*. Greenwich: New York Graphic Society. (This is the most comprehensive English-language treatment on this subject. There are many illustrations but most are black-and-white.)

Charleston, Robert
   1955 *Roman Pottery*. London: Faber and Faber. (This book has excellent photographs of many types of Roman pottery and provides a thorough introduction to red-gloss ware, glazed ware, and coarse ware.)

Chevallier, Raymond
   1976 *Roman Roads*. Berkeley: University of California Press. (Chevallier presents an overview from both an archaeological and inscriptional perspective of the evidence for Roman roads.)

Clark, M. L.
   1956 *The Roman Mind*. London: Cohen & West Ltd. (This is one of the few good books about Roman philosophy. It is outdated, but unfortunately nothing has surpassed it.)

Commager, Steele (ed.)
   1966   *Virgil: A Collection of Critical Essays*. Englewood Cliffs: Prentice-Hall. (Collected in this volume are a number of essays by different scholars on Virgil and his work. While many of these essays are out of date, the volume as a whole can give the reader a good sense for more traditional, literary studies.)

Cornell, Tim
   1995   *The Beginnings of Rome*. New York: Routledge. (This is arguably the best overview of early Roman civilization available, and the sections where Cornell departs from more traditional scholarly conceptions of Rome are particularly noteworthy.)

Cornell, Tim, and John Matthews
   1982   *Atlas of the Roman World*. New York: Facts on File. (Not really an atlas, this book is a good introductory account of Roman history.)

Cowell, F. R.
   1980   *Life in Ancient Rome*. New York: Perigee Books. (This book can be found in most large bookstores. It is very outdated but is very easy to read and relatively comprehensive in its coverage of everyday life. The sometimes inappropriate pictures can be quite amusing.)

Crawford, Michael
   1982   *The Roman Republic*. Cambridge: Harvard University Press. (One of the better discussions of the history of this period, Crawford's book is particularly useful for learning about the sources of Roman history.)

Crook, John
   1977   *Law and Life in Rome*. Ithaca: Cornell University Press. (Crook gives a general discussion of Roman law, but it is more a discussion of the social role and social practice of law in Roman society than a discussion of laws per se.)

   1995   *Legal Advocacy in the Roman World*. Ithaca: Cornell University Press. (This volume describes how advocacy worked, what the sources are for this aspect of legal life, and its wider social setting.)

D'Ambra, Eve
   1998   *Roman Art*. Cambridge: Cambridge University Press. (Quite easy to read, the book begins with a discussion of what the study of art can contribute to one's understanding of Roman social structure. The first chapter is followed by more traditional discussions on art history.)

d'Arms, John
   1981   *Commerce and Social Standing in Ancient Rome*. Cambridge: Harvard University Press. (The relationship between attitudes and actions, specifically in relation to notions of commerce, is discussed here. Also helpful are the author's explanations of the practical aspects of commerce and investment in Rome.)

de Coulanges, Fustel
   1864   *The Ancient City*. New York: Doubleday Books. (A classic work on the concept of the city in the ancient world; even though it is outdated, it is still a useful read.)

de Franciscis, Alfonso

1978 *The Buried Cities: Pompeii and Herculaneum.* Napoli: Interdipress. (This is a glossy, popular book on Pompeii. It basically consists of paragraph-long treatments on the various monuments. It has excellent color photos, and although not very scholarly, it's a useful book for travelers to Pompeii or for people who are just looking for an easy overview.)

Deiss, J. J.

1966 *Herculaneum: Italy's Buried Treasure.* New York: Crowell. (Here is a popular account of Herculaneum, which gives information on both the site and its excavations. There are many pictures but all are in black and white.)

Dilke, Oswald

1971 *The Roman Land Surveyors: An Introduction to the Agrimensores.* Newton Abbot: David and Charles. (A good study with a lot of technical details about many aspects of land surveying.)

1987 *Mathematics and Measurement.* Berkeley: University of California Press. (Intended for general audiences, this is probably the easiest (yet still accurate) account of mathematical issues in the ancient world.)

Dixon, Suzanne

1992 *The Roman Family.* Baltimore: Johns Hopkins University Press. (In one of the best treatments of the subject, Dixon discusses the practices involved in marriage and family life as well as the social meaning of the institution of the family.)

Dodds, Eric

1965 *Pagan and Christian in an Age of Anxiety.* Cambridge: New York: W.W. Norton. (Dodds's volume is an influential and controversial work that argues for similarities between Roman religion and Christianity. Dodds approaches religion using Freudian and Frazerian interpretative categories. See the response to Dodds in the volume edited by Smith and Lounibos [1984].)

Dorey, Thomas (ed.)

1966 *Latin Historians.* London: Routledge & Kegan Paul. (Dorey has edited a volume of essays, written by experts in each subject area, on particular Roman historians, including Polybius, Caesar, Sallust, Livy, Ammianus Marcellinus, and Bede.)

1967 *Latin Biography.* London: Routledge and Kegan Paul. (Each chapter in this collection of essays is devoted to a particular Roman biographer.)

Duckworth, George

1952 *The Nature of Roman Comedy.* Princeton: Princeton University Press. (Written specifically for students, this is essentially a book on Greek New Comedy, and especially about Plautus and Terence. It includes discussions on the background and history of comedy, the presentation of comedy, an analysis of various plays (as well as brief summaries of the plays), and a discussion on the relationship between Roman and Greek comedies.)

Dudley, Donald
   1960   *The Civilization of Rome.* New York: The New American Library. (This is a slightly out of date, but good survey of Roman history. Only 256 pages, it can be considered only an outline of Roman history—but sometimes outlines can be useful.)

Duff, A. M.
   1926   *Freedmen in the Early Roman Empire.* Oxford: Clarendon Press. (An authoritative although outdated overview of many aspects of the lives of freedmen in ancient Rome, with thematically organized chapters.)

Dumézil, Georges
   1970   *Archaic Roman Religion.* 2 vols. Philip Krapp (trans.). Chicago: University of Chicago Press. (This work has been very influential in Roman scholarship on religion. It is an important work but probably not the best book with which to begin one's studies. This is the easiest English version of Dumézil's important but flawed Indo-European hypothesis. His conclusions and viewpoints are not necessarily trustworthy.)

Duncan-Jones, Richard
   1982   *The Economy of the Roman Empire: Quantitative Studies.* Cambridge: Cambridge University Press. (Presented here is an attempt at quantitative methods of investigation of the Roman economy. Noteworthy are the lists of prices in various regions, although there are a lot of problems with the techniques of analysis and the conclusions drawn from those techniques. Nonetheless, this work has been important in modern research on the Roman economy.)

   1990   *Structure and Scale in the Roman Economy.* Cambridge: Cambridge University Press. (Duncan-Jones provides a less quantitatively oriented discussion of Roman economy in this volume than in his 1982 work. Included are important discussions of transportation, labor, agriculture, urbanism, and taxation.)

Dupont, Florence
   1989   *Daily Life in Ancient Rome.* Christopher Woodall (trans.). Cambridge: Basil Blackwell Ltd. (While discussing many aspects of everyday Roman life, Dupont provides insightful analysis of the social meaning of the habits of daily living.)

Earl, Donald
   1967   *The Moral and Political Tradition of Rome.* Ithaca: Cornell University Press. (Earl considers the morality of the Roman nobility through Roman philosophical writings, although he has a shockingly positive bias about the nature of the Roman nobility.)

Ellis, Simon
   2000   *Roman Housing.* London: Gerald Duckworth & Co. Ltd. (This is a good discussion of Roman housing from both an architectural perspective and a social perspective. Chapters on decoration and furniture are quite good. Especially notable is the integration of both archaeological and textual data.)

Errington, Robert
   1972   *The Dawn of Empire: Rome's Rise to World Power.* London: Hamish Hamilton. (Oriented toward nonspecialist readers, this book discusses Roman expansion surrounding the second Punic War.)

Fagan, Garret
1999 *Bathing in Public in the Roman World.* Ann Arbor: University of Michigan Press. (This volume concentrates on the social role of the baths but also includes a collection of inscriptions related to bathing.)

Fantham, Elaine, Helene Peet Foley, and Natalie Boymel Kampen
1995 *Women in the Classical World: Image & Text.* Oxford: Oxford University Press. (Covering Greek and Roman women, the essays collected here are written by a variety of authors and are somewhat uneven. The general format of the articles is to intersperse actual ancient writings with modern scholarly writing.)

Ferguson, John
1970 *The Religions of the Roman Empire.* Ithaca: Cornell University Press. (This book studies Roman religion from a comparative-religion framework.)

Finley, Moses (ed.)
1960 *Slavery in Classical Antiquity.* Cambridge: Heffer. (Another classic work; if one is interested in the subject of slavery from a social-historical or economic standpoint, start with this collection of important statements.)

1973 *The Ancient Economy.* Berkeley: University of California Press. (Finley's classic statement on the nature of ancient economies; scholars of ancient Rome are familiar with this work, although the conclusions are certainly controversial.)

Fowler, William
1911 *The Religious Experience of the Roman People.* London: Macmillan. (Published in this book are a number of lectures given by William Fowler on many aspects of Roman religion. It is an exhaustive work. Although it is out of date, it is still an important work and is frequently cited.)

Fraenkel, Eduard
1957 *Horace.* Oxford: Clarendon Press. (Fraenkel attempts to understand Horace's poetry entirely from a literary perspective and tries to understand the poetry as a Roman was supposed to understand it.)

Frank, Tenney
1927 *An Economic History of Rome.* Baltimore: Johns Hopkins University. (Before editing his five-volume, comprehensive survey of Roman economic issues, Frank published this shorter, preliminary account. It is good to read through this volume before tackling his larger series.)

1933–1940 (ed.) *An Economic Survey of Ancient Rome.* 5 vols. Baltimore: Johns Hopkins University Press. (This is a comprehensive, edited series, detailing various aspects of the Roman economy. Although outdated, it is still a worthwhile source and probably the most inclusive.)

Freeman, Charles
1993 *The World of the Romans.* New York: Oxford University Press. (Readers will find this popular account of Roman civilization easy to read and well written.)

Friedländer, Ludwig
  1910 *Roman Life and Manners under the Early Empire*. London: Routledge & Sons, Ltd. (This is a four-volume encyclopedia on Roman social history. Although very outdated, much of the information is difficult to find elsewhere, and there is nothing available that is more current with a similar scope.)

Frier, Bruce
  1980 *Landlords and Tenants in Imperial Rome*. Princeton: Princeton University Press. (This is an interesting study of real estate in Roman times, especially rental issues. It includes a discussion of the apartments at Ostia, the rental market, and legal issues relating to rental property.)

Futrell, Alison
  1997 *Blood in the Arena*. Austin: University of Texas Press. (This is an easy-to-read, semipopular account of gladiators and Roman arena culture. In terms of the arena, Futrell discusses matters of its origins, religious events, amphitheater construction, and human sacrifice.)

Gardiner, Jane
  1993 *Roman Myths*. Austin: University of Texas Press. (This is a well-illustrated volume, intended for general audiences.)

Garnsey, Peter
  1980 *Non-slave Labour in the Greco-Roman World*. Cambridge: Cambridge Philological Society. (This is a collection of essays by prominent scholars on the topic of labor. The importance of this question in studies of ancient economy is clear from this work. It is a bit technical, however, and not all of the essays are in English.)

Garnsey, Peter, Keith Hopkins, and C. R. Whittaker (eds.)
  1983 *Trade in the Ancient Economy*. Berkeley: University of California Press. (Included within this volume are thirteen articles on a variety of aspects of the classical economy. Most of the articles use Finley's economic models as a starting point, so it is useful to see how his models work when other scholars incorporate them.)

Garnsey, Peter, and Richard Saller
  1987 *The Roman Empire: Economy and Society*. Berkeley: University of California Press. (Written by two prominent scholars; the reader cannot go wrong with this account of Roman civilization.)

Garnsey, Peter, and C. R. Whittaker (eds.)
  1983 *Trade and Famine in Classical Antiquity*. Cambridge: Cambridge Philological Society. (This is a collection of eleven articles presented at a conference, most of which are in English. It is an excellent source of information on the subject of ancient famine, so do not be intimidated by the non-English articles.)

Garzetti, A.
  1974 *From Tiberius to the Antonines*. J. R. Foster (trans.). London: Methuen. (This is a detailed reign-by-reign account of the period noted in the title.)

Gelzer, Matthias
  1968 *Caesar, Politician and Statesman*. Peter Needham (trans.). Cambridge: Cam-

bridge University Press. (Although out of date stylistically, this is still one of the classic accounts of Caesar.)

1969 *The Roman Nobility.* Robin Seager (trans.). New York: Barnes & Noble. (Originally published as two separate volumes in German, this work, geared toward students, describes various aspects of the lives of the nobility in the republic, including patronage and political influence.)

Gibbon, Edward
1776–1788 *The History of the Decline and Fall of the Roman Empire.* (Available in many editions, many of which are abridged, this classic of English-language writing is a necessary read for anyone interested in Rome.)

Gjerstad, Einar
1962 *Legends and Facts of Early Rome.* Lund: C.W.K. Gleerup. (Gjerstad argues for a different chronology of early Rome and for a substantially different early history than more traditional accounts.)

Goodwin, Martin, and Jane Sherwood
1997 *The Roman World 44 B.C.–A.D. 180.* New York: Routledge University Press. (Both the history of the early empire and the major questions asked by modern scholars are the subject of this work.)

Grant, Frederick
1957 *Ancient Roman Religion.* New York: Liberal Arts Press. (This anthology of ancient literature is arranged and selected to present a general overview of Roman religion.)

Grant, Michael
1958 *Roman History from Coins.* Cambridge: Cambridge University Press.
(This is a small book [less than 100 pages] that demonstrates how you can study history through coins.)

1971 *Roman Myth.* New York: Charles Scribner and Sons. (This is a readable discussion of Roman myths. Most of the myths are those recounting the foundation of Rome. Grant does a good job of describing the political uses of myth.)

1974 *The Army of the Caesars.* New York: Charles Scribner's Sons. (This is a good historical study of the army in the empire.)

1978 *History of Rome.* New York: Charles Scribner's Sons. (This is a good, but brief, overview of Roman history from the Etruscan period until the fall of the western empire and is more comprehensive than most one-volume books on the subject.)

1999 *The Collapse and Recovery of the Roman Empire.* New York: Routledge. (This volume tackles the question of why the Roman Empire survived through the troubled 260s–270s C.E. A pretty detailed discussion of a very interesting period, but Grant insists that it is surprising that Rome survived this period.)

Grant, Michael, and Rachel Kitzinger (eds.)
1988 *Civilization of the Ancient Mediterranean: Greece and Rome.* New York: Charles Scribner's Sons. (This is a three-volume encyclopedia, geared toward students and

popular audiences, that provides a good overview of classical civilization and a useful bibliography for selected topics in ancient studies.

Greene, Kevin

1986   *The Archaeology of the Roman Economy.* Berkeley: University of California Press. (This book is geared toward specialists and nonspecialists and provides an excellent discussion of how archaeology can contribute to the study of the Roman economy. It includes sections on transportation, coinage, agriculture, industry, and settlement survey data.)

1992   *Roman Pottery.* Berkeley: University of California Press. (This book is a good introduction to the study of pottery in general and Roman pottery in particular. It is easy to read and emphasizes how archaeologists study Roman pottery more than pottery itself.)

Griffin, Jasper

1985   *Latin Poets and Roman Life.* London and Chapel Hill: University of North Carolina Press. (The interconnectedness of poetry and daily life is the main focus of this study. Griffin demonstrates how Roman literary conventions, which seem artificial to modern readers, were very powerful to ancient readers.)

Grimal, Pierre

1983   *Roman Cities.* G. Michael Woloch (trans.). Madison: University of Wisconsin Press. (Grimal describes Roman urban planning as well as the important, typical structures within a Roman city. The book contains a descriptive catalogue of Roman cities, listing city names (modern and ancient), dates of occupation, locations, and descriptive elements.)

Gruen, Erich

1968   *Roman Politics and the Criminal Courts, 149–78 B.C.* Cambridge: Harvard University Press. (This is an interesting study of Roman political systems through the legal evidence, especially through trials. The way rival Roman families and factions used criminal trials as public forums for disputes and attacks is made clear in Gruen's study.)

1984   *The Hellenistic World and the Coming of Rome.* 2 vols. Berkeley: University of California Press. (Gruen analyzes the institutions of Roman imperialism and provides a historical account of the development of Roman imperialism in the East.)

1995   *The Last Generation of the Roman Republic.* Berkeley: University of California Press. (The period surrounding the end of the republic is discussed in detail.)

Hadas, Moses

1956   *A History of Rome.* New York: Garden City Press. (The history of Rome is recounted in this volume by presenting selections from classical sources. An interesting method of presentation, but the uncritical presentation of sources can be somewhat problematic.)

Hardie, Philip

1998   *Virgil.* Oxford: Oxford University Press. (A brief but very good introduction to Virgil and his poems.)

Harris, W. V.

1979 *War and Imperialism in Republican Rome, 327–70 B.C.* Oxford: Clarendon Press. (This book discusses imperialism, its aims, and attitudes toward war and the nature of conquest in the Republican period.)

Hart, B. H. Liddell

1994 [1926]. *Scipio Africanus: Greater Than Napoleon.* New York: Da Capo Press. (Written from the perspective of a military historian, this is a study of Scipio Africanus and his military strategy, with detailed descriptions of battles.)

Hayes, John W.

1980 *Late Roman Pottery with Supplement.* London: British School at Rome. (Not an easy read, but it is the most important book on this topic and the most thorough presentation of Hayes's ceramic typology. The 1980 edition has a valuable supplement.)

1997 *Handbook of Mediterranean Roman Pottery.* London: British Museum Press. (Perfect for the beginner, this book discusses specific forms and more general issues in Roman ceramic studies.)

Healy, John

1978 *Mining and Metallurgy in the Greek and Roman World.* London: Thames & Hudson. (For an overview of mining in the classical period, this is the best work. It tells what was mined and how it was mined.)

Henig, Martin (ed.)

1983 *Handbook of Roman Art: A Survey of the Visual Arts of the Roman World.* Oxford: Phaidon. (Henig has collected a selection of essays on a variety of topics in Roman art [such as architecture, sculpture, and mosaics.] What makes this handbook useful is that each essay is written by a specialist on the subject.)

Heurgon, Jacques

1973 *The Rise of Rome to 264 B.C.* James Willis (trans.). Berkeley: University of California Press. (Major issues in the study of Rome are presented here, especially those that have been prominent in non-English-speaking scholarly circles.)

Higgins, Reynold

1966 *Greek and Roman Jewelry.* Berkeley: University of California Press. (Although there is only one chapter explicitly devoted to Roman jewelry, the first half of the book treats important technological issues.)

Holmes, T. Rice

1928–1931 *The Architect of the Roman Empire.* 2 vols. Oxford: Clarendon Press. (The first volume is a detailed narrative of events leading up to the establishment of the principate. The second volume is centered on Augustus, the architect of the Roman Empire.)

Hopkins, Keith

1978 *Sociological Studies in Roman History I: Conquerors and Slaves.* Cambridge: Cambridge University Press. (Discusses issues of slavery and imperial domination using sociological methods. The important contribution of this book is the models for social change Hopkins suggests and his demonstration of the applicability of sociology to ancient studies.)

1983   *Sociological Studies in Roman History II: Death and Renewal.* Cambridge: Cambridge University Press. (Another series of sociological studies; the topics in this volume are all somewhat related to death, including games, succession, and mortuary customs.)

Hunter, Richard
1985   *The New Comedy of Greece and Rome.* Cambridge: Cambridge University Press. (Specifically geared toward undergraduates, most of this book is about Greek manifestations of Greek New Comedy. But because Roman adaptations of Greek New Comedy are very heavily based on the Greek prototypes, this book provides a very useful account of the genre in Roman times as well.)

Huskinson, Janet
2000   *Experiencing Rome.* New York: Routledge. (This book was written with upper-level undergraduates in mind. It contains eleven essays on Roman culture, all with a heavy emphasis on analysis.)

Jashemski, W. F.
1979   *The Gardens of Pompeii, Herculaneum and the Villas Destroyed by Vesuvius.* New York: Caratzas Brothers. (This is probably the most thorough account of gardens in ancient Rome. It is well illustrated, and most of Jashemski's arguments are based on archaeology and art history.)

1993   *The Gardens of Pompeii, Herculaneum and the Villas Destroyed by Vesuvius: Appendices.* New York: Caratzas Brothers. (Not as explicitly related to the first volume as one might think, this book contains three appendices. The first describes every excavated Vesuvian garden. The second is a catalogue of Roman garden paintings. And the third includes evidence of Roman flora and fauna.)

Jolowicz, Herbert
1954   *Historical Introduction to Roman Law.* Cambridge: Cambridge University Press. (A very dense discussion of the history of Roman law, this is a thorough work. It provides much of the historical context for Roman law that is lacking in other works on the subject.)

Jones, A. H. M.
1964   *The Later Roman Empire, 294–602.* Oxford: Clarendon Press. (Jones suggests that it is useful to compare the eastern and western empires. The contrasts and comparisons he draws are instructive.)

1974   *The Roman Economy: Studies in Ancient Economic and Administrative History.* Peter Brunt (ed.). Oxford: Blackwell. (Collected here are some important essays by Jones on major issues in Roman economy. Some of the articles are general, but most are geared toward scholars. This is an important collection because of Jones's contribution to the subject.)

Kagan, Donald
1992   *The End of the Roman Empire: Decline or Transformation?* 3rd ed. Lexington: D.C.

Heath and Company. (This is an anthology of important scholarly works on the problem of the fall of Roman civilization, with some introduction and commentary.)

Katz, Solomon

1955 *The Decline of Rome and the Rise of Mediaeval Europe.* Ithaca: Cornell University Press. (Katz describes how much of Roman civilization [law, art, language] continued into medieval civilization. This was a very important work when it first came out, basically instituting a new field of study and integrating medieval and classical scholarship.)

Keller, Donald, and David Rupp (eds.)

1983 *Archaeological Survey in the Mediterranean Area.* Oxford: BAR International Series. (This is an eclectic collection of articles, many of which do not deal with Roman times. It opens with some methodological discussion about surveying in general. Also included are a number of reports [mostly preliminary] about survey work throughout the region.)

Kennedy, George

1972 *The Art of Rhetoric in the Roman World.* Princeton: Princeton University Press. (Written with students in mind, this is a thorough account of rhetoric from a chronological perspective.)

Keppie, Lawrence

1983 *Colonisation and Veteran Settlement in Italy 47–14 B.C.* London: British School at Rome. (Colonies and their impact are the key issues addressed by Keppie. Most of the volume is concerned about those colonies settled by veterans and the nature of that relocation.)

Kleiner, Diana (ed.)

1996 *I Claudia: Women in Ancient Rome.* New Haven: Yale University Art Gallery. Kleiner's volume was created to accompany a museum exhibition and is filled with essays by a number of scholars. There are three main sections [not including the introductory sections on art and gender theory] that revolve around women in the public, private, and funerary realms.

2000 *I Claudia II: Women in Roman Art and Society.* Austin: University of Texas Press. (This book, while ostensibly a companion volume to *I Claudia,* is not an exhibition catalogue but a series of articles on women in Rome, with somewhat of an emphasis on art-historical evidence.)

Klingaman, William

1986 *The First Century.* New York: HarperCollins Publishers. (This book encompasses the entire first century C.E., including the Roman world. It is interesting to put Roman civilization in context with other civilizations. The prose is very readable, but sometimes contains unreliable information. Klingaman frequently makes assertions that cannot be backed up from a scholarly standpoint, so use this book with care.)

Kraus, Theodore

1975 *Pompeii and Herculaneum: The Living Cities of the Dead.* New York: H.N. Abrams. (Kraus's book is very large, not in page numbers but in the size of the book. The chapters are arranged according to various subjects, such as "Man," "Gods," and "Art.")

Laurence, Roy
1999   *The Roads of Roman Italy.* New York: Routledge. (Laurence provides good information on the Roman-period roads in Italy. He puts the issue of transportation into the social context of Roman civilization and illustrates the connection between roads and Roman ideas of territory.)

Lawrence, Arnold
1972   *Greek and Roman Sculpture.* New York: Harper & Row. (There are five chapters in this book specific to Roman sculpture, but the first three provide important information on the study of ancient sculpture in general.)

le Glay, Marcel, Jean-Louis Voisin, and Yann Le Bohec
2001   *A History of Rome.* 2nd ed. Antonia Nevill (trans.). Malden: Blackwell. (This book provides an excellent overview of Roman history from earliest times until 395 C.E. but concentrates mostly on political history.)

Levick, Barbara
2000   *The Government of the Roman Empire: A Sourcebook.* 2nd ed. New York: Routledge. (This is a thematically organized anthology of translated ancient texts relating to Roman governance, economy, and law.)

Ling, Roger
1991   *Roman Painting.* Cambridge: Cambridge University Press. (Actually a discussion of wall painting, this book provides the easiest introduction to Mau's categories of Pompeiian wall paintings; probably easier than reading Mau's book. It also has chapters on aspects of wall painting, including mythological/historical paintings, techniques, and patrons.)

Lot, Ferdinand
1961   *The End of the Ancient World and the Beginnings of the Middle Ages.* New York: HarperTorch Books. (This is a good study, because it encompasses both the fall of Rome and the early medieval period. It illustrates how Roman institutions were transformed in medieval times.)

Luttwak, Edward
1976   *The Grand Strategy of the Roman Empire.* Baltimore: Johns Hopkins University Press. (Written from the perspective of a military historian and strategist, this book details the development of imperial military strategy and warfare, tying these developments to specific historical situations.)

Lyne, R.O.A.M.
1980   *The Latin Love Poets from Catullus to Horace.* Oxford: Oxford University Press. (Designed for students, Lyne's introduction to love poetry includes theme-based discussions as well as sections devoted to particular poets.)

MacDonald, William
1976   *The Pantheon.* Cambridge: Harvard University Press. (Although this is prima-

rily a discussion of the Pantheon [with a description, study of its meaning, and principles of its design and construction], MacDonald uses other Roman architecture to better understand his subject, making the book relevant beyond just the Pantheon.)

1982   *The Architecture of the Roman Empire I.* New Haven: Yale University Press. (Not an overview of the subject, but this book includes interesting chapters on Nero's palace, Domitian's palace, Trajan's markets, and the Pantheon. There are also more general discussions of construction and design as well as individual architects.)

1986   *The Architecture of the Roman Empire II.* New Haven: Yale University Press. (Very different from MacDonald's first volume, this book discusses imperial perspective from the context of its urban environment.)

MacMullen, Ramsay
1963   *Soldier and Civilian in the Later Roman Empire.* Cambridge: Harvard University Press. (The novelty of this book is that it discusses the lives and roles of soldiers when *not* at war.)

1966   *Enemies of the Roman Order: Treason, Unrest, and Alienation in the Empire.* Cambridge: Harvard University Press. (MacMullen's book details many important aspects of the decline of Rome as well as Roman military history and techniques in the imperial period.)

1976   *Roman Government's Response to Crisis, A.D. 235–337.* New Haven: Yale University Press. (Good description of the events of the period presented from a social-historical point of view.)

1981   *Paganism in the Roman Empire.* New Haven: Yale University Press. (Provided in this volume is a discussion of Roman religion from what is essentially a philosophical perspective. It has a very good discussion of paganism as a category and how it can be a useful category for understanding Roman religion.)

Marsh, Frank Burr
1963   *A History of the Roman World from 146 to 30 B.C.* 3rd ed. London: Methuen. (Although it concentrates on political and military history, this book is well organized and detailed.)

Mau, August
1982 [1902]   *Pompeii: Its Life and Art.* F. W. Kelsey (trans.). 2nd ed. New York: Caratzas Brothers. (Mau's work is one of the most important works on Roman art history ever written. Although there has been much more excavated at Pompeii since the time this book was written, the art-historical categories Mau recognized are still used in Roman studies today. This book is worth reading; it is one of those books that is talked about more than it is actually read.)

McKay, Alexander
1975   *Houses, Villas and Palaces in the Roman World.* Ithaca: Cornell University Press. (Domestic housing is the major theme of this book. But the reader should be careful when using it, as it is filled with errors. Unfortunately, there is no book that covers the same ground that this book does.)

Meier, Christian

1982   *Caesar.* David McLintock (trans.). New York: Basic Books. (This is an influential biography of Caesar, to which many of the other biographies on the man refer. There is a heavy emphasis on the military campaigns. The English translation is geared toward a popular audience, so there is no bibliography or footnotes.)

Meiggs, Russel

1973   *Roman Ostia.* 2nd ed. Oxford: Clarendon Press. (This is the classic account of Ostia. It is a very substantial book, discussing the history of Ostia, aspects of urban life at Ostia, and elements of urban planning.)

Millar, Fergus

1977   *The Emperor in the Roman World.* Ithaca: Cornell University Press. (Millar's book is an exhaustive overview of the role of the office of emperor in Roman times. Not a discussion of specific emperors, this book examines the social and political roles of emperors.)

Mommsen, Theodor

1871   *History of Rome.* 4 vols. New York: Scribner. (This is one of the masterpieces of Roman scholarship. Originally intended as a five-volume work, this book is one of the platforms on which modern Roman scholarship is based.)

Nicolet, C.

1980   *The World of the Citizen in Republican Rome.* P.S. Falla (trans.). Berkeley: University of California Press. (The concept of the citizen and issues related to citizenship are discussed in this volume. Nicolet's book is a very useful study on this topic.)

North, John

1976   "Conservatism and Change in Roman Religion." *Papers of the British School at Rome:* 44. (This is one of the most cited articles on the subject of Roman religion. It is crucial to read it to be able to understand much of the current scholarly work on this subject.)

2000   *Roman Religion.* Oxford: Oxford University Press. (This is a short monograph on major issues in the study of Roman religion with useful discussions on approaches to the study of Roman religion.)

Norwood, Gilbert

1923   *The Art of Terence.* New York: Russel & Russel. (Although Norwood paraphrases and comments on Terence's plays, unfortunately he does not translate Latin phrases, making this book difficult for a beginner.)

Ogilvie, R.M.

1969   *The Romans and Their Gods.* London: Chatto & Windus. (This is a classic overview that is still frequently cited. It is not a bad source of information, although it should be read alongside more recent accounts.)

1976   *Early Rome and the Etruscans.* Atlantic Highlands: Humanities Press. (The textual evidence for early Roman and Etruscan civilization is presented, but because the book does not consider the archaeological evidence, the accuracy of the conclusions is questionable.)

Pallotino, Massimo
1991   *A History of Earliest Italy.* Martin Ryle and Kate Soper (trans.). Ann Arbor: University of Michigan Press. (The early history of Italy, not just Rome, is presented in this volume, but most important are the historiographic issues that Pallotino discusses.)

Parker, Henry William
1958   *The Roman Legions.* New York: Barnes & Noble, Inc. (Slightly out of date, this book nevertheless provides an accessible account of life in the Roman legions. The daily life of soldier, the various reforms, and legion tactics are all discussed. The appendixes provided are useful reference tools about specific legions.)

Parkin, Tim
1992   *Demography and Roman Society.* Baltimore: Johns Hopkins University Press. (A good introduction to the methodology of Roman demography and the evidence that is available.)

Percival, John
1975   *The Roman Villa: An Historical Introduction.* Berkeley: University of California Press. (This general survey of the Roman villa describes the physical manifestations of the villa as well as its social and economic role in Roman times and has an especially good discussion of regional variations.)

Plass, Paul
1995   *The Game of Death in Ancient Rome.* Madison: University of Wisconsin Press. (There are two main sections in this book. The first centers on gladiatorial combat and the second discusses the phenomenon of political suicide. The link between these two seemingly unconnected subjects is Plass's discussion of the social role of violence in Roman civilization.)

Polanyi, Karl, Conrad Arensberg, and Harry Pearson (eds.)
1957   *Trade and Market in the Early Empires.* Chicago: Henry Regnery Company. (This is a collection of articles by different authors and is the most important statement of the substantivist school of economics. This is an extremely important work in the history of ancient economic scholarship. Whether or not you agree with the perspective, it is important to be familiar with this work.)

Potter, D.S., and D.J. Mattingly (eds.)
1999   *Life, Death, and Entertainment in the Roman Empire.* Ann Arbor: University of Michigan Press. (Intended for classroom use, this is a collection of essays on various aspects of Roman social history. The essays were written and collected with teaching in mind, so they are very clear and readable.)

Quinn, K.
1969   *Latin Explorations.* 2nd ed. London: Routledge and Kegan Paul. (Quinn's book is essentially a discussion of six major Roman poets. It is not a good introduction, as

Quinn primarily deals with issues that he believed had not been dealt with well in previous scholarship. It has been an influential work, and for that reason may be helpful in one's continued studies of Rome.)

1999 [1959]   *The Catullan Revolution.* 2nd ed. London: Bristol Classical Press. (Although not well regarded when it first appeared, this has been a very influential book. It argues that Catullus led a new literary movement in Rome.)

Raaflaub, Kurt (ed.)
1986   *Social Struggles in Archaic Rome.* Berkeley: University of California Press. (The Conflict of the Orders is treated in twelve essays by prominent scholars. For interpretation and analysis of the conflict, this is an excellent resource.)

Rawson, Beryl (ed.)
1991   *Marriage, Divorce, and Children in Ancient Rome.* Oxford: Clarendon Press. (Nine essays regarding the Roman family—by different scholars on various issues—are collected here.)

Rawson, Elizabeth
1975   *Cicero: A Portrait.* London: Allen Lane. (Rawson provides a good overview of Cicero and especially brings out his place within Roman traditions.)

Rickman, Geoffrey
1980   *The Corn Supply of Ancient Rome.* Oxford: Clarendon Press. (Rickman's study is the authoritative work on the history of cereal crops in the city of Rome. It is structured along chronological lines and gives a good historical account of the city's changing relationship to this important type of crop.)

Rodgers, William
1964 [1937]   *Greek and Roman Naval Warfare.* Annapolis: Naval Institute Press. (This is a thorough overview of Greek and Roman naval warfare. Written from the perspective of a U.S. Navy vice admiral, the description of military strategy and tactics is truly informative. There are some factual errors, but these are more than made up for by the insight into how naval combat plays out.)

Rose, H.J.
1948   *Ancient Roman Religion.* New York: Hutchinson's University Library. (Rose's volume is a classical account of Roman religion that has not stood the test of time. Arguments made by Rose are often directly attacked by later scholars and usually for good reason. Comments such as "the Romans were a much slower-witted people" should make modern readers uncomfortable.)

Rostovtzeff, Michael
1957   *Social and Economic History of the Roman Empire.* Oxford: Oxford University Press. (This is one of the most important works on Roman history and economy. The author is one of the most well-respected scholars and this work is still widely quoted today.)

Saller, Richard
1982   *Personal Patronage under the Early Roman Empire.* Cambridge: Cambridge Uni-

versity Press. (The patron-client relationship is examined in detail in Saller's monograph. He attempts to investigate actual examples of patronage, and much of the discussion is philological.)

1994 *Patriarchy, Property and Death in the Roman Family.* Cambridge: Cambridge University Press. (This is an excellent study of demographic issues related to Roman families. There are three major sections in this work: a demographic study, a discussion of family, and property issues within the Roman family. The true strength of this work lies in its ability to integrate statistical evidence with discussion of Roman families and come to interesting conclusions about social history.)

Salmon, Edward Togo
  1966 *A History of the Roman World from 30 B.C. to A.D. 138.* 5th ed. (This is a detailed historical account, organized according to the reign of each emperor in the period.)

Scarre, Chris
  1995 *Chronicle of the Roman Emperors.* New York: Thames & Hudson Ltd. (Scarre's book provides information about each of the emperors. The book was written for general audiences, and Scarre is sometimes not critical enough in his use of ancient historical accounts, but the book is full of information and is very easy to use and read.)

Schatzman, Israel
  1975 *Senatorial Wealth and Roman Politics.* Bruxelles: Latonus. (This is an important work investigating the economic circumstances and motivations of senators. Part 3 lists senators by name and discusses each individual, a useful tool for more advanced study.)

Scheidel, Walter (ed.)
  2001 *Debating Roman Demography.* Leiden: Brill. (Contained within this volume are five articles on Roman demography. The first is an overview of the history of the subject in Roman scholarship and provides a very good discussion of the major issues and the problems for incorporating demographic studies. The other articles are rooted in specific problems, but are nonetheless interesting and of high quality. This book, however, is not meant for nonspecialists.)

Scullard, H. H.
  1961 *A History of the Roman World 753 to 146 B.C.* London: Methuen. (This is a traditional political and military history of Rome—dependable, but out of date.)

  1976 *From the Gracchi to Nero.* 4th ed. London: Methuen. (This is a traditional, political-military history, with extensive notes. It is well organized and has clear discussions of the complicated political situations of this period.)

  1981 *Festivals and Ceremonies of the Roman Republic.* Ithaca: Cornell University Press. (This is the best source on Roman festivals available in English. It is most valuable as a reference tool, as the majority of the book is a day-by-day guide to all of the most important festivals of the Romans. The appendixes include valuable information about festivals unavailable elsewhere.)

Seaford, R.

1978   *Pompeii.* New York: Thames & Hudson. (Seaford's book is not geared toward specialists. It is well illustrated and contains sections on economy, politics, villas [and their paintings], religion, and the destruction of Pompeii.)

Sear, Frank

1982   *Roman Architecture.* Ithaca: Cornell University Press. (This introduction to the subject consists of two types of chapters: chapters about particular periods and chapters about particular architectural concepts.)

Shelton, Jo-Ann

1988   *As the Romans Did.* Oxford: Oxford University Press. (Shelton's book is a collection of translations of ancient sources, thematically arranged. It is a staple of university classrooms. The translations are good and the commentary is engaging. It is an excellent teaching and learning resource.)

Sherwin-White, Adrian

1963   *Roman Society and Law in the New Testament.* Oxford: Clarendon Press. (Here is an interesting book about the legal and institutional settings of the New Testament. Because this book was written from the perspective of a Roman scholar and not a biblical scholar, it gives a very different [and useful] take on the New Testament, providing a lot of background that was assumed knowledge by New Testament authors.)

1973   *The Roman Citizenship.* 2nd ed. Oxford: Clarendon Press. (This is a classic account of the issue of citizenship, although it is now outdated. This book is pretty dense reading. The first half of the book deals with the period of the republic, and the second half deals with the period of the principate.)

1984   *Roman Foreign Policy in the Greek East.* Norman: University of Oklahoma Press. (Rome's military and political relationship to Greece is explored in this monograph.)

Sinnigen, William, and Arthur Boak

1977   *A History of Rome to A.D. 565.* 6th ed. New York: Macmillan. (The first edition was written by Boak but has been substantially revised after his death by Sinnigen; this is a good textbook of Roman political and military history.)

Smith, Robert, and John Lounibos (eds.)

1984   *Pagan and Christian Anxiety: A Response to E.R. Dodds.* New York: University Press of America. (The result of a conference at Princeton, this volume is a collection of essays responding to the arguments put forward by Eric Dodds.)

Stahl, William

1962   *Roman Science.* Madison: University of Wisconsin Press. (This is the standard account of Roman science and is a necessary read if one is interested in this subject. It describes the development of Roman science from what is essentially a chronological perspective.)

Starr, Chester, Jr.

1971   *Ancient Romans.* New York: Oxford University Press. (This is a frequently cited, short introduction to Rome.)

Stockton, David

1971   *Cicero: A Political Biography*. London: Oxford University Press. (This biography concentrates on Cicero's role in political life, rather than his many other contributions. By singling out this aspect of Cicero's life, Stockton is able to explore a number of interesting issues about Roman society.)

1979   *The Gracchi*. Oxford: Clarendon Press. (This is a good discussion of the politics and laws during the time of the Gracchi.)

Strong, Donald

1988 [1976]   *Roman Art*. Hammondsworth: Penguin Books. (Strong provides a brief overview of Roman art from a chronological perspective. With the exception of the first two chapters, the book is organized by groups of emperors. This can be rather misleading, because art does not always change with regime.)

Strong, Donald, and David Brown

1976   *Roman Crafts*. London: Duckworth. (There are nineteen chapters in this book that describe Roman craft activity in different media. The discussions are well illustrated, with good explanations, especially from a production standpoint.)

Syme, Sir Ronald

1939   *The Roman Revolution*. Oxford: Oxford University Press. (This is a classic account of the transformation from republic to principate. Written from a political perspective, this book does a good job of describing the rise of important families.)

1958   *Tacitus*. 2 vols. Oxford: Clarendon Press. (Syme's biography of Tacitus is a classic work. It provides a comprehensive biography of Tacitus and a substantial discussion of his works and history writing in general.)

1978   *History in Ovid*. Oxford: Clarendon Press. (Another classic work of Syme's, this book provides an ample discussion of the historical context of Ovid. It is difficult reading, with untranslated Latin passages and many sentence fragments, but is a relatively important work.)

Taylor, Lily Ross

1949   *Party Politics in the Age of Caesar*. Berkeley: University of California Press. (Taylor provides a good description of the various political parties that operated during Caesar's time. It is a helpful explanation of the major players and groups.)

Toynbee, Arnold

1965a *Art of the Romans*. London: Thames & Hudson. (The amount of illustrations in this volume is unfortunately low. Even though the discussions are wide ranging, they can be difficult to follow without images.)

1965b *Hannibal's Legacy*. 2 vols. London: Oxford University Press. (This is an extremely detailed study of the setting and aftermath of the second Punic War.)

Toynbee, Jocelyn

1971   *Death and Burial in the Roman World*. Ithaca: Cornell University Press. (This is the best English source on Roman mortuary traditions. It is cited frequently and is well respected. It discusses the beliefs and rituals behind burial, cemetery types, and grave goods. It integrates archaeological and textual data in a very useful fashion.)

Treggiari, Susan

1969 *Roman Freedmen during the Republic.* Oxford: Clarendon Press. (This is a thorough discussion of all aspects of the lives of freedmen during the Republican period, including legal aspects, careers, politics, religion, family, and children.)

Turcan, Robert

2000 *The Gods of Ancient Rome.* Antonio Nevill (trans.). New York: Routledge Press. (This is a general introduction to Roman religion, although the title is somewhat misleading, as it has only minimal discussion of Roman gods per se. The translation is very readable, and it has good discussions of domestic religion, state religion, and imported religious traditions.)

Vag, David

1999 *Coinage and the History of the Roman Empire.* 2 vols. Chicago: Fitzroy Dearborn Publishers. (The first volume provides biographies of Roman officials and historical summaries, and the second volume provides an introduction to numismatics and a catalog of coins with their relative ancient values.)

Veyne, Paul (ed.)

1987 *A History of Private Life: From Pagan Rome to Byzantium.* Arthur Goldhammer (trans.). Cambridge: Harvard University Press. (The first volume of the History of Private Life series, this book contains articles by five scholars, three on Roman issues. The views are relatively traditional and in some ways out of date. However, the descriptions of Roman life are quite vivid.)

Wacher, John (ed.)

1987 *The Roman World.* 2 vols. New York: Routledge & Kegan Paul. (A two-volume work, with essays by different scholars on certain aspects of Rome in the imperial period. The individual essays are quite good, but the choice of topics is relatively idiosyncratic.)

Wallace-Hadrill, Andrew

1994 *Houses and Society in Pompeii and Herculaneum.* Princeton: Princeton University Press. (This is a very influential study of the household in Roman times, based mostly on the evidence from the Vesuvian cities. Wallace-Hadrill sees the household as socially meaningful space and attempts to understand these meanings. His analysis is very good, but it is often repeated in shorter form in other articles. However, this is the most complete account of his ideas.)

Walsh, Patrick

1970 *The Roman Novel.* Cambridge: Cambridge University Press. (Written for students, this book traces the development of Roman novels from their origins in other genres.)

Walters, Henry

1905 *History of Ancient Pottery.* 2 vols. New York: Charles Scribner's Sons. (This was a pioneering work on the subject, though now very out of date. The second volume describes Roman pottery and has valuable information on production and styles.)

Ward-Perkins, John

1977   *Roman Architecture.* New York: Electa/Rizzoli. (With beautiful illustrations and top plans, there are chapters on the Republican period, the Augustan Age, and concrete architecture, among other topics.)

1981   *Roman Imperial Architecture.* New Haven: Yale University Press.(Originally published as one volume with Boëthius in 1978, this is one of the most important and well-respected books on this subject. It covers architecture in Italy and in the rest of the Empire but does not deal with the art of the period.)

Watson, Alan

1970   *The Law of the Ancient Romans.* Dallas: Southern Methodist University Press. (Here is a brief, easy overview of Roman law, organized into discussions of the history of law and the types of law that existed in Rome.)

Webster, Graham

1969   *The Roman Imperial Army.* Totowa: Barnes & Noble Press. (Here is a sound presentation on all aspects of the imperial army, with chapters on the frontier and borders, camps and forts, combat, and peacetime activities.)

West, David

1967   *Reading Horace.* Edinburgh: Edinburgh Press. (This is a small book that provides a good introduction to Horace and his works, specifically designed for nonspecialists.)

Wheeler, Sir Mortimer

1964   *Roman Art and Architecture.* New York: Thames & Hudson. (Wheeler was one of the most influential modern archaeologists, important in all fields, not just Roman studies, for his pioneering field techniques. This is a good book, organized according to type of art. Most interesting is the chapter on collecting in Roman times.)

Wheelock, Frederic

1995   *Wheelock's Latin.* 5th ed. R. A. LaFleur (trans.). New York: HarperCollins. (*Wheelock's* is *the* Latin grammar textbook. It is probably the most used introductory Latin textbook. You can use this book as an aid for classroom study, or the very motivated can use this book for self-study.)

White, Keith

1967   *Agricultural Implements of the Roman World.* Cambridge: Cambridge University Press. (This is very similar to White's *Farm Equipment of the Roman World,* but geared toward terms relating to the raising of crops.)

1970   *Roman Farming.* Ithaca: Cornell University Press. (This is the classic study on Roman farming. It deals with many aspects of Roman agriculture in technical detail [but not unreadable technical detail]. For questions about Roman agriculture, go here first.)

1975   *Farm Equipment of the Roman World.* Cambridge: Cambridge University Press. (The goal of White's book is to identify the names of various kinds of farm equipment, and that is precisely what he does, using textual and archaeological data. This is more of a reference book than the kind of book that one would sit down and read.)

Whittaker, C. R. (ed.)
1993   *Land, City and Trade in the Roman Empire.* Brookfield: Ashgate Publishing Ltd. (This is a collection of fifteen important essays on Roman economy by prominent Roman scholars. None of the essays was written for this publication. They have been collected from other publications and confusingly retain the same formatting [including page numbers!] of their original sources.)

Wiedemann, Thomas
1989   *Adults and Children in the Roman Empire.* New Haven: Yale University Press. (Using textual data, Wiedemann traces the changing attitudes toward children and about childhood through the first four centuries C.E. He studies the issue from a number of perspectives—demographic, legal, etc.)

1995   *Emperors and Gladiators.* New York: Routledge Press. (Although a good general introduction to gladiatorial combat is not provided by this volume, I think it is an important book for beginners to read nonetheless. Wiedemann discusses the social significance of gladiators, avoiding the kinds of disparaging commentary provided by most writers on this topic. In other words, he attempts to understand gladiators from a Roman perspective, not a modern perspective.)

1997   *Slavery.* Oxford: Oxford University Press. (A brief monograph on the subject of slavery in Greek and Roman society. The individual chapters are good, and especially noteworthy are Wiedemann's comments on the problems of studying ancient slavery, given American historical circumstances.)

Wilkinson, L. P.
1955   *Ovid Recalled.* Portway: C. Chivera. (Written for a nonspecialist but Latin-reading audience. Wilkinson provides a biography of Ovid as well as literary commentary.)

1962   *Ovid Surveyed.* Cambridge: Cambridge University Press. (This is an abridged version of Wilkinson's 1955 work, *Ovid Recalled.*)

Williams, Gordon
1968   *Tradition and Originality in Roman Poetry.* Oxford: Clarendon Press. (This book was written with the goal of situating Roman poetry within its historical context.)

1983   *The Nature of Roman Poetry.* London: Oxford University Press. (This is a simplified version of *Tradition and Originality in Roman Poetry.*)

Wiseman, T.P.
1985   *Catullus and His World: A Reappraisal.* Cambridge: Cambridge University Press. (This is a mixture of biography and literary criticism and is a useful introduction to the setting of Catullus.)

Wiseman, Timothy

1971   *New Men in the Roman Senate.* London: Oxford University Press. (Wiseman attempts to identify all of the senators of municipal or equestrian origin in the period 139 B.C.E. to 14 C.E. As well as a discussion on the subject, Wiseman also lists all of the names of these identified senators with some biographic information.)

Yavetz, Zvi

1969   *Plebs and Princeps.* London: Oxford University Press. (The relationship between the plebs and nobility in the principate is the primary topic of Yavetz's book. It includes a good discussion of the ways in which the urban crowd could affect the Roman political scene.)

1983   *Julius Caesar and His Public Image.* Ithaca: Cornell University Press. (A good study of Caesar, but what makes this volume noteworthy is the first chapter, which discusses the history of scholarship on Julius Caesar.)

Zanker, Paul

1998   *Pompeii: Public and Private Life.* Deborah Schneider (trans.). Cambridge: Cambridge University Press. (Zanker's book is an excellent study on understanding the social meaning of Roman architecture—both state architecture and the architecture of the home. The descriptions of how space and design affect the individual are an important contribution. This book, however, is not an overview of Pompeii or its archaeology.)

Index

ABOUT THE AUTHOR

KEVIN McGEOUGH was born in Ontario and grew up in Alberta, Canada. McGeough received a B.A. in history from the University of Lethbridge and an M.T.S. degree from Harvard Divinity School; he expects to receive a Ph.D. from the University of Pennsylvania shortly. Recently he has returned to the University of Lethbridge and accepted an appointment as Assistant Professor in Archaeology for the Geography Department. Outside of school, McGeough is an avid film fan.